The Larger Catechism

This edition © Christian Focus Publications, 2018
Hardback ISBN: 978-1-5271-0240-8

Published in 2018
by
Christian Focus Publications
Geanies House, Fearn, Ross-shire,
IV20 1TW, Great Britain.
www.christianfocus.com

Cover design by Daniel van Straaten

Printed & bound by Bell & Bain Ltd, Glasgow

THE
LARGER CATECHISM:

Agreed upon by the Assembly of Divines at Westminster, with the assistance of Commissioners from the Church of Scotland, as a part of the covenanted uniformity in religion betwixt the churches of Christ in the kingdoms of Scotland, England, and Ireland.

AND

Approved Anno 1648, by the General Assembly of the Church of Scotland, to be a directory for catechising such as have made some proficiency in the knowledge of the grounds of religion,

WITH

The proofs from the Scripture.

Assembly at EDINBURGH, July 2, 1648. Sess. 10.
Act approving the LARGER CATECHISM.

THE General Assembly having exactly examined and seriously considered the LARGER CATECHISM, agreed upon by the Assembly of Divines sitting at Westminster, with assistance of Commissioners from this Kirk, copies thereof being printed, and sent to Presbyteries, for the more exact trial thereof; and publick intimation being frequently made in this Assembly, that every one that had any doubts or objections upon it might put them in; do find, upon due examination thereof, That the said Catechism is agreeable to the word of God, and in nothing contrary to the received doctrine, worship, discipline, and government of this Kirk; a necessary part of the intended uniformity in religion, and a rich treasure for increasing knowledge among the people of God: and therefore the Assembly, as they bless the Lord that so excellent a Catechism is prepared, so they approve the same, as a part of uniformity; agreeing, for their part, that it be a common Catechism for the three kingdoms, and a Directory for catechising such as have made some proficiency in the knowledge of the grounds of religion.

1. What is the chief and highest end of man?

A. Man's chief and highest end is to glorify God, [1] and fully to enjoy him forever. [2]

Proofs

[1] **Romans 11:36:** For of him, and through him, and to him, *are* all things: to whom *be* glory for ever. Amen. **1 Corinthians 10:31:** Whether therefore ye eat, or drink, or whatsoever ye do, do all to the glory of God.

[2] **Psalm 73:24-28:** Thou shalt guide me with thy counsel, and afterward receive me to glory. Whom have I in heaven *but thee*? and *there is* none upon earth *that* I desire beside thee. My flesh and my heart faileth: *but* God *is* the strength of my heart, and my portion for ever. For, lo, they that are far from thee shall perish: thou hast destroyed all them that go a whoring from thee. But *it is* good for me to draw near to God: I have put my trust in the Lord GOD, that I may declare all thy works. **John 17:21-23:** That they all may be one; as thou, Father, *art* in me, and I in thee, that they also may be one in us: that the world may believe that thou hast sent me. And the glory which thou gavest me I have given them; that they may be one, even as we are one: I in them, and thou in me, that they may be made perfect in one; and that the world may know that thou hast sent me, and hast loved them, as thou hast loved me.

2. How doth it appear that there is a God?

A. The very light of nature in man, and the works of God, declare plainly that there is a God; [1] but his Word and Spirit only do sufficiently and effectually reveal him unto men for their salvation. [2]

Proofs

[1] **Romans 1:19-20:** Because that which may be known of God is manifest in them; for God hath shewed *it* unto them. For the invisible things of him from the creation of the world are clearly seen, being understood by the things that are made, *even* his eternal power and Godhead; so that they are without excuse ... **Psalm 19:1-3:** The heavens declare the glory of God; and the firmament sheweth his handywork. Day unto day uttereth speech, and night unto night sheweth knowledge. *There is* no speech nor language, *where* their voice

is not heard. **Acts 17:28:** For in him we live, and move, and have our being; as certain also of your own poets have said, For we are also his offspring.

[2] **1 Corinthians 2:9-10:** But as it is written, Eye hath not seen, nor ear heard, neither have entered into the heart of man, the things which God hath prepared for them that love him. But God hath revealed *them* unto us by his Spirit: for the Spirit searcheth all things, yea, the deep things of God. **2 Timothy 3:15-17:** And that from a child thou hast known the holy scriptures, which are able to make thee wise unto salvation through faith which is in Christ Jesus. All scripture *is* given by inspiration of God, and *is* profitable for doctrine, for reproof, for correction, for instruction in righteousness: That the man of God may be perfect, thoroughly furnished unto all good works. **Isaiah 59:21:** As for me, this is my covenant with them, saith the LORD; My spirit that *is* upon thee, and my words which I have put in thy mouth, shall not depart out of thy mouth, nor out of the mouth of thy seed, nor out of the mouth of thy seed's seed, saith the LORD, from henceforth and for ever.

3. What is the Word of God?

A. The Holy Scriptures of the Old and New Testament are the Word of God, [1] the only rule of faith and obedience. [2]

Proofs

[1] **2 Timothy 3:16:** All scripture *is* given by inspiration of God, and *is* profitable for doctrine, for reproof, for correction, for instruction in righteousness. **2 Peter 1:19-21:** We have also a more sure word of prophecy; whereunto ye do well that ye take heed, as unto a light that shineth in a dark place, until the day dawn, and the day star arise in your hearts: Knowing this first, that no prophecy of the scripture is of any private interpretation. For the prophecy came not in old time by the will of man: but holy men of God spake *as they were* moved by the Holy Ghost.

[2] **Ephesians 2:20:** And are built upon the foundation of the apostles and prophets, Jesus Christ himself being the chief corner stone … **Revelation 22:18-19:** For I testify unto every man that heareth the words of the prophecy of this book, If any man shall add unto these things, God shall add unto him the plagues that are written in this book: And if any man shall take away from the words

of the book of this prophecy, God shall take away his part out of the book of life, and out of the holy city, and *from* the things which are written in this book. **Isaiah 8:20:** To the law and to the testimony: if they speak not according to this word, *it is* because *there is* no light in them. **Luke 16:29, 31:** Abraham saith unto him, They have Moses and the prophets; let them hear them ... And he said unto him, If they hear not Moses and the prophets, neither will they be persuaded, though one rose from the dead. **Galatians 1:8-9:** But though we, or an angel from heaven, preach any other gospel unto you than that which we have preached unto you, let him be accursed. As we said before, so say I now again, if any *man* preach any other gospel unto you than that ye have received, let him be accursed. **2 Timothy 3:15-16:** And that from a child thou hast known the holy scriptures, which are able to make thee wise unto salvation through faith which is in Christ Jesus. All scripture *is* given by inspiration of God, and *is* profitable for doctrine, for reproof, for correction, for instruction in righteousness ...

4. How doth it appear that the Scriptures are of the Word of God?

A. The Scriptures manifest themselves to be the Word of God, by their majesty [1] and purity; [2] by the consent of all the parts, [3] and the scope of the whole, which is to give all glory to God; [4] by their light and power to convince and convert sinners, to comfort and build up believers unto salvation: [5] but the Spirit of God bearing witness by and with the Scriptures in the heart of man is alone able fully to persuade it that they are the very Word of God. [6]

Proofs

[1] **Hosea 8:12:** I have written to him the great things of my law, *but* they were counted as a strange thing. **1 Corinthians 2:6-7, 13:** Howbeit we speak wisdom among them that are perfect: yet not the wisdom of this world, nor of the princes of this world, that come to nought: But we speak the wisdom of God in a mystery, *even* the hidden *wisdom*, which God ordained before the world unto our glory: ... Which things also we speak, not in the words which man's wisdom teacheth, but which the Holy Ghost teacheth; comparing spiritual things with spiritual. **Psalm 119:18, 129:** Open thou mine eyes, that

I may behold wondrous things out of thy law … Thy testimonies *are* wonderful: therefore doth my soul keep them.

[2] **Psalm 12:6:** The words of the LORD *are* pure words: *as* silver tried in a furnace of earth, purified seven times. **Psalm 119:140:** Thy word *is* very pure: therefore thy servant loveth it.

[3] **Acts 10:43:** To him give all the prophets witness, that through his name whosoever believeth in him shall receive remission of sins. **Acts 26:22:** Having therefore obtained help of God, I continue unto this day, witnessing both to small and great, saying none other things than those which the prophets and Moses did say should come …

[4] **Romans 3:19, 27:** Now we know that what things soever the law saith, it saith to them who are under the law: that every mouth may be stopped, and all the world may become guilty before God … Where *is* boasting then? It is excluded. By what law? of works? Nay: but by the law of faith.

[5] **Acts 18:28:** For he mightily convinced the Jews, *and that* publickly, shewing by the scriptures that Jesus was Christ. **Hebrews 4:12:** For the word of God *is* quick, and powerful, and sharper than any twoedged sword, piercing even to the dividing asunder of soul and spirit, and of the joints and marrow, and *is* a discerner of the thoughts and intents of the heart. **James 1:18:** Of his own will begat he us with the word of truth, that we should be a kind of firstfruits of his creatures. **Psalm 19:7-9:** The law of the LORD *is* perfect, converting the soul: the testimony of the LORD *is* sure, making wise the simple. The statutes of the LORD *are* right, rejoicing the heart: the commandment of the LORD *is* pure, enlightening the eyes. The fear of the LORD *is* clean, enduring for ever: the judgments of the LORD *are* true *and* righteous altogether. **Romans 15:4:** For whatsoever things were written aforetime were written for our learning, that we through patience and comfort of the scriptures might have hope. **Acts 20:32:** And now, brethren, I commend you to God, and to the word of his grace, which is able to build you up, and to give you an inheritance among all them which are sanctified.

[6] **John 16:13-14:** Howbeit when he, the Spirit of truth, is come, he will guide you into all truth: for he shall not speak of himself; but whatsoever he shall hear, *that* shall he speak: and he will shew you things to come. He shall glorify me: for he shall receive of mine, and

shall shew *it* unto you. **1 John 2:20, 27:** But ye have an unction from the Holy One, and ye know all things ... But the anointing which ye have received of him abideth in you, and ye need not that any man teach you: but as the same anointing teacheth you of all things, and is truth, and is no lie, and even as it hath taught you, ye shall abide in him. **John 20:31:** But these are written, that ye might believe that Jesus is the Christ, the Son of God; and that believing ye might have life through his name.

5. What do the Scriptures principally teach?

A. The Scriptures principally teach what man is to believe concerning God, and what duty God requires of man. [1]

Proof

[1] **2 Timothy 1:13:** Hold fast the form of sound words, which thou hast heard of me, in faith and love which is in Christ Jesus.

WHAT MAN OUGHT TO BELIEVE CONCERNING GOD

6. What do the Scriptures make known of God?

A. The Scriptures make known what God is, [1] the persons in the Godhead, [2] his decrees, [3] and the execution of his decrees. [4]

Proofs

[1] **Hebrews 11:6:** But without faith *it is* impossible to please *him*: for he that cometh to God must believe that he is, and *that* he is a rewarder of them that diligently seek him.

[2] **1 John 5:7:** For there are three that bear record in heaven, the Father, the Word, and the Holy Ghost: and these three are one.

[3] **Acts 15:14-15, 18:** Simeon hath declared how God at the first did visit the Gentiles, to take out of them a people for his name. And to this agree the words of the prophets; as it is written ... Known unto God are all his works from the beginning of the world.

[4] **Acts 4:27-28:** For of a truth against thy holy child Jesus, whom thou hast anointed, both Herod, and Pontius Pilate, with the Gentiles, and the people of Israel, were gathered together, For to do whatsoever thy hand and thy counsel determined before to be done.

7. What is God?

A. God is a Spirit, [1] in and of himself infinite in being,[2] glory [3] blessedness, [4] and perfection; [5] all-sufficient, [6] eternal, [7] unchangeable, [8] incomprehensible, [9] everywhere present, [10] almighty, [11] knowing all things, [12] most wise, [13] most holy, [14] most just, [15] most merciful and gracious, long-suffering, and abundant in goodness and truth. [16]

Proofs

[1] **John 4:24:** God *is* a Spirit: and they that worship him must worship *him* in spirit and in truth.

[2] **Exodus 3:14:** And God said unto Moses, I AM THAT I AM: and he said, Thus shalt thou say unto the children of Israel, I AM hath sent me unto you. **Job 11:7-9:** Canst thou by searching find out God? canst thou find out the Almighty unto perfection? *It is* as high as heaven; what canst thou do? deeper than hell; what canst thou know? The measure thereof *is* longer than the earth, and broader than the sea.

[3] **Acts 7:2:** And he said, Men, brethren, and fathers, hearken; The God of glory appeared unto our father Abraham, when he was in Mesopotamia, before he dwelt in Charran …

[4] **1 Timothy 6:15:** Which in his times he shall shew, *who is* the blessed and only Potentate, the King of kings, and Lord of lords …

[5] **Matthew 5:48:** Be ye therefore perfect, even as your Father which is in heaven is perfect.

[6] **Genesis 17:1:** And when Abram was ninety years old and nine, the LORD appeared to Abram, and said unto him, I *am* the Almighty God; walk before me, and be thou perfect.

[7] **Psalm 90:2:** Before the mountains were brought forth, or ever thou hadst formed the earth and the world, even from everlasting to everlasting, thou *art* God.

[8] **Malachi 3:6:** For I *am* the LORD, I change not; therefore ye sons of Jacob are not consumed. **James 1:17:** Every good gift and every perfect gift is from above, and cometh down from the Father of lights, with whom is no variableness, neither shadow of turning.

[9] **1 Kings 8:27:** But will God indeed dwell on the earth? behold, the heaven and heaven of heavens cannot contain thee; how much less this house that I have builded?

[10] **Psalm 139:1-13:** O LORD, thou hast searched me, and known *me*. Thou knowest my downsitting and mine uprising, thou understandest my thought afar off. Thou compassest my path and my lying down, and art acquainted *with* all my ways. For *there is* not a word in my tongue, *but*, lo, O LORD, thou knowest it altogether. Thou hast beset me behind and before, and laid thine hand upon me. *Such* knowledge *is* too wonderful for me; it is high, I cannot *attain* unto it. Whither shall I go from thy spirit? or whither shall I flee from thy presence? If I ascend up into heaven, thou *art* there: if I make my bed in hell, behold, thou *art there*. *If* I take the wings of the morning, *and* dwell in the uttermost parts of the sea; Even there shall thy hand lead me, and thy right hand shall hold me. If I say, Surely the darkness shall cover me; even the night shall be light about me. Yea, the darkness hideth not from thee; but the night shineth as the day: the darkness and the light *are* both alike *to thee*. For thou hast possessed my reins: thou hast covered me in my mother's womb.

[11] **Revelation 4:8:** And the four beasts had each of them six wings about *him*; and *they were* full of eyes within: and they rest not day and night, saying, Holy, holy, holy, Lord God Almighty, which was, and is, and is to come.

[12] **Hebrews 4:13:** Neither is there any creature that is not manifest in his sight: but all things *are* naked and opened unto the eyes of him with whom we have to do. **Psalm 147:5:** Great *is* our Lord, and of great power: his understanding *is* infinite.

[13] **Romans 16:27:** To God only wise, *be* glory through Jesus Christ for ever. Amen.

[14] **Isaiah 6:3:** And one cried unto another, and said, Holy, holy, holy, *is* the LORD of hosts: the whole earth *is* full of his glory. **Revelation 15:4:** Who shall not fear thee, O Lord, and glorify thy name? for *thou* only *art* holy: for all nations shall come and worship before thee; for thy judgments are made manifest.

[15] **Deuteronomy 32:4:** *He is* the Rock, his work *is* perfect: for all his ways *are* judgment: a God of truth and without iniquity, just and right *is* he.

[16] **Exodus 34:6:** And the LORD passed by before him, and proclaimed, The LORD, The LORD God, merciful and gracious, longsuffering, and abundant in goodness and truth …

8. Are there more Gods than one?

A. There is but one only, the living and true God.[1]

Proofs

[1] **Deuteronomy 6:4:** Hear, O Israel: The LORD our God *is* one LORD … **1 Corinthians 8:4, 6:** As concerning therefore the eating of those things that are offered in sacrifice unto idols, we know that an idol *is* nothing in the world, and that *there is* none other God but one … But to us *there is but* one God, the Father, of whom *are* all things, and we in him; and one Lord Jesus Christ, by whom *are* all things, and we by him. **Jeremiah 10:10:** But the LORD *is* the true God, he *is* the living God, and an everlasting king: at his wrath the earth shall tremble, and the nations shall not be able to abide his indignation.

9. How many persons are there in the Godhead?

A There be three persons in the Godhead, the Father, the Son, and the Holy Ghost; and these three are one true, eternal God, the same in substance, equal in power and glory; although distinguished by their personal properties.[1]

Proofs

[1] **1 John 5:7:** For there are three that bear record in heaven, the Father, the Word, and the Holy Ghost: and these three are one. **Matthew 3:16–17:** And Jesus, when he was baptized, went up straightway out of the water: and, lo, the heavens were opened unto him, and he saw the Spirit of God descending like a dove, and lighting upon him: And lo a voice from heaven, saying, This is my beloved Son, in whom I am well pleased. **Matthew 28:19:** Go ye therefore, and teach all nations, baptizing them in the name of the Father, and of the Son, and of the Holy Ghost … **2 Corinthians 13:14:** The grace of the Lord Jesus Christ, and the love of God, and the communion of the Holy Ghost, *be* with you all. Amen. **John 10:30:** I and *my* Father are one.

10. What are the personal properties of the three persons in the Godhead?

A. It is proper to the Father to beget the Son, [1] and to the Son to be begotten of the Father, [2] and to the Holy Ghost to proceed from the Father and the Son from all eternity. [3]

Proofs

[1] **Hebrews 1:5-6, 8:** For unto which of the angels said he at any time, Thou art my Son, this day have I begotten thee? And again, I will be to him a Father, and he shall be to me a Son? And again, when he bringeth in the firstbegotten into the world, he saith, And let all the angels of God worship him ... But unto the Son *he saith*, Thy throne, O God, *is* for ever and ever: a sceptre of righteousness *is* the sceptre of thy kingdom.

[2] **John 1:14, 18:** And the Word was made flesh, and dwelt among us, (and we beheld his glory, the glory as of the only begotten of the Father,) full of grace and truth ... No man hath seen God at any time; the only begotten Son, which is in the bosom of the Father, he hath declared *him*.

[3] **John 15:26:** But when the Comforter is come, whom I will send unto you from the Father, *even* the Spirit of truth, which proceedeth from the Father, he shall testify of me ...**Galatians 4:6:** And because ye are sons, God hath sent forth the Spirit of his Son into your hearts, crying, Abba, Father.

11. How doth it appear that the Son and the Holy Ghost are God equal with the Father?

A. The Scriptures manifest that the Son and the Holy Ghost are God equal with the Father, ascribing unto them such names, [1] attributes, [2] works, [3] and worship, [4] as are proper to God only.

Proofs

[1] **Isaiah 6:3, 5, 8:** And one cried unto another, and said, Holy, holy, holy, *is* the LORD of hosts: the whole earth *is* full of his glory ... Then said I, Woe is me! for I am undone; because I *am* a man of unclean lips, and I dwell in the midst of a people of unclean lips: for mine eyes have seen the King, the LORD of hosts ... Also I heard the voice of the Lord, saying, Whom shall I send, and who

will go for us? Then said I, Here *am* I; send me. [Compare with] **John 12:41:** These things said Esaias, when he saw his glory, and spake of him. [And with] **Acts 28:25:** And when they agreed not among themselves, they departed, after that Paul had spoken one word, Well spake the Holy Ghost by Esaias the prophet unto our fathers ... **1 John 5:20:** And we know that the Son of God is come, and hath given us an understanding, that we may know him that is true, and we are in him that is true, *even* in his Son Jesus Christ. This is the true God, and eternal life. **Acts 5:3-4:** But Peter said, Ananias, why hath Satan filled thine heart to lie to the Holy Ghost, and to keep back *part* of the price of the land? Whiles it remained, was it not thine own? and after it was sold, was it not in thine own power? why hast thou conceived this thing in thine heart? thou hast not lied unto men, but unto God.

[2] **John 1:1:** In the beginning was the Word, and the Word was with God, and the Word was God. **Isaiah 9:6:** For unto us a child is born, unto us a son is given: and the government shall be upon his shoulder: and his name shall be called Wonderful, Counsellor, The mighty God, The everlasting Father, The Prince of Peace. **John 2:24-25:** But Jesus did not commit himself unto them, because he knew all *men*, And needed not that any should testify of man: for he knew what was in man. **1 Corinthians 2:10-11:** But God hath revealed *them* unto us by his Spirit: for the Spirit searcheth all things, yea, the deep things of God. For what man knoweth the things of a man, save the spirit of man which is in him? even so the things of God knoweth no man, but the Spirit of God.

[3] **Colossians 1:16:** For by him were all things created, that are in heaven, and that are in earth, visible and invisible, whether *they be* thrones, or dominions, or principalities, or powers: all things were created by him, and for him ... **Genesis 1:2:** And the earth was without form, and void; and darkness *was* upon the face of the deep. And the Spirit of God moved upon the face of the waters.

[4] **Matthew 28:19:** Go ye therefore, and teach all nations, baptizing them in the name of the Father, and of the Son, and of the Holy Ghost ... **2 Corinthians 13:14:** The grace of the Lord Jesus Christ, and the love of God, and the communion of the Holy Ghost *be* with you all. Amen.

12. What are the decrees of God?

A. God's decrees are the wise, free, and holy acts of the counsel of his will, [1] whereby, from all eternity, he hath, for his own glory, unchangeably foreordained whatsoever comes to pass in time, [2] especially concerning angels and men.

Proofs

[1] **Ephesians 1:11:** In whom also we have obtained an inheritance, being predestinated according to the purpose of him who worketh all things after the counsel of his own will ...**Romans 11:33:** O the depth of the riches both of the wisdom and knowledge of God! how unsearchable *are* his judgments, and his ways past finding out! **Romans 9:14-15, 18:** What shall we say then? Is *there* unrighteousness with God? God forbid. For he saith to Moses, I will have mercy on whom I will have mercy, and I will have compassion on whom I will have compassion ... Therefore hath he mercy on whom he will *have mercy*, and whom he will he hardeneth.

[2] **Ephesians 1:4, 11:** According as he hath chosen us in him before the foundation of the world, that we should be holy and without blame before him in love ... In whom also we have obtained an inheritance, being predestinated according to the purpose of him who worketh all things after the counsel of his own will ... **Romans 9:22-23:** *What* if God, willing to shew *his* wrath, and to make his power known, endured with much longsuffering the vessels of wrath fitted to destruction: And that he might make known the riches of his glory on the vessels of mercy, which he had afore prepared unto glory ... **Psalm 33:11:** The counsel of the LORD standeth for ever, the thoughts of his heart to all generations.

13. What hath God especially decreed concerning angels and men?

A. God, by an eternal and immutable decree, out of his mere love, for the praise of his glorious grace, to be manifested in due time, hath elected some angels to glory; [1] and in Christ hath chosen some men to eternal life, and the means thereof: [2] and also, according to his sovereign power, and the unsearchable counsel of his own will, (whereby he extendeth or withholdeth favour as he pleaseth), hath passed by and foreordained the rest to dishonour and wrath, to be for their sin inflicted, to the praise of the glory of his justice.[3]

Proofs

[1] **1 Timothy 5:21:** I charge *thee* before God, and the Lord Jesus Christ, and the elect angels, that thou observe these things without preferring one before another, doing nothing by partiality.

[2] **Ephesians 1:4-6:** According as he hath chosen us in him before the foundation of the world, that we should be holy and without blame before him in love: Having predestinated us unto the adoption of children by Jesus Christ to himself, according to the good pleasure of his will, To the praise of the glory of his grace, wherein he hath made us accepted in the beloved. **2 Thessalonians 2:13-14:** But we are bound to give thanks alway to God for you, brethren beloved of the Lord, because God hath from the beginning chosen you to salvation through sanctification of the Spirit and belief of the truth: Whereunto he called you by our gospel, to the obtaining of the glory of our Lord Jesus Christ.

[3] **Romans 9:17-18, 21-22:** For the scripture saith unto Pharaoh, Even for this same purpose have I raised thee up, that I might shew my power in thee, and that my name might be declared throughout all the earth. Therefore hath he mercy on whom he will *have mercy*, and whom he will he hardeneth … Hath not the potter power over the clay, of the same lump to make one vessel unto honour, and another unto dishonour? *What* if God, willing to shew *his* wrath, and to make his power known, endured with much longsuffering the vessels of wrath fitted to destruction … **Matthew 11:25-26:** At that time Jesus answered and said, I thank thee, O Father, Lord of heaven and earth, because thou hast hid these things from the wise and prudent, and hast revealed them unto babes. Even so, Father: for so it seemed good in thy sight. **2 Timothy 2:20:** But in a great house there are not only vessels of gold and of silver, but also of wood and of earth; and some to honour, and some to dishonour. **Jude 4:** For there are certain men crept in unawares, who were before of old ordained to this condemnation, ungodly men, turning the grace of our God into lasciviousness, and denying the only Lord God, and our Lord Jesus Christ. **1 Peter 2:8:** And a stone of stumbling, and a rock of offence,

even to them which stumble at the word, being disobedient: whereunto also they were appointed.

14. How doth God execute his decrees?

A. God executeth his decrees in the works of creation and providence, according to his infallible foreknowledge, and the free and immutable counsel of his own will. [1]

Proof

[1] **Ephesians 1:11:** In whom also we have obtained an inheritance, being predestinated according to the purpose of him who worketh all things after the counsel of his own will …

15. What is the work of creation?

A. The work of creation is that wherein God did in the beginning, by the word of his power, make of nothing the world, and all things therein, for himself, within the space of six days, and all very good.[1]

Proofs

[1] **Genesis 1 (entire). Hebrews 11:3:** Through faith we understand that the worlds were framed by the word of God, so that things which are seen were not made of things which do appear. **Proverbs 16:4:** The LORD hath made all *things* for himself: yea, even the wicked for the day of evil.

16. How did God create angels?

A. God created all the angels, [1] spirits, [2] immortal, [3] holy, [4] excelling in knowledge, [5] mighty in power, [6] to execute his commandments, and to praise his name, [7] yet subject to change. [8]

Proofs

[1] **Colossians 1:16:** For by him were all things created, that are in heaven, and that are in earth, visible and invisible, whether *they be* thrones, or dominions, or principalities, or powers: all things were created by him, and for him …

[2] **Psalm 104:4:** Who maketh his angels spirits; his ministers a flaming fire …

[3] **Matthew 22:30:** For in the resurrection they neither marry, nor are given in marriage, but are as the angels of God in heaven.

[4] **Matthew 25:31:** When the Son of man shall come in his glory, and all the holy angels with him, then shall he sit upon the throne of his glory …

[5] **2 Samuel 14:17:** Then thine handmaid said, The word of my lord the king shall now be comfortable: for as an angel of God, so is my lord the king to discern good and bad: therefore the LORD thy God will be with thee. **Matthew 24:36:** But of that day and hour knoweth no *man*, no, not the angels of heaven, but my Father only.

[6] **2 Thessalonians 1:7:** And to you who are troubled rest with us, when the Lord Jesus shall be revealed from heaven with his mighty angels …

[7] **Psalm 103:20-21:** Bless the LORD, ye his angels, that excel in strength, that do his commandments, hearkening unto the voice of his word. Bless ye the LORD, all *ye* his hosts; *ye* ministers of his, that do his pleasure.

[8] **2 Peter 2:4:** For if God spared not the angels that sinned, but cast *them* down to hell, and delivered *them* into chains of darkness, to be reserved unto judgment …

17. How did God create man?

A. After God had made all other creatures, he created man male and female; [1] formed the body of the man of the dust of the ground, [2] and the woman of the rib of the man, [3] endued them with living, reasonable, and immortal souls; [4] made them after his own image, [5] in knowledge, [6] righteousness, and holiness; [7] having the law of God written in their hearts, [8] and power to fulfil it, [9] and dominion over the creatures; [10] yet subject to fall. [11]

Proofs

[1] **Genesis 1:27:** So God created man in his *own* image, in the image of God created he him; male and female created he them.

[2] **Genesis 2:7:** And the LORD God formed man of the dust of the ground, and breathed into his nostrils the breath of life; and man became a living soul.

[3] **Genesis 2:22:** And the rib, which the Lord God had taken from man, made he a woman, and brought her unto the man.

[4] **Genesis 2:7:** And the Lord God formed man of the dust of the ground, and breathed into his nostrils the breath of life; and man became a living soul. **Job 35:11:** Who teacheth us more than the beasts of the earth, and maketh us wiser than the fowls of heaven? **Ecclesiastes 12:7:** Then shall the dust return to the earth as it was: and the spirit shall return unto God who gave it. **Matthew 10:28:** And fear not them which kill the body, but are not able to kill the soul: but rather fear him which is able to destroy both soul and body in hell. **Luke 23:43:** And Jesus said unto him, Verily I say unto thee, To day shalt thou be with me in paradise.

[5] **Genesis 1:27:** So God created man in his *own* image, in the image of God created he him; male and female created he them.

[6] **Colossians 3:10:** And have put on the new *man*, which is renewed in knowledge after the image of him that created him …

[7] **Ephesians 4:24:** And that ye put on the new man, which after God is created in righteousness and true holiness.

[8] **Romans 2:14-15:** For when the Gentiles, which have not the law, do by nature the things contained in the law, these, having not the law, are a law unto themselves: Which shew the work of the law written in their hearts, their conscience also bearing witness, and *their* thoughts the mean while accusing or else excusing one another …

[9] **Ecclesiastes 7:29:** Lo, this only have I found, that God hath made man upright; but they have sought out many inventions.

[10] **Genesis 1:28:** And God blessed them, and God said unto them, Be fruitful, and multiply, and replenish the earth, and subdue it: and have dominion over the fish of the sea, and over the fowl of the air, and over every living thing that moveth upon the earth.

[11] **Genesis 3:6:** And when the woman saw that the tree *was* good for food, and that it *was* pleasant to the eyes, and a tree to be desired to make *one* wise, she took of the fruit thereof, and did eat, and gave also unto her husband with her; and he did eat. **Ecclesiastes 7:29:** Lo, this only have I found, that God hath made man upright; but they have sought out many inventions.

18. What are God's works of providence?

A. God's works of providence are his most holy, [1] wise, [2] and powerful preserving [3] and governing [4] all his creatures; ordering them, and all their actions, [5] to his own glory.[6]

Proofs

[1] **Psalm 145:17:** The LORD *is* righteous in all his ways, and holy in all his works.

[2] **Psalm 104:24:** O LORD, how manifold are thy works! in wisdom hast thou made them all: the earth is full of thy riches. **Isaiah 28:29:** This also cometh forth from the LORD of hosts, which is wonderful in counsel, *and* excellent in working.

[3] **Hebrews 1:3:** Who being the brightness of *his* glory, and the express image of his person, and upholding all things by the word of his power, when he had by himself purged our sins, sat down on the right hand of the Majesty on high ...

[4] **Psalm 103:19:** The LORD hath prepared his throne in the heavens; and his kingdom ruleth over all.

[5] **Matthew 10:29-31:** Are not two sparrows sold for a farthing? and one of them shall not fall on the ground without your Father. But the very hairs of your head are all numbered. Fear ye not therefore, ye are of more value than many sparrows. **Genesis 45:7:** And God sent me before you to preserve you a posterity in the earth, and to save your lives by a great deliverance.

[6] **Romans 11:36:** For of him, and through him, and to him, *are* all things: to whom *be* glory for ever. Amen. **Isaiah 63:14:** As a beast goeth down into the valley, the Spirit of the LORD caused him to rest: so didst thou lead thy people, to make thyself a glorious name.

19. What is God's providence towards the angels?

A. God by his providence permitted some of the angels, wilfully and irrecoverably, to fall into sin and damnation, [1] limiting and ordering that, and all their sins, to his own glory; [2] and established the rest in holiness and happiness; [3] employing them all, [4] at his pleasure, in the administrations of his power, mercy, and justice.[5]

Proofs

[1] **Jude 6:** And the angels which kept not their first estate, but left their own habitation, he hath reserved in everlasting chains under darkness unto the judgment of the great day. **2 Peter 2:4:** For if God spared not the angels that sinned, but cast *them* down to hell, and delivered *them* into chains of darkness, to be reserved unto judgment … **Hebrews 2:16:** For verily he took not on *him the nature of* angels; but he took on *him* the seed of Abraham. **John 8:44:** Ye are of *your* father the devil, and the lusts of your father ye will do. He was a murderer from the beginning, and abode not in the truth, because there is no truth in him. When he speaketh a lie, he speaketh of his own: for he is a liar, and the father of it.

[2] **Job 1:12:** And the LORD said unto Satan, Behold, all that he hath *is* in thy power; only upon himself put not forth thine hand. So Satan went forth from the presence of the LORD. **Matthew 8:31:** So the devils besought him, saying, If thou cast us out, suffer us to go away into the herd of swine.

[3] **1 Timothy 5:21:** I charge *thee* before God, and the Lord Jesus Christ, and the elect angels, that thou observe these things without preferring one before another, doing nothing by partiality. **Mark 8:38:** Whosoever therefore shall be ashamed of me and of my words in this adulterous and sinful generation; of him also shall the Son of man be ashamed, when he cometh in the glory of his Father with the holy angels. **Hebrews 12:22:** But ye are come unto mount Sion, and unto the city of the living God, the heavenly Jerusalem, and to an innumerable company of angels …

[4] **Psalm 104:4:** Who maketh his angels spirits; his ministers a flaming fire …

[5] **2 Kings 19:35:** And it came to pass that night, that the angel of the LORD went out, and smote in the camp of the Assyrians an hundred fourscore and five thousand: and when they arose early in the morning, behold, they *were* all dead corpses. **Hebrews 1:14:** Are they not all ministering spirits, sent forth to minister for them who shall be heirs of salvation?

20. What was the providence of God toward man in the estate in which he was created?

A. The providence of God toward man in the estate in which he was created was the placing him in paradise, appointing him to dress it, giving him liberty to eat of the fruit of the earth; [1] putting the creatures under his dominion, [2] and ordaining marriage for his help; [3] affording him communion with himself; [4] instituting the sabbath; [5]entering into a covenant of life with him, upon condition of personal, perfect, and perpetual obedience, [6] of which the tree of life was a pledge; [7] and forbidding to eat of the tree of knowledge of good and evil, upon the pain of death.[8]

Proofs

[1] **Genesis 2:8, 15-16:** And the LORD God planted a garden eastward in Eden; and there he put the man whom he had formed … And the LORD God took the man, and put him into the garden of Eden to dress it and to keep it. And the LORD God commanded the man, saying, Of every tree of the garden thou mayest freely eat …

[2] **Genesis 1:28:** And God blessed them, and God said unto them, Be fruitful, and multiply, and replenish the earth, and subdue it: and have dominion over the fish of the sea, and over the fowl of the air, and over every living thing that moveth upon the earth.

[3] **Genesis 2:18:** And the LORD God said, *It* is not good that the man should be alone; I will make him an help meet for him.

[4] **Genesis 1:26-29:** And God said, Let us make man in our image, after our likeness: and let them have dominion over the fish of the sea, and over the fowl of the air, and over the cattle, and over all the earth, and over every creeping thing that creepeth upon the earth. So God created man in his *own* image, in the image of God created he him; male and female created he them. And God blessed them, and God said unto them, Be fruitful, and multiply, and replenish the earth, and subdue it: and have dominion over the fish of the sea, and over the fowl of the air, and over every living thing that moveth upon the earth. And God said, Behold, I have given you every herb bearing seed, which is upon the face of all the earth, and every tree, in the which *is* the fruit of a tree yielding seed; to you it shall be for meat. **Genesis 3:8:** And they heard the voice of the LORD God walking in the garden in the cool of the day: and Adam and his wife hid themselves from the presence of the LORD God amongst the trees of the garden.

[5] **Genesis 2:3:** And God blessed the seventh day, and sanctified it: because that in it he had rested from all his work which God created and made.

[6] **Galatians 3:12:** And the law is not of faith: but, The man that doeth them shall live in them. **Romans 10:5:** For Moses describeth the righteousness which is of the law, That the man which doeth those things shall live by them.

[7] **Genesis 2:9:** And out of the ground made the LORD God to grow every tree that is pleasant to the sight, and good for food; the tree of life also in the midst of the garden, and the tree of knowledge of good and evil.

[8] **Genesis 2:17:** But of the tree of the knowledge of good and evil, thou shalt not eat of it: for in the day that thou eatest thereof thou shalt surely die.

21. Did man continue in that estate wherein God at first created him?

A. Our first parents being left to the freedom of their own will, through the temptation of Satan, transgressed the commandment of God in eating the forbidden fruit, and thereby fell from the estate of innocency wherein they were created.[1]

Proofs

[1] **Genesis 3:6-8, 13:** And when the woman saw that the tree *was* good for food, and that it *was* pleasant to the eyes, and a tree to be desired to make *one* wise, she took of the fruit thereof, and did eat, and gave also unto her husband with her; and he did eat. And the eyes of them both were opened, and they knew that they *were* naked; and they sewed fig leaves together, and made themselves aprons. And they heard the voice of the LORD God walking in the garden in the cool of the day: and Adam and his wife hid themselves from the presence of the LORD God amongst the trees of the garden ... And the LORD God said unto the woman, What *is* this *that* thou hast done? And the woman said, The serpent beguiled me, and I did eat. **Ecclesiastes 7:29:** Lo, this only have I found, that God hath made man upright; but they have sought out many inventions. **2 Corinthians 11:3:** But I fear, lest by any means,

as the serpent beguiled Eve through his subtilty, so your minds should be corrupted from the simplicity that is in Christ.

22. Did all mankind fall in that first transgression?

A. The covenant being made with Adam as a public person, not for himself only, but for his posterity, all mankind descending from him by ordinary generation, [1] sinned in him, and fell with him in that first transgression. [2]

Proofs

[1] **Acts 17:26:** And hath made of one blood all nations of men for to dwell on all the face of the earth, and hath determined the times before appointed, and the bounds of their habitation …

[2] **Genesis 2:16-17:** And the LORD God commanded the man, saying, Of every tree of the garden thou mayest freely eat: But of the tree of the knowledge of good and evil, thou shalt not eat of it: for in the day that thou eatest thereof thou shalt surely die. [Compare with] **Romans 5:12-20:** Wherefore, as by one man sin entered into the world, and death by sin; and so death passed upon all men, for that all have sinned: (For until the law sin was in the world: but sin is not imputed when there is no law. Nevertheless death reigned from Adam to Moses, even over them that had not sinned after the similitude of Adam's transgression, who is the figure of him that was to come. But not as the offence, so also *is* the free gift. For if through the offence of one many be dead, much more the grace of God, and the gift by grace, *which is* by one man, Jesus Christ, hath abounded unto many. And not as *it was* by one that sinned, *so is* the gift: for the judgment *was* by one to condemnation, but the free gift *is* of many offences unto justification. For if by one man's offence death reigned by one; much more they which receive abundance of grace and of the gift of righteousness shall reign in life by one, Jesus Christ.) Therefore as by the offence of one *judgment came* upon all men to condemnation; even so by the righteousness of one *the free gift came* upon all men unto justification of life. For as by one man's disobedience many were made sinners, so by the obedience of one shall many be made righteous. Moreover the law entered, that the offence might abound. But where sin abounded, grace did much more abound … **1 Corinthians 15:21-22:** For since by man *came* death, by man *came* also the resurrection of the dead. For as in Adam all die, even so in Christ shall all be made alive.

23. Into what estate did the fall bring mankind?

A. The fall brought mankind into an estate of sin and misery.[1]

Proofs

[1] **Romans 5:12:** Wherefore, as by one man sin entered into the world, and death by sin; and so death passed upon all men, for that all have sinned … **Romans 3:23:** For all have sinned, and come short of the glory of God …

24. What is sin?

A. Sin is any want of conformity unto, or transgression of, any law of God, given as a rule to the reasonable creature. [1]

Proofs

[1] **1 John 3:4:** Whosoever committeth sin transgresseth also the law: for sin is the transgression of the law. **Galatians 3:10, 12:** For as many as are of the works of the law are under the curse: for it is written, Cursed *is* every one that continueth not in all things which are written in the book of the law to do them … And the law is not of faith: but, The man that doeth them shall live in them.

25. Wherein consisteth the sinfulness of that estate whereinto man fell?

A. The sinfulness of that estate whereinto man fell, consisteth in the guilt of Adam's first sin, [1] the want of that righteousness wherein he was created, and the corruption of his nature, whereby he is utterly indisposed, disabled, and made opposite unto all that is spiritually good, and wholly inclined to all evil, and that continually;[2] which is commonly called original sin, and from which do proceed all actual transgressions. [3]

Proofs

[1] **Romans 5:12, 19:** Wherefore, as by one man sin entered into the world, and death by sin; and so death passed upon all men, for that all have sinned … For as by one man's disobedience many were made sinners, so by the obedience of one shall many be made righteous.

[2] **Romans 3:10-19:** As it is written, There is none righteous, no, not one: There is none that understandeth, there is none that seeketh after God. They are all gone out of the way, they are together become unprofitable; there is none that doeth good, no, not one. Their throat

is an open sepulchre; with their tongues they have used deceit; the poison of asps *is* under their lips: Whose mouth is full of cursing and bitterness: Their feet *are* swift to shed blood: Destruction and misery *are* in their ways: And the way of peace have they not known: There is no fear of God before their eyes. Now we know that what things soever the law saith, it saith to them who are under the law: that every mouth may be stopped, and all the world may become guilty before God. **Ephesians 2:1-3:** And you *hath he quickened*, who were dead in trespasses and sins; Wherein in time past ye walked according to the course of this world, according to the prince of the power of the air, the spirit that now worketh in the children of disobedience: Among whom also we all had our conversation in times past in the lusts of our flesh, fulfilling the desires of the flesh and of the mind; and were by nature the children of wrath, even as others. **Romans 5:6:** For when we were yet without strength, in due time Christ died for the ungodly. **Romans 8:7-8:** Because the carnal mind *is* enmity against God: for it is not subject to the law of God, neither indeed can be. So then they that are in the flesh cannot please God. **Genesis 6:5:** And God saw that the wickedness of man *was* great in the earth, and *that* every imagination of the thoughts of his heart *was* only evil continually.

[3] **James 1:14-15:** But every man is tempted, when he is drawn away of his own lust, and enticed. Then when lust hath conceived, it bringeth forth sin: and sin, when it is finished, bringeth forth death. **Matthew 15:19:** For out of the heart proceed evil thoughts, murders, adulteries, fornications, thefts, false witness, blasphemies …

26. How is original sin conveyed from our first parents unto their posterity?

A. Original sin is conveyed from our first parents unto their posterity by natural generation, so as all that proceed from them in that way are conceived and born in sin. [1]

Proofs

[1] **Psalm 51:5:** Behold, I was shapen in iniquity; and in sin did my mother conceive me. **Job 14:4:** Who can bring a clean *thing* out of an unclean? not one. **Job 15:14:** What *is* man, that he should be clean? and *he which is* born of a woman, that he should be righteous? **John 3:6:** That which is born of the flesh is flesh; and that which is born of the Spirit is spirit.

27. What misery did the fall bring upon mankind?

A. The fall brought upon mankind the loss of communion with God, [1] his displeasure and curse; so as we are by nature children of wrath, [2] bond-slaves to Satan, [3] and justly liable to all punishments in this world, and that which is to come. [4]

Proofs

[1] **Genesis 3:8, 10, 24:** And they heard the voice of the LORD God walking in the garden in the cool of the day: and Adam and his wife hid themselves from the presence of the LORD God amongst the trees of the garden ... And he said, I heard thy voice in the garden, and I was afraid, because I was naked; and I hid myself ... So he drove out the man; and he placed at the east of the garden of Eden Cherubims, and a flaming sword which turned every way, to keep the way of the tree of life.

[2] **Ephesians 2:2-3:** Wherein in time past ye walked according to the course of this world, according to the prince of the power of the air, the spirit that now worketh in the children of disobedience: Among whom also we all had our conversation in times past in the lusts of our flesh, fulfilling the desires of the flesh and of the mind; and were by nature the children of wrath, even as others.

[3] **2 Timothy 2:26:** And *that* they may recover themselves out of the snare of the devil, who are taken captive by him at his will.

[4] **Genesis 2:17:** But of the tree of the knowledge of good and evil, thou shalt not eat of it: for in the day that thou eatest thereof thou shalt surely die. **Lamentations 3:39:** Wherefore doth a living man complain, a man for the punishment of his sins? **Romans 6:23:** For the wages of sin is death; but the gift of God *is* eternal life through Jesus Christ our Lord. **Matthew 25:41:** Then shall he say also unto them on the left hand, Depart from me, ye cursed, into everlasting fire, prepared for the devil and his angels ... **Matthew 25:46:** And these shall go away into everlasting punishment: but the righteous into life eternal. **Jude 7:** Even as Sodom and Gomorrha, and the cities about them in like manner, giving themselves over to fornication, and going after strange flesh, are set forth for an example, suffering the vengeance of eternal fire.

28. What are the punishments of sin in this world?

A. The punishments of sin in this world are either inward, as blindness of mind, [1] a reprobate sense, [2] strong delusions, [3] hardness of heart, [4] horror of conscience, [5] and vile affections; [6] or outward, as the curse of God upon the creatures for our sakes, [7] and all other evils that befall us in our bodies, names, estates, relations, and employments; [8] together with death itself. [9]

Proofs

[1] **Ephesians 4:18:** Having the understanding darkened, being alienated from the life of God through the ignorance that is in them, because of the blindness of their heart …

[2] **Romans 1:28:** And even as they did not like to retain God in *their* knowledge, God gave them over to a reprobate mind, to do those things which are not convenient …

[3] **2 Thessalonians 2:11:** And for this cause God shall send them strong delusion, that they should believe a lie …

[4] **Romans 2:5:** But after thy hardness and impenitent heart treasurest up unto thyself wrath against the day of wrath and revelation of the righteous judgment of God …

[5] **Isaiah 33:14:** The sinners in Zion are afraid; fearfulness hath surprised the hypocrites. Who among us shall dwell with the devouring fire? who among us shall dwell with everlasting burnings? **Genesis 4:13:** And Cain said unto the LORD, My punishment *is* greater than I can bear. **Matthew 27:4:** Saying, I have sinned in that I have betrayed the innocent blood. And they said, What *is that* to us? see thou *to that*.

[6] **Romans 1:26:** For this cause God gave them up unto vile affections: for even their women did change the natural use into that which is against nature …

[7] **Genesis 3:17:** And unto Adam he said, Because thou hast hearkened unto the voice of thy wife, and hast eaten of the tree, of which I commanded thee, saying, Thou shalt not eat of it: cursed *is* the ground for thy sake; in sorrow shalt thou eat *of* it all the days of thy life …

[8] **Deuteronomy 28:15–18:** But it shall come to pass, if thou wilt not hearken unto the voice of the LORD thy God, to observe to do all his

commandments and his statutes which I command thee this day; that all these curses shall come upon thee, and overtake thee: Cursed *shalt* thou *be* in the city, and cursed *shalt* thou be in the field. Cursed *shall be* thy basket and thy store. Cursed *shall be* the fruit of thy body, and the fruit of thy land, the increase of thy kine, and the flocks of thy sheep. [See the rest of the chapter.]

[9] **Romans 6:21, 23:** What fruit had ye then in those things whereof ye are now ashamed? for the end of those things *is* death … For the wages of sin *is* death; but the gift of God *is* eternal life through Jesus Christ our Lord.

29. What are the punishments of sin in the world to come?

A. The punishments of sin in the world to come, are everlasting separation from the comfortable presence of God, and most grievous torments in soul and body, without intermission, in hell-fire forever.[1]

Proofs

[1] **2 Thessalonians 1:9:** Who shall be punished with everlasting destruction from the presence of the Lord, and from the glory of his power … **Mark 9:43-44, 46, 48:** And if thy hand offend thee, cut it off: it is better for thee to enter into life maimed, than having two hands to go into hell, into the fire that never shall be quenched: Where their worm dieth not, and the fire is not quenched. **Luke 16:24:** And he cried and said, Father Abraham, have mercy on me, and send Lazarus, that he may dip the tip of his finger in water, and cool my tongue; for I am tormented in this flame.

30. Doth God leave all mankind to perish in the estate of sin and misery?

A. God doth not leave all men to perish in the estate of sin and misery, [1] into which they fell by the breach of the first covenant, commonly called the *covenant of works*; [2] but of his mere love and mercy delivereth his elect out of it, and bringeth them into an estate of salvation by the second covenant, commonly called the *covenant of grace*.[3]

Proofs

[1] **1 Thessalonians 5:9:** For God hath not appointed us to wrath, but to obtain salvation by our Lord Jesus Christ …

[2] **Galatians 3:10, 12:** For as many as are of the works of the law are under the curse: for it is written, Cursed *is* every one that continueth not in all things which are written in the book of the law to do them … And the law is not of faith: but, The man that doeth them shall live in them.

[3] **Titus 3:4-7:** But after that the kindness and love of God our Saviour toward man appeared, Not by works of righteousness which we have done, but according to his mercy he saved us, by the washing of regeneration, and renewing of the Holy Ghost; Which he shed on us abundantly through Jesus Christ our Saviour; That being justified by his grace, we should be made heirs according to the hope of eternal life. **Galatians 3:21:** *Is* the law then against the promises of God? God forbid: for if there had been a law given which could have given life, verily righteousness should have been by the law. **Romans 3:20-22:**Therefore by the deeds of the law there shall no flesh be justified in his sight: for by the law *is* the knowledge of sin. But now the righteousness of God without the law is manifested, being witnessed by the law and the prophets; Even the righteousness of God *which is* by faith of Jesus Christ unto all and upon all them that believe: for there is no difference …

31. With whom was the covenant of grace made?

A. The covenant of grace was made with Christ as the second Adam, and in him with all the elect as his seed. [1]

Proofs

[1] **Galatians 3:16:** Now to Abraham and his seed were the promises made. He saith not, And to seeds, as of many; but as of one, And to thy seed, which is Christ. **Romans 5:15-21:** (… But not as the offence, so also *is* the free gift. For if through the offence of one many be dead, much more the grace of God, and the gift by grace, *which is* by one man, Jesus Christ, hath abounded unto many. And not as *it was* by one that sinned, *so is* the gift: for the judgment *was* by one to condemnation, but the free gift *is* of many offences unto justification. For if by one man's offence death reigned by one; much more they which receive abundance of grace and of the gift of righteousness shall reign in life by one, Jesus Christ.) Therefore as by the offence of one *judgment came* upon all men

to condemnation; even so by the righteousness of one *the free gift came* upon all men unto justification of life. For as by one man's disobedience many were made sinners, so by the obedience of one shall many be made righteous. Moreover the law entered, that the offence might abound. But where sin abounded, grace did much more abound: That as sin hath reigned unto death, even so might grace reign through righteousness unto eternal life by Jesus Christ our Lord. **Isaiah 53:10–11:** Yet it pleased the LORD to bruise him; he hath put *him* to grief: when thou shalt make his soul an offering for sin, he shall see *his* seed, he shall prolong *his* days, and the pleasure of the LORD shall prosper in his hand. He shall see of the travail of his soul, *and* shall be satisfied: by his knowledge shall my righteous servant justify many; for he shall bear their iniquities.

32. How is the grace of God manifested in the second covenant?

A. The grace of God is manifested in the second covenant, in that he freely provideth and offereth to sinners a Mediator, [1] and life and salvation by him; [2] and requiring faith as the condition to interest them in him, [3] promiseth and giveth his Holy Spirit [4] to all his elect, to work in them that faith, [5] with all other saving graces; [6] and to enable them unto all holy obedience, [7]as the evidence of the truth of their faith [8] and thankfulness to God, [9] and as the way which he hath appointed them to salvation. [10]

Proofs

[1] **Genesis 3:15:** And I will put enmity between thee and the woman, and between thy seed and her seed; it shall bruise thy head, and thou shalt bruise his heel. **Isaiah 42:6:** I the LORD have called thee in righteousness, and will hold thine hand, and will keep thee, and give thee for a covenant of the people, for a light of the Gentiles … **John 6:27:** Labour not for the meat which perisheth, but for that meat which endureth unto everlasting life, which the Son of man shall give unto you: for him hath God the Father sealed.

[2] **1 John 5:11–12:** And this is the record, that God hath given to us eternal life, and this life is in his Son. He that hath the Son hath life; *and* he that hath not the Son of God hath not life.

[3] **John 3:16:** For God so loved the world, that he gave his only begotten Son, that whosoever believeth in him should not perish, but have everlasting life. **John 1:12:** But as many as received him, to them gave he power to become the sons of God, *even* to them that believe on his name …

[4] **Proverbs 1:23:** Turn you at my reproof: behold, I will pour out my spirit unto you, I will make known my words unto you.

[5] **2 Corinthians 4:13:** We having the same spirit of faith, according as it is written, I believed, and therefore have I spoken; we also believe, and therefore speak …

[6] **Galatians 5:22-23:** But the fruit of the Spirit is love, joy, peace, longsuffering, gentleness, goodness, faith, Meekness, temperance: against such there is no law.

[7] **Ezekiel 36:27:** And I will put my spirit within you, and cause you to walk in my statutes, and ye shall keep my judgments, and do *them*.

[8] **James 2:18, 22:** Yea, a man may say, Thou hast faith, and I have works: shew me thy faith without thy works, and I will shew thee my faith by my works … Seest thou how faith wrought with his works, and by works was faith made perfect?

[9] **2 Corinthians 5:14-15:** For the love of Christ constraineth us; because we thus judge, that if one died for all, then were all dead: And *that* he died for all, that they which live should not henceforth live unto themselves, but unto him which died for them, and rose again.

[10] **Ephesians 2:10:** For we are his workmanship, created in Christ Jesus unto good works, which God hath before ordained that we should walk in them.

33. Was the covenant of grace always administered after one and the same manner?

A. The covenant of grace was not always administered after the same manner, but the administrations of it under the Old Testament were different from those under the New. [1]

Proof

[1] **2 Corinthians 3:6-9:** Who also hath made us able ministers of the new testament; not of the letter, but of the spirit: for the letter killeth, but the spirit giveth life. But if the ministration of death, written *and* engraven in stones, was glorious, so that the children of

Israel could not stedfastly behold the face of Moses for the glory of his countenance; which *glory* was to be done away: How shall not the ministration of the spirit be rather glorious? For if the ministration of condemnation *be* glory, much more doth the ministration of righteousness exceed in glory.

34. How was the covenant of grace administered under the Old Testament?

A. The covenant of grace was administered under the Old Testament, by promises, [1] prophecies, [2] sacrifices, [3] circumcision, [4] the passover, [5] and other types and ordinances, which did all foresignify Christ then to come, and were for that time sufficient to build up the elect in faith in the promised Messiah, [6] by whom they then had full remission of sin, and eternal salvation. [7]

Proofs

[1] **Romans 15:8:** Now I say that Jesus Christ was a minister of the circumcision for the truth of God, to confirm the promises *made* unto the fathers ...

[2] **Acts 3:20, 24:** And he shall send Jesus Christ, which before was preached unto you ... Yea, and all the prophets from Samuel and those that follow after, as many as have spoken, have likewise foretold of these days.

[3] **Hebrews 10:1:** For the law having a shadow of good things to come, *and* not the very image of the things, can never with those sacrifices which they offered year by year continually make the comers thereunto perfect.

[4] **Romans 4:11:** And he received the sign of circumcision, a seal of the righteousness of the faith which *he had yet* being uncircumcised: that he might be the father of all them that believe, though they be not circumcised; that righteousness might be imputed unto them also ...

[5] **1 Corinthians 5:7:** Purge out therefore the old leaven, that ye may be a new lump, as ye are unleavened. For even Christ our passover is sacrificed for us ...

[6] **Hebrews chapters 8, 9, 10 (entire). Hebrews 11:13:** These all died in faith, not having received the promises, but having seen them

afar off, and were persuaded of *them*, and embraced *them*, and confessed that they were strangers and pilgrims on the earth.

[7] **Galatians 3:7-9, 14:** Know ye therefore that they which are of faith, the same are the children of Abraham. And the scripture, foreseeing that God would justify the heathen through faith, preached before the gospel unto Abraham, *saying*, In thee shall all nations be blessed. So then they which be of faith are blessed with faithful Abraham ... That the blessing of Abraham might come on the Gentiles through Jesus Christ; that we might receive the promise of the Spirit through faith.

35. How is the covenant of grace administered under the New Testament?

A. Under the New Testament, when Christ the substance was exhibited, the same covenant of grace was and still is to be administered in the preaching of the Word, [1] and the administration of the sacraments of Baptism [2] and the Lord's Supper; [3] in which grace and salvation are held forth in more fullness, evidence, and efficacy, to all nations. [4]

Proofs

[1] **Mark 16:15:** And he said unto them, Go ye into all the world, and preach the gospel to every creature.

[2] **Matthew 28:19-20:** Go ye therefore, and teach all nations, baptizing them in the name of the Father, and of the Son, and of the Holy Ghost: Teaching them to observe all things whatsoever I have commanded you: and, lo, I am with you alway, even unto the end of the world. Amen.

[3] **1 Corinthians 11:23-25:** For I have received of the Lord that which also I delivered unto you, That the Lord Jesus the *same* night in which he was betrayed took bread: And when he had given thanks, he brake *it*, and said, Take, eat: this is my body, which is broken for you: this do in remembrance of me. After the same manner also *he took* the cup, when he had supped, saying, This cup is the new testament in my blood: this do ye, as oft as ye drink *it*, in remembrance of me.

[4] **2 Corinthians 3:6-9:** Who also hath made us able ministers of the new testament; not of the letter, but of the spirit: for the letter killeth, but the spirit giveth life. But if the ministration of death, written *and* engraven in stones, was glorious, so that the children of Israel could not

stedfastly behold the face of Moses for the glory of his countenance; which *glory* was to be done away: How shall not the ministration of the spirit be rather glorious? For if the ministration of condemnation *be* glory, much more doth the ministration of righteousness exceed in glory. [See the rest of the chapter.] **Hebrews 8:6, 10-11:** But now hath he obtained a more excellent ministry, by how much also he is the mediator of a better covenant, which was established upon better promises ... For this *is* the covenant that I will make with the house of Israel after those days, saith the Lord; I will put my laws into their mind, and write them in their hearts: and I will be to them a God, and they shall be to me a people: And they shall not teach every man his neighbour, and every man his brother, saying, Know the Lord: for all shall know me, from the least to the greatest. **Matthew 28:19:** Go ye therefore, and teach all nations, baptizing them in the name of the Father, and of the Son, and of the Holy Ghost ...

36. Who is the Mediator of the covenant of grace?

A. The only Mediator of the covenant of grace is the Lord Jesus Christ, [1] who, being the eternal Son of God, of one substance and equal with the Father, [2] in the fullness of time became man, [3] and so was and continues to be God and man, in two entire distinct natures, and one person, forever. [4]

Proofs

[1] **1 Timothy 2:5:** For *there* is one God, and one mediator between God and men, the man Christ Jesus ...

[2] **John 1:1, 14:** In the beginning was the Word, and the Word was with God, and the Word was God ... And the Word was made flesh, and dwelt among us, (and we beheld his glory, the glory as of the only begotten of the Father,) full of grace and truth. **John 10:30:** I and *my* Father are one. **Philippians 2:6:** Who, being in the form of God, thought it not robbery to be equal with God ...

[3] **Galatians 4:4:** But when the fulness of the time was come, God sent forth his Son, made of a woman, made under the law ...

[4] **Luke 1:35:** And the angel answered and said unto her, The Holy Ghost shall come upon thee, and the power of the Highest shall overshadow thee: therefore also that holy thing which shall be born of thee shall be called the Son of God. **Romans 9:5:** Whose *are* the

fathers, and of whom as concerning the flesh Christ *came*, who is over all, God blessed for ever. Amen. **Colossians 2:9:** For in him dwelleth all the fulness of the Godhead bodily. **Hebrews 7:24-25:** But this *man*, because he continueth ever, hath an unchangeable priesthood. Wherefore he is able also to save them to the uttermost that come unto God by him, seeing he ever liveth to make intercession for them.

37. How did Christ, being the Son of God, become man?

A Christ the Son of God became man, by taking to himself a true body, and a reasonable soul, [1] being conceived by the power of the Holy Ghost in the womb of the virgin Mary, of her substance, and born of her, [2] yet without sin. [3]

Proofs

[1] **John 1:14:** And the Word was made flesh, and dwelt among us, (and we beheld his glory, the glory as of the only begotten of the Father,) full of grace and truth. **Matthew 26:38:** Then saith he unto them, My soul is exceeding sorrowful, even unto death: tarry ye here, and watch with me.

[2] **Luke 1:27, 31, 35, 42:** To a virgin espoused to a man whose name was Joseph, of the house of David; and the virgin's name *was* Mary ... And, behold, thou shalt conceive in thy womb, and bring forth a son, and shalt call his name JESUS ... And the angel answered and said unto her, The Holy Ghost shall come upon thee, and the power of the Highest shall overshadow thee: therefore also that holy thing which shall be born of thee shall be called the Son of God ... And she spake out with a loud voice, and said, Blessed *art* thou among women, and blessed *is* the fruit of thy womb. **Galatians 4:4:** But when the fulness of the time was come, God sent forth his Son, made of a woman, made under the law ...

[3] **Hebrews 4:15:** For we have not an high priest which cannot be touched with the feeling of our infirmities; but was in all points tempted like as *we are, yet* without sin. **Hebrews 7:26:** For such an high priest became us, *who is* holy, harmless, undefiled, separate from sinners, and made higher than the heavens ...

38. Why was it requisite that the Mediator should be God?

A. It was requisite that the Mediator should be God, that he might sustain and keep the human nature from sinking under the infinite wrath of God, and the power of death, [1] give worth and efficacy to his sufferings, obedience, and intercession; [2] and to satisfy God's justice, [3]procure his favour, [4] purchase a peculiar people, [5]give his Spirit to them, [6] conquer all their enemies, [7]and bring them to everlasting salvation. [8]

Proofs

[1] **Acts 2:24-25:** Whom God hath raised up, having loosed the pains of death: because it was not possible that he should be holden of it. For David speaketh concerning him, I foresaw the Lord always before my face, for he is on my right hand, that I should not be moved ... **Romans 1:4:** And declared *to be* the Son of God with power, according to the spirit of holiness, by the resurrection from the dead ... [Compare with] **Romans 4:25:** Who was delivered for our offences, and was raised again for our justification. **Hebrews 9:14:** How much more shall the blood of Christ, who through the eternal Spirit offered himself without spot to God, purge your conscience from dead works to serve the living God?

[2] **Acts 20:28:** Take heed therefore unto yourselves, and to all the flock, over the which the Holy Ghost hath made you overseers, to feed the church of God, which he hath purchased with his own blood. **Hebrews 9:14:** How much more shall the blood of Christ, who through the eternal Spirit offered himself without spot to God, purge your conscience from dead works to serve the living God? **Hebrews 7:25-28:** Wherefore he is able also to save them to the uttermost that come unto God by him, seeing he ever liveth to make intercession for them. For such an high priest became us, *who is* holy, harmless, undefiled, separate from sinners, and made higher than the heavens; Who needeth not daily, as those high priests, to offer up sacrifice, first for his own sins, and then for the people's: for this he did once, when he offered up himself. For the law maketh men high priests which have infirmity; but the word of the oath, which was since the law, *maketh* the Son, who is consecrated for evermore.

[3] **Romans 3:24-26:** Being justified freely by his grace through the redemption that is in Christ Jesus: Whom God hath set forth *to be* a propitiation through faith in his blood, to declare his righteousness for the remission of sins that are past, through the forbearance of God; To declare, *I say*, at this time his righteousness: that he might be just, and the justifier of him which believeth in Jesus.

[4] **Ephesians 1:6:** To the praise of the glory of his grace, wherein he hath made us accepted in the beloved. **Matthew 3:17:** And lo a voice from heaven, saying, This is my beloved Son, in whom I am well pleased.

[5] **Titus 2:13-14:** Looking for that blessed hope, and the glorious appearing of the great God and our Saviour Jesus Christ; Who gave himself for us, that he might redeem us from all iniquity, and purify unto himself a peculiar people, zealous of good works.

[6] **Galatians 4:6:** And because ye are sons, God hath sent forth the Spirit of his Son into your hearts, crying, Abba, Father.

[7] **Luke 1:68-69, 71, 74:** Blessed *be* the Lord God of Israel; for he hath visited and redeemed his people, And hath raised up an horn of salvation for us in the house of his servant David … That we should be saved from our enemies, and from the hand of all that hate us … That he would grant unto us, that we being delivered out of the hand of our enemies might serve him without fear …

[8] **Hebrews 5:8-9:** Though he were a Son, yet learned he obedience by the things which he suffered; And being made perfect, he became the author of eternal salvation unto all them that obey him … **Hebrews 9:11-15:** But Christ being come an high priest of good things to come, by a greater and more perfect tabernacle, not made with hands, that is to say, not of this building; Neither by the blood of goats and calves, but by his own blood he entered in once into the holy place, having obtained eternal redemption *for us*. For if the blood of bulls and of goats, and the ashes of an heifer sprinkling the unclean, sanctifieth to the purifying of the flesh: How much more shall the blood of Christ, who through the eternal Spirit offered himself without spot to God, purge your conscience from dead works to serve the living God? And for this cause he is the mediator of the new testament, that by means of death, for the redemption of the transgressions *that were* under the first testament, they which are called might receive the promise of eternal inheritance.

39. Why was it requisite that the Mediator should be man?

A. It was requisite that the Mediator should be man, that he might advance our nature, [1] perform obedience to the law, [2] suffer and make intercession for us in our nature, [3] have a fellow-feeling of our infirmities; [4] that we might receive the adoption of sons, [5] and have comfort and access with boldness unto the throne of grace. [6]

Proofs

[1] **Hebrews 2:16:** For verily he took not on *him the nature of* angels; but he took on *him* the seed of Abraham.

[2] **Galatians 4:4:** But when the fulness of the time was come, God sent forth his Son, made of a woman, made under the law …

[3] **Hebrews 2:14:** Forasmuch then as the children are partakers of flesh and blood, he also himself likewise took part of the same; that through death he might destroy him that had the power of death, that is, the devil … **Hebrews 7:24-25:** But this *man*, because he continueth ever, hath an unchangeable priesthood. Wherefore he is able also to save them to the uttermost that come unto God by him, seeing he ever liveth to make intercession for them.

[4] **Hebrews 4:15:** For we have not an high priest which cannot be touched with the feeling of our infirmities; but was in all points tempted like as *we are, yet* without sin.

[5] **Galatians 4:5:** To redeem them that were under the law, that we might receive the adoption of sons.

[6] **Hebrews 4:16:** Let us therefore come boldly unto the throne of grace, that we may obtain mercy, and find grace to help in time of need.

40. Why was it requisite that the Mediator should be God and man in one person?

A. It was requisite that the Mediator, who was to reconcile God and man, should himself be both God and man, and this in one person, that the proper works of each nature might be accepted of God for us, [1] and relied on by us as the works of the whole person. [2]

Proofs

[1] **Matthew 1:21, 23:** And she shall bring forth a son, and thou shalt call his name JESUS: for he shall save his people from their sins … Behold, a virgin shall be with child, and shall bring forth a son, and they shall call his name Emmanuel, which being interpreted is, God with us. **Matthew 3:17:** And lo a voice from heaven, saying, This is my beloved Son, in whom I am well pleased. **Hebrews 9:14:** How

much more shall the blood of Christ, who through the eternal Spirit offered himself without spot to God, purge your conscience from dead works to serve the living God?

[2] **1 Peter 2:6:** Wherefore also it is contained in the scripture, Behold, I lay in Sion a chief corner stone, elect, precious: and he that believeth on him shall not be confounded.

41. Why was our Mediator called Jesus?

A. Our Mediator was called Jesus, because he saveth his people from their sins. [1]

Proof

[1] **Matthew 1:21:** And she shall bring forth a son, and thou shalt call his name JESUS: for he shall save his people from their sins.

42. Why was our Mediator called Christ?

A. Our Mediator was called Christ, because he was anointed with the Holy Ghost above measure, [1] and so set apart, and fully furnished with all authority and ability, [2] to execute the offices of prophet, [3] priest, [4] and king of his church, [5] in the estate both of his humiliation and exaltation.

Proofs

[1] **John 3:34:** For he whom God hath sent speaketh the words of God: for God giveth not the Spirit by measure *unto him*. **Psalm 45:7:** Thou lovest righteousness, and hatest wickedness: therefore God, thy God, hath anointed thee with the oil of gladness above thy fellows.

[2] **John 6:27:** Labour not for the meat which perisheth, but for that meat which endureth unto everlasting life, which the Son of man shall give unto you: for him hath God the Father sealed. **Matthew 28:18-20:** And Jesus came and spake unto them, saying, All power is given unto me in heaven and in earth. Go ye therefore, and teach all nations, baptizing them in the name of the Father, and of the Son, and of the Holy Ghost: Teaching them to observe all things whatsoever I have commanded you: and, lo, I am with you alway, *even* unto the end of the world. Amen.

[3] **Acts 3:21-22:** Whom the heaven must receive until the times of restitution of all things, which God hath spoken by the mouth of all his holy prophets since the world began. For Moses truly said

unto the fathers, A prophet shall the Lord your God raise up unto you of your brethren, like unto me; him shall ye hear in all things whatsoever he shall say unto you. **Luke 4:18, 21:** The Spirit of the Lord is upon me, because he hath anointed me to preach the gospel to the poor; he hath sent me to heal the brokenhearted, to preach deliverance to the captives, and recovering of sight to the blind, to set at liberty them that are bruised … And he began to say unto them, This day is this scripture fulfilled in your ears.

[4] **Hebrews 5:5-7:** So also Christ glorified not himself to be made an high priest; but he that said unto him, Thou art my Son, to day have I begotten thee. As he saith also in another *place,* Thou *art* a priest for ever after the order of Melchisedec. Who in the days of his flesh, when he had offered up prayers and supplications with strong crying and tears unto him that was able to save him from death, and was heard in that he feared … **Hebrews 4:14-15:** Seeing then that we have a great high priest, that is passed into the heavens, Jesus the Son of God, let us hold fast *our* profession. For we have not an high priest which cannot be touched with the feeling of our infirmities; but was in all points tempted like as *we are, yet* without sin.

[5] **Psalm 2:6:** Yet have I set my king upon my holy hill of Zion. **Matthew 21:5:** Tell ye the daughter of Sion, Behold, thy King cometh unto thee, meek, and sitting upon an ass, and a colt the foal of an ass. **Isaiah 9:6-7:** For unto us a child is born, unto us a son is given: and the government shall be upon his shoulder: and his name shall be called Wonderful, Counsellor, The mighty God, The everlasting Father, The Prince of Peace. Of the increase of *his* government and peace *there shall be* no end, upon the throne of David, and upon his kingdom, to order it, and to establish it with judgment and with justice from henceforth even for ever. The zeal of the LORD of hosts will perform this. **Philippians 2:8-11:** And being found in fashion as a man, he humbled himself, and became obedient unto death, even the death of the cross. Wherefore God also hath highly exalted him, and given him a name which is above every name: That at the name of Jesus every knee should bow, of *things* in heaven, and *things* in earth, and *things* under the earth; And *that* every tongue should confess that Jesus Christ *is* Lord, to the glory of God the Father.

43. How doth Christ execute the office of prophet?

A. Christ executeth the office of a prophet, in his revealing to the church, [1] in all ages, by his Spirit and Word, [2]in divers ways of administration, [3] the whole will of God, [4] in all things concerning their edification and salvation. [5]

Proofs

[1] **John 1:18:** No man hath seen God at any time; the only begotten Son, which is in the bosom of the Father, he hath declared *him*.

[2] **1 Peter 1:10-12:** Of which salvation the prophets have inquired and searched diligently, who prophesied of the grace *that should come* unto you: Searching what, or what manner of time the Spirit of Christ which was in them did signify, when it testified beforehand the sufferings of Christ, and the glory that should follow. Unto whom it was revealed, that not unto themselves, but unto us they did minister the things, which are now reported unto you by them that have preached the gospel unto you with the Holy Ghost sent down from heaven; which things the angels desire to look into.

[3] **Hebrews 1:1-2:** God, who at sundry times and in divers manners spake in time past unto the fathers by the prophets, Hath in these last days spoken unto us by *his* Son, whom he hath appointed heir of all things, by whom also he made the worlds …

[4] **John 15:15:** Henceforth I call you not servants; for the servant knoweth not what his lord doeth: but I have called you friends; for all things that I have heard of my Father I have made known unto you.

[5] **Acts 20:32:** And now, brethren, I commend you to God, and to the word of his grace, which is able to build you up, and to give you an inheritance among all them which are sanctified. **Ephesians 4:11-13:** And he gave some, apostles; and some, prophets; and some, evangelists; and some, pastors and teachers; For the perfecting of the saints, for the work of the ministry, for the edifying of the body of Christ: Till we all come in the unity of the faith, and of the knowledge of the Son of God, unto a perfect man, unto the measure of the stature of the fulness of Christ … **John 20:31:** But these are written, that ye might believe that Jesus is the Christ, the Son of God; and that believing ye might have life through his name.

44. How doth Christ execute the office of a priest?

A. Christ executeth the office of a priest, in his once offering himself a sacrifice without spot to God, [1] to be a reconciliation for the sins of his people; [2] and in making continual intercession for them. [3]

Proofs

[1] **Hebrews 9:14, 28:** How much more shall the blood of Christ, who through the eternal Spirit offered himself without spot to God, purge your conscience from dead works to serve the living God? ... So Christ was once offered to bear the sins of many; and unto them that look for him shall he appear the second time without sin unto salvation.

[2] **Hebrews 2:17:** Wherefore in all things it behoved him to be made like unto *his* brethren, that he might be a merciful and faithful high priest in things *pertaining* to God, to make reconciliation for the sins of the people.

[3] **Hebrews 7:25:** Wherefore he is able also to save them to the uttermost that come unto God by him, seeing he ever liveth to make intercession for them.

45. How doth Christ execute the office of a king?

A. Christ executeth the office of a king, in calling out of the world a people to himself, [1] and giving them officers, [2] laws, [3] and censures, by which he visibly governs them; [4] in bestowing saving grace upon his elect, [5] rewarding their obedience, [6] and correcting them for their sins, [7] preserving and supporting them under all their temptations and sufferings, [8] restraining and overcoming all their enemies, [9] and powerfully ordering all things for his own glory, [10] and their good; [11] and also in taking vengeance on the rest, who know not God, and obey not the gospel. [12]

Proofs

[1] **Acts 15:14-16:** Simeon hath declared how God at the first did visit the Gentiles, to take out of them a people for his name. And to this agree the words of the prophets; as it is written, After this I will return, and will build again the tabernacle of David, which is fallen down; and I will build again the ruins thereof, and I will set it

up ... **Isaiah 55:4-5:** Behold, I have given him *for* a witness to the people, a leader and commander to the people. Behold, thou shalt call a nation *that* thou knowest not, and nations *that* knew not thee shall run unto thee because of the LORD thy God, and for the Holy One of Israel; for he hath glorified thee. **Genesis 49:10:** The sceptre shall not depart from Judah, nor a lawgiver from between his feet, until Shiloh come; and unto him *shall* the gathering of the people be. **Psalm 110:3:** Thy people *shall be* willing in the day of thy power, in the beauties of holiness from the womb of the morning: thou hast the dew of thy youth.

[2] **Ephesians 4:11-12:** And he gave some, apostles; and some, prophets; and some, evangelists; and some, pastors and teachers; For the perfecting of the saints, for the work of the ministry, for the edifying of the body of Christ ... **1 Corinthians 12:28:** And God hath set some in the church, first apostles, secondarily prophets, thirdly teachers, after that miracles, then gifts of healings, helps, governments, diversities of tongues.

[3] **Isaiah 33:22:** For the LORD *is* our judge, the LORD *is* our lawgiver, the LORD *is* our king; he will save us.

[4] **Matthew 18:17-18:** And if he shall neglect to hear them, tell *it* unto the church: but if he neglect to hear the church, let him be unto thee as an heathen man and a publican. Verily I say unto you, Whatsoever ye shall bind on earth shall be bound in heaven: and whatsoever ye shall loose on earth shall be loosed in heaven. **1 Corinthians 5:4-5:** In the name of our Lord Jesus Christ, when ye are gathered together, and my spirit, with the power of our Lord Jesus Christ, To deliver such an one unto Satan for the destruction of the flesh, that the spirit may be saved in the day of the Lord Jesus.

[5] **Acts 5:31:** Him hath God exalted with his right hand *to* be a Prince and a Saviour, for to give repentance to Israel, and forgiveness of sins.

[6] **Revelation 22:12:** And, behold, I come quickly; and my reward *is* with me, to give every man according as his work shall be. **Revelation 2:10**: Fear none of those things which thou shalt suffer: behold, the devil shall cast *some* of you into prison, that ye may be tried; and ye shall have tribulation ten days: be thou faithful unto death, and I will give thee a crown of life.

[7] **Revelation 3:19:** As many as I love, I rebuke and chasten: be zealous therefore, and repent.

[8] **Isaiah 63:9:** In all their affliction he was afflicted, and the angel of his presence saved them: in his love and in his pity he redeemed them; and he bare them, and carried them all the days of old.

[9] **1 Corinthians 15:25:** For he must reign, till he hath put all enemies under his feet. **Psalm 110:1-2**: The LORD said unto my Lord, Sit thou at my right hand, until I make thine enemies thy footstool. The LORD shall send the rod of thy strength out of Zion: rule thou in the midst of thine enemies.

[10] **Romans 14:10-11:** But why dost thou judge thy brother? or why dost thou set at nought thy brother? for we shall all stand before the judgment seat of Christ. For it is written, *As* I live, saith the Lord, every knee shall bow to me, and every tongue shall confess to God.

[11] **Romans 8:28:** And we know that all things work together for good to them that love God, to them who are the called according to *his* purpose.

[12] **2 Thessalonians 1:8-9:** In flaming fire taking vengeance on them that know not God, and that obey not the gospel of our Lord Jesus Christ: Who shall be punished with everlasting destruction from the presence of the Lord, and from the glory of his power ... **Psalm 2:8-9:** Ask of me, and I shall give *thee* the heathen *for* thine inheritance, and the uttermost parts of the earth *for* thy possession. Thou shalt break them with a rod of iron; thou shalt dash them in pieces like a potter's vessel.

46. What was the estate of Christ's humiliation?

A. The estate of Christ's humiliation was that low condition, wherein he for our sakes, emptying himself of his glory, took upon him the form of a servant, in his conception and birth, life, death, and after his death, until his resurrection. [1]

Proofs

[1] **Philippians 2:6-8:** Who, being in the form of God, thought it not robbery to be equal with God: But made himself of no reputation, and took upon him the form of a servant, and was made in the likeness of men: And being found in fashion as a man, he humbled himself, and became obedient unto death, even the death of the cross. **Luke 1:31:** And, behold, thou shalt conceive in thy womb, and bring forth a son, and shalt call his name JESUS. **2 Corinthians 8:9:** For ye know the grace of our Lord Jesus Christ, that, though he was rich, yet

for your sakes he became poor, that ye through his poverty might be rich. **Acts 2:24:** Whom God hath raised up, having loosed the pains of death: because it was not possible that he should be holden of it.

47. How did Christ humble himself in his conception and birth?

A. Christ humbled himself in his conception and birth, in that, being from all eternity the Son of God, in the bosom of the Father, he was pleased in the fullness of time to become the son of man, made of a woman of low estate, and to be born of her, with divers circumstances of more than ordinary abasement. [1]

Proofs

[1] **John 1:14, 18:** And the Word was made flesh, and dwelt among us, (and we beheld his glory, the glory as of the only begotten of the Father,) full of grace and truth … No man hath seen God at any time; the only begotten Son, which is in the bosom of the Father, he hath declared *him*. **Galatians 4:4:** But when the fulness of the time was come, God sent forth his Son, made of a woman, made under the law … **Luke 2:7:** And she brought forth her firstborn son, and wrapped him in swaddling clothes, and laid him in a manger; because there was no room for them in the inn.

48. How did Christ humble himself in his life?

A. Christ humbled himself in his life, by subjecting himself to the law, [1] which he perfectly fulfilled; [2] and by conflicting with the indignities of the world, [3] temptations of Satan, [4] and infirmities in his flesh, whether common to the nature of man, or particularly accompanying that of his low condition. [5]

Proofs

[1] **Galatians 4:4:** But when the fulness of the time was come, God sent forth his Son, made of a woman, made under the law …

[2] **Matthew 5:17:** Think not that I am come to destroy the law, or the prophets: I am not come to destroy, but to fulfil. **Romans 5:19:** For as by one man's disobedience many were made sinners, so by the obedience of one shall many be made righteous.

[3] **Psalm 22:6:** But I *am* a worm, and no man; a reproach of men, and despised of the people. **Hebrews 12:2-3:** Looking unto Jesus the author and finisher of *our* faith; who for the joy that was set before him endured the cross, despising the shame, and is set down at the right hand of the throne of God. For consider him that endured such contradiction of sinners against himself, lest ye be wearied and faint in your minds.

[4] **Matthew 4:1-12:** Then was Jesus led up of the spirit into the wilderness to be tempted of the devil … **Luke 4:13:** And when the devil had ended all the temptation, he departed from him for a season.

[5] **Hebrews 2:17-18:** Wherefore in all things it behoved him to be made like unto *his* brethren, that he might be a merciful and faithful high priest in things *pertaining* to God, to make reconciliation for the sins of the people. For in that he himself hath suffered being tempted, he is able to succour them that are tempted. **Hebrews 4:15:** For we have not an high priest which cannot be touched with the feeling of our infirmities; but was in all points tempted like as *we are, yet* without sin. **Isaiah 52:13-14:** Behold, my servant shall deal prudently, he shall be exalted and extolled, and be very high. As many were astonied at thee; his visage was so marred more than any man, and his form more than the sons of men …

49. How did Christ humble himself in his death?

A. Christ humbled himself in his death, in that having been betrayed by Judas, [1] forsaken by his disciples, [2] scorned and rejected by the world, [3] condemned by Pilate, and tormented by his persecutors; [4] having also conflicted with the terrors of death, and the powers of darkness, felt and borne the weight of God's wrath, [5] he laid down his life an offering for sin, [6] enduring the painful, shameful, and cursed death of the cross. [7]

Proofs

[1] **Matthew 27:4:** Saying, I have sinned in that I have betrayed the innocent blood. And they said, What *is that* to us? see thou *to that*.

[2] **Matthew 26:56:** But all this was done, that the scriptures of the prophets might be fulfilled. Then all the disciples forsook him, and fled.

[3] **Isaiah 53:2-3:** For he shall grow up before him as a tender plant, and as a root out of a dry ground: he hath no form nor comeliness; and

when we shall see him, *there is* no beauty that we should desire him. He is despised and rejected of men; a man of sorrows, and acquainted with grief: and we hid as it were *our* faces from him; he was despised, and we esteemed him not.

[4] **Matthew 27:26-50:** Then released he Barabbas unto them: and when he had scourged Jesus, he delivered *him* to be crucified ... **John 19:34:** But one of the soldiers with a spear pierced his side, and forthwith came there out blood and water.

[5] **Luke 22:44:** And being in an agony he prayed more earnestly: and his sweat was as it were great drops of blood falling down to the ground. **Matthew 27:46:** And about the ninth hour Jesus cried with a loud voice, saying, Eli, Eli, lama sabachthani? that is to say, My God, my God, why hast thou forsaken me?

[6] **Isaiah 53:10:** Yet it pleased the LORD to bruise him; he hath put *him* to grief: when thou shalt make his soul an offering for sin, he shall see *his* seed, he shall prolong *his* days, and the pleasure of the LORD shall prosper in his hand.

[7] **Philippians 2:8:** And being found in fashion as a man, he humbled himself, and became obedient unto death, even the death of the cross. **Hebrews 12:2:** Looking unto Jesus the author and finisher of *our* faith; who for the joy that was set before him endured the cross, despising the shame, and is set down at the right hand of the throne of God. **Galatians 3:13:** Christ hath redeemed us from the curse of the law, being made a curse for us: for it is written, Cursed *is* every one that hangeth on a tree ...

50. Wherein consisted Christ's humiliation after his death?

A. Christ's humiliation after his death consisted in his being buried, [1] and continuing in the state of the dead, and under the power of death till the third day; [2] which hath been otherwise expressed in these words, *He descended into hell.*

Proofs

[1] **1 Corinthians 15:3-4:** For I delivered unto you first of all that which I also received, how that Christ died for our sins according to the scriptures; And that he was buried, and that he rose again the third day according to the scriptures ...

[2] **Psalm 16:10:** For thou wilt not leave my soul in hell; neither wilt thou suffer thine Holy One to see corruption. **Acts 2:24–27, 31:** Whom God hath raised up, having loosed the pains of death: because it was not possible that he should be holden of it. For David speaketh concerning him, I foresaw the Lord always before my face, for he is on my right hand, that I should not be moved: Therefore did my heart rejoice, and my tongue was glad; moreover also my flesh shall rest in hope: Because thou wilt not leave my soul in hell, neither wilt thou suffer thine Holy One to see corruption ... He seeing this before spake of the resurrection of Christ, that his soul was not left in hell, neither his flesh did see corruption. **Romans 6:9:** Knowing that Christ being raised from the dead dieth no more; death hath no more dominion over him. **Matthew 12:40:** For as Jonas was three days and three nights in the whale's belly; so shall the Son of man be three days and three nights in the heart of the earth.

51. What was the estate of Christ's exaltation?

A. The estate of Christ's exaltation comprehendeth his resurrection, [1] ascension, [2] sitting at the right hand of the Father, [3] and his coming again to judge the world. [4]

Proofs

[1] **1 Corinthians 15:4:** And that he was buried, and that he rose again the third day according to the scriptures ...

[2] **Mark 16:19:** So then after the Lord had spoken unto them, he was received up into heaven, and sat on the right hand of God.

[3] **Ephesians 1:20:** Which he wrought in Christ, when he raised him from the dead, and set *him* at his own right hand in the heavenly *places* ...

[4] **Acts 1:11:** Which also said, Ye men of Galilee, why stand ye gazing up into heaven? this same Jesus, which is taken up from you into heaven, shall so come in like manner as ye have seen him go into heaven. **Acts 17:31:** Because he hath appointed a day, in the which he will judge the world in righteousness by *that* man whom he hath ordained; *whereof* he hath given assurance unto all *men*, in that he hath raised him from the dead.

52. How was Christ exalted in his resurrection?

A. Christ was exalted in his resurrection, in that, not having seen corruption in death (of which it was not possible for him to be held), [1] and having the very same body in which he suffered, with the essential properties thereof, [2] (but without mortality, and other common infirmities belonging to this life), really united to his soul, [3] he rose again from the dead the third day by his own power; [4] whereby he declared himself to be the Son of God, [5] to have satisfied divine justice, [6] to have vanquished death, and him that had the power of it, [7] and to be Lord of quick and dead: [8] all which he did as a public person, [9]the head of his church, [10] for their justification, [11] quickening in grace, [12] support against enemies, [13] and to assure them of their resurrection from the dead at the last day. [14]

Proofs

[1] **Acts 2:24, 27:** Whom God hath raised up, having loosed the pains of death: because it was not possible that he should be holden of it ... Because thou wilt not leave my soul in hell, neither wilt thou suffer thine Holy One to see corruption.

[2] **Luke 24:39:** Behold my hands and my feet, that it is I myself: handle me, and see; for a spirit hath not flesh and bones, as ye see me have.

[3] **Romans 6:9:** Knowing that Christ being raised from the dead dieth no more; death hath no more dominion over him. **Revelation 1:18.** *I am* he that liveth, and was dead; and, behold, I am alive for evermore, Amen; and have the keys of hell and of death.

[4] **John 10:18:** No man taketh it from me, but I lay it down of myself. I have power to lay it down, and I have power to take it again. This commandment have I received of my Father.

[5] **Romans 1:4:** And declared *to be* the Son of God with power, according to the spirit of holiness, by the resurrection from the dead ...

[6] **Romans 8:34:** Who *is* he that condemneth? *It is* Christ that died, yea rather, that is risen again, who is even at the right hand of God, who also maketh intercession for us.

[7] **Hebrews 2:14:** Forasmuch then as the children are partakers of flesh and blood, he also himself likewise took part of the same; that through death he might destroy him that had the power of death, that is, the devil ...

[8] **Romans 14:9:** For to this end Christ both died, and rose, and revived, that he might be Lord both of the dead and living.

[9] **1 Corinthians 15:21-22:** For since by man *came* death, by man *came* also the resurrection of the dead. For as in Adam all die, even so in Christ shall all be made alive.

[10] **Ephesians 1:20-23:** Which he wrought in Christ, when he raised him from the dead, and set *him* at his own right hand in the heavenly *places*, Far above all principality, and power, and might, and dominion, and every name that is named, not only in this world, but also in that which is to come: And hath put all *things* under his feet, and gave him *to be* the head over all *things* to the church, Which is his body, the fulness of him that filleth all in all. **Colossians 1:18:** And he is the head of the body, the church: who is the beginning, the firstborn from the dead; that in all *things* he might have the preeminence.

[11] **Romans 4:25:** Who was delivered for our offences, and was raised again for our justification.

[12] **Ephesians 2:1, 5-6:** And you *hath he quickened*, who were dead in trespasses and sins ... Even when we were dead in sins, hath quickened us together with Christ, (by grace ye are saved;) And hath raised *us* up together, and made *us* sit together in heavenly *places* in Christ Jesus ... **Colossians 2:12:** Buried with him in baptism, wherein also ye are risen with *him* through the faith of the operation of God, who hath raised him from the dead.

[13] **1 Corinthians 15:25-27:** For he must reign, till he hath put all enemies under his feet. The last enemy *that* shall be destroyed *is* death. For he hath put all things under his feet. But when he saith all things are put under *him, it is* manifest that he is excepted, which did put all things under him.

[14] **1 Corinthians 15:20:** But now is Christ risen from the dead, *and* become the firstfruits of them that slept.

53. How was Christ exalted in his ascension?

A. Christ was exalted in his ascension, in that having after his resurrection often appeared unto and conversed with his apostles, speaking to them of the things pertaining to the kingdom of God, [1] and giving them commission to preach the gospel to all nations, [2] forty days after his resurrection, he, in our nature, and as our head, [3] triumphing over enemies, [4] visibly went up into the highest heavens, there to receive gifts for men, [5] to raise up our affections thither, [6] and to prepare a place for us, [7] where he himself is, and shall continue till his second coming at the end of the world. [8]

Proofs

[1] **Acts 1:2-3:** Until the day in which he was taken up, after that he through the Holy Ghost had given commandments unto the apostles whom he had chosen: To whom also he shewed himself alive after his passion by many infallible proofs, being seen of them forty days, and speaking of the things pertaining to the kingdom of God ...

[2] **Matthew 28:19-20:** Go ye therefore, and teach all nations, baptizing them in the name of the Father, and of the Son, and of the Holy Ghost: Teaching them to observe all things whatsoever I have commanded you: and, lo, I am with you alway, *even* unto the end of the world. Amen.

[3] **Hebrews 6:20:** Whither the forerunner is for us entered, *even* Jesus, made an high priest for ever after the order of Melchisedec.

[4] **Ephesians 4:8:** Wherefore he saith, When he ascended up on high, he led captivity captive, and gave gifts unto men.

[5] **Acts 1:9-11:** And when he had spoken these things, while they beheld, he was taken up; and a cloud received him out of their sight. And while they looked stedfastly toward heaven as he went up, behold, two men stood by them in white apparel; Which also said, Ye men of Galilee, why stand ye gazing up into heaven? this same Jesus, which is taken up from you into heaven, shall so come in like manner as ye have seen him go into heaven. **Ephesians 4:10:** He that descended is the same also that ascended up far above all heavens, that he might fill all things. **Psalm 68:18:** Thou hast ascended on high, thou hast led captivity captive: thou hast received gifts for men; yea, *for* the rebellious also, that the LORD God might dwell *among them*.

[6] **Colossians 3:1-2:** If ye then be risen with Christ, seek those things which are above, where Christ sitteth on the right hand of God. Set your affection on things above, not on things on the earth.

[7] **John 14:3:** And if I go and prepare a place for you, I will come again, and receive you unto myself; that where I am, *there* ye may be also.

[8] **Acts 3:21:** Whom the heaven must receive until the times of restitution of all things, which God hath spoken by the mouth of all his holy prophets since the world began.

54. How is Christ exalted in his sitting at the right hand of God?

A. Christ is exalted in his sitting at the right hand of God, in that as God-man he is advanced to the highest favour with God the Father, [1] with all fullness of joy, [2] glory, [3] and power over all things in heaven and earth; [4] and doth gather and defend his church, and subdue their enemies; furnisheth his ministers and people with gifts and graces, [5] and maketh intercession for them. [6]

Proofs

[1] **Philippians 2:9:** Wherefore God also hath highly exalted him, and given him a name which is above every name …

[2] **Acts 2:28:** Thou hast made known to me the ways of life; thou shalt make me full of joy with thy countenance. [Compare with] **Psalm 16:11:** Thou wilt shew me the path of life: in thy presence *is* fulness of joy; at thy right hand *there are* pleasures for evermore.

[3] **John 17:5:** And now, O Father, glorify thou me with thine own self with the glory which I had with thee before the world was.

[4] **Ephesians 1:22:** And hath put all things under his feet, and gave him to be the head over all *things* to the church … **1 Peter 3:22:** Who is gone into heaven, and is on the right hand of God; angels and authorities and powers being made subject unto him.

[5] **Ephesians 4:10-12:** (… He that descended is the same also that ascended up far above all heavens, that he might fill all things.) And he gave some, apostles; and some, prophets; and some, evangelists; and some, pastors and teachers; For the perfecting of the saints, for the work of the ministry, for the edifying of the body of Christ … **Psalm 110:1:** The LORD said unto my Lord, Sit thou at my right hand, until I make thine enemies thy footstool. [See the Psalm throughout.]

[6] **Romans 8:34:** Who *is* he that condemneth? *It is* Christ that died, yea rather, that is risen again, who is even at the right hand of God, who also maketh intercession for us.

55. How doeth Christ make intercession?

A. Christ maketh intercession, by his appearing in our nature continually before the Father in heaven, [1] in the merit of his obedience and sacrifice on earth, [2] declaring his will to have it applied to all believers; [3] answering all accusations against them, [4] and procuring for them quiet of conscience, notwithstanding daily failings, [5] access with boldness to the throne of grace, [6] and acceptance of their persons [7] and services. [8]

Proofs

[1] **Hebrews 9:12, 24:** Neither by the blood of goats and calves, but by his own blood he entered in once into the holy place, having obtained eternal redemption *for us* … For Christ is not entered into the holy places made with hands, *which are* the figures of the true; but into heaven itself, now to appear in the presence of God for us …

[2] **Hebrews 1:3:** Who being the brightness of *his* glory, and the express image of his person, and upholding all things by the word of his power, when he had by himself purged our sins, sat down on the right hand of the Majesty on high …

[3] **John 3:16:** For God so loved the world, that he gave his only begotten Son, that whosoever believeth in him should not perish, but have everlasting life. **John 17:9, 20, 24:** I pray for them: I pray not for the world, but for them which thou hast given me; for they are thine … Neither pray I for these alone, but for them also which shall believe on me through their word … Father, I will that they also, whom thou hast given me, be with me where I am; that they may behold my glory, which thou hast given me: for thou lovedst me before the foundation of the world.

[4] **Romans 8:33-34:** Who shall lay any thing to the charge of God's elect? *It is* God that justifieth. Who *is* he that condemneth? *It is* Christ that died, yea rather, that is risen again, who is even at the right hand of God, who also maketh intercession for us.

[5] **Romans 5:1-2:** Therefore being justified by faith, we have peace with God through our Lord Jesus Christ: By whom also we have access by faith into this grace wherein we stand, and rejoice in hope of the glory of God. **1 John 2:1-2:** My little children, these things write I unto you, that ye sin not. And if any man sin, we have an advocate with the Father, Jesus Christ the righteous: And he is the propitiation for our sins: and not for ours only, but also for *the sins of* the whole world.

[6] **Hebrews 4:16:** Let us therefore come boldly unto the throne of grace, that we may obtain mercy, and find grace to help in time of need.

[7] **Ephesians 1:6:** To the praise of the glory of his grace, wherein he hath made us accepted in the beloved.

[8] **1 Peter 2:5:** Ye also, as lively stones, are built up a spiritual house, an holy priesthood, to offer up spiritual sacrifices, acceptable to God by Jesus Christ.

56. How is Christ to be exalted in his coming again to judge the world?

A. Christ is to be exalted in his coming again to judge the world, in that he, who was unjustly judged and condemned by wicked men, [1] shall come again at the last day in great power, [2] and in the full manifestation of his own glory, and of his Father's, with all his holy angels, [3] with a shout, with the voice of the archangel, and with the trumpet of God, [4] to judge the world in righteousness. [5]

Proofs

[1] **Acts 3:14-15:** But ye denied the Holy One and the Just, and desired a murderer to be granted unto you; And killed the Prince of life, whom God hath raised from the dead; whereof we are witnesses.

[2] **Matthew 24:30:** And then shall appear the sign of the Son of man in heaven: and then shall all the tribes of the earth mourn, and they shall see the Son of man coming in the clouds of heaven with power and great glory.

[3] **Luke 9:26:** For whosoever shall be ashamed of me and of my words, of him shall the Son of man be ashamed, when he shall come in his own glory, and *in his* Father's, and of the holy angels. **Matthew 25:31:** When the Son of man shall come in his glory, and all the holy angels with him, then shall he sit upon the throne of his glory …

[4] **1 Thessalonians 4:16:** For the Lord himself shall descend from heaven with a shout, with the voice of the archangel, and with the trump of God: and the dead in Christ shall rise first ...

[5] **Acts 17:31:** Because he hath appointed a day, in the which he will judge the world in righteousness by *that* man whom he hath ordained; *whereof* he hath given assurance unto all *men*, in that he hath raised him from the dead.

57. What benefits hath Christ procured by his mediation?

A. Christ, by his mediation, hath procured redemption, [1]with all other benefits of the covenant of grace.[2]

Proofs

[1] **Hebrews 9:12:** Neither by the blood of goats and calves, but by his own blood he entered in once into the holy place, having obtained eternal redemption *for us*.

[2] **2 Corinthians 1:20:** For all the promises of God in him *are* yea, and in him Amen, unto the glory of God by us.

58. How do we come to be made partakers of the benefits which Christ hath procured?

A. We are made partakers of the benefits which Christ hath procured, by the application of them unto us, [1]which is the work especially of God the Holy Ghost. [2]

Proofs

[1] **John 1:11-12:** He came unto his own, and his own received him not. But as many as received him, to them gave he power to become the sons of God, *even* to them that believe on his name.

[2] **Titus 3:5-6:** Not by works of righteousness which we have done, but according to his mercy he saved us, by the washing of regeneration, and renewing of the Holy Ghost; Which he shed on us abundantly through Jesus Christ our Saviour ...

59. Who are made partakers of redemption through Christ?

A. Redemption is certainly applied, and effectually communicated, to all those for whom Christ hath purchased it: [1] who are in time by the Holy Ghost enabled to believe in Christ according to the gospel. [2]

Proofs

[1] **Ephesians 1:13-14:** In whom ye also *trusted,* after that ye heard the word of truth, the gospel of your salvation: in whom also after that ye believed, ye were sealed with that holy Spirit of promise, Which is the earnest of our inheritance until the redemption of the purchased possession, unto the praise of his glory. **John 6:37, 39:** All that the Father giveth me shall come to me; and him that cometh to me I will in no wise cast out ... And this is the Father's will which hath sent me, that of all which he hath given me I should lose nothing, but should raise it up again at the last day. **John 10:15-16:** As the Father knoweth me, even so know I the Father: and I lay down my life for the sheep. And other sheep I have, which are not of this fold: them also I must bring, and they shall hear my voice; and there shall be one fold, *and* one shepherd.

[2] **Ephesians 2:8:** For by grace are ye saved through faith; and that not of yourselves: *it is* the gift of God ... **2 Corinthians 4:13:** We having the same spirit of faith, according as it is written, I believed, and therefore have I spoken; we also believe, and therefore speak ...

60. **Can they who have never heard the gospel, and so know not Jesus Christ, nor believe in him, be saved by their living according to the light of nature?**

A. They who, having never heard the gospel, [1] know not Jesus Christ, [2] and believe not in him, cannot be saved, [3] be they never so diligent to frame their lives according to the light of nature, [4] or the laws of that religion which they profess; [5] neither is there salvation in any other, but in Christ alone, [6] who is the Saviour only of his body the church.[7]

Proofs

[1] **Romans 10:14:** How then shall they call on him in whom they have not believed? and how shall they believe in him of whom they have not heard? and how shall they hear without a preacher?

[2] **2 Thessalonians 1:8-9:** In flaming fire taking vengeance on them that know not God, and that obey not the gospel of our Lord Jesus Christ: Who shall be punished with everlasting

destruction from the presence of the Lord, and from the glory of his power … **Ephesians 2:12:** That at that time ye were without Christ, being aliens from the commonwealth of Israel, and strangers from the covenants of promise, having no hope, and without God in the world … **John 1:10-12:** He was in the world, and the world was made by him, and the world knew him not. He came unto his own, and his own received him not. But as many as received him, to them gave he power to become the sons of God, *even* to them that believe on his name …

[3] **John 8:24:** I said therefore unto you, that ye shall die in your sins: for if ye believe not that I am *he*, ye shall die in your sins. **Mark 16:16:** He that believeth and is baptized shall be saved; but he that believeth not shall be damned.

[4] **1 Corinthians 1:20-24:** Where *is* the wise? where *is* the scribe? where *is* the disputer of this world? hath not God made foolish the wisdom of this world? For after that in the wisdom of God the world by wisdom knew not God, it pleased God by the foolishness of preaching to save them that believe. For the Jews require a sign, and the Greeks seek after wisdom: But we preach Christ crucified, unto the Jews a stumblingblock, and unto the Greeks foolishness; But unto them which are called, both Jews and Greeks, Christ the power of God, and the wisdom of God.

[5] **John 4:22:** Ye worship ye know not what: we know what we worship: for salvation is of the Jews. **Romans 9:31-32:** But Israel, which followed after the law of righteousness, hath not attained to the law of righteousness. Wherefore? Because *they sought* it not by faith, but as it were by the works of the law. For they stumbled at that stumblingstone … **Philippians 3:4-9:** Though I might also have confidence in the flesh. If any other man thinketh that he hath whereof he might trust in the flesh, I more: Circumcised the eighth day, of the stock of Israel, *of* the tribe of Benjamin, an Hebrew of the Hebrews; as touching the law, a Pharisee; Concerning zeal, persecuting the church; touching the righteousness which is in the law, blameless. But what things were gain to me, those I counted loss for Christ. Yea doubtless, and I count all things *but* loss for the excellency of the knowledge of Christ Jesus my Lord: for whom I have suffered the loss of all things, and do count them *but* dung, that I may win Christ, And be found in him, not having mine own righteousness,

which is of the law, but that which is through the faith of Christ, the righteousness which is of God by faith ...

[6] **Acts 4:12:** Neither is there salvation in any other: for there is none other name under heaven given among men, whereby we must be saved.

[7] **Ephesians 5:23:** For the husband is the head of the wife, even as Christ is the head of the church: and he is the saviour of the body.

61. Are all they saved who hear the gospel, and live in the church?

A. All that hear the gospel, and live in the visible church, are not saved; but they only who are true members of the church invisible. [1]

Proofs

[1] **John 12:38-40:** That the saying of Esaias the prophet might be fulfilled, which he spake, Lord, who hath believed our report? and to whom hath the arm of the Lord been revealed? Therefore they could not believe, because that Esaias said again, He hath blinded their eyes, and hardened their heart; that they should not see with *their* eyes, nor understand with *their* heart, and be converted, and I should heal them. **Romans 9:6:** Not as though the word of God hath taken none effect. For they *are* not all Israel, which are of Israel. **Matthew 22:14:** For many are called, but few *are* chosen. **Matthew 7:21:** Not every one that saith unto me, Lord, Lord, shall enter into the kingdom of heaven; but he that doeth the will of my Father which is in heaven. **Romans 11:7:** What then? Israel hath not obtained that which he seeketh for; but the election hath obtained it, and the rest were blinded ...

62. What is the visible church?

A. The visible church is a society made up of all such as in all ages and places of the world do profess the true religion, [1] and of their children. [2]

Proofs

[1] **1 Corinthians 1:2:** Unto the church of God which is at Corinth, to them that are sanctified in Christ Jesus, called *to be* saints, with all that in every place call upon the name of Jesus Christ our Lord, both theirs and

ours ... **1 Corinthians 12:13:** For by one Spirit are we all baptized into one body, whether *we be* Jews or Gentiles, whether *we be* bond or free; and have been all made to drink into one Spirit. **Romans 15:9-12:** And that the Gentiles might glorify God for *his* mercy; as it is written, For this cause I will confess to thee among the Gentiles, and sing unto thy name. And again he saith, Rejoice, ye Gentiles, with his people. And again, Praise the Lord, all ye Gentiles; and laud him, all ye people. And again, Esaias saith, There shall be a root of Jesse, and he that shall rise to reign over the Gentiles; in him shall the Gentiles trust. **Revelation 7:9:** After this I beheld, and, lo, a great multitude, which no man could number, of all nations, and kindreds, and people, and tongues, stood before the throne, and before the Lamb, clothed with white robes, and palms in their hands ... **Psalm 2:8:** Ask of me, and I shall give *thee* the heathen *for* thine inheritance, and the uttermost parts of the earth *for* thy possession. **Psalm 22:27-31:** All the ends of the world shall remember and turn unto the LORD: and all the kindreds of the nations shall worship before thee. For the kingdom *is* the LORD'S: and he *is* the governor among the nations. All *they that be* fat upon earth shall eat and worship: all they that go down to the dust shall bow before him: and none can keep alive his own soul. A seed shall serve him; it shall be accounted to the Lord for a generation. They shall come, and shall declare his righteousness unto a people that shall be born, that he hath done *this*. **Psalm 45:17:** I will make thy name to be remembered in all generations: therefore shall the people praise thee for ever and ever. **Matthew 28:19-20:** Go ye therefore, and teach all nations, baptizing them in the name of the Father, and of the Son, and of the Holy Ghost: Teaching them to observe all things whatsoever I have commanded you: and, lo, I am with you alway, *even* unto the end of the world. Amen. **Isaiah 59:21:** As for me, this *is* my covenant with them, saith the LORD; My spirit that *is* upon thee, and my words which I have put in thy mouth, shall not depart out of thy mouth, nor out of the mouth of thy seed, nor out of the mouth of thy seed's seed, saith the LORD, from henceforth and for ever.

[2] **1 Corinthians 7:14:** For the unbelieving husband is sanctified by the wife, and the unbelieving wife is sanctified by the husband: else were your children unclean; but now are they holy. **Acts 2:39:** For the promise is unto you, and to your children, and to all that are afar off, *even* as many as the Lord our God shall call. **Romans 11:16:** For if the firstfruit be holy, the lump *is* also *holy*: and if the root *be* holy, so *are*

the branches. **Genesis 17:7:** And I will establish my covenant between me and thee and thy seed after thee in their generations for an everlasting covenant, to be a God unto thee, and to thy seed after thee.

63. What are the special privileges of the visible church?

A. The visible church hath the privilege of being under God's special care and government; [1] of being protected and preserved in all ages, notwithstanding the opposition of all enemies; [2] and of enjoying the communion of saints, the ordinary means of salvation, [3] and offers of grace by Christ to all the members of it in the ministry of the gospel, testifying, that whosoever believes in him shall be saved, [4] and excluding none that will come unto him. [5]

Proofs

[1] **Isaiah 4:5-6:** And the LORD will create upon every dwelling place of mount Zion, and upon her assemblies, a cloud and smoke by day, and the shining of a flaming fire by night: for upon all the glory *shall be* a defence. And there shall be a tabernacle for a shadow in the daytime from the heat, and for a place of refuge, and for a covert from storm and from rain. **1 Timothy 4:10;** For therefore we both labour and suffer reproach, because we trust in the living God, who is the Saviour of all men, specially of those that believe.

[2] **Psalm 115:1-2, 9;** Not unto us, O LORD, not unto us, but unto thy name give glory, for thy mercy, *and* for thy truth's sake. Wherefore should the heathen say, Where *is* now their God? … O Israel, trust thou in the LORD: he *is* their help and their shield.[See the Psalm throughout.] **Isaiah 31:4-5:** For thus hath the LORD spoken unto me, Like as the lion and the young lion roaring on his prey, when a multitude of shepherds is called forth against him, *he* will not be afraid of their voice, nor abase himself for the noise of them: so shall the LORD of hosts come down to fight for mount Zion, and for the hill thereof. As birds flying, so will the LORD of hosts defend Jerusalem; defending also he will deliver *it; and* passing over he will preserve it. **Zechariah 12:2-4, 8-9:** Behold, I will make Jerusalem a cup of trembling unto all the people round about, when they shall be in the siege both against Judah *and* against Jerusalem. And in that day will I make Jerusalem a burdensome stone for all people: all that burden

themselves with it shall be cut in pieces, though all the people of the earth be gathered together against it. In that day, saith the LORD, I will smite every horse with astonishment, and his rider with madness: and I will open mine eyes upon the house of Judah, and will smite every horse of the people with blindness ... In that day shall the LORD defend the inhabitants of Jerusalem; and he that is feeble among them at that day shall be as David; and the house of David *shall be* as God, as the angel of the LORD before them. And it shall come to pass in that day, *that* I will seek to destroy all the nations that come against Jerusalem.

[3] **Acts 2:39, 42:** For the promise is unto you, and to your children, and to all that are afar off, *even* as many as the Lord our God shall call ... And they continued stedfastly in the apostles' doctrine and fellowship, and in breaking of bread, and in prayers.

[4] **Psalm 147:19-20:** He sheweth his word unto Jacob, his statutes and his judgments unto Israel. He hath not dealt so with any nation: and *as for his* judgments, they have not known them. Praise ye the LORD. **Romans 9:4:** Who are Israelites; to whom *pertaineth* the adoption, and the glory, and the covenants, and the giving of the law, and the service *of God*, and the promises ... **Ephesians 4:11-12:** And he gave some, apostles; and some, prophets; and some, evangelists; and some, pastors and teachers; For the perfecting of the saints, for the work of the ministry, for the edifying of the body of Christ ... **Mark 16:15-16:** And he said unto them, Go ye into all the world, and preach the gospel to every creature. He that believeth and is baptized shall be saved; but he that believeth not shall be damned.

[5] **John 6:37:** All that the Father giveth me shall come to me; and him that cometh to me I will in no wise cast out.

64. What is the invisible church?

A. The invisible church is the whole number of the elect, that have been, are, or shall be gathered into one under Christ the head. [1]

Proofs

[1] **Ephesians 1:10:** That in the dispensation of the fulness of times he might gather together in one all things in Christ, both which are in heaven, and which are on earth; *even* in him ... **Ephesians 1:22-23:** And hath put all *things* under his feet, and gave him to be the head over all *things* to the church, Which is his body, the fulness of him that filleth all in all. **John 10:16:** And other sheep I have, which are not of this fold:

them also I must bring, and they shall hear my voice; and there shall be one fold, *and* one shepherd. **John 11:52:** And not for that nation only, but that also he should gather together in one the children of God that were scattered abroad.

65. What special benefits do the members of the invisible church enjoy by Christ?

A. The members of the invisible church by Christ enjoy union and communion with him in grace and glory. [1]

Proofs

[1] **John 17:21:** That they all may be one; as thou, Father, *art* in me, and I in thee, that they also may be one in us: that the world may believe that thou hast sent me. **Ephesians 2:5-6:** Even when we were dead in sins, hath quickened us together with Christ, (by grace ye are saved;) And hath raised *us* up together, and made us sit together in heavenly places in Christ Jesus ... **John 17:24:** Father, I will that they also, whom thou hast given me, be with me where I am; that they may behold my glory, which thou hast given me: for thou lovedst me before the foundation of the world.

66. What is the union which the elect have with Christ?

A. The union which the elect have with Christ is the work of God's grace, [1] whereby they are spiritually and mystically, yet really and inseparably, joined to Christ as their head and husband, [2] which is done in their effectual calling. [3]

Proofs

[1] **Ephesians 1:22:** And hath put all *things* under his feet, and gave him *to be* the head over all *things* to the church ... **Ephesians 2:6-8:** And hath raised *us* up together, and made *us* sit together in heavenly *places* in Christ Jesus: That in the ages to come he might shew the exceeding riches of his grace in *his* kindness toward us through Christ Jesus. For by grace are ye saved through faith; and that not of yourselves: *it is* the gift of God ...

[2] **1 Corinthians 6:17:** But he that is joined unto the Lord is one spirit. **John 10:28:** And I give unto them eternal life; and they shall never perish, neither shall any *man* pluck them out of my hand. **Ephesians 5:23, 30:** For the husband is the head of the wife, even as Christ is the head of the church: and he is the saviour of the body ... For we are members of his body, of his flesh, and of his bones.

[3] **1 Peter 5:10:** But the God of all grace, who hath called us unto his eternal glory by Christ Jesus, after that ye have suffered a while, make you perfect, stablish, strengthen, settle *you*. **1 Corinthians 1:9:** God *is* faithful, by whom ye were called unto the fellowship of his Son Jesus Christ our Lord.

67. What is effectual calling?

A. Effectual calling is the work of God's almighty power and grace, [1] whereby (out of his free and special love to his elect, and from nothing in them moving him thereunto) [2] he doth, in his accepted time, invite and draw them to Jesus Christ, by his Word and Spirit; [3] savingly enlightening their minds, [4] renewing and powerfully determining their wills, [5] so as they (although in themselves dead in sin) are hereby made willing and able freely to answer his call, and to accept and embrace the grace offered and conveyed therein. [6]

Proofs

[1] **John 5:25:** Verily, verily, I say unto you, The hour is coming, and now is, when the dead shall hear the voice of the Son of God: and they that hear shall live. **Ephesians 1:18-20:** The eyes of your understanding being enlightened; that ye may know what is the hope of his calling, and what the riches of the glory of his inheritance in the saints, And what *is* the exceeding greatness of his power to usward who believe, according to the working of his mighty power, Which he wrought in Christ, when he raised him from the dead, and set *him* at his own right hand in the heavenly *places*. **2 Timothy 1:8-9:** Be not thou therefore ashamed of the testimony of our Lord, nor of me his prisoner: but be thou partaker of the afflictions of the gospel according to the power of God; Who hath saved us, and called *us* with an holy calling, not according to our works, but according to his own purpose and grace, which was given us in Christ Jesus before the world began …

[2] **Titus 3:4-5:** But after that the kindness and love of God our Saviour toward man appeared, Not by works of righteousness which we have done, but according to his mercy he saved us, by the washing of regeneration, and renewing of the Holy Ghost … **Ephesians 2:4-5, 7-9:** But God, who is rich in mercy, for his great love wherewith he loved us, Even when we were dead in sins, hath quickened us together with Christ, (by grace ye are saved;) … That in the ages to come he

might shew the exceeding riches of his grace in *his* kindness toward us through Christ Jesus. For by grace are ye saved through faith; and that not of yourselves: *it is* the gift of God: Not of works, lest any man should boast. **Romans 9:11:** For *the children* being not yet born, neither having done any good or evil, that the purpose of God according to election might stand, not of works, but of him that calleth ...

[3] **2 Corinthians 5:20:** Now then we are ambassadors for Christ, as though God did beseech *you* by us: we pray *you* in Christ's stead, be ye reconciled to God. [Compare with] **2 Corinthians 6:1-2:** We then, as workers together *with him*, beseech *you* also that ye receive not the grace of God in vain. (For he saith, I have heard thee in a time accepted, and in the day of salvation have I succoured thee: behold, now *is* the accepted time; behold, now *is* the day of salvation.) **John 6:44:** No man can come to me, except the Father which hath sent me draw him: and I will raise him up at the last day. **2 Thessalonians 2:13-14:** But we are bound to give thanks alway to God for you, brethren beloved of the Lord, because God hath from the beginning chosen you to salvation through sanctification of the Spirit and belief of the truth: Whereunto he called you by our gospel, to the obtaining of the glory of our Lord Jesus Christ.

[4] **Acts 26:18:** To open their eyes, *and* to turn *them* from darkness to light, and *from* the power of Satan unto God, that they may receive forgiveness of sins, and inheritance among them which are sanctified by faith that is in me. **1 Corinthians 2:10, 12:** But God hath revealed *them* unto us by his Spirit: for the Spirit searcheth all things, yea, the deep things of God ... Now we have received, not the spirit of the world, but the spirit which is of God; that we might know the things that are freely given to us of God.

[5] **Ezekiel 11:19:** And I will give them one heart, and I will put a new spirit within you; and I will take the stony heart out of their flesh, and will give them an heart of flesh ... **Ezekiel 36:26-27:** A new heart also will I give you, and a new spirit will I put within you: and I will take away the stony heart out of your flesh, and I will give you an heart of flesh. And I will put my spirit within you, and cause you to walk in my statutes, and ye shall keep my judgments, and do *them*. **John 6:45:** It is written in the prophets, And they shall be all taught of God. Every man therefore that hath heard, and hath learned of the Father, cometh unto me.

[6] **Ephesians 2:5:** Even when we were dead in sins, hath quickened us together with Christ, (by grace ye are saved;) … **Philippians 2:13:** For it is God which worketh in you both to will and to do of *his* good pleasure. **Deuteronomy 30:6:** And the LORD thy God will circumcise thine heart, and the heart of thy seed, to love the LORD thy God with all thine heart, and with all thy soul, that thou mayest live.

68. Are the elect only effectually called?

A. All the elect, and they only, are effectually called: [1] although others may be, and often are, outwardly called by the ministry of the Word, [2] and have some common operations of the Spirit; [3] who, for their wilful neglect and contempt of the grace offered to them, being justly left in their unbelief, do never truly come to Jesus Christ. [4]

Proofs

[1] **Acts 13:48:** And when the Gentiles heard this, they were glad, and glorified the word of the Lord: and as many as were ordained to eternal life believed.

[2] **Matthew 22:14:** For many are called, but few *are* chosen.

[3] **Matthew 7:22:** Many will say to me in that day, Lord, Lord, have we not prophesied in thy name? and in thy name have cast out devils? and in thy name done many wonderful works? **Matthew 13:20-21:** But he that received the seed into stony places, the same is he that heareth the word, and anon with joy receiveth it; Yet hath he not root in himself, but dureth for a while: for when tribulation or persecution ariseth because of the word, by and by he is offended. **Hebrews 6:4-6:** For *it is* impossible for those who were once enlightened, and have tasted of the heavenly gift, and were made partakers of the Holy Ghost, And have tasted the good word of God, and the powers of the world to come, If they shall fall away, to renew them again unto repentance; seeing they crucify to themselves the Son of God afresh, and put *him* to an open shame.

[4] **John 12:38-40:** That the saying of Esaias the prophet might be fulfilled, which he spake, Lord, who hath believed our report? and to whom hath the arm of the Lord been revealed? Therefore they could not believe, because that Esaias said again, He hath blinded their eyes,

and hardened their heart; that they should not see with *their* eyes, nor understand with *their* heart, and be converted, and I should heal them. **Acts 28:25-27:** And when they agreed not among themselves, they departed, after that Paul had spoken one word, Well spake the Holy Ghost by Esaias the prophet unto our fathers, Saying, Go unto this people, and say, Hearing ye shall hear, and shall not understand; and seeing ye shall see, and not perceive: For the heart of this people is waxed gross, and their ears are dull of hearing, and their eyes have they closed; lest they should see with *their* eyes, and hear with *their* ears, and understand with *their* heart, and should be converted, and I should heal them. **John 6:64-65:** But there are some of you that believe not. For Jesus knew from the beginning who they were that believed not, and who should betray him. And he said, Therefore said I unto you, that no man can come unto me, except it were given unto him of my Father. **Psalm 81:11-12:** But my people would not hearken to my voice; and Israel would none of me. So I gave them up unto their own hearts' lust: *and* they walked in their own counsels.

69. What is the communion in grace which the members of the invisible church have with Christ?

A. The communion in grace which the members of the invisible church have with Christ is their partaking of the virtue of his mediation, in their justification, [1] adoption, [2] sanctification, and whatever else, in this life, manifests their union with him [3]

Proofs

[1] **Romans 8:30:** Moreover whom he did predestinate, them he also called: and whom he called, them he also justified: and whom he justified, them he also glorified.

[2] **Ephesians 1:5:** Having predestinated us unto the adoption of children by Jesus Christ to himself, according to the good pleasure of his will …

[3] **1 Corinthians 1:30:** But of him are ye in Christ Jesus, who of God is made unto us wisdom, and righteousness, and sanctification, and redemption …

70. What is justification?

A. Justification is an act of God's free grace unto sinners, [1] in which he pardoneth all their sins, accepteth and accounteth their persons righteous in his sight; [2] not for any thing wrought in them, or done by them, [3] but only for the perfect obedience and full satisfaction of Christ, by God imputed to them, [4] and received by faith alone. [5]

Proofs

[1] **Romans 3:22, 24-25:** Even the righteousness of God *which is* by faith of Jesus Christ unto all and upon all them that believe: for there is no difference … Being justified freely by his grace through the redemption that is in Christ Jesus: Whom God hath set forth *to be* a propitiation through faith in his blood, to declare his righteousness for the remission of sins that are past, through the forbearance of God … **Romans 4:5:** But to him that worketh not, but believeth on him that justifieth the ungodly, his faith is counted for righteousness.

[2] **2 Corinthians 5:19, 21:** To wit, that God was in Christ, reconciling the world unto himself, not imputing their trespasses unto them; and hath committed unto us the word of reconciliation … For he hath made him *to be* sin for us, who knew no sin; that we might be made the righteousness of God in him. **Romans 3:22, 24-25, 27-28.** Even the righteousness of God *which is* by faith of Jesus Christ unto all and upon all them that believe: for there is no difference … Being justified freely by his grace through the redemption that is in Christ Jesus: Whom God hath set forth *to be* a propitiation through faith in his blood, to declare his righteousness for the remission of sins that are past, through the forbearance of God … Where *is* boasting then? It is excluded. By what law? of works? Nay: but by the law of faith. Therefore we conclude that a man is justified by faith without the deeds of the law.

[3] **Titus 3:5, 7:** Not by works of righteousness which we have done, but according to his mercy he saved us, by the washing of regeneration, and renewing of the Holy Ghost … That being justified by his grace, we should be made heirs according to the hope of eternal life. **Ephesians 1:7:** In whom we have redemption through his blood, the forgiveness of sins, according to the riches of his grace …

[4] **Romans 5:17-19:** (… For if by one man's offence death reigned by one; much more they which receive abundance of grace and of the gift of righteousness shall reign in life by one, Jesus Christ.) Therefore as by the offence of one *judgment came* upon all men to condemnation; even so by the righteousness of one *the free gift came* upon all men unto

justification of life. For as by one man's disobedience many were made sinners, so by the obedience of one shall many be made righteous. **Romans 4:6-8:** Even as David also describeth the blessedness of the man, unto whom God imputeth righteousness without works, *Saying*, Blessed *are* they whose iniquities are forgiven, and whose sins are covered. Blessed *is* the man to whom the Lord will not impute sin.

[5] **Acts 10:43:** To him give all the prophets witness, that through his name whosoever believeth in him shall receive remission of sins. **Galatians 2:16:** Knowing that a man is not justified by the works of the law, but by the faith of Jesus Christ, even we have believed in Jesus Christ, that we might be justified by the faith of Christ, and not by the works of the law: for by the works of the law shall no flesh be justified. **Philippians 3:9:** And be found in him, not having mine own righteousness, which is of the law, but that which is through the faith of Christ, the righteousness which is of God by faith …

71. How is justification an act of God's free grace?

A. Although Christ, by his obedience and death, did make a proper, real, and full satisfaction to God's justice on the behalf of them that are justified; [1] yet in as much as God accepteth the satisfaction from a surety, which he might have demanded of them, and did provide this surety, his own only Son, [2] imputing his righteousness to them, and requiring nothing of them [3] for their justification but faith, [4] which also is his gift, [5] their justification is to them of free grace. [6]

Proofs

[1] **Romans 5:8-10, 19:** But God commendeth his love toward us, in that, while we were yet sinners, Christ died for us. Much more then, being now justified by his blood, we shall be saved from wrath through him. For if, when we were enemies, we were reconciled to God by the death of his Son, much more, being reconciled, we shall be saved by his life … For as by one man's disobedience many were made sinners, so by the obedience of one shall many be made righteous.

[2] **1 Timothy 2:5-6:** For *there is* one God, and one mediator between God and men, the man Christ Jesus; Who gave himself a ransom for all, to be testified in due time. **Hebrews 10:10:** By the which will we are sanctified through the offering of the body of Jesus Christ

once *for all.* **Matthew 20:28:** Even as the Son of man came not to be ministered unto, but to minister, and to give his life a ransom for many. **Daniel 9:24, 26:** Seventy weeks are determined upon thy people and upon thy holy city, to finish the transgression, and to make an end of sins, and to make reconciliation for iniquity, and to bring in everlasting righteousness, and to seal up the vision and prophecy, and to anoint the most Holy … And after threescore and two weeks shall Messiah be cut off, but not for himself: and the people of the prince that shall come shall destroy the city and the sanctuary; and the end thereof *shall be* with a flood, and unto the end of the war desolations are determined. **Isaiah 53:4-6, 10-12:** Surely he hath borne our griefs, and carried our sorrows: yet we did esteem him stricken, smitten of God, and afflicted. But he *was* wounded for our transgressions, *he was* bruised for our iniquities: the chastisement of our peace was upon him; and with his stripes we are healed. All we like sheep have gone astray; we have turned every one to his own way; and the LORD hath laid on him the iniquity of us all … Yet it pleased the LORD to bruise him; he hath put *him* to grief: when thou shalt make his soul an offering for sin, he shall see *his* seed, he shall prolong *his* days, and the pleasure of the LORD shall prosper in his hand. He shall see of the travail of his soul, *and* shall be satisfied: by his knowledge shall my righteous servant justify many; for he shall bear their iniquities. Therefore will I divide him *a portion* with the great, and he shall divide the spoil with the strong; because he hath poured out his soul unto death: and he was numbered with the transgressors; and he bare the sin of many, and made intercession for the transgressors. **Hebrews 7:22:** By so much was Jesus made a surety of a better testament. **Romans 8:32:** He that spared not his own Son, but delivered him up for us all, how shall he not with him also freely give us all things? **1 Peter 1:18-19:** Forasmuch as ye know that ye were not redeemed with corruptible things, *as* silver and gold, from your vain conversation *received* by tradition from your fathers; But with the precious blood of Christ, as of a lamb without blemish and without spot …

[3] **2 Corinthians 5:21:** For he hath made him *to be* sin for us, who knew no sin; that we might be made the righteousness of God in him.

[4] **Romans 3:24-25:** Being justified freely by his grace through the redemption that is in Christ Jesus: Whom God hath set forth *to be* a propitiation through faith in his blood, to declare his righteousness for the remission of sins that are past, through the forbearance of God …

[5] **Ephesians 2:8:** For by grace are ye saved through faith; and that not of yourselves: *it is* the gift of God …

[6] **Ephesians 1:7:** In whom we have redemption through his blood, the forgiveness of sins, according to the riches of his grace …

72. What is justifying faith?

A. Justifying faith is a saving grace, [1] wrought in the heart of a sinner by the Spirit [2] and Word of God, [3] whereby he, being convinced of his sin and misery, and of the disability in himself and all other creatures to recover him out of his lost condition, [4] not only assenteth to the truth of the promise of the gospel, [5] but receiveth and resteth upon Christ and his righteousness, therein held forth, for pardon of sin, [6] and for the accepting and accounting of his person righteous in the sight of God for salvation. [7]

Proofs

[1] **Hebrews 10:39:** But we are not of them who draw back unto perdition; but of them that believe to the saving of the soul.

[2] **2 Corinthians 4:13:** We having the same spirit of faith, according as it is written, I believed, and therefore have I spoken; we also believe, and therefore speak … **Ephesians 1:17-19:** That the God of our Lord Jesus Christ, the Father of glory, may give unto you the spirit of wisdom and revelation in the knowledge of him: The eyes of your understanding being enlightened; that ye may know what is the hope of his calling, and what the riches of the glory of his inheritance in the saints, And what *is* the exceeding greatness of his power to usward who believe, according to the working of his mighty power …

[3] **Romans 10:14-17:** How then shall they call on him in whom they have not believed? and how shall they believe in him of whom they have not heard? and how shall they hear without a preacher? And how shall they preach, except they be sent? as it is written, How beautiful are the feet of them that preach the gospel of peace, and bring glad tidings of good things! But they have not all obeyed the gospel. For Esaias saith, Lord, who hath believed our report? So then faith *cometh* by hearing, and hearing by the word of God.

[4] **Acts 2:37:** Now when they heard *this*, they were pricked in their heart, and said unto Peter and to the rest of the apostles, Men *and*

brethren, what shall we do? **Acts 16:30:** And brought them out, and said, Sirs, what must I do to be saved? **John 16:8-9:** And when he is come, he will reprove the world of sin, and of righteousness, and of judgment: Of sin, because they believe not on me ... **Romans 5:6:** For when we were yet without strength, in due time Christ died for the ungodly. **Ephesians 2:1:** And you *hath he quickened,* who were dead in trespasses and sins ... **Acts 4:12:** Neither is there salvation in any other: for there is none other name under heaven given among men, whereby we must be saved.

[5] **Ephesians 1:13:** In whom ye also *trusted*, after that ye heard the word of truth, the gospel of your salvation: in whom also after that ye believed, ye were sealed with that holy Spirit of promise ...

[6] **John 1:12:** But as many as received him, to them gave he power to become the sons of God, *even* to them that believe on his name ... **Acts 16:31:** And they said, Believe on the Lord Jesus Christ, and thou shalt be saved, and thy house. **Acts 10:43:** To him give all the prophets witness, that through his name whosoever believeth in him shall receive remission of sins.

[7] **Philippians 3:9:** And be found in him, not having mine own righteousness, which is of the law, but that which is through the faith of Christ, the righteousness which is of God by faith ... **Acts 15:11:** But we believe that through the grace of the Lord Jesus Christ we shall be saved, even as they.

73. How doth faith justify a sinner in the sight of God?

A. Faith justifies a sinner in the sight of God, not because of those other graces which do always accompany it, or of good works that are the fruits of it, [1] nor as if the grace of faith, or any act thereof, were imputed to him for his justification; [2] but only as it is an instrument by which he receiveth and applieth Christ and his righteousness. [3]

Proofs

[1] **Galatians 3:11:** But that no man is justified by the law in the sight of God, *it is* evident: for, The just shall live by faith. **Romans 3:28:** Therefore we conclude that a man is justified by faith without the deeds of the law.

[2] **Romans 4:5:** But to him that worketh not, but believeth on him that justifieth the ungodly, his faith is counted for righteousness. [Compare with] **Romans 10:10:** For with the heart man believeth unto righteousness; and with the mouth confession is made unto salvation.

[3] **John 1:12:** But as many as received him, to them gave he power to become the sons of God, *even* to them that believe on his name ... **Philippians 3:9:** And be found in him, not having mine own righteousness, which is of the law, but that which is through the faith of Christ, the righteousness which is of God by faith ... **Galatians 2:16:** Knowing that a man is not justified by the works of the law, but by the faith of Jesus Christ, even we have believed in Jesus Christ, that we might be justified by the faith of Christ, and not by the works of the law: for by the works of the law shall no flesh be justified.

74. What is adoption?

A. Adoption is an act of the free grace of God, [1] in and for his only Son Jesus Christ, [2] whereby all those that are justified are received into the number of his children, [3] have his name put upon them, [4] the Spirit of his Son given to them, [5] are under his fatherly care and dispensations, [6] admitted to all the liberties and privileges of the sons of God, made heirs of all the promises, and fellow-heirs with Christ in glory. [7]

Proofs

[1] **1 John 3:1:** Behold, what manner of love the Father hath bestowed upon us, that we should be called the sons of God: therefore the world knoweth us not, because it knew him not.

[2] **Ephesians 1:5:** Having predestinated us unto the adoption of children by Jesus Christ to himself, according to the good pleasure of his will ... **Galatians 4:4-5:** But when the fulness of the time was come, God sent forth his Son, made of a woman, made under the law, To redeem them that were under the law, that we might receive the adoption of sons.

[3] **John 1:12:** But as many as received him, to them gave he power to become the sons of God, *even* to them that believe on his name ...

[4] **2 Corinthians 6:18:** And will be a Father unto you, and ye shall be my sons and daughters, saith the Lord Almighty. **Revelation 3:12:** Him

that overcometh will I make a pillar in the temple of my God, and he shall go no more out: and I will write upon him the name of my God, and the name of the city of my God, *which is* new Jerusalem, which cometh down out of heaven from my God: and *I will write upon him* my new name.

[5] **Galatians 4:6:** And because ye are sons, God hath sent forth the Spirit of his Son into your hearts, crying, Abba, Father.

[6] **Psalm 103:13:** Like as a father pitieth *his* children, *so* the LORD pitieth them that fear him. **Proverbs 14:26:** In the fear of the LORD *is* strong confidence: and his children shall have a place of refuge. **Matthew 6:32:** (For after all these things do the Gentiles seek:) for your heavenly Father knoweth that ye have need of all these things.

[7] **Hebrews 6:12:** That ye be not slothful, but followers of them who through faith and patience inherit the promises. **Romans 8:17:** And if children, then heirs; heirs of God, and joint-heirs with Christ; if so be that we suffer with *him*, that we may be also glorified together.

75. What is sanctification?

A. Sanctification is a work of God's grace, whereby they whom God hath, before the foundation of the world, chosen to be holy, are in time, through the powerful operation of his Spirit [1] applying the death and resurrection of Christ unto them, [2] renewed in their whole man after the image of God; [3] having the seeds of repentance unto life, and all other saving graces, put into their hearts, [4] and those graces so stirred up, increased, and strengthened, [5] as that they more and more die unto sin, and rise unto newness of life. [6]

Proofs

[1] **Ephesians 1:4:** According as he hath chosen us in him before the foundation of the world, that we should be holy and without blame before him in love ... **1 Corinthians 6:11:** And such were some of you: but ye are washed, but ye are sanctified, but ye are justified in the name of the Lord Jesus, and by the Spirit of our God. **2 Thessalonians 2:13:** But we are bound to give thanks alway to God for you, brethren beloved of the Lord, because God hath from the beginning chosen you to salvation through sanctification of the Spirit and belief of the truth.

[2] **Romans 6:4-6:** Therefore we are buried with him by baptism into death: that like as Christ was raised up from the dead by the glory of the Father, even so we also should walk in newness of life. For if we have been planted together in the likeness of his death, we shall be also *in the likeness* of *his* resurrection: Knowing this, that our old man is crucified with *him*, that the body of sin might be destroyed, that henceforth we should not serve sin.

[3] **Ephesians 4:23-24:** And be renewed in the spirit of your mind; And that ye put on the new man, which after God is created in righteousness and true holiness.

[4] **Acts 11:18:** When they heard these things, they held their peace, and glorified God, saying, Then hath God also to the Gentiles granted repentance unto life. **1 John 3:9:** Whosoever is born of God doth not commit sin; for his seed remaineth in him: and he cannot sin, because he is born of God.

[5] **Jude 20:** But ye, beloved, building up yourselves on your most holy faith, praying in the Holy Ghost ... **Hebrews 6:11-12:** And we desire that every one of you do shew the same diligence to the full assurance of hope unto the end: That ye be not slothful, but followers of them who through faith and patience inherit the promises. **Ephesians 3:16-19:** That he would grant you, according to the riches of his glory, to be strengthened with might by his Spirit in the inner man; That Christ may dwell in your hearts by faith; that ye, being rooted and grounded in love, May be able to comprehend with all saints what *is* the breadth, and length, and depth, and height; And to know the love of Christ, which passeth knowledge, that ye might be filled with all the fulness of God. **Colossians 1:10-11:** That ye might walk worthy of the Lord unto all pleasing, being fruitful in every good work, and increasing in the knowledge of God; Strengthened with all might, according to his glorious power, unto all patience and longsuffering with joyfulness ...

[6] **Romans 6:4, 6, 14:** Therefore we are buried with him by baptism into death: that like as Christ was raised up from the dead by the glory of the Father, even so we also should walk in newness of life ... Knowing this, that our old man is crucified with *him*, that the body of sin might be destroyed, that henceforth we should not serve sin ... For sin shall not have dominion over you: for ye are not under the law, but under

grace. **Galatians 5:24:** And they that are Christ's have crucified the flesh with the affections and lusts.

76. What is repentance unto life?

A. Repentance unto life is a saving grace, [1] wrought in the heart of a sinner by the Spirit [2] and Word of God, [3] whereby, out of the sight and sense, not only of the danger, [4] but also of the filthiness and odiousness of his sins, [5] and upon the apprehension of God's mercy in Christ to such as are penitent, [6] he so grieves for [7] and hates his sins, [8] as that he turns from them all to God, [9] purposing and endeavouring constantly to walk with him in all the ways of new obedience. [10]

Proofs

[1] **2 Timothy 2:25:** In meekness instructing those that oppose themselves; if God peradventure will give them repentance to the acknowledging of the truth …

[2] **Zechariah 12:10:** And I will pour upon the house of David, and upon the inhabitants of Jerusalem, the spirit of grace and of supplications: and they shall look upon me whom they have pierced, and they shall mourn for him, as one mourneth for *his* only *son*, and shall be in bitterness for him, as one that is in bitterness for *his* firstborn.

[3] **Acts 11:18, 20-21:** When they heard these things, they held their peace, and glorified God, saying, Then hath God also to the Gentiles granted repentance unto life … And some of them were men of Cyprus and Cyrene, which, when they were come to Antioch, spake unto the Grecians, preaching the Lord Jesus. And the hand of the Lord was with them: and a great number believed, and turned unto the Lord.

[4] **Ezekiel 18:28, 30, 32:** Because he considereth, and turneth away from all his transgressions that he hath committed, he shall surely live, he shall not die … Therefore I will judge you, O house of Israel, every one according to his ways, saith the Lord God. Repent, and turn *yourselves* from all your transgressions; so iniquity shall not be your ruin … For I have no pleasure in the death of him that dieth, saith the Lord God: wherefore turn *yourselves*, and live ye. **Luke 15:17-18:** And when he came to himself, he said, How many hired servants of my father's have bread enough and to spare, and I perish with hunger! I will arise and go to my father, and will say unto him, Father, I have sinned against

heaven, and before thee ... **Hosea 2:6-7:** Therefore, behold, I will hedge up thy way with thorns, and make a wall, that she shall not find her paths. And she shall follow after her lovers, but she shall not overtake *them*; and she shall seek them, but shall not find them: then shall she say, I will go and return to my first husband; for then *was it* better with me than now.

[5] **Ezekiel 36:31:** Then shall ye remember your own evil ways, and your doings that *were* not good, and shall *lothe* yourselves in your own sight for your iniquities and for your abominations. **Isaiah 30:22:** Ye shall defile also the covering of thy graven images of silver, and the ornament of thy molten images of gold: thou shalt cast them away as a menstruous cloth; thou shalt say unto it, Get thee hence.

[6] **Joel 2:12-13:** Therefore also now, saith the LORD, turn ye *even* to me with all your heart, and with fasting, and with weeping, and with mourning: And rend your heart, and not your garments, and turn unto the LORD your God: for he *is* gracious and merciful, slow to anger, and of great kindness, and repenteth him of the evil.

[7] **Jeremiah 31:18-19:** I have surely heard Ephraim bemoaning himself *thus*; Thou hast chastised me, and I was chastised, as a bullock unaccustomed *to the yoke*: turn thou me, and I shall be turned; for thou *art* the LORD my God. Surely after that I was turned, I repented; and after that I was instructed, I smote upon *my* thigh: I was ashamed, yea, even confounded, because I did bear the reproach of my youth.

[8] **2 Corinthians 7:11:** For behold this selfsame thing, that ye sorrowed after a godly sort, what carefulness it wrought in you, yea, *what* clearing of yourselves, yea, *what* indignation, yea, *what* fear, yea, *what* vehement desire, yea, *what* zeal, yea, *what* revenge! In all *things* ye have approved yourselves to be clear in this matter.

[9] **Acts 26:18:** To open their eyes, *and* to turn *them* from darkness to light, and *from* the power of Satan unto God, that they may receive forgiveness of sins, and inheritance among them which are sanctified by faith that is in me. **Ezekiel 14:6:** Therefore say unto the house of Israel, Thus saith the Lord GOD; Repent, and turn *yourselves* from your idols; and turn away your faces from all your abominations. **1 Kings 8:47-48:** *Yet* if they shall bethink themselves in the land whither they were carried captives, and repent, and make supplication unto thee in the land of them that carried them captives,

saying, We have sinned, and have done perversely, we have committed wickedness; And *so* return unto thee with all their heart, and with all their soul, in the land of their enemies, which led them away captive, and pray unto thee toward their land, which thou gavest unto their fathers, the city which thou hast chosen, and the house which I have built for thy name …

[10] **Psalm 119:6, 59, 128:** Then shall I not be ashamed, when I have respect unto all thy commandments … I thought on my ways, and turned my feet unto thy testimonies … Therefore I esteem all *thy* precepts *concerning* all *things to be* right; *and* I hate every false way. **Luke 1:6:** And they were both righteous before God, walking in all the commandments and ordinances of the Lord blameless. **2 Kings 23:25:** And like unto him was there no king before him, that turned to the LORD with all his heart, and with all his soul, and with all his might, according to all the law of Moses; neither after him arose there *any* like him.

77. Wherein do justification and sanctification differ?

A. Although sanctification be inseparably joined with justification, [1] yet they differ, in that God in justification imputeth the righteousness of Christ; [2] in sanctification of his Spirit infuseth grace, and enableth to the exercise thereof; [3] in the former, sin is pardoned; [4] in the other, it is subdued: [5] the one doth equally free all believers from the revenging wrath of God, and that perfectly in this life, that they never fall into condemnation; [6] the other is neither equal in all, [7] nor in this life perfect in any, [8] but growing up to perfection. [9]

Proofs

[1] **1 Corinthians 6:11:** And such were some of you: but ye are washed, but ye are sanctified, but ye are justified in the name of the Lord Jesus, and by the Spirit of our God. **1 Corinthians 1:30:** But of him are ye in Christ Jesus, who of God is made unto us wisdom, and righteousness, and sanctification, and redemption …

[2] **Romans 4:6, 8:** Even as David also describeth the blessedness of the man, unto whom God imputeth righteousness without works … Blessed *is* the man to whom the Lord will not impute sin.

[3] **Ezekiel 36:27:** And I will put my spirit within you, and cause you to walk in my statutes, and ye shall keep my judgments, and do *them*.

[4] **Romans 3:24-25:** Being justified freely by his grace through the redemption that is in Christ Jesus: Whom God hath set forth *to be* a propitiation through faith in his blood, to declare his righteousness for the remission of sins that are past, through the forbearance of God …

[5] **Romans 6:6, 14:** Knowing this, that our old man is crucified with *him*, that the body of sin might be destroyed, that henceforth we should not serve sin … For sin shall not have dominion over you: for ye are not under the law, but under grace.

[6] **Romans 8:33-34:** Who shall lay any thing to the charge of God's elect? *It is* God that justifieth. Who *is* he that condemneth? *It is* Christ that died, yea rather, that is risen again, who is even at the right hand of God, who also maketh intercession for us.

[7] **1 John 2:12-14:** I write unto you, little children, because your sins are forgiven you for his name's sake. I write unto you, fathers, because ye have known him *that is* from the beginning. I write unto you, young men, because ye have overcome the wicked one. I write unto you, little children, because ye have known the Father. I have written unto you, fathers, because ye have known him *that is* from the beginning. I have written unto you, young men, because ye are strong, and the word of God abideth in you, and ye have overcome the wicked one. **Hebrews 5:12-14:** For when for the time ye ought to be teachers, ye have need that one teach you again which *be* the first principles of the oracles of God; and are become such as have need of milk, and not of strong meat. For every one that useth milk *is* unskilful in the word of righteousness: for he is a babe. But strong meat belongeth to them that are of full age, *even* those who by reason of use have their senses exercised to discern both good and evil.

[8] **1 John 1:8, 10:** If we say that we have no sin, we deceive ourselves, and the truth is not in us … If we say that we have not sinned, we make him a liar, and his word is not in us.

[9] **2 Corinthians 7:1:** Having therefore these promises, dearly beloved, let us cleanse ourselves from all filthiness of the flesh and spirit, perfecting holiness in the fear of God. **Philippians 3:12-14:** Not as though I had already attained, either were already perfect: but I follow after, if that I may apprehend that for which also I am apprehended of Christ Jesus. Brethren, I count not myself to have apprehended: but *this*

one thing *I do,* forgetting those things which are behind, and reaching forth unto those things which are before, I press toward the mark for the prize of the high calling of God in Christ Jesus.

78. Whence ariseth the imperfection of sanctification in believers?

A. The imperfection of sanctification in believers ariseth from the remnants of sin abiding in every part of them, and the perpetual lustings of the flesh against the spirit; whereby they are often foiled with temptations, and fall into many sins, [1] are hindered in all their spiritual services, [2] and their best works are imperfect and defiled in the sight of God. [3]

Proofs

[1] **Romans 7:18, 23:** For I know that in me (that is, in my flesh,) dwelleth no good thing: for to will is present with me; but *how* to perform that which is good I find not … But I see another law in my members, warring against the law of my mind, and bringing me into captivity to the law of sin which is in my members. **Mark 14:66:** And as Peter was beneath in the palace, there cometh one of the maids of the high priest … [See the rest of the chapter.] **Galatians 2:11-12:** But when Peter was come to Antioch, I withstood him to the face, because he was to be blamed. For before that certain came from James, he did eat with the Gentiles: but when they were come, he withdrew and separated himself, fearing them which were of the circumcision.

[2] **Hebrews 12:1:** Wherefore seeing we also are compassed about with so great a cloud of witnesses, let us lay aside every weight, and the sin which doth so easily beset *us*, and let us run with patience the race that is set before us …

[3] **Isaiah 64:6:** But we are all as an unclean *thing*, and all our righteousnesses *are* as filthy rags; and we all do fade as a leaf; and our iniquities, like the wind, have taken us away. **Exodus 28:38:** And it shall be upon Aaron's forehead, that Aaron may bear the iniquity of the holy things, which the children of Israel shall hallow in all their holy gifts; and it shall be always upon his forehead, that they may be accepted before the LORD.

79. May not true believers, by reason of their imperfections, and the many temptations and sins they are overtaken with, fall away from the state of grace?

A. True believers, by reason of the unchangeable love of God, [1] and his decree and covenant to give them perseverance, [2] their inseparable union with Christ, [3] his continual intercession for them, [4] and the Spirit and seed of God abiding in them, [5] can neither totally nor finally fall away from the state of grace, [6] but are kept by the power of God through faith unto salvation. [7]

Proofs

[1] **Jeremiah 31:3:** The LORD hath appeared of old unto me, *saying*, Yea, I have loved thee with an everlasting love: therefore with lovingkindness have I drawn thee.

[2] **2 Timothy 2:19:** Nevertheless the foundation of God standeth sure, having this seal, The Lord knoweth them that are his. And, Let every one that nameth the name of Christ depart from iniquity. **Hebrews 13:20-21:** Now the God of peace, that brought again from the dead our Lord Jesus, that great shepherd of the sheep, through the blood of the everlasting covenant, Make you perfect in every good work to do his will, working in you that which is wellpleasing in his sight, through Jesus Christ; to whom *be* glory for ever and ever. Amen. **2 Samuel 23:5:** Although my house *be* not so with God; yet he hath made with me an everlasting covenant, ordered in all *things*, and sure: for *this is* all my salvation, and all *my* desire, although he make *it* not to grow.

[3] **1 Corinthians 1:8-9:** Who shall also confirm you unto the end, *that ye may be* blameless in the day of our Lord Jesus Christ. God *is* faithful, by whom ye were called unto the fellowship of his Son Jesus Christ our Lord.

[4] **Hebrews 7:25:** Wherefore he is able also to save them to the uttermost that come unto God by him, seeing he ever liveth to make intercession for them. **Luke 22:32:** But I have prayed for thee, that thy faith fail not: and when thou art converted, strengthen thy brethren.

[5] **1 John 3:9:** Whosoever is born of God doth not commit sin; for his seed remaineth in him: and he cannot sin, because he is born

of God. **1 John 2:27:** But the anointing which ye have received of him abideth in you, and ye need not that any man teach you: but as the same anointing teacheth you of all things, and is truth, and is no lie, and even as it hath taught you, ye shall abide in him.

[6] **Jeremiah 32:40:** And I will make an everlasting covenant with them, that I will not turn away from them, to do them good; but I will put my fear in their hearts, that they shall not depart from me. **John 10:28:** And I give unto them eternal life; and they shall never perish, neither shall any man pluck them out of my hand.

[7] **1 Peter 1:5:** Who are kept by the power of God through faith unto salvation ready to be revealed in the last time.

80. Can true believers be infallibly assured that they are in the estate of grace, and that they shall persevere therein unto salvation?

A. Such as truly believe in Christ, and endeavour to walk in all good conscience before him, [1] may, without extraordinary revelation, by faith grounded upon the truth of God's promises, and by the Spirit enabling them to discern in themselves those graces to which the promises of life are made, [2] and bearing witness with their spirits that they are the children of God, [3] be infallibly assured that they are in the estate of grace, and shall persevere therein unto salvation. [4]

Proofs

[1] **1 John 2:3:** And hereby we do know that we know him, if we keep his commandments.

[2] **1 Corinthians 2:12:** Now we have received, not the spirit of the world, but the spirit which is of God; that we might know the things that are freely given to us of God. **1 John 3:14, 18-19, 21, 24:** We know that we have passed from death unto life, because we love the brethren. He that loveth not *his* brother abideth in death … My little children, let us not love in word, neither in tongue; but in deed and in truth. And hereby we know that we are of the truth, and shall assure our hearts before him … Beloved, if our heart condemn us not, then have we confidence toward God … And he that keepeth his commandments dwelleth in him, and he in him. And hereby we know that he abideth in us, by the Spirit which he hath given us. **1 John 4:13, 16:** Hereby know we that we dwell in him, and

he in us, because he hath given us of his Spirit … And we have known and believed the love that God hath to us. God is love; and he that dwelleth in love dwelleth in God, and God in him. **Hebrews 6:11-12:** And we desire that every one of you do shew the same diligence to the full assurance of hope unto the end: That ye be not slothful, but followers of them who through faith and patience inherit the promises.

[3] **Romans 8:16:** The Spirit itself beareth witness with our spirit, that we are the children of God …

[4] **1 John 5:13:** These things have I written unto you that believe on the name of the Son of God; that ye may know that ye have eternal life, and that ye may believe on the name of the Son of God.

81. Are all true believers at all times assured of their present being in the estate of grace, and that they shall be saved?

A. Assurance of grace and salvation not being of the essence of faith, [1] true believers may wait long before they obtain it; [2] and, after the enjoyment thereof, may have it weakened and intermitted, through manifold distempers, sins, temptations, and desertions; [3] yet they are never left without such a presence and support of the Spirit of God as keeps them from sinking into utter despair. [4]

Proofs

[1] **Ephesians 1:13:** In whom ye also *trusted*, after that ye heard the word of truth, the gospel of your salvation: in whom also after that ye believed, ye were sealed with that holy Spirit of promise …

[2] **Isaiah 50:10:** Who *is* among you that feareth the LORD, that obeyeth the voice of his servant, that walketh *in* darkness, and hath no light? let him trust in the name of the LORD, and stay upon his God. **Psalm 88:1-3, 6-7, 9-10, 13-15:** O LORD God of my salvation, I have cried day *and* night before thee: Let my prayer come before thee: incline thine ear unto my cry; For my soul is full of troubles: and my life draweth nigh unto the grave … Thou hast laid me in the lowest pit, in darkness, in the deeps. Thy wrath lieth hard upon me, and thou hast afflicted *me* with all thy waves. Selah … Mine eye mourneth by reason of affliction: LORD, I have called daily upon thee, I have stretched out my hands unto thee. Wilt thou shew wonders to the dead? shall the dead arise *and* praise thee? Selah … But unto thee

have I cried, O LORD; and in the morning shall my prayer prevent thee. LORD, why castest thou off my soul? *why* hidest thou thy face from me? I *am* afflicted and ready to die from *my* youth up: *while* I suffer thy terrors I am distracted.

[3] **Psalm 77:1-12:** I cried unto God with my voice, *even* unto God with my voice; and he gave ear unto me. In the day of my trouble I sought the Lord: my sore ran in the night, and ceased not: my soul refused to be comforted. I remembered God, and was troubled: I complained, and my spirit was overwhelmed. Selah. Thou holdest mine eyes waking: I am so troubled that I cannot speak. I have considered the days of old, the years of ancient times. I call to remembrance my song in the night: I commune with mine own heart: and my spirit made diligent search. Will the Lord cast off for ever? and will he be favourable no more? Is his mercy clean gone for ever? doth *his* promise fail for evermore? Hath God forgotten to be gracious? hath he in anger shut up his tender mercies? Selah. And I said, This *is my* infirmity: *but I will remember* the years of the right hand of the most High. I will remember the works of the LORD: surely I will remember thy wonders of old. I will meditate also of all thy work, and talk of thy doings. **Song of Solomon 5:2-3, 6:** I sleep, but my heart waketh: *it is* the voice of my beloved that knocketh, *saying*, Open to me, my sister, my love, my dove, my undefiled: for my head is filled with dew, *and* my locks with the drops of the night. I have put off my coat; how shall I put it on? I have washed my feet; how shall I defile them? … I opened to my beloved; but my beloved had withdrawn himself, *and* was gone: my soul failed when he spake: I sought him, but I could not find him; I called him, but he gave me no answer. **Psalm 51:8, 12:** Make me to hear joy and gladness; *that* the bones *which* thou hast broken may rejoice … Restore unto me the joy of thy salvation; and uphold me *with thy* free spirit. **Psalm 31:22:** For I said in my haste, I am cut off from before thine eyes: nevertheless thou heardest the voice of my supplications when I cried unto thee. **Psalm 22:1:** My God, my God, why hast thou forsaken me? *why art thou so* far from helping me, *and from* the words of my roaring?

[4] **1 John 3:9:** Whosoever is born of God doth not commit sin; for his seed remaineth in him: and he cannot sin, because he is born of God. **Job 13:15:** Though he slay me, yet will I trust in him: but I will maintain mine own ways before him. **Psalm 73:15, 23:** If I say,

I will speak thus; behold, I should offend *against* the generation of thy children ... Nevertheless I *am* continually with thee: thou hast holden *me* by my right hand. **Isaiah 54:7-10**: For a small moment have I forsaken thee; but with great mercies will I gather thee. In a little wrath I hid my face from thee for a moment; but with everlasting kindness will I have mercy on thee, saith the LORD thy Redeemer. For this *is as* the waters of Noah unto me: for *as* I have sworn that the waters of Noah should no more go over the earth; so have I sworn that I would not be wroth with thee, nor rebuke thee. For the mountains shall depart, and the hills be removed; but my kindness shall not depart from thee, neither shall the covenant of my peace be removed, saith the LORD that hath mercy on thee.

82. What is the communion in glory which the members of the invisible church have with Christ?

A. The communion in glory which the members of the invisible church have with Christ, is in this life, [1] immediately after death, [2] and at last perfected at the resurrection and day of judgment. [3]

Proofs

[1] **2 Corinthians 3:18:** But we all, with open face beholding as in a glass the glory of the Lord, are changed into the same image from glory to glory, *even* as by the Spirit of the Lord.

[2] **Luke 23:43:** And Jesus said unto him, Verily I say unto thee, To day shalt thou be with me in paradise.

[3] **1 Thessalonians 4:17:** Then we which are alive *and* remain shall be caught up together with them in the clouds to meet the Lord in the air: and so shall we ever be with the Lord.

83. What is the communion in glory with Christ which the members of the invisible church enjoy in this life?

A. The members of the invisible church have communicated to them in this life the first-fruits of glory with Christ, as they are members of him their head, and so in him are interested in that glory which he is fully possessed of; [1] and, as an earnest thereof, enjoy the sense of God's love, [2] peace of conscience, joy in the Holy Ghost, and hope of glory; [3]

as, on the contrary, sense of God's revenging wrath, horror of conscience, and a fearful expectation of judgment, are to the wicked the beginning of their torments which they shall endure after death. [4]

Proofs

[1] **Ephesians 2:5-6:** Even when we were dead in sins, hath quickened us together with Christ, (by grace ye are saved;) And hath raised *us* up together, and made *us* sit together in heavenly *places* in Christ Jesus ...

[2] **Romans 5:5:** And hope maketh not ashamed; because the love of God is shed abroad in our hearts by the Holy Ghost which is given unto us. **2 Corinthians 1:22:** Who hath also sealed us, and given the earnest of the Spirit in our hearts.

[3] **Romans 5:1-2:** Therefore being justified by faith, we have peace with God through our Lord Jesus Christ: By whom also we have access by faith into this grace wherein we stand, and rejoice in hope of the glory of God. **Romans 14:17:** For the kingdom of God is not meat and drink; but righteousness, and peace, and joy in the Holy Ghost.

[4] **Genesis 4:13:** And Cain said unto the LORD, My punishment is greater than I can bear. **Matthew 27:4:** Saying, I have sinned in that I have betrayed the innocent blood. And they said, What *is that* to us? see thou *to that*. **Hebrews 10:27:** But a certain fearful looking for of judgment and fiery indignation, which shall devour the adversaries. **Romans 2:9:** Tribulation and anguish, upon every soul of man that doeth evil, of the Jew first, and also of the Gentile ... **Mark 9:44:** Where their worm dieth not, and the fire is not quenched.

84. Shall all men die?

A. Death being threatened as the wages of sin, [1] it is appointed unto all men once to die; [2] for that all have sinned. [3]

Proofs

[1] **Romans 6:23:** For the wages of sin *is* death; but the gift of God *is* eternal life through Jesus Christ our Lord.

[2] **Hebrews 9:27:** And as it is appointed unto men once to die, but after this the judgment ...

[3] **Romans 5:12:** Wherefore, as by one man sin entered into the world, and death by sin; and so death passed upon all men, for that all have sinned …

85. Death, being the wages of sin, why are not the righteous delivered from death, seeing all their sins are forgiven in Christ?

A. The righteous shall be delivered from death itself at the last day, and even in death are delivered from the sting and curse of it; [1] so that, although they die, yet it is out of God's love, [2] to free them perfectly from sin and misery, [3] and to make them capable of further communion with Christ in glory, which they then enter upon. [4]

Proofs

[1] **1 Corinthians 15:26, 55-57:** The last enemy *that* shall be destroyed *is* death … O death, where *is* thy sting? O grave, where *is* thy victory? The sting of death *is* sin; and the strength of sin *is* the law. But thanks *be* to God, which giveth us the victory through our Lord Jesus Christ. **Hebrews 2:15:** And deliver them who through fear of death were all their lifetime subject to bondage.

[2] **Isaiah 57:1-2:** The righteous perisheth, and no man layeth *it* to heart: and merciful men *are* taken away, none considering that the righteous is taken away from the evil *to come*. He shall enter into peace: they shall rest in their beds, *each one* walking *in* his uprightness. **2 Kings 22:20:** Behold therefore, I will gather thee unto thy fathers, and thou shalt be gathered into thy grave in peace; and thine eyes shall not see all the evil which I will bring upon this place. And they brought the king word again.

[3] **Revelation 14:13:** And I heard a voice from heaven saying unto me, Write, Blessed *are* the dead which die in the Lord from henceforth: Yea, saith the Spirit, that they may rest from their labours; and their works do follow them. **Ephesians 5:27:** That he might present it to himself a glorious church, not having spot, or wrinkle, or any such thing; but that it should be holy and without blemish.

[4] **Luke 23:43:** And Jesus said unto him, Verily I say unto thee, To day shalt thou be with me in paradise. **Philippians 1:23:** For I am in

a strait betwixt two, having a desire to depart, and to be with Christ; which is far better …

86. What is the communion in glory with Christ, which the members of the invisible church enjoy immediately after death?

A. The communion in glory with Christ, which the members of the invisible church enjoy immediately after death is, in that their souls are then made perfect in holiness, [1]and received into the highest heavens, [2] where they behold the face of God in light and glory, [3] waiting for the full redemption of their bodies, [4] which even in death continue united to Christ, [5] and rest in their graves as in their beds, [6] till at the last day they be again united to their souls. [7] Whereas the souls of the wicked are at their death cast into hell, where they remain in torments and utter darkness, and their bodies kept in their graves, as in their prisons, till the resurrection and judgment of the great day. [8]

Proofs

[1] **Hebrews 12:23:** To the general assembly and church of the first-born, which are written in heaven, and to God the Judge of all, and to the spirits of just men made perfect …

[2] **2 Corinthians 5:1, 6, 8:** For we know that if our earthly house of *this* tabernacle were dissolved, we have a building of God, an house not made with hands, eternal in the heavens … Therefore *we are* always confident, knowing that, whilst we are at home in the body, we are absent from the Lord … We are confident, *I say*, and willing rather to be absent from the body, and to be present with the Lord. **Philippians 1:23:** For I am in a strait betwixt two, having a desire to depart, and to be with Christ; which is far better … [Compare with] **Acts 3:21:** Whom the heaven must receive until the times of restitution of all things, which God hath spoken by the mouth of all his holy prophets since the world began. [And with] **Ephesians 4:10:** He that descended is the same also that ascended up far above all heavens, that he might fill all things.

[3] **1 John 3:2:** Beloved, now are we the sons of God, and it doth not yet appear what we shall be: but we know that, when he shall appear, we shall be like him; for we shall see him as he is. **1 Corinthians 13:12:** For

now we see through a glass, darkly; but then face to face: now I know in part; but then shall I know even as also I am known.

[4] **Romans 8:23:** And not only *they*, but ourselves also, which have the firstfruits of the Spirit, even we ourselves groan within ourselves, waiting for the adoption, *to wit*, the redemption of our body. **Psalm 16:9:** Therefore my heart is glad, and my glory rejoiceth: my flesh also shall rest in hope.

[5] **1 Thessalonians 4:14:** For if we believe that Jesus died and rose again, even so them also which sleep in Jesus will God bring with him.

[6] **Isaiah 57:2:** He shall enter into peace: they shall rest in their beds, *each one* walking *in* his uprightness.

[7] **Job 19:26-27:** And *though* after my skin *worms* destroy this *body*, yet in my flesh shall I see God: Whom I shall see for myself, and mine eyes shall behold, and not another; *though* my reins be consumed within me.

[8] **Luke 16:23-24:** And in hell he lift up his eyes, being in torments, and seeth Abraham afar off, and Lazarus in his bosom. And he cried and said, Father Abraham, have mercy on me, and send Lazarus, that he may dip the tip of his finger in water, and cool my tongue; for I am tormented in this flame. **Acts 1:25:** That he may take part of this ministry and apostleship, from which Judas by transgression fell, that he might go to his own place. **Jude 6-7:** And the angels which kept not their first estate, but left their own habitation, he hath reserved in everlasting chains under darkness unto the judgment of the great day. Even as Sodom and Gomorrha, and the cities about them in like manner, giving themselves over to fornication, and going after strange flesh, are set forth for an example, suffering the vengeance of eternal fire.

87. What are we to believe concerning the resurrection?

A. We are to believe that at the last day there shall be a general resurrection of the dead, both of the just and unjust: [1] when they that are then found alive shall in a moment be changed; and the selfsame bodies of the dead which were laid in the grave, being then again united to their souls forever, shall be raised up by the power of Christ. [2] The bodies of the just, by the Spirit of Christ, and by virtue of his resurrection as their head, shall be raised in power, spiritual, incorruptible, and made like to his glorious body; [3] and the bodies of the wicked shall be raised up in dishonour by him, as an offended judge. [4]

Proofs

[1] **Acts 24:15:** And have hope toward God, which they themselves also allow, that there shall be a resurrection of the dead, both of the just and unjust.

[2] **1 Corinthians 15:51-53:** Behold, I shew you a mystery; We shall not all sleep, but we shall all be changed, In a moment, in the twinkling of an eye, at the last trump: for the trumpet shall sound, and the dead shall be raised incorruptible, and we shall be changed. For this corruptible must put on incorruption, and this mortal *must* put on immortality. **1 Thessalonians 4:15-17:** For this we say unto you by the word of the Lord, that we which are alive *and* remain unto the coming of the Lord shall not prevent them which are asleep. For the Lord himself shall descend from heaven with a shout, with the voice of the archangel, and with the trump of God: and the dead in Christ shall rise first: Then we which are alive *and* remain shall be caught up together with them in the clouds to meet the Lord in the air: and so shall we ever be with the Lord. **John 5:28-29:** Marvel not at this: for the hour is coming, in the which all that are in the graves shall hear his voice, And shall come forth; they that have done good, unto the resurrection of life; and they that have done evil, unto the resurrection of damnation.

[3] **1 Corinthians 15:21-23, 42-44:** For since by man *came* death, by man *came* also the resurrection of the dead. For as in Adam all die, even so in Christ shall all be made alive. But every man in his own order: Christ the firstfruits; afterward they that are Christ's at his coming … So also *is* the resurrection of the dead. It is sown in corruption; it is raised in incorruption: It is sown in dishonour; it is raised in glory: it is sown in weakness; it is raised in power: It is sown a natural body; it is raised a spiritual body. There is a natural body, and there is a spiritual body. **Philippians 3:21:** Who shall change our vile body, that it may be fashioned like unto his glorious body, according to the working whereby he is able even to subdue all things unto himself.

[4] **John 5:27-29:** And hath given him authority to execute judgment also, because he is the Son of man. Marvel not at this: for the hour is coming, in the which all that are in the graves shall hear his voice, And shall come forth; they that have done good, unto the

resurrection of life; and they that have done evil, unto the resurrection of damnation. **Matthew 25:33:** And he shall set the sheep on his right hand, but the goats on the left.

88. What shall immediately follow after the resurrection?

A. Immediately after the resurrection shall follow the general and final judgment of angels and men: [1] the day and hour whereof no man knoweth, that all may watch and pray, and be ever ready for the coming of the Lord. [2]

Proofs

[1] **2 Peter 2:4, 6-7, 14-15:** For if God spared not the angels that sinned, but cast *them* down to hell, and delivered *them* into chains of darkness, to be reserved unto judgment ... And turning the cities of Sodom and Gomorrha into ashes condemned *them* with an overthrow, making *them* an ensample unto those that after should live ungodly; And delivered just Lot, vexed with the filthy conversation of the wicked ... Having eyes full of adultery, and that cannot cease from sin; beguiling unstable souls: an heart they have exercised with covetous practices; cursed children: Which have forsaken the right way, and are gone astray, following the way of Balaam *the son* of Bosor, who loved the wages of unrighteousness ... **Matthew 25:46:** And these shall go away into everlasting punishment: but the righteous into life eternal.

[2] **Matthew 24:36, 42, 44:** But of that day and hour knoweth no *man*, no, not the angels of heaven, but my Father only ... Watch therefore: for ye know not what hour your Lord doth come ... Therefore be ye also ready: for in such an hour as ye think not the Son of man cometh. **Luke 21:35-36:** For as a snare shall it come on all them that dwell on the face of the whole earth. Watch ye therefore, and pray always, that ye may be accounted worthy to escape all these things that shall come to pass, and to stand before the Son of man.

89. What shall be done to the wicked at the day of judgment?

A. At the day of judgment, the wicked shall be set on Christ's left hand, [1] and, upon clear evidence, and full conviction of their own consciences, [2] shall have the fearful but just sentence of condemnation pronounced against them; [3] and thereupon shall be cast out from the favourable presence of God, and the glorious fellowship with Christ, his saints, and all his holy angels, into hell, to be punished with unspeakable torments, both of body and soul, with the devil and his angels forever. [4]

Proofs

[1] **Matthew 25:33:** And he shall set the sheep on his right hand, but the goats on the left.

[2] **Romans 2:15-16:** (... Which shew the work of the law written in their hearts, their conscience also bearing witness, and *their* thoughts the mean while accusing or else excusing one another;) In the day when God shall judge the secrets of men by Jesus Christ according to my gospel.

[3] **Matthew 25:41-43:** Then shall he say also unto them on the left hand, Depart from me, ye cursed, into everlasting fire, prepared for the devil and his angels: For I was an hungered, and ye gave me no meat: I was thirsty, and ye gave me no drink: I was a stranger, and ye took me not in: naked, and ye clothed me not: sick, and in prison, and ye visited me not.

[4] **Luke 16:26:** And beside all this, between us and you there is a great gulf fixed: so that they which would pass from hence to you cannot; neither can they pass to us, that *would come* from thence. **2 Thessalonians 1:8-9:** In flaming fire taking vengeance on them that know not God, and that obey not the gospel of our Lord Jesus Christ: Who shall be punished with everlasting destruction from the presence of the Lord, and from the glory of his power ...

90. What shall be done to the righteous at the day of judgment?

A. At the day of judgment, the righteous, being caught up to Christ in the clouds, [1] shall be set on his right hand, and there openly acknowledged and acquitted, [2] shall join with him in the judging of reprobate angels and men, [3] and shall be received into heaven, [4] where they shall be fully and forever freed from all sin and misery; [5] filled with inconceivable joys, [6] made perfectly holy and happy both in body and soul, in the company of innumerable saints and holy angels, [7] but especially in the immediate vision and fruition of God the Father, of our Lord Jesus Christ, and of the Holy Spirit, to all eternity. [8] And this is the perfect and full communion, which the members of the invisible church shall enjoy with Christ in glory, at the resurrection and day of judgment.

Proofs

[1] **1 Thessalonians 4:17:** Then we which are alive *and* remain shall be caught up together with them in the clouds to meet the Lord in the air: and so shall we ever be with the Lord.

[2] **Matthew 25:33:** And he shall set the sheep on his right hand, but the goats on the left. **Matthew 10:32:** Whosoever therefore shall confess me before men, him will I confess also before my Father which is in heaven.

[3] **1 Corinthians 6:2-3:** Do ye not know that the saints shall judge the world? and if the world shall be judged by you, are ye unworthy to judge the smallest matters? Know ye not that we shall judge angels? how much more things that pertain to this life?

[4] **Matthew 25:34, 46:** Then shall the King say unto them on his right hand, Come, ye blessed of my Father, inherit the kingdom prepared for you from the foundation of the world ... And these shall go away into everlasting punishment: but the righteous into life eternal.

[5] **Ephesians 5:27:** That he might present it to himself a glorious church, not having spot, or wrinkle, or any such thing; but that it should be holy and without blemish. **Revelation 14:13:** And I heard a voice from heaven saying unto me, Write, Blessed *are* the dead which die in the Lord from henceforth: Yea, saith the Spirit, that they may rest from their labours; and their works do follow them.

[6] **Psalm 16:11:** Thou wilt shew me the path of life: in thy presence is fulness of joy; at thy right hand *there are* pleasures for evermore.

[7] **Hebrews 12:22-23:** But ye are come unto mount Sion, and unto the city of the living God, the heavenly Jerusalem, and to an innumerable company of angels, To the general assembly and church of the firstborn, which are written in heaven, and to God the Judge of all, and to the spirits of just men made perfect ...

[8] **1 John 3:2:** Beloved, now are we the sons of God, and it doth not yet appear what we shall be: but we know that, when he shall appear, we shall be like him; for we shall see him as he is. **1 Corinthians 13:12:** For now we see through a glass, darkly; but then face to face: now I know in part; but then shall I know even as

also I am known. 1 **Thessalonians 4:17-18:** Then we which are alive *and* remain shall be caught up together with them in the clouds to meet the Lord in the air: and so shall we ever be with the Lord. Wherefore comfort one another with these words.

91. What is the duty which God requireth of man?

A. The duty which God requireth of man is obedience to his revealed will. [1]

Proofs

[1] **Romans 12:1-2:** I beseech you therefore, brethren, by the mercies of God, that ye present your bodies a living sacrifice, holy, acceptable unto God, *which is* your reasonable service. And be not conformed to this world: but be ye transformed by the renewing of your mind, that ye may prove what *is* that good, and acceptable, and perfect, will of God. **Micah 6:8:** He hath shewed thee, O man, what is good; and what doth the LORD require of thee, but to do justly, and to love mercy, and to walk humbly with thy God? **1 Samuel 15:22:** And Samuel said, Hath the LORD *as great* delight in burnt offerings and sacrifices, as in obeying the voice of the LORD? Behold, to obey *is* better than sacrifice, *and* to hearken than the fat of rams.

92. What did God at first reveal unto man as the rule of his obedience?

A. The rule of obedience revealed to Adam in the estate of innocence, and to all mankind in him, besides a special command not to eat of the fruit of the tree knowledge of good and evil, was the moral law. [1]

Proofs

[1] **Genesis 1:26-27:** And God said, Let us make man in our image, after our likeness: and let them have dominion over the fish of the sea, and over the fowl of the air, and over the cattle, and over all the earth, and over every creeping thing that creepeth upon the earth. So God created man in his *own* image, in the image of God created he him; male and female created he them. **Romans 2:14-15:** For when the Gentiles, which have not the law, do by nature the things contained in the law, these, having not the law, are a law unto themselves: Which shew the work of the law written in their hearts, their conscience also bearing witness, and *their* thoughts the mean while accusing or else excusing

one another ... **Romans 10:5:** For Moses describeth the righteousness which is of the law, That the man which doeth those things shall live by them. **Genesis 2:17:** But of the tree of the knowledge of good and evil, thou shalt not eat of it: for in the day that thou eatest thereof thou shalt surely die.

93. What is the moral law?

A. The moral law is the declaration of the will of God to mankind, directing and binding every one to personal, perfect, and perpetual conformity and obedience thereunto, in the frame and disposition of the whole man, soul and body, [1] and in performance of all those duties of holiness and righteousness which he oweth to God and man: [2] promising life upon the fulfilling, and threatening death upon the breach of it. [3]

Proofs

[1] **Deuteronomy 5:1-3, 31, 33:** And Moses called all Israel, and said unto them, Hear, O Israel, the statutes and judgments which I speak in your ears this day, that ye may learn them, and keep, and do them. The LORD our God made a covenant with us in Horeb. The LORD made not this covenant with our fathers, but with us, *even* us, who *are* all of us here alive this day ... But as for thee, stand thou here by me, and I will speak unto thee all the commandments, and the statutes, and the judgments, which thou shalt teach them, that they may do *them* in the land which I give them to possess it ... Ye shall walk in all the ways which the LORD your God hath commanded you, that ye may live, and *that it may be* well with you, and *that* ye may prolong *your* days in the land which ye shall possess. **Luke 10:26-27:** He said unto him, What is written in the law? how readest thou? And he answering said, Thou shalt love the Lord thy God with all thy heart, and with all thy soul, and with all thy strength, and with all thy mind; and thy neighbour as thyself. **Galatians 3:10:** For as many as are of the works of the law are under the curse: for it is written, Cursed *is* every one that continueth not in all things which are written in the book of the law to do them. **1 Thessalonians 5:23:** And the very God of peace sanctify you wholly; and *I pray God* your whole spirit and soul and body be preserved blameless unto the coming of our Lord Jesus Christ.

[2] **Luke 1:75:** In holiness and righteousness before him, all the days of our life. **Acts 24:16:** And herein do I exercise myself, to have always a conscience void of offence toward God, and *toward* men.

[3] **Romans 10:5:** For Moses describeth the righteousness which is of the law, That the man which doeth those things shall live by them. **Galatians 3:10:** For as many as are of the works of the law are under the curse: for it is written, Cursed *is* every one that continueth not in all things which are written in the book of the law to do them. **Galatians 3:12:** And the law is not of faith: but, The man that doeth them shall live in them.

94. Is there any use of the moral law to man since the fall?

A. Although no man, since the fall, can attain to righteousness and life by the moral law: [1] yet there is great use thereof, as well common to all men, as peculiar either to the unregenerate, or the regenerate. [2]

Proofs

[1] **Romans 8:3:** For what the law could not do, in that it was weak through the flesh, God sending his own Son in the likeness of sinful flesh, and for sin, condemned sin in the flesh … **Galatians 2:16:** Knowing that a man is not justified by the works of the law, but by the faith of Jesus Christ, even we have believed in Jesus Christ, that we might be justified by the faith of Christ, and not by the works of the law: for by the works of the law shall no flesh be justified.

[2] **1 Timothy 1:8:** But we know that the law *is* good, if a man use it lawfully …

95. Of what use is the moral law to all men?

A. The moral law is of use to all men, to inform them of the holy nature and the will of God, [1] and of their duty, binding them to walk accordingly; [2] to convince them of their disability to keep it, and of the sinful pollution of their nature, hearts, and lives; [3] to humble them in the sense of their sin and misery, [4] and thereby help them to a clearer sight of the need they have of Christ, [5] and of the perfection of his obedience. [6]

Proofs

[1] **Leviticus 11:44-45:** For I *am* the LORD your God: ye shall therefore sanctify yourselves, and ye shall be holy; for I *am* holy: neither shall ye defile yourselves with any manner of creeping thing that creepeth upon the earth. For I *am* the LORD that bringeth you up out of the land of Egypt, to be your God: ye shall therefore be holy, for I *am* holy.**Leviticus 20:7-8:** Sanctify yourselves therefore, and be ye holy: for I *am* the LORD your God. And ye shall keep my statutes, and do them: I *am* the LORD which sanctify you. **Romans 7:12:** Wherefore the law *is* holy, and the commandment holy, and just, and good.

[2] **Micah 6:8:** He hath shewed thee, O man, what *is* good; and what doth the LORD require of thee, but to do justly, and to love mercy, and to walk humbly with thy God? **James 2:10-11:** For whosoever shall keep the whole law, and yet offend in one *point*, he is guilty of all. For he that said, Do not commit adultery, said also, Do not kill. Now if thou commit no adultery, yet if thou kill, thou art become a transgressor of the law.

[3] **Psalm 19:11-12:** Moreover by them is thy servant warned: *and* in keeping of them *there is* great reward. Who can understand *his* errors? cleanse thou me from secret *faults*. **Romans 3:20:** Therefore by the deeds of the law there shall no flesh be justified in his sight: for by the law is the knowledge of sin. **Romans 7:7:** What shall we say then? *Is* the law sin? God forbid. Nay, I had not known sin, but by the law: for I had not known lust, except the law had said, Thou shalt not covet.

[4] **Romans 3:9, 23:** What then? are we better *than they*? No, in no wise: for we have before proved both Jews and Gentiles, that they are all under sin … For all have sinned, and come short of the glory of God …

[5] **Galatians 3:21-22:** *Is* the law then against the promises of God? God forbid: for if there had been a law given which could have given life, verily righteousness should have been by the law. But the scripture hath concluded all under sin, that the promise by faith of Jesus Christ might be given to them that believe.

[6] **Romans 10:4:** For Christ *is* the end of the law for righteousness to every one that believeth.

96. What particular use is there of the moral law to unregenerate men?

A. The moral law is of use to unregenerate men to awaken their consciences to flee from wrath to come, [1] and to drive them to Christ; [2] or, upon their continuance in the estate and way of sin, to leave them inexcusable, [3]and under the curse thereof. [4]

Proofs

[1] **1 Timothy 1:9-10:** Knowing this, that the law is not made for a righteous man, but for the lawless and disobedient, for the ungodly and for sinners, for unholy and profane, for murderers of fathers and murderers of mothers, for manslayers, For whoremongers, for them that defile themselves with mankind, for menstealers, for liars, for perjured persons, and if there be any other thing that is contrary to sound doctrine ...

[2] **Galatians 3:24:** Wherefore the law was our schoolmaster *to bring us* unto Christ, that we might be justified by faith.

[3] **Romans 1:20:** For the invisible things of him from the creation of the world are clearly seen, being understood by the things that are made, *even* his eternal power and Godhead; so that they are without excuse. [Compare with] **Romans 2:15:** Which shew the work of the law written in their hearts, their conscience also bearing witness, and *their* thoughts the mean while accusing or else excusing one another ...

[4] **Galatians 3:10:** For as many as are of the works of the law are under the curse: for it is written, Cursed *is* every one that continueth not in all things which are written in the book of the law to do them.

97. What special use is there of the moral law to the regenerate?

A. Although they that are regenerate, and believe in Christ, be delivered from the moral law as a covenant of works, [1] so as thereby they are neither justified [2] nor condemned; [3]yet, besides the general uses thereof common to them with all men, it is of special use, to show them how much they are bound to Christ for his fulfilling it, and enduring the curse thereof in their stead, and for their good; [4] and thereby to provoke them to more thankfulness, [5] and to express the same in their greater care to conform themselves thereunto as the rule of their obedience. [6]

Proofs

[1] **Romans 6:14:** For sin shall not have dominion over you: for ye are not under the law, but under grace. **Romans 7:4, 6:** Wherefore, my brethren, ye also are become dead to the law by the body of Christ; that ye should be married to another, *even* to him who is raised from the dead, that we should bring forth fruit unto God … But now we are delivered from the law, that being dead wherein we were held; that we should serve in newness of spirit, and not *in* the oldness of the letter. **Galatians 4:4-5:** But when the fulness of the time was come, God sent forth his Son, made of a woman, made under the law, To redeem them that were under the law, that we might receive the adoption of sons.

[2] **Romans 3:20:** Therefore by the deeds of the law there shall no flesh be justified in his sight: for by the law *is* the knowledge of sin.

[3] **Galatians 5:23:** Meekness, temperance: against such there is no law. **Romans 8:1:** *There is* therefore now no condemnation to them which are in Christ Jesus, who walk not after the flesh, but after the Spirit.

[4] **Romans 7:24-25:** O wretched man that I am! who shall deliver me from the body of this death? I thank God through Jesus Christ our Lord. So then with the mind I myself serve the law of God; but with the flesh the law of sin. **Galatians 3:13-14:** Christ hath redeemed us from the curse of the law, being made a curse for us: for it is written, Cursed *is* every one that hangeth on a tree: That the blessing of Abraham might come on the Gentiles through Jesus Christ; that we might receive the promise of the Spirit through faith. **Romans 8:3-4:** For what the law could not do, in that it was weak through the flesh, God sending his own Son in the likeness of sinful flesh, and for sin, condemned sin in the flesh: That the righteousness of the law might be fulfilled in us, who walk not after the flesh, but after the Spirit.

[5] **Luke 1:68-69, 74-75:** Blessed *be* the Lord God of Israel; for he hath visited and redeemed his people, And hath raised up an horn of salvation for us in the house of his servant David … That he would grant unto us, that we being delivered out of the hand of our enemies might serve him without fear, In holiness and righteousness before him, all the days of our life. **Colossians 1:12-14:** Giving thanks unto the

Father, which hath made us meet to be partakers of the inheritance of the saints in light: Who hath delivered us from the power of darkness, and hath translated *us* into the kingdom of his dear Son: In whom we have redemption through his blood, *even* the forgiveness of sins ...

[6] **Romans 7:22:** For I delight in the law of God after the inward man ... **Romans 12:2:** And be not conformed to this world: but be ye transformed by the renewing of your mind, that ye may prove what *is* that good, and acceptable, and perfect, will of God. **Titus 2:11-14:** For the grace of God that bringeth salvation hath appeared to all men, Teaching us that, denying ungodliness and worldly lusts, we should live soberly, righteously, and godly, in this present world; Looking for that blessed hope, and the glorious appearing of the great God and our Saviour Jesus Christ; Who gave himself for us, that he might redeem us from all iniquity, and purify unto himself a peculiar people, zealous of good works.

98. Where is the moral law summarily comprehended?

A. The moral law is summarily comprehended in the ten commandments, which were delivered by the voice of God upon Mount Sinai, and written by him in two tables of stone, [1] and are recorded in the twentieth chapter of Exodus: the four first commandments containing our duty to God, and the other six our duty to man. [2]

Proofs

[1] **Deuteronomy 10:4:** And he wrote on the tables, according to the first writing, the ten commandments, which the LORD spake unto you in the mount out of the midst of the fire in the day of the assembly: and the LORD gave them unto me. **Exodus 34:1-4:** And the LORD said unto Moses, Hew thee two tables of stone like unto the first: and I will write upon *these* tables the words that were in the first tables, which thou brakest. And be ready in the morning, and come up in the morning unto mount Sinai, and present thyself there to me in the top of the mount. And no man shall come up with thee, neither let any man be seen throughout all the mount; neither let the flocks nor herds feed before that mount. And he hewed two tables of stone like unto the first; and Moses rose up early in the morning, and went up unto mount Sinai, as the LORD had commanded him, and took in his hand the two tables of stone.

[2] **Matthew 22:37-40:** Jesus said unto him, Thou shalt love the Lord thy God with all thy heart, and with all thy soul, and with all thy mind. This is the first and great commandment. And the second *is* like unto it, Thou shalt love thy neighbour as thyself. On these two commandments hang all the law and the prophets.

99. What rules are to be observed for the right understanding of the ten commandments?

A. For the right understanding of the ten commandments, these rules are to be observed:

1. That the law is perfect, and bindeth everyone to full conformity in the whole man unto the righteousness thereof, and unto entire obedience forever; so as to require the utmost perfection of every duty, and to forbid the least degree of every sin. [1]
2. That it is spiritual, and so reacheth the understanding, will, affections, and all other powers of the soul; as well as words, works, and gestures. [2]
3. That one and the same thing, in divers respects, is required or forbidden in several commandments. [3]
4. That as, where a duty is commanded, the contrary sin is forbidden; [4] and, where a sin is forbidden, the contrary duty is commanded: [5] so, where a promise is annexed, the contrary threatening is included; [6] and, where a threatening is annexed, the contrary promise is included. [7]
5. That what God forbids, is at no time to be done; [8] what he commands, is always our duty; [9] and yet every particular duty is not to be done at all times. [10]
6. That under one sin or duty, all of the same kind are forbidden or commanded: together with all the causes, means, occasions, and appearances thereof, and provocations thereunto. [11]
7. That what is forbidden or commanded to ourselves, we are bound, according to our places to endeavour that it

may be avoided or performed by others, according to the duty of their places. [12]

8. That in what is commanded to others, we are bound, according to our places and callings, to be helpful to them: [13] and to take heed of partaking with others in what is forbidden them. [14]

Proofs

[1] **Psalm 19:7:** The law of the LORD *is* perfect, converting the soul: the testimony of the LORD *is* sure, making wise the simple. **James 2:10:** For whosoever shall keep the whole law, and yet offend in one *point*, he is guilty of all. **Matthew 5:21-22:** Ye have heard that it was said by them of old time, Thou shalt not kill; and whosoever shall kill shall be in danger of the judgment: But I say unto you, That whosoever is angry with his brother without a cause shall be in danger of the judgment: and whosoever shall say to his brother, Raca, shall be in danger of the council: but whosoever shall say, Thou fool, shall be in danger of hell fire.

[2] **Romans 7:14:** For we know that the law is spiritual: but I am carnal, sold under sin. **Deuteronomy 6:5:** And thou shalt love the LORD thy God with all thine heart, and with all thy soul, and with all thy might. [Compare with] **Matthew 22:37-39:** Jesus said unto him, Thou shalt love the Lord thy God with all thy heart, and with all thy soul, and with all thy mind. This is the first and great commandment. And the second *is* like unto it, Thou shalt love thy neighbour as thyself. **Matthew 5:21-22, 27-28, 33-34, 37-39, 43-44:** Ye have heard that it was said by them of old time, Thou shalt not kill; and whosoever shall kill shall be in danger of the judgment: But I say unto you, That whosoever is angry with his brother without a cause shall be in danger of the judgment: and whosoever shall say to his brother, Raca, shall be in danger of the council: but whosoever shall say, Thou fool, shall be in danger of hell fire ... Ye have heard that it was said by them of old time, Thou shalt not commit adultery: But I say unto you, That whosoever looketh on a woman to lust after her hath committed adultery with her already in his heart ... Again, ye have heard that it hath been said by them of old time, Thou shalt not forswear thyself, but shalt perform unto the Lord thine oaths: But I say unto you, Swear not at all; neither by heaven; for it is God's throne ... But let your

communication be, Yea, yea; Nay, nay: for whatsoever is more than these cometh of evil. Ye have heard that it hath been said, An eye for an eye, and a tooth for a tooth: But I say unto you, That ye resist not evil: but whosoever shall smite thee on thy right cheek, turn to him the other also ... Ye have heard that it hath been said, Thou shalt love thy neighbour, and hate thine enemy. But I say unto you, Love your enemies, bless them that curse you, do good to them that hate you, and pray for them which despitefully use you, and persecute you ...

[3] **Colossians 3:5:** Mortify therefore your members which are upon the earth; fornication, uncleanness, inordinate affection, evil concupiscence, and covetousness, which is idolatry ... **Amos 8:5:** Saying, When will the new moon be gone, that we may sell corn? and the sabbath, that we may set forth wheat, making the ephah small, and the shekel great, and falsifying the balances by deceit? **Proverbs 1:19:** So *are* the ways of every one that is greedy of gain; *which* taketh away the life of the owners thereof. **1 Timothy 6:10:** For the love of money is the root of all evil: which while some coveted after, they have erred from the faith, and pierced themselves through with many sorrows.

[4] **Isaiah 58:13:** If thou turn away thy foot from the sabbath, *from* doing thy pleasure on my holy day; and call the sabbath a delight, the holy of the LORD, honourable; and shalt honour him, not doing thine own ways, nor finding thine own pleasure, nor speaking *thine own words* ... **Deuteronomy 6:13:** Thou shalt fear the LORD thy God, and serve him, and shalt swear by his name. [Compare with] **Matthew 4:9-10:** And saith unto him, All these things will I give thee, if thou wilt fall down and worship me. Then saith Jesus unto him, Get thee hence, Satan: for it is written, Thou shalt worship the Lord thy God, and him only shalt thou serve. **Matthew 15:4-6:** For God commanded, saying, Honour thy father and mother: and, He that curseth father or mother, let him die the death. But ye say, Whosoever shall say to *his* father or *his* mother, *It is* a gift, by whatsoever thou mightest be profited by me; And honour not his father or his mother, *he shall be free*. Thus have ye made the commandment of God of none effect by your tradition.

[5] **Matthew 5:21-25:** Ye have heard that it was said by them of old time, Thou shalt not kill; and whosoever shall kill shall be in danger of the judgment: But I say unto you, That whosoever is angry with his brother without a cause shall be in danger of the judgment: and

whosoever shall say to his brother, Raca, shall be in danger of the council: but whosoever shall say, Thou fool, shall be in danger of hell fire. Therefore if thou bring thy gift to the altar, and there rememberest that thy brother hath ought against thee; Leave there thy gift before the altar, and go thy way; first be reconciled to thy brother, and then come and offer thy gift. Agree with thine adversary quickly, whiles thou art in the way with him; lest at any time the adversary deliver thee to the judge, and the judge deliver thee to the officer, and thou be cast into prison. **Ephesians 4:28:** Let him that stole steal no more: but rather let him labour, working with *his* hands the thing which is good, that he may have to give to him that needeth.

[6] **Exodus 20:12:** Honour thy father and thy mother: that thy days may be long upon the land which the LORD thy God giveth thee. [Compare with] **Proverbs 30:17:** The eye *that* mocketh at *his* father, and despiseth to obey *his* mother, the ravens of the valley shall pick it out, and the young eagles shall eat it.

[7] **Jeremiah 18:7-8:** *At what* instant I shall speak concerning a nation, and concerning a kingdom, to pluck up, and to pull down, and to destroy *it*; If that nation, against whom I have pronounced, turn from their evil, I will repent of the evil that I thought to do unto them. **Exodus 20:7:** Thou shalt not take the name of the LORD thy God in vain; for the LORD will not hold him guiltless that taketh his name in vain. **Psalm 15:1, 4-5:** Lord, who shall abide in thy tabernacle? who shall dwell in thy holy hill? ... In whose eyes a vile person is contemned; but he honoureth them that fear the LORD. He that sweareth to *his own* hurt, and changeth not. *He that* putteth not out his money to usury, nor taketh reward against the innocent. He that doeth these *things* shall never be moved. **Psalm 24:4-5:** He that hath clean hands, and a pure heart; who hath not lifted up his soul unto vanity, nor sworn deceitfully. He shall receive the blessing from the LORD, and righteousness from the God of his salvation.

[8] **Job 13:7-8:** Will ye speak wickedly for God? and talk deceitfully for him? Will ye accept his person? will ye contend for God? **Romans 3:8:** And not *rather*, (as we be slanderously reported, and as some affirm that we say,) Let us do evil, that good may come? whose damnation is just. **Job 36:21:** Take heed, regard not iniquity: for this hast thou chosen rather than affliction. **Hebrews 11:25:** Choosing

rather to suffer affliction with the people of God, than to enjoy the pleasures of sin for a season …

[9] **Deuteronomy 4:8-9:** And what nation *is there so* great, that hath statutes and judgments *so* righteous as all this law, which I set before you this day? Only take heed to thyself, and keep thy soul diligently, lest thou forget the things which thine eyes have seen, and lest they depart from thy heart all the days of thy life: but teach them thy sons, and thy sons' sons …

[10] **Matthew 12:7:** But if ye had known what *this* meaneth, I will have mercy, and not sacrifice, ye would not have condemned the guiltless.

[11] **Matthew 5:21-22, 27-28:** Ye have heard that it was said by them of old time, Thou shalt not kill; and whosoever shall kill shall be in danger of the judgment: But I say unto you, That whosoever is angry with his brother without a cause shall be in danger of the judgment: and whosoever shall say to his brother, Raca, shall be in danger of the council: but whosoever shall say, Thou fool, shall be in danger of hell fire … Ye have heard that it was said by them of old time, Thou shalt not commit adultery: But I say unto you, That whosoever looketh on a woman to lust after her hath committed adultery with her already in his heart. **Matthew 15:4-6:** For God commanded, saying, Honour thy father and mother: and, He that curseth father or mother, let him die the death. But ye say, Whosoever shall say to *his* father or *his* mother, *It is* a gift, by whatsoever thou mightest be profited by me; And honour not his father or his mother, *he shall be free*. Thus have ye made the commandment of God of none effect by your tradition. **Hebrews 10:24-25:** And let us consider one another to provoke unto love and to good works: Not forsaking the assembling of ourselves together, as the manner of some *is*; but exhorting *one another*: and so much the more, as ye see the day approaching. **1 Thessalonians 5:22:** Abstain from all appearance of evil. **Jude 23:** And others save with fear, pulling *them* out of the fire; hating even the garment spotted by the flesh. **Galatians 5:26:** Let us not be desirous of vain glory, provoking one another, envying one another. **Colossians 3:21:** Fathers, provoke not your children *to anger*, lest they be discouraged.

[12] **Exodus 20:10:** But the seventh day *is* the sabbath of the Lord thy God: *in it* thou shalt not do any work, thou, nor thy son, nor thy daughter, thy manservant, nor thy maidservant, nor thy cattle, nor

thy stranger that *is* within thy gates … **Leviticus 19:17:** Thou shalt not hate thy brother in thine heart: thou shalt in any wise rebuke thy neighbour, and not suffer sin upon him. **Genesis 18:19:** For I know him, that he will command his children and his household after him, and they shall keep the way of the LORD, to do justice and judgment; that the LORD may bring upon Abraham that which he hath spoken of him. **Joshua 24:15:** And if it seem evil unto you to serve the LORD, choose you this day whom ye will serve; whether the gods which your fathers served that *were* on the other side of the flood, or the gods of the Amorites, in whose land ye dwell: but as for me and my house, we will serve the LORD. **Deuteronomy 6:6-7:** And these words, which I command thee this day, shall be in thine heart: And thou shalt teach them diligently unto thy children, and shalt talk of them when thou sittest in thine house, and when thou walkest by the way, and when thou liest down, and when thou risest up.

[13] **2 Corinthians 1:24:** Not for that we have dominion over your faith, but are helpers of your joy: for by faith ye stand.

[14] **1 Timothy 5:22:** Lay hands suddenly on no man, neither be partaker of other men's sins: keep thyself pure. **Ephesians 5:11:** And have no fellowship with the unfruitful works of darkness, but rather reprove *them*.

100. What special things are we to consider in the ten commandments?

A. We are to consider in the ten commandments, the preface, the substance of the commandments themselves, and several reasons annexed to some of them, the more to enforce them.

101. What is the preface to the ten commandments?

A. The preface to the ten commandments is contained in these words, *I am the Lord thy God, which have brought thee out of the land of Egypt, out of the house of bondage.* [1] Wherein God manifesteth his sovereignty, as being JEHOVAH, the eternal, immutable, and almighty God; [2] having his being in and of himself, [3] and giving being to all his words [4] and works: [5] and that he is a God in covenant, as with Israel of old, so with all his people; [6] who, as he brought them out of their bondage in Egypt, so he delivereth us from our spiritual thraldom; [7] and that therefore we are bound to take him for our God alone, and to keep all his commandments. [8]

Proofs

[1] **Exodus 20:2:** I *am* the LORD thy God, which have brought thee out of the land of Egypt, out of the house of bondage.

[2] **Isaiah 44:6:** Thus saith the LORD the King of Israel, and his redeemer the LORD of hosts; I *am* the first, and I *am* the last; and beside me *there is* no God.

[3] **Exodus 3:14:** And God said unto Moses, I AM THAT I AM: and he said, Thus shalt thou say unto the children of Israel, I AM hath sent me unto you.

[4] **Exodus 6:3:** And I appeared unto Abraham, unto Isaac, and unto Jacob, by *the name of* God Almighty, but by my name JEHOVAH was I not known to them.

[5] **Acts 17:24, 28:** God that made the world and all things therein, seeing that he is Lord of heaven and earth, dwelleth not in temples made with hands … For in him we live, and move, and have our being; as certain also of your own poets have said, For we are also his offspring.

[6] **Genesis 17:7:** And I will establish my covenant between me and thee and thy seed after thee in their generations for an everlasting covenant, to be a God unto thee, and to thy seed after thee. [Compare with] **Romans 3:29:** *Is he* the God of the Jews only? *is he* not also of the Gentiles? Yes, of the Gentiles also …

[7] **Luke 1:74-75:** That he would grant unto us, that we being delivered out of the hand of our enemies might serve him without fear, In holiness and righteousness before him, all the days of our life.

[8] **1 Peter 1:15, 16-18:** But as he which hath called you is holy, so be ye holy in all manner of conversation … Because it is written, Be ye holy; for I am holy. And if ye call on the Father, who without respect of persons judgeth according to every man's work, pass the time of your sojourning *here* in fear: Forasmuch as ye know that ye were not redeemed with corruptible things, *as* silver and gold, from your vain conversation *received* by tradition from your fathers … **Leviticus 18:30:** Therefore shall *ye* keep mine ordinance, that ye commit *not any* one of these abominable customs, which were committed before you, and that ye defile not yourselves

therein: I *am* the LORD your God. **Leviticus 19:37:** Therefore shall ye observe all my statutes, and all my judgments, and do them: I *am* the LORD.

102. What is the sum of the four commandments which contain our duty to God?

A. The sum of the four commandments containing our duty to God is, to love the Lord our God with all our heart, and with all our soul, and with all our strength, and with all our mind. [1]

Proof

[1] **Luke 10:27:** And he answering said, Thou shalt love the Lord thy God with all thy heart, and with all thy soul, and with all thy strength, and with all thy mind; and thy neighbour as thyself.

103. Which is the first commandment?

A. The first commandment is, *Thou shall have no other gods before me.* [1]

Proof

[1] **Exodus 20:3:** Thou shalt have no other gods before me.

104. What are the duties required in the first commandment?

A. The duties required in the first commandment are, the knowing and acknowledging of God to be the only true God, and our God; [1] and to worship and glorify him accordingly, [2] by thinking, [3] meditating, [4] remembering, [5] highly esteeming, [6] honouring, [7] adoring, [8] choosing, [9] loving, [10] desiring, [11] fearing of him; [12] believing him; [13] trusting, [14] hoping, [15] delighting, [16] rejoicing in him; [17] being zealous for him; [18] calling upon him, giving all praise and thanks, [19] and yielding all obedience and submission to him with the whole man; [20] being careful in all things to please him, [21] and sorrowful when in any thing he is offended; [22] and walking humbly with him. [23]

Proofs

[1] **1 Chronicles 28:9:** And thou, Solomon my son, know thou the God of thy father, and serve him with a perfect heart and with a

willing mind: for the LORD searcheth all hearts, and understandeth all the imaginations of the thoughts: if thou seek him, he will be found of thee; but if thou forsake him, he will cast thee off for ever. **Deuteronomy 26:7:** And when we cried unto the LORD God of our fathers, the LORD heard our voice, and looked on our affliction, and our labour, and our oppression ... **Isaiah 43:10:** Ye *are* my witnesses, saith the LORD, and my servant whom I have chosen: that ye may know and believe me, and understand that I *am* he: before me there was no God formed, neither shall there be after me. **Jeremiah 14:22:** Are there *any* among the vanities of the Gentiles that can cause rain? or can the heavens give showers? *art* not thou he, O LORD our God? therefore we will wait upon thee: for thou hast made all these *things*.

[2] **Psalm 95:6-7:** O come, let us worship and bow down: let us kneel before the LORD our maker. For he *is* our God; and we *are* the people of his pasture, and the sheep of his hand. To day if ye will hear his voice ... **Matthew 4:10:** Then saith Jesus unto him, Get thee hence, Satan: for it is written, Thou shalt worship the Lord thy God, and him only shalt thou serve. **Psalm 29:2:** Give unto the LORD the glory due unto his name; worship the LORD in the beauty of holiness.

[3] **Malachi 3:16:** Then they that feared the LORD spake often one to another: and the LORD hearkened, and heard *it*, and a book of remembrance was written before him for them that feared the LORD, and that thought upon his name.

[4] **Psalm 63:6:** When I remember thee upon my bed, *and* meditate on thee in the night watches.

[5] **Ecclesiastes 12:1:** Remember now thy Creator in the days of thy youth, while the evil days come not, nor the years draw nigh, when thou shalt say, I have no pleasure in them ...

[6] **Psalm 71:19:** Thy righteousness also, O God, *is* very high, who hast done great things: O God, who *is* like unto thee!

[7] **Malachi 1:6:** A son honoureth *his* father, and a servant his master: if then I *be* a father, where *is* mine honour? and if I *be* a master, where *is* my fear? saith the LORD of hosts unto you, O priests, that despise my name. And ye say, Wherein have we despised thy name?

[8] **Isaiah 45:23:** I have sworn by myself, the word is gone out of my mouth *in* righteousness, and shall not return, That unto me every knee shall bow, every tongue shall swear.

[9] **Joshua 24:15, 22:** And if it seem evil unto you to serve the LORD, choose you this day whom ye will serve; whether the gods which your fathers served that *were* on the other side of the flood, or the gods of the Amorites, in whose land ye dwell: but as for me and my house, we will serve the LORD … And Joshua said unto the people, Ye *are* witnesses against yourselves that ye have chosen you the LORD, to serve him. And they said, *We are* witnesses.

[10] **Deuteronomy 6:5:** And thou shalt love the LORD thy God with all thine heart, and with all thy soul, and with all thy might.

[11] **Psalm 73:25:** Whom have I in heaven *but thee?* and *there is* none upon earth *that* I desire beside thee.

[12] **Isaiah 8:13:** Sanctify the LORD of hosts himself; and *let* him *be* your fear, and *let* him *be* your dread.

[13] **Exodus 14:31:** And Israel saw that great work which the LORD did upon the Egyptians: and the people feared the LORD, and believed the LORD, and his servant Moses.

[14] **Isaiah 26:4:** Trust ye in the LORD for ever: for in the LORD JEHOVAH *is* everlasting strength …

[15] **Psalm 130:7:** Let Israel hope in the LORD: for with the LORD *there is* mercy, and with him *is* plenteous redemption.

[16] **Psalm 37:4:** Delight thyself also in the LORD; and he shall give thee the desires of thine heart.

[17] **Psalm 32:11:** Be glad in the LORD, and rejoice, ye righteous: and shout for joy, all *ye that are* upright in heart.

[18] **Romans 12:11:** Not slothful in business; fervent in spirit; serving the Lord … [Compare with] **Numbers 25:11:** Phinehas, the son of Eleazar, the son of Aaron the priest, hath turned my wrath away from the children of Israel, while he was zealous for my sake among them, that I consumed not the children of Israel in my jealousy.

[19] **Philippians 4:6:** Be careful for nothing; but in every thing by prayer and supplication with thanksgiving let your requests be made known unto God.

[20] **Jeremiah 7:23:** But this thing commanded I them, saying, Obey my voice, and I will be your God, and ye shall be my people: and walk ye in all the ways that I have commanded you, that it may be well

unto you. **James 4:7:** Submit yourselves therefore to God. Resist the devil, and he will flee from you.

[21] **1 John 3:22:** And whatsoever we ask, we receive of him, because we keep his commandments, and do those things that are pleasing in his sight.

[22] **Jeremiah 31:18:** I have surely heard Ephraim bemoaning himself *thus*; Thou hast chastised me, and I was chastised, as a bullock unaccustomed *to the yoke*: turn thou me, and I shall be turned; for thou *art* the LORD my God. **Psalm 119:136:** Rivers of waters run down mine eyes, because they keep not thy law.

[23] **Micah 6:8:** He hath shewed thee, O man, what *is* good; and what doth the LORD require of thee, but to do justly, and to love mercy, and to walk humbly with thy God?

105. What are the sins forbidden in the first commandment?

A. The sins forbidden in the first commandment are, atheism, in denying or not having a God; [1] idolatry, in having or worshipping more gods than one, or any with or instead of the true God; [2] the not having and avouching him for God, and our God; [3] the omission or neglect of anything due to him, required in this commandment; [4] ignorance, [5] forgetfulness, [6] misapprehensions, [7] false opinions, [8] unworthy and wicked thoughts of him; [9] bold and curious searching into his secrets; [10] all profaneness, [11] hatred of God; [12] self-love, [13] self-seeking, [14] and all other inordinate and immoderate setting of our mind, will, or affections upon other things, and taking them off from him in whole or in part; [15] vain credulity, [16] unbelief, [17] heresy, [18] misbelief, [19] distrust, [20] despair, [21] incorrigibleness, [22] and insensibleness under judgments, [23] hardness of heart, [24] pride, [25] presumption, [26] carnal security, [27] tempting of God; [28] using unlawful means, [29] and trusting in lawful means; [30] carnal delights and joys; [31] corrupt, blind and indiscreet zeal; [32] lukewarmness, [33] and deadness in the things of God; [34] estranging ourselves, and apostatizing from God; [35] praying, or giving any religious worship, to saints, angels, or any other creatures; [36] all compacts and consulting with the devil, [37] and hearkening to his suggestions; [38] making men the lords of our faith and conscience; [39] slighting and despising God and his commands; [40] resisting and grieving of his Spirit, [41] discontent and impatience at his dispensations, charging him foolishly for the evils he inflicts on us; [42]and ascribing the praise of any good we either are, have or can do, to fortune, [43] idols, [44] ourselves, [45] or any other creature. [46]

Proofs

[1] **Psalm 14:1:** The fool hath said in his heart, *There is* no God. They are corrupt, they have done abominable works, *there is* none that doeth good. **Ephesians 2:12:** That at that time ye were without Christ, being aliens from the commonwealth of Israel, and strangers from the covenants of promise, having no hope, and without God in the world ...

[2] **Jeremiah 2:27-28:** Saying to a stock, Thou *art* my father; and to a stone, Thou hast brought me forth: for they have turned *their* back unto me, and not *their* face: but in the time of their trouble they will say, Arise, and save us. But where *are* thy gods that thou hast made thee? let them arise, if they can save thee in the time of thy trouble: for *according* to the number of thy cities are thy gods, O Judah. [Compare with] **1 Thessalonians 1:9:** For they themselves shew of us what manner of entering in we had unto you, and how ye turned to God from idols to serve the living and true God ...

[3] **Psalm 81:11:** But my people would not hearken to my voice; and Israel would none of me.

[4] **Isaiah 43:22-24:** But thou hast not called upon me, O Jacob; but thou hast been weary of me, O Israel. Thou hast not brought me the small cattle of thy burnt offerings; neither hast thou honoured me with thy sacrifices. I have not caused thee to serve with an offering, nor wearied thee with incense. Thou hast bought me no sweet cane with money, neither hast thou filled me with the fat of thy sacrifices: but thou hast made me to serve with thy sins, thou hast wearied me with thine iniquities.

[5] **Jeremiah 4:22:** For my people *is* foolish, they have not known me; they *are* sottish children, and they have none understanding: they *are* wise

to do evil, but to do good they have no knowledge. **Hosea 4:1, 6:** Hear the word of the LORD, ye children of Israel: for the LORD hath a controversy with the inhabitants of the land, because *there is* no truth, nor mercy, nor knowledge of God in the land … My people are destroyed for lack of knowledge: because thou hast rejected knowledge, I will also reject thee, that thou shalt be no priest to me: seeing thou hast forgotten the law of thy God, I will also forget thy children.

[6] **Jeremiah 2:32:** Can a maid forget her ornaments, *or* a bride her attire? yet my people have forgotten me days without number.

[7] **Acts 17:23, 29:** For as I passed by, and beheld your devotions, I found an altar with this inscription, TO THE UNKNOWN GOD. Whom therefore ye ignorantly worship, him declare I unto you … Forasmuch then as we are the offspring of God, we ought not to think that the Godhead is like unto gold, or silver, or stone, graven by art and man's device.

[8] **Isaiah 40:18:** To whom then will ye liken God? or what likeness will ye compare unto him?

[9] **Psalm 50:21:** These *things* hast thou done, and I kept silence; thou thoughtest that I was altogether *such an one* as thyself: *but* I will reprove thee, and set *them* in order before thine eyes.

[10] **Deuteronomy 29:29:** The secret *things* belong unto the LORD our God: but those *things which are* revealed *belong* unto us and to our children for ever, that we may do all the words of this law.

[11] **Titus 1:16:** They profess that they know God; but in works they deny *him*, being abominable, and disobedient, and unto every good work reprobate. **Hebrews 12:16:** Lest there *be* any fornicator, or profane person, as Esau, who for one morsel of meat sold his birthright.

[12] **Romans 1:30:** Backbiters, haters of God, despiteful, proud, boasters, inventors of evil things, disobedient to parents …

[13] **2 Timothy 3:2:** For men shall be lovers of their own selves, covetous, boasters, proud, blasphemers, disobedient to parents, unthankful, unholy …

[14] **Philippians 2:21:** For all seek their own, not the things which are Jesus Christ's.

[15] **1 John 2:15-16:** Love not the world, neither the things *that are* in the world. If any man love the world, the love of the Father is not in him. For all that *is* in the world, the lust of the flesh, and the lust

of the eyes, and the pride of life, is not of the Father, but is of the world. **1 Samuel 2:29:** Wherefore kick ye at my sacrifice and at mine offering, which I have commanded *in my* habitation; and honourest thy sons above me, to make yourselves fat with the chiefest of all the offerings of Israel my people? **Colossians 3:2, 5:** Set your affection on things above, not on things on the earth … Mortify therefore your members which are upon the earth; fornication, uncleanness, inordinate affection, evil concupiscence, and covetousness, which is idolatry …

[16] **1 John 4:1:** Beloved, believe not every spirit, but try the spirits whether they are of God: because many false prophets are gone out into the world.

[17] **Hebrews 3:12:** Take heed, brethren, lest there be in any of you an evil heart of unbelief, in departing from the living God.

[18] **Galatians 5:20:** Idolatry, witchcraft, hatred, variance, emulations, wrath, strife, seditions, heresies … **Titus 3:10:** A man that is an heretick after the first and second admonition reject …

[19] **Acts 26:9:** I verily thought with myself, that I ought to do many things contrary to the name of Jesus of Nazareth.

[20] **Psalm 78:22:** Because they believed not in God, and trusted not in his salvation …

[21] **Genesis 4:13:** And Cain said unto the LORD, My punishment *is* greater than I can bear.

[22] **Jeremiah 5:3:** O LORD, *are* not thine eyes upon the truth? thou hast stricken them, but they have not grieved; thou hast consumed them, *but* they have refused to receive correction: they have made their faces harder than a rock; they have refused to return.

[23] **Isaiah 42:25:** Therefore he hath poured upon him the fury of his anger, and the strength of battle: and it hath set him on fire round about, yet he knew not; and it burned him, yet he laid *it* not to heart.

[24] **Romans 2:5:** But after thy hardness and impenitent heart treasurest up unto thyself wrath against the day of wrath and revelation of the righteous judgment of God …

[25] **Jeremiah 13:15:** Hear ye, and give ear; be not proud: for the LORD hath spoken.

[26] **Psalm 19:13:** Keep back thy servant also from presumptuous *sins*; let them not have dominion over me: then shall I be upright, and I shall be innocent from the great transgression.

[27] **Zephaniah 1:12:** And it shall come to pass at that time, *that* I will search Jerusalem with candles, and punish the men that are settled on their lees: that say in their heart, The LORD will not do good, neither will he do evil.

[28] **Matthew 4:7:** Jesus said unto him, It is written again, Thou shalt not tempt the Lord thy God.

[29] **Romans 3:8:** And not *rather*, (as we be slanderously reported, and as some affirm that we say,) Let us do evil, that good may come? whose damnation is just.

[30] **Jeremiah 17:5:** Thus saith the LORD; Cursed *be* the man that trusteth in man, and maketh flesh his arm, and whose heart departeth from the LORD.

[31] **2 Timothy 3:4:** Traitors, heady, highminded, lovers of pleasures more than lovers of God …

[32] **Galatians 4:17:** They zealously affect you, but not well; yea, they would exclude you, that ye might affect them.**John 16:2:** They shall put you out of the synagogues: yea, the time cometh, that whosoever killeth you will think that he doeth God service. **Romans 10:2:** For I bear them record that they have a zeal of God, but not according to knowledge. **Luke 9:54-55:** And when his disciples James and John saw *this*, they said, Lord, wilt thou that we command fire to come down from heaven, and consume them, even as Elias did? But he turned, and rebuked them, and said, Ye know not what manner of spirit ye are of.

[33] **Revelation 3:16:** So then because thou art lukewarm, and neither cold nor hot, I will spue thee out of my mouth.

[34] **Revelation 3:1:** And unto the angel of the church in Sardis write; These things saith he that hath the seven Spirits of God, and the seven stars; I know thy works, that thou hast a name that thou livest, and art dead.

[35] **Ezekiel 14:5:** That I may take the house of Israel in their own heart, because they are all estranged from me through their idols. **Isaiah 1:4-5:** Ah sinful nation, a people laden with iniquity, a seed of evildoers, children that are corrupters: they have forsaken the LORD,

they have provoked the Holy One of Israel unto anger, they are gone away backward. Why should ye be stricken any more? ye will revolt more and more: the whole head is sick, and the whole heart faint.

[36] **Romans 10:13-14:** For whosoever shall call upon the name of the Lord shall be saved. How then shall they call on him in whom they have not believed? and how shall they believe in him of whom they have not heard? and how shall they hear without a preacher? **Hosea 4:12:** My people ask counsel at their stocks, and their staff declareth unto them: for the spirit of whoredoms hath caused *them* to err, and they have gone a whoring from under their God. **Acts 10:25-26:** And as Peter was coming in, Cornelius met him, and fell down at his feet, and worshipped *him*. But Peter took him up, saying, Stand up; I myself also am a man. **Revelation 19:10:** And I fell at his feet to worship him. And he said unto me, See *thou do it* not: I am thy fellowservant, and of thy brethren that have the testimony of Jesus: worship God: for the testimony of Jesus is the spirit of prophecy. **Matthew 4:10:** Then saith Jesus unto him, Get thee hence, Satan: for it is written, Thou shalt worship the Lord thy God, and him only shalt thou serve. **Colossians 2:18:** Let no man beguile you of your reward in a voluntary humility and worshipping of angels, intruding into those things which he hath not seen, vainly puffed up by his fleshly mind … **Romans 1:25:** Who changed the truth of God into a lie, and worshipped and served the creature more than the Creator, who is blessed for ever. Amen.

[37] **Leviticus 20:6:** And the soul that turneth after such as have familiar spirits, and after wizards, to go a whoring after them, I will even set my face against that soul, and will cut him off from among his people. **1 Samuel 28:7, 11:** Then said Saul unto his servants, Seek me a woman that hath a familiar spirit, that I may go to her, and inquire of her. And his servants said to him, Behold, *there is* a woman that hath a familiar spirit at Endor … Then said the woman, Whom shall I bring up unto thee? And he said, Bring me up Samuel. [Compare with] **1 Chronicles 10:13-14:** So Saul died for his transgression which he committed against the LORD, *even* against the word of the LORD, which he kept not, and also for asking *counsel* of *one that had* a familiar spirit, to inquire *of it*; And inquired not of the LORD: therefore he slew him, and turned the kingdom unto David the son of Jesse.

[38] **Acts 5:3:** But Peter said, Ananias, why hath Satan filled thine heart to lie to the Holy Ghost, and to keep back *part* of the price of the land?

[39] **2 Corinthians 1:24:** Not for that we have dominion over your faith, but are helpers of your joy: for by faith ye stand. **Matthew 23:9:** And call no *man* your father upon the earth: for one is your Father, which is in heaven.

[40] **Deuteronomy 32:15:** But Jeshurun waxed fat, and kicked: thou art waxen fat, thou art grown thick, thou art covered *with fatness*; then he forsook God *which* made him, and lightly esteemed the Rock of his salvation. **2 Samuel 12:9:** Wherefore hast thou despised the commandment of the LORD, to do evil in his sight? thou hast killed Uriah the Hittite with the sword, and hast taken his wife *to be* thy wife, and hast slain him with the sword of the children of Ammon. **Proverbs 13:13:** Whoso despiseth the word shall be destroyed: but he that feareth the commandment shall be rewarded.

[41] **Acts 7:51:** Ye stiffnecked and uncircumcised in heart and ears, ye do always resist the Holy Ghost: as your fathers *did*, so *do* ye. **Ephesians 4:30:** And grieve not the holy Spirit of God, whereby ye are sealed unto the day of redemption.

[42] **Psalm 73:2-3, 13-15, 22:** But as for me, my feet were almost gone; my steps had well nigh slipped. For I was envious at the foolish, *when* I saw the prosperity of the wicked ... Verily I have cleansed my heart *in* vain, and washed my hands in innocency. For all the day long have I been plagued, and chastened every morning. If I say, I will speak thus; behold, I should offend *against* the generation of thy children ... So foolish *was* I, and ignorant: I was *as* a beast before thee. **Job 1:22:** In all this Job sinned not, nor charged God foolishly.

[43] **1 Samuel 6:7-9:** Now therefore make a new cart, and take two milch kine, on which there hath come no yoke, and tie the kine to the cart, and bring their calves home from them: And take the ark of the LORD, and lay it upon the cart; and put the jewels of gold, which ye return him *for* a trespass offering, in a coffer by the side thereof; and send it away, that it may go. And see, if it goeth up by the way of his own coast to Bethshemesh, *then* he hath done us this great evil: but if not, then we shall know that *it is* not his hand *that* smote us: it was a chance *that* happened to us.

[44] **Daniel 5:23:** But hast lifted up thyself against the Lord of heaven; and they have brought the vessels of his house before thee, and thou, and thy lords, thy wives, and thy concubines, have drunk wine in them; and thou hast praised the gods of silver, and gold, of brass, iron, wood, and stone, which see not, nor hear, nor know: and the God in whose hand thy breath *is*, and whose *are* all thy ways, hast thou not glorified ...

[45] **Deuteronomy 8:17:** And thou say in thine heart, My power and the might of *mine* hand hath gotten me this wealth. **Daniel 4:30:** The king spake, and said, Is not this great Babylon, that I have built for the house of the kingdom by the might of my power, and for the honour of my majesty?

[46] **Habakkuk 1:16:** Therefore they sacrifice unto their net, and burn incense unto their drag; because by them their portion *is* fat, and their meat plenteous.

106. What are we specially taught by these words *before me* in the first commandment?

A. These words before me or before my face, in the first commandment, teach us that God, who seeth all things, taketh special notice of, and is much displeased with, the sin of having any other God: that so it may be an argument to dissuade from it, and to aggravate it as a most impudent provocation: [1] as also to persuade us to do as in his sight, whatever we do in his service. [2]

Proofs

[1] **Ezekiel 8:5-6:** Then said he unto me, Son of man, lift up thine eyes now the way toward the north. So I lifted up mine eyes the way toward the north, and behold northward at the gate of the altar this image of jealousy in the entry. He said furthermore unto me, Son of man, seest thou what they do? *even* the great abominations that the house of Israel committeth here, that I should go far off from my sanctuary? but turn thee yet again, *and* thou shalt see greater abominations. [See the rest of the chapter.]**Psalm 44:20-21:** If we have forgotten the name of our God, or stretched out our hands to a strange god; Shall not God search this out? for he knoweth the secrets of the heart.

[2] **1 Chronicles 28:9:** And thou, Solomon my son, know thou the God of thy father, and serve him with a perfect heart and with a willing mind: for the LORD searcheth all hearts, and understandeth all the

imaginations of the thoughts: if thou seek him, he will be found of thee; but if thou forsake him, he will cast thee off for ever.

107. Which is the second commandment?

A. The second commandment is, *Thou shalt not make unto thee any graven image, or any likeness of anything that is in heaven above, or that is in the earth beneath, or that is in the water under the earth. Thou shalt not bow down thyself to them, nor serve them: for I the Lord thy God am a jealous God, visiting the iniquity of the fathers upon the children unto the third and fourth generation of them that hate me; and showing mercy unto thousands of them that love me, and keep my commandments.* [1]

Proof

[1] **Exodus 20:4-6:** Thou shalt not make unto thee any graven image, or any likeness *of any thing* that *is* in heaven above, or that *is* in the earth beneath, or that *is* in the water under the earth: Thou shalt not bow down thyself to them, nor serve them: for I the LORD thy God *am* a jealous God, visiting the iniquity of the fathers upon the children unto the third and fourth *generation* of them that hate me; And shewing mercy unto thousands of them that love me, and keep my commandments.

108. What are the duties required in the second commandment?

A. The duties required in the second commandment are, the receiving, observing, and keeping pure and entire, all such religious worship and ordinances as God hath instituted in his Word; [1] particularly prayer and thanksgiving in the name of Christ; [2] the reading, preaching, and hearing of the Word; [3] the administration and receiving of the sacraments; [4] church government and discipline; [5] the ministry and maintainance thereof; [6] religious fasting; [7] swearing by the name of God; [8] and vowing unto him; [9] as also the disapproving, detesting, opposing all false worship; [10] and, according to each one's place and calling, removing it, and all monuments of idolatry. [11]

Proofs

[1] **Deuteronomy 32:46-47:** And he said unto them, Set your hearts unto all the words which I testify among you this day, which ye shall command your children to observe to do, all the words of this law. For

it *is* not a vain thing for you; because it *is* your life: and through this thing ye shall prolong *your* days in the land, whither ye go over Jordan to possess it. **Matthew 28:20:** Teaching them to observe all things whatsoever I have commanded you: and, lo, I am with you alway, *even* unto the end of the world. Amen. **Acts 2:42:** And they continued stedfastly in the apostles' doctrine and fellowship, and in breaking of bread, and in prayers. **1 Timothy 6:13-14:** I give thee charge in the sight of God, who quickeneth all things, and *before* Christ Jesus, who before Pontius Pilate witnessed a good confession; That thou keep *this* commandment without spot, unrebukeable, until the appearing of our Lord Jesus Christ …

[2] **Philippians 4:6:** Be careful for nothing; but in every thing by prayer and supplication with thanksgiving let your requests be made known unto God. **Ephesians 5:20:** Giving thanks always for all things unto God and the Father in the name of our Lord Jesus Christ …

[3] **Deuteronomy 17:18-19:** And it shall be, when he sitteth upon the throne of his kingdom, that he shall write him a copy of this law in a book out of *that which is* before the priests the Levites: And it shall be with him, and he shall read therein all the days of his life: that he may learn to fear the Lord his God, to keep all the words of this law and these statutes, to do them … **Acts 15:21:** For Moses of old time hath in every city them that preach him, being read in the synagogues every sabbath day. **2 Timothy 4:2:** Preach the word; be instant in season, out of season; reprove, rebuke, exhort with all longsuffering and doctrine. **James 1:21-22:** Wherefore lay apart all filthiness and superfluity of naughtiness, and receive with meekness the engrafted word, which is able to save your souls. But be ye doers of the word, and not hearers only, deceiving your own selves. **Acts 10:33:** Immediately therefore I sent to thee; and thou hast well done that thou art come. Now therefore are we all here present before God, to hear all things that are commanded thee of God.

[4] **Matthew 28:19:** Go ye therefore, and teach all nations, baptizing them in the name of the Father, and of the Son, and of the Holy Ghost … **1 Corinthians 11:23-30:** For I have received of the Lord that which also I delivered unto you, That the Lord Jesus the *same* night in which he was betrayed took bread: And when he had given thanks, he brake *it*, and said, Take, eat: this is my body, which is broken for you: this do in remembrance of me. After the same manner also *he took*

the cup, when he had supped, saying, This cup is the new testament in my blood: this do ye, as oft as ye drink *it*, in remembrance of me. For as often as ye eat this bread, and drink this cup, ye do shew the Lord's death till he come. Wherefore whosoever shall eat this bread, and drink *this* cup of the Lord, unworthily, shall be guilty of the body and blood of the Lord. But let a man examine himself, and so let him eat of *that* bread, and drink of *that* cup. For he that eateth and drinketh unworthily, eateth and drinketh damnation to himself, not discerning the Lord's body. For this cause many *are* weak and sickly among you, and many sleep.

[5] **Matthew 18:15-17:** Moreover if thy brother shall trespass against thee, go and tell him his fault between thee and him alone: if he shall hear thee, thou hast gained thy brother. But if he will not hear *thee, then* take with thee one or two more, that in the mouth of two or three witnesses every word may be established. And if he shall neglect to hear them, tell *it* unto the church: but if he neglect to hear the church, let him be unto thee as an heathen man and a publican. **Matthew 16:19:** And I will give unto thee the keys of the kingdom of heaven: and whatsoever thou shalt bind on earth shall be bound in heaven: and whatsoever thou shalt loose on earth shall be loosed in heaven. **1 Corinthians 5** [entire]. **1 Corinthians 12:28:** And God hath set some in the church, first apostles, secondarily prophets, thirdly teachers, after that miracles, then gifts of healings, helps, governments, diversities of tongues.

[6] **Ephesians 4:11-12:** And he gave some, apostles; and some, prophets; and some, evangelists; and some, pastors and teachers; For the perfecting of the saints, for the work of the ministry, for the edifying of the body of Christ ... **1 Timothy 5:17-18**. Let the elders that rule well be counted worthy of double honour, especially they who labour in the word and doctrine. For the scripture saith, Thou shalt not muzzle the ox that treadeth out the corn. And, The labourer *is* worthy of his reward. **1 Corinthians 9:7-15:** Who goeth a warfare any time at his own charges? who planteth a vineyard, and eateth not of the fruit thereof? or who feedeth a flock, and eateth not of the milk of the flock? Say I these things as a man? or saith not the law the same also? For it is written in the law of Moses, Thou shalt not muzzle the mouth of the ox that treadeth out the corn. Doth God take care for oxen? Or saith he *it* altogether for our sakes? For our sakes, no doubt, *this* is written: that he that ploweth should plow in hope; and that

he that thresheth in hope should be partaker of his hope. If we have sown unto you spiritual things, *is it* a great thing if we shall reap your carnal things? If others be partakers of *this* power over you, *are* not we rather? Nevertheless we have not used this power; but suffer all things, lest we should hinder the gospel of Christ. Do ye not know that they which minister about holy things live *of the things* of the temple? and they which wait at the altar are partakers with the altar? Even so hath the Lord ordained that they which preach the gospel should live of the gospel. But I have used none of these things: neither have I written these things, that it should be so done unto me: for *it were* better for me to die, than that any man should make my glorying void.

[7] **Joel 2:12-13:** Therefore also now, saith the LORD, turn ye *even* to me with all your heart, and with fasting, and with weeping, and with mourning: And rend your heart, and not your garments, and turn unto the LORD your God: for he *is* gracious and merciful, slow to anger, and of great kindness, and repenteth him of the evil. **1 Corinthians 7:5:** Defraud ye not one the other, except *it be* with consent for a time, that ye may give yourselves to fasting and prayer; and come together again, that Satan tempt you not for your incontinency.

[8] **Deuteronomy 6:13:** Thou shalt fear the LORD thy God, and serve him, and shalt swear by his name.

[9] **Isaiah 19:21:** And the LORD shall be known to Egypt, and the Egyptians shall know the LORD in that day, and shall do sacrifice and oblation; yea, they shall vow a vow unto the LORD, and perform *it*. **Psalm 76:11:** Vow, and pay unto the LORD your God: let all that be round about him bring presents unto him that ought to be feared.

[10] **Acts 17:16-17:** Now while Paul waited for them at Athens, his spirit was stirred in him, when he saw the city wholly given to idolatry. Therefore disputed he in the synagogue with the Jews, and with the devout persons, and in the market daily with them that met with him. **Psalm 16:4:** Their sorrows shall be multiplied *that* hasten *after* another *god*: their drink offerings of blood will I not offer, nor take up their names into my lips.

[11] **Deuteronomy 7:5:** But thus shall ye deal with them; ye shall destroy their altars, and break down their images, and cut down their groves, and burn their graven images with fire. **Isaiah 30:22:** Ye shall defile also the covering of thy graven images of silver, and the

ornament of thy molten images of gold: thou shalt cast them away as a menstruous cloth; thou shalt say unto it, Get thee hence.

109. What are the sins forbidden in the second commandment?

A. The sins forbidden in the second commandment are, all devising, [1] counselling, [2] commanding, [3] using, [4] and anywise approving, any religious worship not instituted by God himself; [5] tolerating a false religion; the making any representation of God, of all or of any of the three persons, either inwardly in our mind, or outwardly in any kind of image or likeness of any creature whatsoever; [6] all worshipping of it, [7] or God in it or by it; [8] the making of any representation of feigned deities, [9] and all worship of them, or service belonging to them, [10] all superstitious devices, [11] corrupting the worship of God, [12] adding to it, or taking from it, [13] whether invented and taken up to ourselves, [14] or received by tradition from others, [15] though under the title of antiquity, [16] custom, [17] devotion, [18] good intent, or any other pretence whatsoever; [19] simony; [20] sacrilege; [21] all neglect, [22] contempt, [23] hindering, [24] and opposing the worship and ordinances which God hath appointed. [25]

Proofs

[1] **Numbers 15:39:** And it shall be unto you for a fringe, that ye may look upon it, and remember all the commandments of the LORD, and do them; and that ye seek not after your own heart and your own eyes, after which ye use to go a whoring …

[2] **Deuteronomy 13:6-8:** If thy brother, the son of thy mother, or thy son, or thy daughter, or the wife of thy bosom, or thy friend, which *is* as thine own soul, entice thee secretly, saying, Let us go and serve other gods, which thou hast not known, thou, nor thy fathers; *Namely*, of the gods of the people which are round about you, nigh unto thee, or far off from thee, from the one end of the earth even unto the *other* end of the earth; Thou shalt not consent unto him, nor hearken unto him; neither shall thine eye pity him, neither shalt thou spare, neither shalt thou conceal him …

[3] **Hosea 5:11:** Ephraim *is* oppressed *and* broken in judgment, because he willingly walked after the commandment. **Micah 6:16:** For the statutes of Omri are kept, and all the works of the house of Ahab, and ye walk in their counsels; that I should make thee a desolation, and the inhabitants thereof an hissing: therefore ye shall bear the reproach of my people.

[4] **1 Kings 11:33:** Because that they have forsaken me, and have worshipped Ashtoreth the goddess of the Zidonians, Chemosh the god of the Moabites, and Milcom the god of the children of Ammon, and have not walked in my ways, to do *that which is* right in mine eyes, and *to keep* my statutes and my judgments, as *did* David his father. **1 Kings 12:33:** So he offered upon the altar which he had made in Bethel the fifteenth day of the eighth month, *even* in the month which he had devised of his own heart; and ordained a feast unto the children of Israel: and he offered upon the altar, and burnt incense.

[5] **Deuteronomy 12:30-32:** Take heed to thyself that thou be not snared by following them, after that they be destroyed from before thee; and that thou inquire not after their gods, saying, How did these nations serve their gods? even so will I do likewise. Thou shalt not do so unto the LORD thy God: for every abomination to the LORD, which he hateth, have they done unto their gods; for even their sons and their daughters they have burnt in the fire to their gods. What thing soever I command you, observe to do it: thou shalt not add thereto, nor diminish from it. **Zechariah 13:2-3:** And it shall come to pass in that day, saith the LORD of hosts, *that* I will cut off the names of the idols out of the land, and they shall no more be remembered: and also I will cause the prophets and the unclean spirit to pass out of the land. And it shall come to pass, that when any shall yet prophesy, then his father and his mother that begat him shall say unto him, Thou shalt not live; for thou speakest lies in the name of the LORD: and his father and his mother that begat him shall thrust him through when he prophesieth. **Revelation 2:2, 14, 20:** I know thy works, and thy labour, and thy patience, and how thou canst not bear them which are evil: and thou hast tried them which say they are apostles, and are not, and hast found them liars ... But I have a few things against thee, because thou hast there them that hold the doctrine of Balaam, who taught Balac to cast a stumblingblock before the children of Israel, to eat things sacrificed unto idols, and to commit fornication ... Notwithstanding

I have a few things against thee, because thou sufferest that woman Jezebel, which calleth herself a prophetess, to teach and to seduce my servants to commit fornication, and to eat things sacrificed unto idols. **Revelation 17:12, 16-17:** And the ten horns which thou sawest are ten kings, which have received no kingdom as yet; but receive power as kings one hour with the beast ... And the ten horns which thou sawest upon the beast, these shall hate the whore, and shall make her desolate and naked, and shall eat her flesh, and burn her with fire. For God hath put in their hearts to fulfil his will, and to agree, and give their kingdom unto the beast, until the words of God shall be fulfilled.

[6] **Deuteronomy 4:15-19:** Take ye therefore good heed unto yourselves; for ye saw no manner of similitude on the day *that* the LORD spake unto you in Horeb out of the midst of the fire: Lest ye corrupt *yourselves*, and make you a graven image, the similitude of any figure, the likeness of male or female, The likeness of any beast that *is* on the earth, the likeness of any winged fowl that flieth in the air, The likeness of any thing that creepeth on the ground, the likeness of any fish that *is* in the waters beneath the earth: And lest thou lift up thine eyes unto heaven, and when thou seest the sun, and the moon, and the stars, *even* all the host of heaven, shouldest be driven to worship them, and serve them, which the LORD thy God hath divided unto all nations under the whole heaven. **Acts 17:29:** Forasmuch then as we are the offspring of God, we ought not to think that the Godhead is like unto gold, or silver, or stone, graven by art and man's device. **Romans 1:21-23, 25:** Because that, when they knew God, they glorified *him* not as God, neither were thankful; but became vain in their imaginations, and their foolish heart was darkened. Professing themselves to be wise, they became fools, And changed the glory of the uncorruptible God into an image made like to corruptible man, and to birds, and fourfooted beasts, and creeping things ... Who changed the truth of God into a lie, and worshipped and served the creature more than the Creator, who is blessed for ever. Amen.

[7] **Daniel 3:18:** But if not, be it known unto thee, O king, that we will not serve thy gods, nor worship the golden image which thou hast set up. **Galatians 4:8:** Howbeit then, when ye knew not God, ye did service unto them which by nature are no gods.

[8] **Exodus 32:5:** And when Aaron saw *it*, he built an altar before it; and Aaron made proclamation, and said, To morrow *is* a feast to the LORD.

[9] **Exodus 32:8:** They have turned aside quickly out of the way which I commanded them: they have made them a molten calf, and have worshipped it, and have sacrificed thereunto, and said, These *be* thy gods, O Israel, which have brought thee up out of the land of Egypt.

[10] **1 Kings 18:26, 28:** And they took the bullock which was given them, and they dressed *it*, and called on the name of Baal from morning even until noon, saying, O Baal, hear us. But *there was* no voice, nor any that answered. And they leaped upon the altar which was made … And they cried aloud, and cut themselves after their manner with knives and lancets, till the blood gushed out upon them. **Isaiah 65:11:** But ye *are* they that forsake the LORD, that forget my holy mountain, that prepare a table for that troop, and that furnish the drink offering unto that number.

[11] **Acts 17:22:** Then Paul stood in the midst of Mars' hill, and said, *Ye* men of Athens, I perceive that in all things ye are too superstitious. **Colossians 2:21-23:** (Touch not; taste not; handle not; Which all are to perish with the using;) after the commandments and doctrines of men … Which things have indeed a shew of wisdom in will worship, and humility, and neglecting of the body; not in any honour to the satisfying of the flesh.

[12] **Malachi 1:7-8, 14:** Ye offer polluted bread upon mine altar; and ye say, Wherein have we polluted thee? In that ye say, The table of the LORD *is* contemptible. And if ye offer the blind for sacrifice, *is it* not evil? and if ye offer the lame and sick, *is it* not evil? offer it now unto thy governor; will he be pleased with thee, or accept thy person? saith the LORD of hosts … But cursed *be* the deceiver, which hath in his flock a male, and voweth, and sacrificeth unto the LORD a corrupt thing: for I *am* a great King, saith the LORD of hosts, and my name *is* dreadful among the heathen.

[13] **Deuteronomy 4:2:** Ye shall not add unto the word which I command you, neither shall ye diminish *ought* from it, that ye may keep the commandments of the LORD your God which I command you.

[14] **Psalm 106:39:** Thus were they defiled with their own works, and went a whoring with their own inventions.

[15] **Matthew 15:9:** But in vain they do worship me, teaching *for* doctrines the commandments of men.

[16] **1 Peter 1:18:** Forasmuch as ye know that ye were not redeemed with corruptible things, *as* silver and gold, from your vain conversation *received* by tradition from your fathers …

[17] **Jeremiah 44:17:** But we will certainly do whatsoever thing goeth forth out of our own mouth, to burn incense unto the queen of heaven, and to pour out drink offerings unto her, as we have done, we, and our fathers, our kings, and our princes, in the cities of Judah, and in the streets of Jerusalem: for *then* had we plenty of victuals, and were well, and saw no evil.

[18] **Isaiah 65:3-5:** A people that provoketh me to anger continually to my face; that sacrificeth in gardens, and burneth incense upon altars of brick; Which remain among the graves, and lodge in the monuments, which eat swine's flesh, and broth of abominable *things is in* their vessels; Which say, Stand by thyself, come not near to me; for I am holier than thou. These *are* a smoke in my nose, a fire that burneth all the day. **Galatians 1:13-14:** For ye have heard of my conversation in time past in the Jews' religion, how that beyond measure I persecuted the church of God, and wasted it: And profited in the Jews' religion above many my equals in mine own nation, being more exceedingly zealous of the traditions of my fathers.

[19] **1 Samuel 13:11-12:** And Samuel said, What hast thou done? And Saul said, Because I saw that the people were scattered from me, and that *thou* camest not within the days appointed, and *that* the Philistines gathered themselves together at Michmash; Therefore said I, The Philistines will come down now upon me to Gilgal, and I have not made supplication unto the LORD: I forced myself therefore, and offered a burnt offering. **1 Samuel 15:21:** But the people took of the spoil, sheep and oxen, the chief of the things which should have been utterly destroyed, to sacrifice unto the LORD thy God in Gilgal.

[20] **Acts 8:18:** And when Simon saw that through laying on of the apostles' hands the Holy Ghost was given, he offered them money …

[21] **Romans 2:22:** Thou that sayest a man should not commit adultery, dost thou commit adultery? thou that abhorrest idols, dost thou commit sacrilege? **Malachi 3:8:** Will a man rob God? Yet ye have robbed me. But ye say, Wherein have we robbed thee? In tithes and offerings.

[22] **Exodus 4:24-26:** And it came to pass by the way in the inn, that the LORD met him, and sought to kill him. Then Zipporah took a sharp stone, and cut off the foreskin of her son, and cast *it* at his feet, and said, Surely a bloody husband *art* thou to me. So he let him go: then she said, A bloody husband *thou art,* because of the circumcision.

[23] **Matthew 22:5:** But they made light of *it*, and went their ways, one to his farm, another to his merchandise ... **Malachi 1:7, 13:** Ye offer polluted bread upon mine altar; and ye say, Wherein have we polluted thee? In that ye say, The table of the LORD *is* contemptible ... Ye said also, Behold, what a weariness *is it!* and ye have snuffed at it, saith the LORD of hosts; and ye brought *that which was* torn, and the lame, and the sick; thus ye brought an offering: should I accept this of your hand? saith the LORD.

[24] **Matthew 23:13:** But woe unto you, scribes and Pharisees, hypocrites! for ye shut up the kingdom of heaven against men: for ye neither go in *yourselves,* neither suffer ye them that are entering to go in.

[25] **Acts 13:44-45:** And the next sabbath day came almost the whole city together to hear the word of God. But when the Jews saw the multitudes, they were filled with envy, and spake against those things which were spoken by Paul, contradicting and blaspheming. **1 Thessalonians 2:15-16:** Who both killed the Lord Jesus, and their own prophets, and have persecuted us; and they please not God, and are contrary to all men: Forbidding us to speak to the Gentiles that they might be saved, to fill up their sins alway: for the wrath is come upon them to the uttermost.

110. What are the reasons annexed to the second commandment, the more to enforce it?

A. The reasons annexed to the second commandment, the more to enforce it, contained in these words, *For I the Lord thy God am a jealous God, visiting the iniquity of the fathers upon the children unto the third and fourth generation of them that hate me; and showing mercy unto thousands of them that love me, and keep my commandments;* [1] are, besides God's sovereignty over us, and propriety in us, [2] his fervent zeal for his own worship, [3] and his revengeful indignation against all false worship, as being a spiritual whoredom; [4]accounting the breakers of this commandment such as hate him, and threatening to punish them unto divers generations; [5] and esteeming the observers of it such as love him and keep his commandments, and promising mercy to them unto many generations. [6]

Proofs

[1] **Exodus 20:5-6:** Thou shalt not bow down thyself to them, nor serve them: for I the LORD thy God *am* a jealous God, visiting the iniquity of the fathers upon the children unto the third and fourth *generation* of them that hate me; And shewing mercy unto thousands of them that love me, and keep my commandments.

[2] **Psalm 45:11:** So shall the king greatly desire thy beauty: for he *is* thy Lord; and worship thou him. **Revelation 15:3-4:** And they sing the song of Moses the servant of God, and the song of the Lamb, saying, Great and marvellous *are* thy works, Lord God Almighty; just and true *are* thy ways, thou King of saints. Who shall not fear thee, O Lord, and glorify thy name? for *thou* only *art* holy: for all nations shall come and worship before thee; for thy judgments are made manifest.

[3] **Exodus 34:13-14:** But ye shall destroy their altars, break their images, and cut down their groves: For thou shalt worship no other god: for the LORD, whose name *is* Jealous, *is* a jealous God ...

[4] **1 Corinthians 10:20-22:** But *I say*, that the things which the Gentiles sacrifice, they sacrifice to devils, and not to God: and I would not that ye should have fellowship with devils. Ye cannot drink the cup of the Lord, and the cup of devils: ye cannot be partakers of the Lord's table, and of the table of devils. Do we provoke the Lord to jealousy? are we stronger than he? **Jeremiah 7:18-20:** The children gather wood, and the fathers kindle the fire, and the women knead *their* dough, to make cakes to the queen of heaven, and to pour out drink offerings unto other gods, that they may provoke me to anger. Do they provoke me to anger? saith the LORD: *do they not provoke* themselves to the confusion of their own faces? Therefore thus saith the Lord GOD; Behold, mine anger and my fury shall be poured out upon this place, upon man, and upon beast, and upon the trees of the field, and upon the fruit of the ground; and it shall burn, and shall not be quenched. **Ezekiel 16:26-27:** Thou hast also committed fornication with the Egyptians thy neighbours, great of

flesh; and hast increased thy whoredoms, to provoke me to anger. Behold, therefore I have stretched out my hand over thee, and have diminished thine ordinary *food*, and delivered thee unto the will of them that hate thee, the daughters of the Philistines, which are ashamed of thy lewd way. **Deuteronomy 32:16-20:** They provoked him to jealousy with strange *gods*, with abominations provoked they him to anger. They sacrificed unto devils, not to God; to gods whom they knew not, to new *gods that* came newly up, whom your fathers feared not. Of the Rock *that* begat thee thou art unmindful, and hast forgotten God that formed thee. And when the LORD saw *it*, he abhorred *them*, because of the provoking of his sons, and of his daughters. And he said, I will hide my face from them, I will see what their end *shall be*: for they are a very froward generation, children in whom *is* no faith.

[5] **Hosea 2:2-4:** Plead with your mother, plead: for she *is* not my wife, neither *am* I her husband: let her therefore put away her whoredoms out of her sight, and her adulteries from between her breasts; Lest I strip her naked, and set her as in the day that she was born, and make her as a wilderness, and set her like a dry land, and slay her with thirst. And I will not have mercy upon her children; for they *be* the children of whoredoms.

[6] **Deuteronomy 5:29:** O that there were such an heart in them, that they would fear me, and keep all my commandments always, that it might be well with them, and with their children for ever!

111. Which is the third commandment?

A. The third commandment is, *Thou shalt not take the name of the Lord thy God in vain: for the Lord will not hold him guiltless that taketh his name in vain.* [1]

Proof

[1] **Exodus 20:7:** Thou shalt not take the name of the LORD thy God in vain; for the LORD will not hold him guiltless that taketh his name in vain.

112. What is required in the third commandment?

A. The third commandment requires, That the name of God, his titles, attributes, [1] ordinances, [2] the Word,[3] sacraments, [4] prayer, [5] oaths, [6] vows, [7] lots, [8] his works, [9] and whatsoever else there is whereby he makes himself known, be holily and reverently used in thought, [10] meditation, [11] word, [12] and writing; [13] by an holy profession, [14] and answerable conversation, [15] to the glory of God, [16] and the good of ourselves, [17]and others. [18]

Proofs

[1] **Matthew 6:9:** After this manner therefore pray ye: Our Father which art in heaven, Hallowed be thy name. **Deuteronomy 28:58:** If thou wilt not observe to do all the words of this law that are written in this book, that thou mayest fear this glorious and fearful name, THE LORD THY GOD. **Psalm 29:2:** Give unto the LORD the glory due unto his name; worship the LORD in the beauty of holiness. **Psalm 68:4:** Sing unto God, sing praises to his name: extol him that rideth upon the heavens by his name JAH, and rejoice before him. **Revelation 15:3-4:** And they sing the song of Moses the servant of God, and the song of the Lamb, saying, Great and marvellous *are* thy works, Lord God Almighty; just and true are thy ways, thou King of saints. Who shall not fear thee, O Lord, and glorify thy name? for *thou* only *art* holy: for all nations shall come and worship before thee; for thy judgments are made manifest.

[2] **Malachi 1:14:** But cursed *be* the deceiver, which hath in his flock a male, and voweth, and sacrificeth unto the LORD a corrupt thing: for I *am* a great King, saith the LORD of hosts, and my name *is* dreadful among the heathen. **Ecclesiastes 5:1:** Keep thy foot when thou goest to the house of God, and be more ready to hear, than to give the sacrifice of fools: for they consider not that they do evil.

[3] **Psalm 138:2:** I will worship toward thy holy temple, and praise thy name for thy lovingkindness and for thy truth: for thou hast magnified thy word above all thy name.

[4] **1 Corinthians 11:24-25, 28-29:** And when he had given thanks, he brake *it*, and said, Take, eat: this is my body, which is broken for you: this do in remembrance of me. After the same manner also *he took* the cup, when he had supped, saying, This cup is the new testament in my blood: this do ye, as oft as ye drink *it*, in remembrance of me ... But let a man examine himself, and so let him eat of *that* bread, and drink of *that* cup. For he that eateth and drinketh unworthily, eateth and drinketh damnation to himself, not discerning the Lord's body.

[5] **1 Timothy 2:8:** I will therefore that men pray every where, lifting up holy hands, without wrath and doubting.

[6] **Jeremiah 4:2:** And thou shalt swear, The LORD liveth, in truth, in judgment, and in righteousness; and the nations shall bless themselves in him, and in him shall they glory.

[7] **Ecclesiastes 5:2, 4-6:** Be not rash with thy mouth, and let not thine heart be hasty to utter *any* thing before God: for God *is* in heaven, and thou upon earth: therefore let thy words be few ... When thou vowest a vow unto God, defer not to pay it; for *he hath* no pleasure in fools: pay that which thou hast vowed. Better *is it* that thou shouldest not vow, than that thou shouldest vow and not pay. Suffer not thy mouth to cause thy flesh to sin; neither say thou before the angel, that it *was* an error: wherefore should God be angry at thy voice, and destroy the work of thine hands?

[8] **Acts 1:24, 26:**And they prayed, and said, Thou, Lord, which knowest the hearts of all *men*, shew whether of these two thou hast chosen ... And they gave forth their lots; and the lot fell upon Matthias; and he was numbered with the eleven apostles.

[9] **Job 36:24:** Remember that thou magnify his work, which men behold.

[10] **Malachi 3:16:** Then they that feared the LORD spake often one to another: and the LORD hearkened, and heard *it*, and a book of remembrance was written before him for them that feared the LORD, and that thought upon his name.

[11] **Psalm 8:1, 3-4, 9:** O LORD our Lord, how excellent *is* thy name in all the earth! who hast set thy glory above the heavens ... When I consider thy heavens, the work of thy fingers, the moon and the stars, which thou hast ordained; What is man, that thou art mindful of him? and the son of man, that thou visitest him? ... O LORD our Lord, how excellent *is* thy name in all the earth!

[12] **Colossians 3:17:** And whatsoever ye do in word or deed, *do* all in the name of the Lord Jesus, giving thanks to God and the Father by him. **Psalm 105:2, 5:** Sing unto him, sing psalms unto him: talk ye of all his wondrous works ... Remember his marvellous works that he hath done; his wonders, and the judgments of his mouth ...

[13] **Psalm 102:18:** This shall be written for the generation to come: and the people which shall be created shall praise the LORD.

[14] **1 Peter 3:15:** But sanctify the Lord God in your hearts: and *be* ready always to *give* an answer to every man that asketh you a reason of the hope that is in you with meekness and fear … **Micah 4:5:** For all people will walk every one in the name of his god, and we will walk in the name of the LORD our God for ever and ever.

[15] **Philippians 1:27:** Only let your conversation be as it becometh the gospel of Christ: that whether I come and see you, or else be absent, I may hear of your affairs, that ye stand fast in one spirit, with one mind striving together for the faith of the gospel …

[16] **1 Corinthians 10:31:** Whether therefore ye eat, or drink, or whatsoever ye do, do all to the glory of God.

[17] **Jeremiah 32:39:** And I will give them one heart, and one way, that they may fear me for ever, for the good of them, and of their children after them …

[18] **1 Peter 2:12:** Having your conversation honest among the Gentiles: that, whereas they speak against you as evildoers, they may by *your* good works, which they shall behold, glorify God in the day of visitation.

113. What are the sins forbidden in the third commandment?

A. The sins forbidden in the third commandment are, the not using of God's name as is required; [1] and the abuse of it in an ignorant, [2] vain, [3] irreverent, profane, [4] superstitious [5] or wicked mentioning or otherwise using his titles, attributes, [6] ordinances, [7] or works, [8] by blasphemy, [9] perjury; [10] all sinful cursings, [11] oaths, [12] vows, [13] and lots; [14] violating of our oaths and vows, if lawful; [15] and fulfilling them, if of things unlawful; [16] murmuring and quarrelling at, [17] curious prying into, [18] and misapplying of God's decrees [19] and providences; [20] misinterpreting, [21] misapplying, [22] or any way perverting the Word, or any part of it; [23] to profane jests, [24] curious or unprofitable questions, vain janglings, or the maintaining of false doctrines; [25] abusing it, the creatures, or anything contained under the name of God, to charms, [26] or sinful lusts and practices; [27] the maligning, [28] scorning, [29] reviling, [30] or any wise opposing of God's truth, grace and ways; [31] making profession of religion in hypocrisy, or for sinister ends; [32] being ashamed of it, [33] or a shame to it, by unconformable, [34] unwise, [35] unfruitful, [36] and offensive walking, [37] or backsliding from it. [38]

Proofs

[1] **Malachi 2:2:** If ye will not hear, and if ye will not lay *it* to heart, to give glory unto my name, saith the LORD of hosts, I will even send a curse upon you, and I will curse your blessings: yea, I have cursed them already, because ye do not lay *it* to heart.

[2] **Acts 17:23:** For as I passed by, and beheld your devotions, I found an altar with this inscription, TO THE UNKNOWN GOD. Whom therefore ye ignorantly worship, him declare I unto you.

[3] **Proverbs 30:9:** Lest I be full, and deny *thee*, and say, Who *is* the LORD? or lest I be poor, and steal, and take the name of my God *in vain*.

[4] **Malachi 1:6-7, 12:** A son honoureth *his* father, and a servant his master: if then I *be* a father, where *is* mine honour? and if I *be* a master, where *is* my fear? saith the LORD of hosts unto you, O priests, that despise my name. And ye say, Wherein have we despised thy name? Ye offer polluted bread upon mine altar; and ye say, Wherein have we polluted thee? In that ye say, The table of the LORD *is* contemptible ... But ye have profaned it, in that ye say, The table of the LORD *is* polluted; and the fruit thereof, *even* his meat, *is* contemptible. **Malachi 3:14:** Ye have said, It *is* vain to serve God: and what profit *is it* that we have kept his ordinance, and that we have walked mournfully before the LORD of hosts?

[5] **1 Samuel 4:3-5:** And when the people were come into the camp, the elders of Israel said, Wherefore hath the LORD smitten us to day before the Philistines? Let us fetch the ark of the covenant of the LORD out of Shiloh unto us, that, when it cometh among us, it may save us out of the hand of our enemies. So the people sent to Shiloh, that they might bring from thence the ark of the covenant of the LORD of hosts, which dwelleth *between* the cherubims: and the two sons of Eli, Hophni and Phinehas, *were* there with the ark of the covenant of God. And when the ark of the covenant of the LORD came into the camp, all Israel shouted with a great shout, so that the earth rang again. **Jeremiah 7:4, 9-10, 14, 31:** Trust ye not in lying words, saying,

The temple of the LORD, The temple of the LORD, The temple of the LORD, *are* these … Will ye steal, murder, and commit adultery, and swear falsely, and burn incense unto Baal, and walk after other gods whom ye know not; And come and stand before me in *this* house, which is called by my name, and say, We are delivered to do all these abominations? … Therefore will I do unto this house, which is called by my name, wherein ye trust, and unto the place which I gave to you and to your fathers, as I have done to Shiloh … And they have built the high places of Tophet, which *is* in the valley of the son of Hinnom, to burn their sons and their daughters in the fire; which I commanded *them* not, neither came it into my heart. **Colossians 2:20-22:** Wherefore if ye be dead with Christ from the rudiments of the world, why, as though living in the world, are ye subject to ordinances, (Touch not; taste not; handle not; Which all are to perish with the using;) after the commandments and doctrines of men?

[6] **2 Kings 18:30, 35:** Neither let Hezekiah make you trust in the LORD, saying, The LORD will surely deliver us, and this city shall not be delivered into the hand of the king of Assyria … Who *are* they among all the gods of the countries, that have delivered their country out of mine hand, that the LORD should deliver Jerusalem out of mine hand? **Exodus 5:2:** And Pharaoh said, Who *is* the LORD, that I should obey his voice to let Israel go? I know not the LORD, neither will I let Israel go. **Psalm 139:20:** For they speak against thee wickedly, *and* thine enemies take *thy name* in vain.

[7] **Psalm 50:16-17:** But unto the wicked God saith, What hast thou to do to declare my statutes, or *that* thou shouldest take my covenant in thy mouth? Seeing thou hatest instruction, and castest my words behind thee.

[8] **Isaiah 5:12:** And the harp, and the viol, the tabret, and pipe, and wine, are in their feasts: but they regard not the work of the LORD, neither consider the operation of his hands.

[9] **2 Kings 19:22:** Whom hast thou reproached and blasphemed? and against whom hast thou exalted *thy* voice, and lifted up thine eyes on high? *even* against the Holy *One* of Israel.**Leviticus 24:11:** And the Israelitish woman's son blasphemed the name *of the LORD*, and cursed. And they brought him unto Moses: (and his mother's name *was* Shelomith, the daughter of Dibri, of the tribe of Dan:) …

[10] **Zechariah 5:4:** I will bring it forth, saith the LORD of hosts, and it shall enter into the house of the thief, and into the house of him that sweareth falsely by my name: and it shall remain in the midst of his house, and shall consume it with the timber thereof and the stones thereof. **Zechariah 8:17:** And let none of you imagine evil in your hearts against his neighbour; and love no false oath: for all these *are things* that I hate, saith the LORD.

[11] **1 Samuel 17:43:** And the Philistine said unto David, *Am* I a dog, that thou comest to me with staves? And the Philistine cursed David by his gods. **2 Samuel 16:5:** And when king David came to Bahurim, behold, thence came out a man of the family of the house of Saul, whose name *was* Shimei, the son of Gera: he came forth, and cursed still as he came.

[12] **Jeremiah 5:7:** How shall I pardon thee for this? thy children have forsaken me, and sworn by *them that are* no gods: when I had fed them to the full, they then committed adultery, and assembled themselves by troops in the harlots' houses. **Jeremiah 23:10:** For the land is full of adulterers; for because of swearing the land mourneth; the pleasant places of the wilderness are dried up, and their course is evil, and their force *is* not right.

[13] **Deuteronomy 23:18:** Thou shalt not bring the hire of a whore, or the price of a dog, into the house of the LORD thy God for any vow: for even both these *are* abomination unto the LORD thy God. **Acts 23:12, 14:** And when it was day, certain of the Jews banded together, and bound themselves under a curse, saying that they would neither eat nor drink till they had killed Paul … And they came to the chief priests and elders, and said, We have bound ourselves under a great curse, that we will eat nothing until we have slain Paul.

[14] **Esther 3:7:** In the first month, that *is*, the month Nisan, in the twelfth year of king Ahasuerus, they cast Pur, that *is*, the lot, before Haman from day to day, and from month to month, *to* the twelfth *month*, that *is*, the month Adar. **Esther 9:24:** Because Haman the son of Hammedatha, the Agagite, the enemy of all the Jews, had devised against the Jews to destroy them, and had cast Pur, that *is*, the lot, to consume them, and to destroy them … **Psalm 22:18:** They part my garments among them, and cast lots upon my vesture.

[15] **Psalm 24:4:** He that hath clean hands, and a pure heart; who hath not lifted up his soul unto vanity, nor sworn deceitfully. **Ezekiel 17:16, 18-19:** As I live, saith the Lord GOD, surely in the place *where* the king *dwelleth* that made him king, whose oath he despised, and whose covenant he brake, *even* with him in the midst of Babylon he shall die ... Seeing he despised the oath by breaking the covenant, when, lo, he had given his hand, and hath done all these *things*, he shall not escape. Therefore thus saith the Lord GOD; As I live, surely mine oath that he hath despised, and my covenant that he hath broken, even it will I recompense upon his own head.

[16] **Mark 6:26:** And the king was exceeding sorry; *yet* for his oath's sake, and for their sakes which sat with him, he would not reject her. **1 Samuel 25:22, 32-34:** So and more also do God unto the enemies of David, if I leave of all that *pertain* to him by the morning light any that pisseth against the wall ... And David said to Abigail, Blessed *be* the LORD God of Israel, which sent thee this day to meet me: And blessed *be* thy advice, and blessed *be* thou, which hast kept me this day from coming to *shed* blood, and from avenging myself with mine own hand. For in very deed, *as* the LORD God of Israel liveth, which hath kept me back from hurting thee, except thou hadst hasted and come to meet me, surely there had not been left unto Nabal by the morning light any that pisseth against the wall.

[17] **Romans 9:14, 19-20:** What shall we say then? *Is there* unrighteousness with God? God forbid ... Thou wilt say then unto me, Why doth he yet find fault? *For who* hath resisted his will? Nay but, O man, who art thou that repliest against God? Shall the thing formed say to him that formed *it*, Why hast thou made me thus?

[18] **Deuteronomy 29:29:** The secret *things belong* unto the LORD our God: but those *things which are* revealed *belong* unto us and to our children for ever, that we may do all the words of this law.

[19] **Romans 3:5, 7:** But if our unrighteousness commend the righteousness of God, what shall we say? *Is* God unrighteous who taketh vengeance? (I speak as a man) ... For if the truth of God hath more abounded through my lie unto his glory; why yet am I also judged as a sinner? **Romans 6:1:** What shall we say then? Shall we continue in sin, that grace may abound?

[20] **Ecclesiastes 8:11:** Because sentence against an evil work is not executed speedily, therefore the heart of the sons of men is fully set in them to do evil. **Ecclesiastes 9:3:** This *is* an evil among all *things* that are done under the sun, that *there is* one event unto all: yea, also the heart of the sons of men is full of evil, and madness *is* in their heart while they live, and after that *they go* to the dead. **Psalm 39:** I said, I will take heed to my ways, that I sin not with my tongue …

[21] **Matthew 5:21-22:** Ye have heard that it was said by them of old time, Thou shalt not kill; and whosoever shall kill shall be in danger of the judgment: But I say unto you, That whosoever is angry with his brother without a cause shall be in danger of the judgment: and whosoever shall say to his brother, Raca, shall be in danger of the council: but whosoever shall say, Thou fool, shall be in danger of hell fire … [to the end of the chapter].

[22] **Ezekiel 13:22:** Because with lies ye have made the heart of the righteous sad, whom I have not made sad; and strengthened the hands of the wicked, that he should not return from his wicked way, by promising him life …

[23] **2 Peter 3:16:** As also in all *his* epistles, speaking in them of these things; in which are some things hard to be understood, which they that are unlearned and unstable wrest, as *they do* also the other scriptures, unto their own destruction. **Matthew 22:24-31:** Saying, Master, Moses said, If a man die, having no children, his brother shall marry his wife, and raise up seed unto his brother. Now there were with us seven brethren: and the first, when he had married a wife, deceased, and, having no issue, left his wife unto his brother: Likewise the second also, and the third, unto the seventh. And last of all the woman died also. Therefore in the resurrection whose wife shall she be of the seven? for they all had her. Jesus answered and said unto them, Ye do err, not knowing the scriptures, nor the power of God. For in the resurrection they neither marry, nor are given in marriage, but are as the angels of God in heaven. But as touching the resurrection of the dead, have ye not read that which was spoken unto you by God, saying …

[24] **Isaiah 22:13:** And behold joy and gladness, slaying oxen, and killing sheep, eating flesh, and drinking wine: let us eat and drink; for tomorrow we shall die. **Jeremiah 23:34, 36, 38:** And *as for* the prophet, and the priest, and the people, that shall say, The burden of

the LORD, I will even punish that man and his house ... And the burden of the LORD shall ye mention no more: for every man's word shall be his burden; for ye have perverted the words of the living God, of the LORD of hosts our God ... But since ye say, The burden of the LORD; therefore thus saith the LORD; Because ye say this word, The burden of the LORD, and I have sent unto you, saying, Ye shall not say, The burden of the LORD ...

[25] **1 Timothy 1:4, 6-7:** Neither give heed to fables and endless genealogies, which minister questions, rather than godly edifying which is in faith: *so do* ... From which some having swerved have turned aside unto vain jangling; Desiring to be teachers of the law; understanding neither what they say, nor whereof they affirm. **1 Timothy 6:4-5, 20:** He is proud, knowing nothing, but doting about questions and strifes of words, whereof cometh envy, strife, railings, evil surmisings, Perverse disputings of men of corrupt minds, and destitute of the truth, supposing that gain is godliness: from such withdraw thyself ... O Timothy, keep that which is committed to thy trust, avoiding profane *and* vain babblings, and oppositions of science falsely so called ... **2 Timothy 2:14:** Of these things put them in remembrance, charging *them* before the Lord that they strive not about words to no profit, *but* to the subverting of the hearers. **Titus 3:9:** But avoid foolish questions, and genealogies, and contentions, and strivings about the law; for they are unprofitable and vain.

[26] **Deuteronomy 18:10-14:** There shall not be found among you *any one* that maketh his son or his daughter to pass through the fire, *or* that useth divination, *or* an observer of times, or an enchanter, or a witch, Or a charmer, or a consulter with familiar spirits, or a wizard, or a necromancer. For all that do these things *are* an abomination unto the LORD ... **Acts 19:13:** Then certain of the vagabond Jews, exorcists, took upon them to call over them which had evil spirits the name of the LORD Jesus, saying, We adjure you by Jesus whom Paul preacheth.

[27] **2 Timothy 4:3-4:** For the time will come when they will not endure sound doctrine; but after their own lusts shall they heap to themselves teachers, having itching ears; And they shall turn away *their* ears from the truth, and shall be turned unto fables. **Romans 13:13-14:** Let us walk honestly, as in the day; not in rioting and drunkenness, not in chambering and wantonness, not in strife and envying. But put ye on the Lord Jesus Christ, and make not provision for the flesh, to *fulfil* the

lusts *thereof.* **1 Kings 21:9-10:** And she wrote in the letters, saying, Proclaim a fast, and set Naboth on high among the people: And set two men, sons of Belial, before him, to bear witness against him, saying, Thou didst blaspheme God and the king. And *then* carry him out, and stone him, that he may die. **Jude 4:** For there are certain men crept in unawares, who were before of old ordained to this condemnation, ungodly men, turning the grace of our God into lasciviousness, and denying the only Lord God, and our Lord Jesus Christ.

[28] **Acts 13:45:** But when the Jews saw the multitudes, they were filled with envy, and spake against those things which were spoken by Paul, contradicting and blaspheming. **1 John 3:12:** Not as Cain, *who* was of that wicked one, and slew his brother. And wherefore slew he him? Because his own works were evil, and his brother's righteous.

[29] **Psalm 1:1:** Blessed *is* the man that walketh not in the counsel of the ungodly, nor standeth in the way of sinners, nor sitteth in the seat of the scornful. **2 Peter 3:3:** Knowing this first, that there shall come in the last days scoffers, walking after their own lusts ...

[30] **1 Peter 4:4:** Wherein they think it strange that ye run not with *them* to the same excess of riot, speaking evil of *you* ...

[31] **Acts 13:45-46, 50:** But when the Jews saw the multitudes, they were filled with envy, and spake against those things which were spoken by Paul, contradicting and blaspheming. Then Paul and Barnabas waxed bold, and said, It was necessary that the word of God should first have been spoken to you: but seeing ye put it from you, and judge yourselves unworthy of everlasting life, lo, we turn to the Gentiles ... But the Jews stirred up the devout and honourable women, and the chief men of the city, and raised persecution against Paul and Barnabas, and expelled them out of their coasts. **Acts 4:18:** And they called them, and commanded them not to speak at all nor teach in the name of Jesus. **Acts 19:9:** But when divers were hardened, and believed not, but spake evil of that way before the multitude, he departed from them, and separated the disciples, disputing daily in the school of one Tyrannus. **1 Thessalonians 2:16:** Forbidding us to speak to the Gentiles that they might be saved, to fill up their sins alway: for the wrath is come upon them to the uttermost. **Hebrews 10:29:** Of how much sorer punishment, suppose ye, shall he be thought worthy, who hath trodden under foot the Son of God, and hath counted the blood

of the covenant, wherewith he was sanctified, an unholy thing, and hath done despite unto the Spirit of grace?

[32] **2 Timothy 3:5:** Having a form of godliness, but denying the power thereof: from such turn away. **Matthew 23:14:** Woe unto you, scribes and Pharisees, hypocrites! for ye devour widows' houses, and for a pretence make long prayer: therefore ye shall receive the greater damnation. **Matthew 6:1–2, 5, 16:** Take heed that ye do not your alms before men, to be seen of them: otherwise ye have no reward of your Father which is in heaven. Therefore when thou doest *thine* alms, do not sound a trumpet before thee, as the hypocrites do in the synagogues and in the streets, that they may have glory of men. Verily I say unto you, They have their reward ... And when thou prayest, thou shalt not be as the hypocrites *are*: for they love to pray standing in the synagogues and in the corners of the streets, that they may be seen of men. Verily I say unto you, They have their reward ... Moreover when ye fast, be not, as the hypocrites, of a sad countenance: for they disfigure their faces, that they may appear unto men to fast. Verily I say unto you, They have their reward.

[33] **Mark 8:38:** Whosoever therefore shall be ashamed of me and of my words in this adulterous and sinful generation; of him also shall the Son of man be ashamed, when he cometh in the glory of his Father with the holy angels.

[34] **Psalm 73:14–15:** For all the day long have I been plagued, and chastened every morning. If I say, I will speak thus; behold, I should offend *against* the generation of thy children.

[35] **1 Corinthians 6:5–6:** I speak to your shame. Is it so, that there is not a wise man among you? no, not one that shall be able to judge between his brethren? But brother goeth to law with brother, and that before the unbelievers. **Ephesians 5:15–17:** See then that ye walk circumspectly, not as fools, but as wise, Redeeming the time, because the days are evil. Wherefore be ye not unwise, but understanding what the will of the Lord *is*.

[36] **Isaiah 5:4:** What could have been done more to my vineyard, that I have not done in it? wherefore, when I looked that it should bring forth grapes, brought it forth wild grapes? **2 Peter 1:8–9:** For if these things be in you, and abound, they make *you that ye shall* neither *be* barren nor unfruitful in the knowledge of our Lord Jesus Christ. But

he that lacketh these things is blind, and cannot see afar off, and hath forgotten that he was purged from his old sins.

[37] **Romans 2:23-24:** Thou that makest thy boast of the law, through breaking the law dishonourest thou God? For the name of God is blasphemed among the Gentiles through you, as it is written.

[38] **Galatians 3:1, 3:** O foolish Galatians, who hath bewitched you, that ye should not obey the truth, before whose eyes Jesus Christ hath been evidently set forth, crucified among you? ... Are ye so foolish? having begun in the Spirit, are ye now made perfect by the flesh? **Hebrews 6:6:** If they shall fall away, to renew them again unto repentance; seeing they crucify to themselves the Son of God afresh, and put *him* to an open shame.

114. What reasons are annexed to the third commandment?

A. The reasons annexed to the third commandment, in these words, The *Lord thy God*, and, *For the Lord will not hold him guiltless that taketh his name in vain*, [1] are, because he is the Lord and our God, therefore his name is not to be profaned, or any way abused by us; [2] especially because he will be so far from acquitting and sparing the transgressors of this commandment, as that he will not suffer them to escape his righteous judgment; [3] albeit many such escape the censures and punishments of men. [4]

Proofs

[1] **Exodus 20:7:** Thou shalt not take the name of the LORD thy God in vain; for the LORD will not hold him guiltless that taketh his name in vain.

[2] **Leviticus 19:12:** And ye shall not swear by my name falsely, neither shalt thou profane the name of thy God: I *am* the LORD.

[3] **Ezekiel 36:21-23:** But I had pity for mine holy name, which the house of Israel had profaned among the heathen, whither they went. Therefore say unto the house of Israel, Thus saith the LORD GOD; I do not *this* for your sakes, O house of Israel, but for mine holy name's sake, which ye have profaned among the heathen, whither ye went. And I will sanctify my great name, which was profaned among the heathen, which ye have profaned in the midst of them; and the heathen shall know that I *am* the LORD, saith the Lord GOD, when I shall be

sanctified in you before their eyes. **Deuteronomy 28:58-59:** If thou wilt not observe to do all the words of this law that are written in this book, that thou mayest fear this glorious and fearful name, THE LORD THY GOD; Then the LORD will make thy plagues wonderful, and the plagues of thy seed, *even* great plagues, and of long continuance, and sore sicknesses, and of long continuance. **Zechariah 5:2-4:** And he said unto me, What seest thou? And I answered, I see a flying roll; the length thereof *is* twenty cubits, and the breadth thereof ten cubits. Then said he unto me, This *is* the curse that goeth forth over the face of the whole earth: for every one that stealeth shall be cut off *as* on this side according to it; and every one that sweareth shall be cut off *as* on that side according to it. I will bring it forth, saith the LORD of hosts, and it shall enter into the house of the thief, and into the house of him that sweareth falsely by my name: and it shall remain in the midst of his house, and shall consume it with the timber thereof and the stones thereof.

[4] **1 Samuel 2:12, 17, 22, 24:** Now the sons of Eli *were* sons of Belial; they knew not the LORD ... Wherefore the sin of the young men was very great before the LORD: for men abhorred the offering of the LORD ... Now Eli was very old, and heard all that his sons did unto all Israel; and how they lay with the women that assembled at the door of the tabernacle of the congregation ... Nay, my sons; for *it is* no good report that I hear: ye make the LORD's people to transgress. [Compare with] **1 Samuel 3:13:** For I have told him that I will judge his house for ever for the iniquity which he knoweth; because his sons made themselves vile, and he restrained them not.

115. Which is the fourth commandment?

A. The fourth commandment is, *Remember the sabbath day, to keep it holy. Six days shalt thou labour, and do all thy work; but the seventh day is the sabbath of the Lord thy God: in it thou shalt not do any work, thou, nor thy son, nor thy daughter, thy man-servant, nor thy maid-servant, nor thy cattle, nor thy stranger that is within thy gates. For in six days the Lord made heaven and earth, the sea, and all that in them is, and rested the seventh day: wherefore the Lord blessed the sabbath-day and hallowed it.* [1]

Proof

[1] **Exodus 20:8-11:** Remember the sabbath day, to keep it holy. Six days shalt thou labour, and do all thy work: But the seventh day *is* the sabbath of the LORD thy God: *in it* thou shalt not do any work, thou, nor thy son, nor thy daughter, thy manservant, nor thy maidservant, nor thy cattle, nor thy stranger that *is* within thy gates: For in six days the LORD made heaven and earth, the sea, and all that in them *is*, and rested the seventh day: wherefore the LORD blessed the sabbath day, and hallowed it.

116. What is required in the fourth commandment?

A. The fourth commandment requireth of all men the sanctifying or keeping holy to God such set times as he hath appointed in his Word, expressly one whole day in seven; which was the seventh from the beginning of the world to the resurrection of Christ, and the first day of the week ever since, and so to continue to the end of the world; which is the Christian sabbath, [1] and in the New Testament called *The Lord's day.* [2]

Proofs

[1] **Deuteronomy 5:12-14:** Keep the sabbath day to sanctify it, as the LORD thy God hath commanded thee. Six days thou shalt labour, and do all thy work: But the seventh day is the sabbath of the LORD thy God: *in it* thou shalt not do any work, thou, nor thy son, nor thy daughter, nor thy manservant, nor thy maidservant, nor thine ox, nor thine ass, nor any of thy cattle, nor thy stranger that *is* within thy gates; that thy manservant and thy maidservant may rest as well as thou. **Genesis 2:2-3:** And on the seventh day God ended his work which he had made; and he rested on the seventh day from all his work which he had made. And God blessed the seventh day, and sanctified it: because that in it he had rested from all his work which God created and made. **1 Corinthians 16:1-2:** Now concerning the collection for the saints, as I have given order to the churches of Galatia, even so do ye. Upon the first *day* of the week let every one of you lay by him in store, as *God* hath prospered him, that there be no gatherings when I come. **Acts 20:7:** And upon the first *day* of the week, when the disciples came together to break bread, Paul preached unto them, ready to depart on the morrow; and continued his speech until midnight. **Matthew 5:17-18:** Think not that I am come to destroy the law, or the

prophets: I am not come to destroy, but to fulfil. For verily I say unto you, Till heaven and earth pass, one jot or one tittle shall in no wise pass from the law, till all be fulfilled. **Isaiah 56:2, 4, 6-7:** Blessed *is* the man *that* doeth this, and the son of man *that* layeth hold on it; that keepeth the sabbath from polluting it, and keepeth his hand from doing any evil ... For thus saith the LORD unto the eunuchs that keep my sabbaths, and choose *the things* that please me, and take hold of my covenant ... Also the sons of the stranger, that join themselves to the LORD, to serve him, and to love the name of the LORD, to be his servants, every one that keepeth the sabbath from polluting it, and taketh hold of my covenant; Even them will I bring to my holy mountain, and make them joyful in my house of prayer: their burnt offerings and their sacrifices *shall be* accepted upon mine altar; for mine house shall be called an house of prayer for all people.

[2] **Revelation 1:10:** I was in the Spirit on the Lord's day, and heard behind me a great voice, as of a trumpet ...

117. How is the sabbath or the Lord's day to be sanctified?

A. The sabbath or Lord's day is to be sanctified by an holy resting all the day, [1] not only from such works as are at all times sinful, but even from such worldly employments and recreations as are on other days lawful; [2] and making it our delight to spend the whole time (except so much of it as is to be taken up in works of necessity and mercy [3]) in the public and private exercises of God's worship: [4] and, to that end, we are to prepare our hearts, and with such foresight, diligence, and moderation, to dispose and seasonably dispatch our worldly business, that we may be the more free and fit for the duties of that day. [5]

Proofs

[1] **Exodus 20:8, 10:** Remember the sabbath day, to keep it holy ... But the seventh day *is* the sabbath of the LORD thy God: *in it* thou shalt not do any work, thou, nor thy son, nor thy daughter, thy manservant, nor thy maidservant, nor thy cattle, nor thy stranger that *is* within thy gates ...

[2] **Exodus 16:25-28:** And Moses said, Eat that to day; for to day *is* a sabbath unto the LORD: to day ye shall not find it in the field. Six days ye shall gather it; but on the seventh day, *which is* the sabbath,

in it there shall be none. And it came to pass, *that* there went out *some* of the people on the seventh day for to gather, and they found none. And the LORD said unto Moses, How long refuse ye to keep my commandments and my laws? **Nehemiah 13:15-22:** In those days saw I in Judah *some* treading wine presses on the sabbath, and bringing in sheaves, and lading asses; as also wine, grapes, and figs, and all *manner of* burdens, which they brought into Jerusalem on the sabbath day: and I testified *against them* in the day wherein they sold victuals. There dwelt men of Tyre also therein, which brought fish, and all manner of ware, and sold on the sabbath unto the children of Judah, and in Jerusalem. Then I contended with the nobles of Judah, and said unto them, What evil thing *is* this that ye do, and profane the sabbath day? Did not your fathers thus, and did not our God bring all this evil upon us, and upon this city? yet ye bring more wrath upon Israel by profaning the sabbath. And it came to pass, that when the gates of Jerusalem began to be dark before the sabbath, I commanded that the gates should be shut, and charged that they should not be opened till after the sabbath: and *some* of my servants set I at the gates, that there should no burden be brought in on the sabbath day. So the merchants and sellers of all kind of ware lodged without Jerusalem once or twice. Then I testified against them, and said unto them, Why lodge ye about the wall? if ye do so again, I will lay hands on you. From that time forth came they no *more* on the sabbath. And I commanded the Levites that they should cleanse themselves, and *that* they should come *and* keep the gates, to sanctify the sabbath day. Remember me, O my God, *concerning* this also, and spare me according to the greatness of thy mercy. **Jeremiah 17:21-22:** Thus saith the LORD; Take heed to yourselves, and bear no burden on the sabbath day, nor bring *it* in by the gates of Jerusalem; Neither carry forth a burden out of your houses on the sabbath day, neither do ye any work, but hallow ye the sabbath day, as I commanded your fathers.

[3] **Matthew 12:1-13:** At that time Jesus went on the sabbath day through the corn; and his disciples were an hungred, and began to pluck the ears of corn, and to eat. But when the Pharisees saw it …

[4] **Isaiah 58:13:** If thou turn away thy foot from the sabbath, *from* doing thy pleasure on my holy day; and call the sabbath a delight, the holy of the LORD, honourable; and shalt honour him, not doing thine own ways, nor finding thine own pleasure, nor speaking *thine own*

words ... **Luke 4:16:** And he came to Nazareth, where he had been brought up: and, as his custom was, he went into the synagogue on the sabbath day, and stood up for to read. **Acts 20:7:** And upon the first *day* of the week, when the disciples came together to break bread, Paul preached unto them, ready to depart on the morrow; and continued his speech until midnight. **1 Corinthians 16:1-2:** Now concerning the collection for the saints, as I have given order to the churches of Galatia, even so do ye. Upon the first *day* of the week let every one of you lay by him in store, as *God* hath prospered him, that there be no gatherings when I come. **Psalm 92** [title: A psalm or song for the sabbath-day]. **Isaiah 66:23:** And it shall come to pass, *that* from one new moon to another, and from one sabbath to another, shall all flesh come to worship before me, saith the LORD. **Leviticus 23:3:** Six days shall work be done: but the seventh day *is* the sabbath of rest, an holy convocation; ye shall do no work *therein*: it *is* the sabbath of the LORD in all your dwellings.

[5] **Exodus 20:8:** Remember the sabbath day, to keep it holy. **Luke 23:54, 56:** And that day was the preparation, and the sabbath drew on ... And they returned, and prepared spices and ointments; and rested the sabbath day according to the commandment. **Exodus 16:22, 25-26, 29:** And it came to pass, *that* on the sixth day they gathered twice as much bread, two omers for one *man*: and all the rulers of the congregation came and told Moses ... And Moses said, Eat that to day; for to day is a sabbath unto the LORD: to day ye shall not find it in the field. Six days ye shall gather it; but on the seventh day, *which is* the sabbath, in it there shall be none ... See, for that the LORD hath given you the sabbath, therefore he giveth you on the sixth day the bread of two days; abide ye every man in his place, let no man go out of his place on the seventh day. **Nehemiah 13:19:** And it came to pass, that when the gates of Jerusalem began to be dark before the sabbath, I commanded that the gates should be shut, and charged that they should not be opened till after the sabbath: and *some* of my servants set I at the gates, *that* there should no burden be brought in on the sabbath day.

118. Why is the charge of keeping the sabbath more specially directed to governors of families, and other superiors?

A. The charge of keeping the sabbath is more specially directed to governors of families, and other superiors, because they are bound not only to keep it themselves, but to see that it be observed by all those that are under their charge; and because they are prone ofttimes to hinder them by employments of their own. [1]

Proofs

[1] **Exodus 20:10:** But the seventh day *is* the sabbath of the LORD thy God: *in it* thou shalt not do any work, thou, nor thy son, nor thy daughter, thy manservant, nor thy maidservant, nor thy cattle, nor thy stranger that *is* within thy gates ... **Joshua 24:15:** And if it seem evil unto you to serve the LORD, choose you this day whom ye will serve; whether the gods which your fathers served that *were* on the other side of the flood, or the gods of the Amorites, in whose land ye dwell: but as for me and my house, we will serve the LORD. **Nehemiah 13:15, 17:** In those days saw I in Judah *some* treading wine presses on the sabbath, and bringing in sheaves, and lading asses; as also wine, grapes, and figs, and all *manner* of burdens, which they brought into Jerusalem on the sabbath day: and I testified *against them* in the day wherein they sold victuals ... Then I contended with the nobles of Judah, and said unto them, What evil thing *is* this that ye do, and profane the sabbath day? **Jeremiah 17:20-22:** And say unto them, Hear ye the word of the LORD, ye kings of Judah, and all Judah, and all the inhabitants of Jerusalem, that enter in by these gates: Thus saith the LORD; Take heed to yourselves, and bear no burden on the sabbath day, nor bring *it* in by the gates of Jerusalem; Neither carry forth a burden out of your houses on the sabbath day, neither do ye any work, but hallow ye the sabbath day, as I commanded your fathers. **Exodus 23:12:** Six days thou shalt do thy work, and on the seventh day thou shalt rest: that thine ox and thine ass may rest, and the son of thy handmaid, and the stranger, may be refreshed.

119. What are the sins forbidden in the fourth commandment?

A. The sins forbidden in the fourth commandment are, all omissions of the duties required, [1] all careless, negligent, and unprofitable performing of them, and being weary of them; [2] all profaning the day by idleness, and doing that which is in itself sinful; [3] and by all needless works, words, and thoughts, about our worldly employments and recreations. [4]

Proofs

[1] **Ezekiel 22:26:** Her priests have violated my law, and have profaned mine holy things: they have put no difference between the holy and profane, neither have they shewed *difference* between the unclean and the clean, and have hid their eyes from my sabbaths, and I am profaned among them.

[2] **Acts 20:7, 9:** And upon the first *day* of the week, when the disciples came together to break bread, Paul preached unto them, ready to depart on the morrow; and continued his speech until midnight ... And there sat in a window a certain young man named Eutychus, being fallen into a deep sleep: and as Paul was long preaching, he sunk down with sleep, and fell down from the third loft, and was taken up dead. **Ezekiel 33:30-32:** Also, thou son of man, the children of thy people still are talking against thee by the walls and in the doors of the houses, and speak one to another, every one to his brother, saying, Come, I pray you, and hear what is the word that cometh forth from the LORD. And they come unto thee as the people cometh, and they sit before thee *as* my people, and they hear thy words, but they will not do them: for with their mouth they shew much love, *but* their heart goeth after their covetousness. And, lo, thou *art* unto them as a very lovely song of one that hath a pleasant voice, and can play well on an instrument: for they hear thy words, but they do them not. **Amos 8:5:** Saying, When will the new moon be gone, that we may sell corn? and the sabbath, that we may set forth wheat, making the ephah small, and the shekel great, and falsifying the balances by deceit? **Malachi 1:13:** Ye said also, Behold, what a weariness *is it!* and ye have snuffed at it, saith the LORD of hosts; and ye brought *that which was* torn, and the lame, and the sick; thus ye brought an offering: should I accept this of your hand? saith the LORD.

[3] **Ezekiel 23:38:** Moreover this they have done unto me: they have defiled my sanctuary in the same day, and have profaned my sabbaths.

[4] **Jeremiah 17:24, 27:** And it shall come to pass, if ye diligently hearken unto me, saith the LORD, to bring in no burden through the gates of this city on the sabbath day, but hallow the sabbath day, to do no work therein ... But if ye will not hearken unto me to hallow the sabbath day, and not to bear a burden, even entering in at the gates of Jerusalem on the sabbath day; then will I kindle a fire in the gates

thereof, and it shall devour the palaces of Jerusalem, and it shall not be quenched. **Isaiah 58:13:** If thou turn away thy foot from the sabbath, *from* doing thy pleasure on my holy day; and call the sabbath a delight, the holy of the LORD, honourable; and shalt honour him, not doing thine own ways, nor finding thine own pleasure, nor speaking *thine own* words …

120. What are the reasons annexed to the fourth commandment, the more to enforce it?

A. The reasons annexed to the fourth commandment, the more to enforce it, are taken from the equity of it, God allowing us six days of seven for our own affairs, and reserving but one for himself in these words, *Six days shalt thou labour, and do all thy work*: [1] from God's challenging a special propriety in that day, *The seventh day is the sabbath of the Lord thy God*: [2] from the example of God, who *in six days made heaven and earth, the sea, and all that in them is, and rested the seventh day*: and from that blessing which God put upon that day, not only in sanctifying it to be a day for his service, but in ordaining it to be a means of blessing to us in our sanctifying it; *Wherefore the Lord blessed the sabbath day, and hallowed it.* [3]

Proofs

[1] **Exodus 20:9:** Six days shalt thou labour, and do all thy work …

[2] **Exodus 20:10:** But the seventh day *is* the sabbath of the LORD thy God: *in it* thou shalt not do any work, thou, nor thy son, nor thy daughter, thy manservant, nor thy maidservant, nor thy cattle, nor thy stranger that *is* within thy gates …

[3] **Exodus 20:11:** For *in* six days the LORD made heaven and earth, the sea, and all that in them *is*, and rested the seventh day: wherefore the LORD blessed the sabbath day, and hallowed it.

121. Why is the word *Remember* set in the beginning of the fourth commandment?

A. The word *Remember* is set in the beginning of the fourth commandment, [1] partly, because of the great benefit of remembering it, we being thereby helped in our preparation to keep it, [2] and, in keeping it, better to keep all the rest of the commandments, [3] and to continue a thankful remembrance of the two great benefits of creation and redemption, which contain a short abridgment of religion; [4] and partly, because we are very ready to forget it, [5] for that there is less light of nature for it, [6] and yet it restraineth our natural liberty in things at other times lawful; [7] that it cometh but once in seven days, and many worldly businesses come between, and too often take off our minds from thinking of it, either to prepare for it, or to sanctify it; [8] and that Satan with his instruments labours much to blot out the glory, and even the memory of it, to bring in all irreligion and impiety. [9]

Proofs

[1] **Exodus 20:8:** Remember the sabbath day, to keep it holy.

[2] **Exodus 16:23:** And he said unto them, This *is that* which the LORD hath said, To morrow is the rest of the holy sabbath unto the LORD: bake *that* which ye will bake *to day*, and seethe that ye will seethe; and that which remaineth over lay up for you to be kept until the morning. **Luke 23:54, 56:** And that day was the preparation, and the sabbath drew on ... And they returned, and prepared spices and ointments; and rested the sabbath day according to the commandment. [Compare with] **Mark 15:42:** And now when the even was come, because it was the preparation, that is, the day before the sabbath ... **Nehemiah 13:19:** And it came to pass, that when the gates of Jerusalem began to be dark before the sabbath, I commanded that the gates should be shut, and charged that they should not be opened till after the sabbath: and *some* of my servants set I at the gates, *that* there should no burden be brought in on the sabbath day.

[3] **Psalm 92** [title: A psalm or song for the sabbath-day, 7 compared with vv. 13-14:] Those that be planted in the house of the LORD shall flourish in the courts of our God. They shall still bring forth fruit in old age; they shall be fat and flourishing ... **Ezekiel 20:12, 19-20:** Moreover also I gave them my sabbaths, to be a sign between me and them, that they might know that I *am* the LORD that sanctify them ... I *am* the LORD your God; walk in my statutes, and keep my judgments, and do them; And hallow my sabbaths; and they shall be a sign between me and you, that ye may know that I *am* the LORD your God.

[4] **Genesis 2:2-3:** And on the seventh day God ended his work which he had made; and he rested on the seventh day from all his work which he had made. And God blessed the seventh day, and sanctified it: because that in it he had rested from all his work which God created and made. **Psalm 118:22, 24:** The stone *which* the builders refused is become the head *stone* of the corner … This *is* the day *which* the LORD hath made; we will rejoice and be glad in it. **Acts 4:10-11:** Be it known unto you all, and to all the people of Israel, that by the name of Jesus Christ of Nazareth, whom ye crucified, whom God raised from the dead, *even* by him doth this man stand here before you whole. This is the stone which was set at nought of you builders, which is become the head of the corner. **Revelation 1:10:** I was in the Spirit on the Lord's day, and heard behind me a great voice, as of a trumpet …

[5] **Ezekiel 22:26:** Her priests have violated my law, and have profaned mine holy things: they have put no difference between the holy and profane, neither have they shewed *difference* between the unclean and the clean, and have hid their eyes from my sabbaths, and I am profaned among them.

[6] **Nehemiah 9:14:** And madest known unto them thy holy sabbath, and commandedst them precepts, statutes, and laws, by the hand of Moses thy servant …

[7] **Exodus 34:21:** Six days thou shalt work, but on the seventh day thou shalt rest: in earing time and in harvest thou shalt rest.

[8] **Deuteronomy 5:14-15:** But the seventh day is the sabbath of the LORD thy God: *in it* thou shalt not do any work, thou, nor thy son, nor thy daughter, nor thy manservant, nor thy maidservant, nor thine ox, nor thine ass, nor any of thy cattle, nor thy stranger that *is* within thy gates; that thy manservant and thy maidservant may rest as well as thou. And remember that thou wast a servant in the land of Egypt, and *that* the LORD thy God brought thee out thence through a mighty hand and by a stretched out arm: therefore the LORD thy God commanded thee to keep the sabbath day. **Amos 8:5:** Saying, When will the new moon be gone, that we may sell corn? and the sabbath, that we may set forth wheat, making the ephah small, and the shekel great, and falsifying the balances by deceit?

[9] **Lamentations 1:7:** Jerusalem remembered in the days of her affliction and of her miseries all her pleasant things that she had in

the days of old, when her people fell into the hand of the enemy, and none did help her: the adversaries saw her, *and* did mock at her sabbaths. **Jeremiah 17:21-23:** Thus saith the LORD; Take heed to yourselves, and bear no burden on the sabbath day, nor bring *it* in by the gates of Jerusalem; Neither carry forth a burden out of your houses on the sabbath day, neither do ye any work, but hallow ye the sabbath day, as I commanded your fathers. But they obeyed not, neither inclined their ear, but made their neck stiff, that they might not hear, nor receive instruction. **Nehemiah 13:15-22:** In those days saw I in Judah *some* treading wine presses on the sabbath, and bringing in sheaves, and lading asses; as also wine, grapes, and figs, and all *manner* of burdens, which they brought into Jerusalem on the sabbath day: and I testified *against them* in the day wherein they sold victuals. There dwelt men of Tyre also therein, which brought fish, and all manner of ware, and sold on the sabbath unto the children of Judah, and in Jerusalem. Then I contended with the nobles of Judah, and said unto them, What evil thing *is* this that ye do, and profane the sabbath day? Did not your fathers thus, and did not our God bring all this evil upon us, and upon this city? yet ye bring more wrath upon Israel by profaning the sabbath. And it came to pass, that when the gates of Jerusalem began to be dark before the sabbath, I commanded that the gates should be shut, and charged that they should not be opened till after the sabbath: and *some* of my servants set I at the gates, *that* there should no burden be brought in on the sabbath day. So the merchants and sellers of all kind of ware lodged without Jerusalem once or twice. Then I testified against them, and said unto them, Why lodge ye about the wall? if ye do *so* again, I will lay hands on you. From that time forth came they no *more* on the sabbath. And I commanded the Levites that they should cleanse themselves, and *that* they should come *and* keep the gates, to sanctify the sabbath day. Remember me, O my God, *concerning* this also, and spare me according to the greatness of thy mercy.

122. What is the sum of the six commandments which contain our duty to man?

A. The sum of the six commandments which contain our duty to man, is, to love our neighbour as ourselves, [1]and to do to others what we would have them to do to us. [2]

Proofs

[1] **Matthew 22:39:** And the second *is* like unto it, Thou shalt love thy neighbour as thyself.

[2] **Matthew 7:12:** Therefore all things whatsoever ye would that men should do to you, do ye even so to them: for this is the law and the prophets.

123. Which is the fifth commandment?

A. The fifth commandment is, *Honour thy father and thy mother: that thy days may be long upon the land which the Lord thy God giveth thee.* [1]

Proof

[1] **Exodus 20:12:** Honour thy father and thy mother: that thy days may be long upon the land which the LORD thy God giveth thee.

124. Who are meant by *father* and *mother* in the fifth commandment?

A. By *father* and *mother*, in the fifth commandment, are meant, not only natural parents, [1] but all superiors in age [2] and gifts; [3] and especially such as, by God's ordinance, are over us in place of authority, whether in family, [4] church, [5] or commonwealth. [6]

Proofs

[1] **Proverbs 23:22, 25:** Hearken unto thy father that begat thee, and despise not thy mother when she is old ... Thy father and thy mother shall be glad, and she that bare thee shall rejoice. **Ephesians 6:1-2:** Children, obey your parents in the Lord: for this is right. Honour thy father and mother; which is the first commandment with promise ...

[2] **1 Timothy 5:1-2:** Rebuke not an elder, but intreat *him* as a father; *and* the younger men as brethren; The elder women as mothers; the younger as sisters, with all purity.

[3] **Genesis 4:20-22:** And Adah bare Jabal: he was the father of such as dwell in tents, and *of such as have* cattle. And his brother's name *was* Jubal: he was the father of all such as handle the harp and organ. And Zillah, she also bare Tubalcain, an instructor of every artificer in brass and iron: and the sister of Tubalcain *was* Naamah. **Genesis 45:8:** So now *it was* not you *that* sent me hither, but God: and he hath made me

a father to Pharaoh, and lord of all his house, and a ruler throughout all the land of Egypt.

[4] **2 Kings 5:13:** And his servants came near, and spake unto him, and said, My father, *if* the prophet had bid thee *do some* great thing, wouldest thou not have done *it*? how much rather then, when he saith to thee, Wash, and be clean?

[5] **2 Kings 2:12:** And Elisha saw *it*, and he cried, My father, my father, the chariot of Israel, and the horsemen thereof. And he saw him no more: and he took hold of his own clothes, and rent them in two pieces. **2 Kings 13:14:** Now Elisha was fallen sick of his sickness whereof he died. And Joash the king of Israel came down unto him, and wept over his face, and said, O my father, my father, the chariot of Israel, and the horsemen thereof. **Galatians 4:19:** My little children, of whom I travail in birth again until Christ be formed in you …

[6] **Isaiah 49:23:** And kings shall be thy nursing fathers, and their queens thy nursing mothers: they shall bow down to thee with *their* face toward the earth, and lick up the dust of thy feet; and thou shalt know that I *am* the LORD: for they shall not be ashamed that wait for me.

125. Why are superiors styled *father* and *mother*?

A. Superiors are styled father and mother, both to teach them in all duties toward their inferiors, like natural parents, to express love and tenderness to them, according to their several relations; [1] and to work inferiors to a greater willingness and cheerfulness in performing their duties to their superiors, as to their parents.[2]

Proofs

[1] **Ephesians 6:4:** And, ye fathers, provoke not your children to wrath: but bring them up in the nurture and admonition of the Lord. **2 Corinthians 12:14:** Behold, the third time I am ready to come to you; and I will not be burdensome to you: for I seek not yours, but you: for the children ought not to lay up for the parents, but the parents for the children. **1 Thessalonians 2:7-8, 11:** But we were gentle among you, even as a nurse cherisheth her children: So being affectionately desirous of you, we were willing to have imparted unto you, not the gospel of God only, but also our own souls, because ye were dear unto us … As ye know how we exhorted and comforted and charged every

one of you, as a father *doth* his children ... **Numbers 11:11-12:** And Moses said unto the Lord, Wherefore hast thou afflicted thy servant? and wherefore have I not found favour in thy sight, that thou layest the burden of all this people upon me? Have I conceived all this people? have I begotten them, that thou shouldest say unto me, Carry them in thy bosom, as a nursing father beareth the sucking child, unto the land which thou swarest unto their fathers?

[2] **1 Corinthians 4:14-16:** I write not these things to shame you, but as my beloved sons I warn *you*. For though ye have ten thousand instructors in Christ, yet *have ye* not many fathers: for in Christ Jesus I have begotten you through the gospel. Wherefore I beseech you, be ye followers of me. **2 Kings 5:13:** And his servants came near, and spake unto him, and said, My father, *if* the prophet had bid thee *do some* great thing, wouldest thou not have done *it*? how much rather then, when he saith to thee, Wash, and be clean?

126. What is the general scope of the fifth commandment?

A. The general scope of the fifth commandment is, the performance of those duties which we mutually owe in our several relations, as inferiors, superiors, or equals. [1]

Proofs

[1] **Ephesians 5:21:** Submitting yourselves one to another in the fear of God. **1 Peter 2:17:** Honour all *men*. Love the brotherhood. Fear God. Honour the king. **Romans 12:10:** *Be* kindly affectioned one to another with brotherly love; in honour preferring one another ...

127. What is the honour that inferiors owe to their superiors?

A. The honour which inferiors owe to their superiors is, all due reverence in heart, [1] word, [2] and behaviour; [3] prayer and thanksgiving for them; [4] imitation of their virtues and graces; [5] willing obedience to their lawful commands and counsels; [6] due submission to their corrections; [7] fidelity to, [8] defence, [9] and maintenance of their persons and authority, according to their several ranks, and the nature of their places; [10] bearing with their infirmities, and covering them in love, [11] that so they may be an honour to them and to their government. [12]

Proofs

[1] **Malachi 1:6:** A son honoureth *his* father, and a servant his master: if then I *be* a father, where *is* mine honour? and if I *be* a master, where is my fear? saith the LORD of hosts unto you, O priests, that despise my name. And ye say, Wherein have we despised thy name? **Leviticus 19:3:** Ye shall fear every man his mother, and his father, and keep my sabbaths: I *am* the LORD your God.

[2] **Proverbs 31:28:** Her children arise up, and call her blessed; her husband *also*, and he praiseth her. **1 Peter 3:6:** Even as Sara obeyed Abraham, calling him lord: whose daughters ye are, as long as ye do well, and are not afraid with any amazement.

[3] **Leviticus 19:32:** Thou shalt rise up before the hoary head, and honour the face of the old man, and fear thy God: I *am* the LORD. **1 Kings 2:19:** Bathsheba therefore went unto king Solomon, to speak unto him for Adonijah. And the king rose up to meet her, and bowed himself unto her, and sat down on his throne, and caused a seat to be set for the king's mother; and she sat on his right hand.

[4] **1 Timothy 2:1-2:** I exhort therefore, that, first of all, supplications, prayers, intercessions, *and* giving of thanks, be made for all men; For kings, and *for* all that are in authority; that we may lead a quiet and peaceable life in all godliness and honesty.

[5] **Hebrews 13:7:**Remember them which have the rule over you, who have spoken unto you the word of God: whose faith follow, considering the end of *their* conversation. **Philippians 3:17:** Brethren, be followers together of me, and mark them which walk so as ye have us for an ensample.

[6] **Ephesians 6:1-2, 5-7:** Children, obey your parents in the Lord: for this is right. Honour thy father and mother; which is the first commandment with promise … Servants, be obedient to them that are *your* masters according to the flesh, with fear and trembling, in singleness of your heart, as unto Christ; Not with eyeservice, as menpleasers; but as the servants of Christ, doing the will of God from the heart; With good will doing service, as to the Lord, and not to men … **1 Peter 2:13-14:** Submit yourselves to every ordinance of man for the Lord's sake: whether it be to the king, as supreme; Or unto governors, as unto them that are sent by him for the punishment of evildoers, and for the praise of them that do well. **Romans 13:1-5:** Let every soul be subject unto the higher powers.

For there is no power but of God: the powers that be are ordained of God. Whosoever therefore resisteth the power, resisteth the ordinance of God: and they that resist shall receive to themselves damnation. For rulers are not a terror to good works, but to the evil. Wilt thou then not be afraid of the power? do that which is good, and thou shalt have praise of the same: For he is the minister of God to thee for good. But if thou do that which is evil, be afraid; for he beareth not the sword in vain: for he is the minister of God, a revenger to *execute* wrath upon him that doeth evil. Wherefore *ye* must needs be subject, not only for wrath, but also for conscience sake. **Hebrews 13:17:** Obey them that have the rule over you, and submit yourselves: for they watch for your souls, as they that must give account, that they may do it with joy, and not with grief: for that *is* unprofitable for you. **Proverbs 4:3-4:** For I was my father's son, tender and only *beloved* in the sight of my mother. He taught me also, and said unto me, Let thine heart retain my words: keep my commandments, and live. **Proverbs 23:22:** Hearken unto thy father that begat thee, and despise not thy mother when she is old. **Exodus 18:19, 24:** Hearken now unto my voice, I will give thee counsel, and God shall be with thee: Be thou for the people to God-ward, that thou mayest bring the causes unto God ... So Moses hearkened to the voice of his father in law, and did all that he had said.

[7] **Hebrews 12:9:** Furthermore we have had fathers of our flesh which corrected *us*, and we gave *them* reverence: shall we not much rather be in subjection unto the Father of spirits, and live? **1 Peter 2:18-20:** Servants, *be* subject to *your* masters with all fear; not only to the good and gentle, but also to the froward. For this *is* thankworthy, if a man for conscience toward God endure grief, suffering wrongfully. For what glory *is it*, if, when ye be buffeted for your faults, ye shall take it patiently? but if, when ye do well, and suffer *for it*, ye take it patiently, this *is* acceptable with God.

[8] **Titus 2:9-10:** *Exhort* servants to be obedient unto their own masters, *and* to please *them* well in all *things*; not answering again; Not purloining, but shewing all good fidelity; that they may adorn the doctrine of God our Saviour in all things.

[9] **1 Samuel 26:15-16:** And David said to Abner, *Art* not thou a *valiant* man? and who *is* like to thee in Israel? wherefore then hast thou not kept thy lord the king? for there came one of the people in to destroy the king thy lord. This thing *is* not good that thou hast done.

As the LORD liveth, ye *are* worthy to die, because ye have not kept your master, the LORD'S anointed. And now see where the king's spear *is*, and the cruse of water that *was* at his bolster. **2 Samuel 18:3.** But the people answered, Thou shalt not go forth: for if we flee away, they will not care for us; neither if half of us die, will they care for us: but now *thou art* worth ten thousand of us: therefore now *it is* better that thou succour us out of the city. **Esther 6:2:** And it was found written, that Mordecai had told of Bigthana and Teresh, two of the king's chamberlains, the keepers of the door, who sought to lay hand on the king Ahasuerus.

[10] **Matthew 22:21:** They say unto him, Caesar's. Then saith he unto them, Render therefore unto Caesar the things which are Caesar's; and unto God the things that are God's. **Romans 13:6-7:** For for this cause pay ye tribute also: for they are God's ministers, attending continually upon this very thing. Render therefore to all their dues: tribute to whom tribute *is due*; custom to whom custom; fear to whom fear; honour to whom honour. **1 Timothy 5:17-18:** Let the elders that rule well be counted worthy of double honour, especially they who labour in the word and doctrine. For the scripture saith, Thou shalt not muzzle the ox that treadeth out the corn. And, The labourer *is* worthy of his reward. **Galatians 6:6:** Let him that is taught in the word communicate unto him that teacheth in all good things. **Genesis 45:11:** And there will I nourish thee; for yet *there are* five years of famine; lest thou, and thy household, and all that thou hast, come to poverty. **Genesis 47:12:** And Joseph nourished his father, and his brethren, and all his father's household, with bread, according to *their* families.

[11] **1 Peter 2:18:** Servants, *be* subject to *your* masters with all fear; not only to the good and gentle, but also to the froward. **Proverbs 23:22:** Hearken unto thy father that begat thee, and despise not thy mother when she is old. **Genesis 9:23:** And Shem and Japheth took a garment, and laid *it* upon both their shoulders, and went backward, and covered the nakedness of their father; and their faces *were* backward, and they saw not their father's nakedness.

[12] **Psalm 127:3-5:** Lo, children *are* an heritage of the LORD: *and* the fruit of the womb *is his* reward. As arrows *are* in the hand of a mighty man; so *are* children of the youth. Happy *is* the man that hath his quiver full of them: they shall not be ashamed, but they shall speak with the

enemies in the gate. **Proverbs 31:23:** Her husband is known in the gates, when he sitteth among the elders of the land.

128. What are the sins of inferiors against their superiors?

A. The sins of inferiors against their superiors are, all neglect of the duties required toward them; [1] envying at, [2] contempt of, [3] and rebellion [4] against, their persons [5] and places, [6] in their lawful counsels, [7]commands, and corrections; [8] cursing, mocking [9] and all such refractory and scandalous carriage, as proves a shame and dishonour to them and their government. [10]

Proofs

[1] **Matthew 15:4-6:** For God commanded, saying, Honour thy father and mother: and, He that curseth father or mother, let him die the death. But ye say, Whosoever shall say to *his* father or *his* mother, *It is* a gift, by whatsoever thou mightest be profited by me; And honour not his father or his mother, *he shall be free*. Thus have ye made the commandment of God of none effect by your tradition.

[2] **Numbers 11:28-29:** And Joshua the son of Nun, the servant of Moses, *one* of his young men, answered and said, My lord Moses, forbid them. And Moses said unto him, Enviest thou for my sake? would God that all the LORD's people were prophets, *and* that the LORD would put his spirit upon them!

[3] **1 Samuel 8:7:** And the LORD said unto Samuel, Hearken unto the voice of the people in all that they say unto thee: for they have not rejected thee, but they have rejected me, that I should not reign over them. **Isaiah 3:5:** And the people shall be oppressed, every one by another, and every one by his neighbour: the child shall behave himself proudly against the ancient, and the base against the honourable.

[4] **2 Samuel 15:1-12:** And it came to pass after this, that Absalom prepared him chariots and horses …

[5] **Exodus 21:15:** And he that smiteth his father, or his mother, shall be surely put to death.

[6] **1 Samuel 10:27:** But the children of Belial said, How shall this man save us? And they despised him, and brought him no presents. But he held his peace.

[7] **1 Samuel 2:25:** If one man sin against another, the judge shall judge him: but if a man sin against the LORD, who shall intreat for him? Notwithstanding they hearkened not unto the voice of their father, because the LORD would slay them.

[8] **Deuteronomy 21:18–21:** If a man have a stubborn and rebellious son, which will not obey the voice of his father, or the voice of his mother, and *that*, when they have chastened him, will not hearken unto them: Then shall his father and his mother lay hold on him, and bring him out unto the elders of his city, and unto the gate of his place; And they shall say unto the elders of his city, This our son *is* stubborn and rebellious, he will not obey our voice; *he is* a glutton, and a drunkard. And all the men of his city shall stone him with stones, that he die: so shalt thou put evil away from among you; and all Israel shall hear, and fear.

[9] **Proverbs 30:11, 17:** *There is* a generation *that* curseth their father, and doth not bless their mother ... The eye *that* mocketh at *his* father, and despiseth to obey *his* mother, the ravens of the valley shall pick it out, and the young eagles shall eat it.

[10] **Proverbs 19:26:** He that wasteth *his* father, *and* chaseth away *his* mother, is a son that causeth shame, and bringeth reproach.

129. What is required of superiors towards their inferiors?

A. It is required of superiors, according to that power they receive from God, and that relation wherein they stand, to love, [1] pray for, [2] and bless their inferiors; [3] to instruct, [4] counsel, and admonish them; [5] countenancing, [6] commending, [7] and rewarding such as do well; [8] and discountenancing, [9] reproving, and chastising such as do ill; [10] protecting, [11] and providing for them all things necessary for soul [12] and body: [13] and by grave, wise, holy, and exemplary carriage, to procure glory to God, [14] honour to themselves, [15] and so to preserve that authority which God hath put upon them. [16]

Proofs

[1] **Colossians 3:19:** Husbands, love *your* wives, and be not bitter against them. **Titus 2:4:** That they may teach the young women to be sober, to love their husbands, to love their children ...

[2] **1 Samuel 12:23:** Moreover as for me, God forbid that I should sin against the LORD in ceasing to pray for you: but I will teach you the good and the right way... **Job 1:5:** And it was so, when the days of *their* feasting were gone about, that Job sent and sanctified them, and rose up early in the morning, and offered burnt offerings *according* to the number of them all: for Job said, It may be that my sons have sinned, and cursed God in their hearts. Thus did Job continually.

[3] **1 Kings 8:55-56:** And he stood, and blessed all the congregation of Israel with a loud voice, saying, Blessed *be* the LORD, that hath given rest unto his people Israel, according to all that he promised: there hath not failed one word of all his good promise, which he promised by the hand of Moses his servant. **Hebrews 7:7:** And without all contradiction the less is blessed of the better. **Genesis 49:28:** All these *are* the twelve tribes of Israel: and this *is it* that their father spake unto them, and blessed them; every one according to his blessing he blessed them.

[4] **Deuteronomy 6:6-7:** And these words, which I command thee this day, shall be in thine heart: And thou shalt teach them diligently unto thy children, and shalt talk of them when thou sittest in thine house, and when thou walkest by the way, and when thou liest down, and when thou risest up.

[5] **Ephesians 6:4:** And, ye fathers, provoke not your children to wrath: but bring them up in the nurture and admonition of the Lord.

[6] **1 Peter 3:7:** Likewise, ye husbands, dwell with *them* according to knowledge, giving honour unto the wife, as unto the weaker vessel, and as being heirs together of the grace of life; that your prayers be not hindered.

[7] **1 Peter 2:14:** Or unto governors, as unto them that are sent by him for the punishment of evildoers, and for the praise of them that do well. **Romans 13:3:** For rulers are not a terror to good works, but to the evil. Wilt thou then not be afraid of the power? do that which is good, and thou shalt have praise of the same ...

[8] **Esther 6:3:** And the king said, What honour and dignity hath been done to Mordecai for this? Then said the king's servants that ministered unto him, There is nothing done for him.

[9] **Romans 13:3-4:** For rulers are not a terror to good works, but to the evil. Wilt thou then not be afraid of the power? do that which is good, and thou shalt have praise of the same: For he is the minister of God to thee for good. But if thou do that which is evil, be afraid; for he beareth not the sword in vain: for he is the minister of God, a revenger to *execute* wrath upon him that doeth evil.

[10] **Proverbs 29:15:** The rod and reproof give wisdom: but a child left *to himself* bringeth his mother to shame. **1 Peter 2:14:** Or unto governors, as unto them that are sent by him for the punishment of evildoers, and for the praise of them that do well.

[11] **Job 29:12-17:** Because I delivered the poor that cried, and the fatherless, and *him that had* none to help him. The blessing of him that was ready to perish came upon me: and I caused the widow's heart to sing for joy. I put on righteousness, and it clothed me: my judgment *was* as a robe and a diadem. I was eyes to the blind, and feet *was* I to the lame. I was a father to the poor: and the cause *which* I knew not I searched out. And I brake the jaws of the wicked, and plucked the spoil out of his teeth. **Isaiah 1:10, 17:** Hear the word of the LORD, ye rulers of Sodom; give ear unto the law of our God, ye people of Gomorrah ... Learn to do well; seek judgment, relieve the oppressed, judge the fatherless, plead for the widow.

[12] **Ephesians 6:4:** And, ye fathers, provoke not your children to wrath: but bring them up in the nurture and admonition of the Lord.

[13] **1 Timothy 5:8:** But if any provide not for his own, and specially for those of his own house, he hath denied the faith, and is worse than an infidel.

[14] **1 Timothy 4:12:** Let no man despise thy youth; but be thou an example of the believers, in word, in conversation, in charity, in spirit, in faith, in purity. **Titus 2:3-5:** The aged women likewise, that *they be* in behaviour as becometh holiness, not false accusers, not given to much wine, teachers of good things; That they may teach the young women to be sober, to love their husbands, to love their children, *To be* discreet, chaste, keepers at home, good, obedient to their own husbands, that the word of God be not blasphemed.

[15] **1 Kings 3:28:** And all Israel heard of the judgment which the king had judged; and they feared the king: for they saw that the wisdom of God *was* in him, to do judgment.

[16] **Titus 2:15:** These things speak, and exhort, and rebuke with all authority. Let no man despise thee.

130. What are the sins of superiors?

A. The sins of superiors are, besides the neglect of the duties required of them, [1] and inordinate seeking of themselves, [2] their own glory, [3] ease, profit, or pleasure; [4] commanding things unlawful, [5] or not in the power of inferiors to perform; [6] counselling, [7] encouraging, [8] or favouring them in that which is evil; [9] dissuading, discouraging, or discountenancing them in that which is good; [10] correcting them unduly; [11] careless exposing, or leaving them to wrong, temptation, and danger; [12] provoking them to wrath; [13] or any way dishonouring themselves, or lessening their authority, by an unjust, indiscreet, rigorous, or remiss behaviour. [14]

Proofs

[1] **Ezekiel 34:2-4:** Son of man, prophesy against the shepherds of Israel, prophesy, and say unto them, Thus saith the Lord GOD unto the shepherds; Woe *be* to the shepherds of Israel that do feed themselves! should not the shepherds feed the flocks? Ye eat the fat, and ye clothe you with the wool, ye kill them that are fed: *but* ye feed not the flock. The diseased have ye not strengthened, neither have ye healed that which was sick, neither have ye bound up *that which was* broken, neither have ye brought again that which was driven away, neither have ye sought that which was lost; but with force and with cruelty have ye ruled them.

[2] **Philippians 2:21:** For all seek their own, not the things which are Jesus Christ's.

[3] **John 5:44:** How can ye believe, which receive honour one of another, and seek not the honour that *cometh* from God only? **John 7:18:** He that speaketh of himself seeketh his own glory: but he that seeketh his glory that sent him, the same is true, and no unrighteousness is in him.

[4] **Isaiah 56:10-11:** His watchmen *are* blind: they are all ignorant, they *are* all dumb dogs, they cannot bark; sleeping, lying down, loving to slumber. Yea, *they are* greedy dogs *which* can never have enough, and they *are* shepherds *that* cannot understand: they all look to their own way, every one for his gain, from his quarter. **Deuteronomy 17:17:** Neither

shall he multiply wives to himself, that his heart turn not away: neither shall he greatly multiply to himself silver and gold.

[5] **Daniel 3:4-6:** Then an herald cried aloud, To you it is commanded, O people, nations, and languages, *That* at what time ye hear the sound of the cornet, flute, harp, sackbut, psaltery, dulcimer, and all kinds of musick, ye fall down and worship the golden image that Nebuchadnezzar the king hath set up: And whoso falleth not down and worshippeth shall the same hour be cast into the midst of a burning fiery furnace. **Acts 4:17-18:** But that it spread no further among the people, let us straitly threaten them, that they speak henceforth to no man in this name. And they called them, and commanded them not to speak at all nor teach in the name of Jesus.

[6] **Exodus 5:10-18:** And the taskmasters of the people went out, and their officers, and they spake to the people, saying, Thus saith Pharaoh, I will not give you straw. Go ye, get you straw where ye can find it: yet not ought of your work shall be diminished. So the people were scattered abroad throughout all the land of Egypt to gather stubble instead of straw. And the taskmasters hasted *them*, saying, Fulfil your works, *your* daily tasks, as when there was straw. And the officers of the children of Israel, which Pharaoh's taskmasters had set over them, were beaten, *and* demanded, Wherefore have ye not fulfilled your task in making brick both yesterday and to day, as heretofore? Then the officers of the children of Israel came and cried unto Pharaoh, saying, Wherefore dealest thou thus with thy servants? There is no straw given unto thy servants, and they say to us, Make brick: and, behold, thy servants *are* beaten; but the fault *is* in thine own people. But he said, Ye *are* idle, *ye are* idle: therefore ye say, Let us go *and* do sacrifice to the LORD. Go therefore now, *and* work; for there shall no straw be given you, yet shall ye deliver the tale of bricks. **Matthew 23:2, 4:** Saying, The scribes and the Pharisees sit in Moses' seat ... For they bind heavy burdens and grievous to be borne, and lay *them* on men's shoulders; but they *themselves* will not move them with one of their fingers.

[7] **Matthew 14:8:** And she, being before instructed of her mother, said, Give me here John Baptist's head in a charger. [Compare with] **Mark 6:24:** And she went forth, and said unto her mother, What shall I ask? And she said, The head of John the Baptist.

[8] **2 Samuel 13:28:** Now Absalom had commanded his servants, saying, Mark ye now when Amnon's heart is merry with wine, and when I say unto you, Smite Amnon; then kill him, fear not: have not I commanded you? be courageous, and be valiant.

[9] **1 Samuel 3:13:** For I have told him that I will judge his house for ever for the iniquity which he knoweth; because his sons made themselves vile, and he restrained them not.

[10] **John 7:46-49:** The officers answered, Never man spake like this man. Then answered them the Pharisees, Are ye also deceived? Have any of the rulers or of the Pharisees believed on him? But this people who knoweth not the law are cursed. **Colossians 3:21:** Fathers, provoke not your children *to anger*, lest they be discouraged. **Exodus 5:17:** But he said, Ye *are* idle, *ye are* idle: therefore ye say, Let us go *and* do sacrifice to the LORD.

[11] **1 Peter 2:18-20:** Servants, *be* subject to *your* masters with all fear; not only to the good and gentle, but also to the froward. For this *is* thankworthy, if a man for conscience toward God endure grief, suffering wrongfully. For what glory *is it*, if, when ye be buffeted for your faults, ye shall take it patiently? but if, when ye do well, and suffer *for it*, ye take it patiently, this *is* acceptable with God. **Hebrews 12:10:** For they verily for a few days chastened *us* after their own pleasure; but he for our profit, that we might be partakers of his holiness. **Deuteronomy 25:3:** Forty stripes he may give him, *and* not exceed: lest, *if* he should exceed, and beat him above these with many stripes, then thy brother should seem vile unto thee.

[12] **Genesis 38:11, 26:** Then said Judah to Tamar his daughter in law, Remain a widow at thy father's house, till Shelah my son be grown: for he said, Lest peradventure he die also, as his brethren *did*. And Tamar went and dwelt in her father's house ... And Judah acknowledged *them*, and said, She hath been more righteous than I; because that I gave her not to Shelah my son. And he knew her again no more. **Acts 18:17:** Then all the Greeks took Sosthenes, the chief ruler of the synagogue, and beat *him* before the judgment seat. And Gallio cared for none of those things.

[13] **Ephesians 6:4:** And, ye fathers, provoke not your children to wrath: but bring them up in the nurture and admonition of the Lord.

[14] **Genesis 9:21:** And he drank of the wine, and was drunken; and he was uncovered within his tent. **1 Kings 12:13-16:** And the king

answered the people roughly, and forsook the old men's counsel that they gave him; And spake to them after the counsel of the young men, saying, My father made your yoke heavy, and I will add to your yoke: my father *also* chastised you with whips, but I will chastise you with scorpions. Wherefore the king hearkened not unto the people; for the cause was from the LORD, that he might perform his saying, which the LORD spake by Ahijah the Shilonite unto Jeroboam the son of Nebat. So when all Israel saw that the king hearkened not unto them, the people answered the king, saying, What portion have we in David? neither *have we* inheritance in the son of Jesse: to your tents, O Israel: now see to thine own house, David. So Israel departed unto their tents. **1 Kings 1:6:** And his father had not displeased him at any time in saying, Why hast thou done so? and he also *was a* very goodly *man*; and *his mother* bare him after Absalom. **1 Samuel 2:29-31:** Wherefore kick ye at my sacrifice and at mine offering, which I have commanded *in my* habitation; and honourest thy sons above me, to make yourselves fat with the chiefest of all the offerings of Israel my people? Wherefore the LORD God of Israel saith, I said indeed *that* thy house, and the house of thy father, should walk before me for ever: but now the LORD saith, Be it far from me; for them that honour me I will honour, and they that despise me shall be lightly esteemed. Behold, the days come, that I will cut off thine arm, and the arm of thy father's house, that there shall not be an old man in thine house.

131. What are the duties of equals?

A. The duties of equals are, to regard the dignity and worth of each other, [1] in giving honour to go one before another; [2] and to rejoice in each others' gifts and advancement, as their own. [3]

Proofs

[1] **1 Peter 2:17:** Honour all *men*. Love the brotherhood. Fear God. Honour the king.

[2] **Romans 12:10:** *Be* kindly affectioned one to another with brotherly love; in honour preferring one another …

[3] **Romans 12:15-16:** Rejoice with them that do rejoice, and weep with them that weep. *Be* of the same mind one toward another. Mind not high things, but condescend to men of low estate. Be not wise in your own conceits. **Philippians 2:3-4:** Let nothing *be done* through

strife or vainglory; but in lowliness of mind let each esteem other better than themselves. Look not every man on his own things, but every man also on the things of others.

132. What are the sins of equals?

A. The sins of equals are, besides the neglect of the duties required, [1] the undervaluing of the worth, [2] envying the gifts, [3] grieving at the advancement or prosperity one of another; [4] and usurping pre-eminence one over another. [5]

Proofs

[1] **Romans 13:8:** Owe no man any thing, but to love one another: for he that loveth another hath fulfilled the law.

[2] **2 Timothy 3:3:** Without natural affection, trucebreakers, false accusers, incontinent, fierce, despisers of those that are good ...

[3] **Acts 7:9:** And the patriarchs, moved with envy, sold Joseph into Egypt: but God was with him ... **Galatians 5:26:** Let us not be desirous of vain glory, provoking one another, envying one another.

[4] **Numbers 12:2:** And they said, Hath the LORD indeed spoken only by Moses? hath he not spoken also by us? And the LORD heard *it*. **Esther 6:12-13:** And Mordecai came again to the king's gate. But Haman hasted to his house mourning, and having his head covered. And Haman told Zeresh his wife and all his friends every *thing* that had befallen him. Then said his wise men and Zeresh his wife unto him, If Mordecai *be* of the seed of the Jews, before whom thou hast begun to fall, thou shalt not prevail against him, but shalt surely fall before him.

[5] **3 John 9:** I wrote unto the church: but Diotrephes, who loveth to have the preeminence among them, receiveth us not. **Luke 22:24:** And there was also a strife among them, which of them should be accounted the greatest.

133. What is the reason annexed to the fifth commandment, the more to enforce it?

A. The reason annexed to the fifth commandment, in these words, *That thy days may be long upon the land which the Lord thy God giveth thee*, [1] is an express promise of long life and prosperity, as far as it shall serve for God's glory and their own good, to all such as keep this commandment. [2]

Proofs

[1] **Exodus 20:12:** Honour thy father and thy mother: that thy days may be long upon the land which the LORD thy God giveth thee.

[2] **Deuteronomy 5:16:** Honour thy father and thy mother, as the LORD thy God hath commanded thee; that thy days may be prolonged, and that it may go well with thee, in the land which the LORD thy God giveth thee. **1 Kings 8:25:** Therefore now, LORD God of Israel, keep with thy servant David my father that thou promisedst him, saying, There shall not fail thee a man in my sight to sit on the throne of Israel; so that thy children take heed to their way, that they walk before me as thou hast walked before me. **Ephesians 6:2-3:** Honour thy father and mother; which is the first commandment with promise; That it may be well with thee, and thou mayest live long on the earth.

134. Which is the sixth commandment?

A. The sixth commandment is, *Thou shalt not kill.* [1]

Proof

[1] **Exodus 20:13:** Thou shalt not kill.

135. What are the duties required in the sixth commandment?

A. The duties required in the sixth commandment are all careful studies, and lawful endeavours, to preserve the life of ourselves [1] and others [2] by resisting all thoughts and purposes, [3] subduing all passions, [4] and avoiding all occasions, [5] temptations, [6] and practices, which tend to the unjust taking away the life of any; [7] by just defence thereof against violence, [8] patient bearing of the hand of God, [9] quietness of mind, [10] cheerfulness of spirit; [11] a sober use of meat, [12] drink, [13] physic, [14] sleep, [15] labour, [16] and recreations; [17] by charitable thoughts, [18] love, [19] compassion, [20] meekness, gentleness, kindness; [21] peaceable, [22] mild and courteous speeches and behaviour; [23] forbearance, readiness to be reconciled, patient bearing and forgiving of injuries, and requiting good for evil; [24] comforting and succouring the distressed and protecting and defending the innocent. [25]

Proofs

[1] **Ephesians 5:28-29:** So ought men to love their wives as their own bodies. He that loveth his wife loveth himself. For no man ever yet hated his own flesh; but nourisheth and cherisheth it, even as the Lord the church …

[2] **1 Kings 18:4:** For it was *so*, when Jezebel cut off the prophets of the LORD, that Obadiah took an hundred prophets, and hid them by fifty in a cave, and fed them with bread and water.

[3] **Jeremiah 26:15-16:** But know ye for certain, that if ye put me to death, ye shall surely bring innocent blood upon yourselves, and upon this city, and upon the inhabitants thereof: for of a truth the LORD hath sent me unto you to speak all these words in your ears. Then said the princes and all the people unto the priests and to the prophets; This man *is* not worthy to die: for he hath spoken to us in the name of the LORD our God. **Acts 23:12, 16-17, 21, 27:** And when it was day, certain of the Jews banded together, and bound themselves under a curse, saying that they would neither eat nor drink till they had killed Paul … And when Paul's sister's son heard of their lying in wait, he went and entered into the castle, and told Paul. Then Paul called one of the centurions unto *him*, and said, Bring this young man unto the chief captain: for he hath a certain thing to tell him … But do not thou yield unto them: for there lie in wait for him of them more than forty men, which have bound themselves with an oath, that they will neither eat nor drink till they have killed him: and now are they ready, looking for a promise from thee … This man was taken of the Jews, and should have been killed of them: then came I with an army, and rescued him, having understood that he was a Roman.

[4] **Ephesians 4:26-27:** Be ye angry, and sin not: let not the sun go down upon your wrath: Neither give place to the devil.

[5] **2 Samuel 2:22:** And Abner said again to Asahel, Turn thee aside from following me: wherefore should I smite thee to the ground? how then should I hold up my face to Joab thy brother? **Deuteronomy 22:8:** When thou buildest a new house, then thou shalt make a battlement for thy roof, that thou bring not blood upon thine house, if any man fall from thence.

[6] **Matthew 4:6-7:** And saith unto him, If thou be the Son of God, cast thyself down: for it is written, He shall give his angels charge concerning

thee: and in *their* hands they shall bear thee up, lest at any time thou dash thy foot against a stone. Jesus said unto him, It is written again, Thou shalt not tempt the Lord thy God. **Proverbs 1:10-11, 15-16:** My son, if sinners entice thee, consent thou not. If they say, Come with us, let us lay wait for blood, let us lurk privily for the innocent without cause ... My son, walk not thou in the way with them; refrain thy foot from their path: For their feet run to evil, and make haste to shed blood.

[7] **1 Samuel 24:12:** The LORD judge between me and thee, and the LORD avenge me of thee: but mine hand shall not be upon thee. **1 Samuel 26:9-11:** And David said to Abishai, Destroy him not: for who can stretch forth his hand against the LORD's anointed, and be guiltless? David said furthermore, *As* the LORD liveth, the LORD shall smite him; or his day shall come to die; or he shall descend into battle, and perish. The LORD forbid that I should stretch forth mine hand against the LORD's anointed: but, I pray thee, take thou now the spear that *is* at his bolster, and the cruse of water, and let us go. **Genesis 37:21-22:** And Reuben heard *it*, and he delivered him out of their hands; and said, Let us not kill him. And Reuben said unto them, Shed no blood, *but* cast him into this pit that *is* in the wilderness, and lay no hand upon him; that he might rid him out of their hands, to deliver him to his father again.

[8] **Psalm 82:4:** Deliver the poor and needy: rid *them* out of the hand of the wicked. **Proverbs 24:11-12:** If thou forbear to deliver *them that are* drawn unto death, and *those that are* ready to be slain; If thou sayest, Behold, we knew it not; doth not he that pondereth the heart consider *it*? and he that keepeth thy soul, doth *not* he know *it*? and shall *not* he render to *every* man according to his works? **1 Samuel 14:45:** And the people said unto Saul, Shall Jonathan die, who hath wrought this great salvation in Israel? God forbid: *as* the LORD liveth, there shall not one hair of his head fall to the ground; for he hath wrought with God this day. So the people rescued Jonathan, that he died not.

[9] **James 5:7-11:** Be patient therefore, brethren, unto the coming of the Lord. Behold, the husbandman waiteth for the precious fruit of the earth, and hath long patience for it, until he receive the early and latter rain. Be ye also patient; stablish your hearts: for the coming of the Lord draweth nigh. Grudge not one against another, brethren, lest ye be condemned: behold, the judge standeth before the door. Take, my brethren, the prophets, who have spoken in the name of the Lord, for an example of suffering affliction, and of patience. Behold, we

count them happy which endure. Ye have heard of the patience of Job, and have seen the end of the Lord; that the Lord is very pitiful, and of tender mercy. **Hebrews 12:9:** Furthermore we have had fathers of our flesh which corrected *us*, and we gave *them* reverence: shall we not much rather be in subjection unto the Father of spirits, and live?

[10] **1 Thessalonians 4:11:** And that ye study to be quiet, and to do your own business, and to work with your own hands, as we commanded you … **1 Peter 3:3-4:** Whose adorning let it not be that outward *adorning* of plaiting the hair, and of wearing of gold, or of putting on of apparel; But *let it be* the hidden man of the heart, in that which is not corruptible, *even the ornament* of a meek and quiet spirit, which is in the sight of God of great price. **Psalm 37:8-11:** Cease from anger, and forsake wrath: fret not thyself in any wise to do evil. For evildoers shall be cut off: but those that wait upon the LORD, they shall inherit the earth. For yet a little while, and the wicked *shall* not *be*: yea, thou shalt diligently consider his place, and it *shall* not *be*. But the meek shall inherit the earth; and shall delight themselves in the abundance of peace.

[11] **Proverbs 17:22:** A merry heart doeth good *like* a medicine: but a broken spirit drieth the bones.

[12] **Proverbs 25:16, 27:** Hast thou found honey? eat so much as is sufficient for thee, lest thou be filled therewith, and vomit it … *It is* not good to eat much honey: so *for men* to search their own glory *is not* glory.

[13] **1 Timothy 5:23:** Drink no longer water, but use a little wine for thy stomach's sake and thine often infirmities.

[14] **Isaiah 38:21:** For Isaiah had said, Let them take a lump of figs, and lay *it* for a plaister upon the boil, and he shall recover.

[15] **Psalm 127:2:** *It is* vain for you to rise up early, to sit up late, to eat the bread of sorrows: *for* so he giveth his beloved sleep.

[16] **Ecclesiastes 5:12:** The sleep of a labouring man is sweet, whether he eat little or much: but the abundance of the rich will not suffer him to sleep. **2 Thessalonians 3:10, 12:** For even when we were with you, this we commanded you, that if any would not work, neither should he eat … Now them that are such we command and exhort by our Lord Jesus Christ, that with quietness they work, and eat their own bread. **Proverbs 16:26:** He that laboureth laboureth for himself; for his mouth craveth it of him.

[17] **Ecclesiastes 3:4, 11:** A time to weep, and a time to laugh; a time to mourn, and a time to dance ... He hath made every *thing* beautiful in his time: also he hath set the world in their heart, so that no man can find out the work that God maketh from the beginning to the end.

[18] **1 Samuel 19:4-5:** And Jonathan spake good of David unto Saul his father, and said unto him, Let not the king sin against his servant, against David; because he hath not sinned against thee, and because his works *have been* to thee-ward very good: For he did put his life in his hand, and slew the Philistine, and the LORD wrought a great salvation for all Israel: thou sawest *it*, and didst rejoice: wherefore then wilt thou sin against innocent blood, to slay David without a cause? **1 Samuel 22:13-14:** And Saul said unto him, Why have ye conspired against me, thou and the son of Jesse, in that thou hast given him bread, and a sword, and hast inquired of God for him, that he should rise against me, to lie in wait, as at this day? Then Ahimelech answered the king, and said, And who *is so* faithful among all thy servants as David, which is the king's son in law, and goeth at thy bidding, and is honourable in thine house?

[19] **Romans 13:10:** Love worketh no ill to his neighbour: therefore love *is* the fulfilling of the law.

[20] **Luke 10:33-34:** But a certain Samaritan, as he journeyed, came where he was: and when he saw him, he had compassion *on him*, And went to *him*, and bound up his wounds, pouring in oil and wine, and set him on his own beast, and brought him to an inn, and took care of him.

[21] **Colossians 3:12-13:** Put on therefore, as the elect of God, holy and beloved, bowels of mercies, kindness, humbleness of mind, meekness, longsuffering; Forbearing one another, and forgiving one another, if any man have a quarrel against any: even as Christ forgave you, so also *do* ye.

[22] **James 3:17:** But the wisdom that is from above is first pure, then peaceable, gentle, *and* easy to be intreated, full of mercy and good fruits, without partiality, and without hypocrisy.

[23] **1 Peter 3:8-11:** Finally, *be ye* all of one mind, having compassion one of another, love as brethren, *be* pitiful, *be* courteous: Not rendering evil for evil, or railing for railing: but contrariwise blessing; knowing that ye are thereunto called, that ye should inherit a blessing. For he that will love life, and see good days, let him refrain his tongue from evil, and his lips that they speak no guile: Let him eschew evil, and do good;

let him seek peace, and ensue it. **Proverbs 15:1:** A soft answer turneth away wrath: but grievous words stir up anger. **Judges 8:1-3:** And the men of Ephraim said unto him, Why hast thou served us thus, that thou calledst us not, when thou wentest to fight with the Midianites? And they did chide with him sharply. And he said unto them, What have I done now in comparison of you? *Is* not the gleaning of the grapes of Ephraim better than the vintage of Abiezer? God hath delivered into your hands the princes of Midian, Oreb and Zeeb: and what was I able to do in comparison of you? Then their anger was abated toward him, when he had said that.

[24] **Matthew 5:24:** Leave there thy gift before the altar, and go thy way; first be reconciled to thy brother, and then come and offer thy gift. **Ephesians 4:2, 32:** With all lowliness and meekness, with longsuffering, forbearing one another in love ... And be ye kind one to another, tenderhearted, forgiving one another, even as God for Christ's sake hath forgiven you. **Romans 12:17, 20-21:** Recompense to no man evil for evil. Provide things honest in the sight of all men ... Therefore if thine enemy hunger, feed him; if he thirst, give him drink: for in so doing thou shalt heap coals of fire on his head. Be not overcome of evil, but overcome evil with good.

[25] **1 Thessalonians 5:14:** Now we exhort you, brethren, warn them that are unruly, comfort the feebleminded, support the weak, be patient toward all *men*. **Job 31:19-20:** If I have seen any perish for want of clothing, or any poor without covering; If his loins have not blessed me, and *if* he were *not* warmed with the fleece of my sheep ... **Matthew 25:35-36:** For I was an hungered, and ye gave me meat: I was thirsty, and ye gave me drink: I was a stranger, and ye took me in: Naked, and ye clothed me: I was sick, and ye visited me: I was in prison, and ye came unto me. **Proverbs 31:8-9:** Open thy mouth for the dumb in the cause of all such as are appointed to destruction. Open thy mouth, judge righteously, and plead the cause of the poor and needy.

136. What are the sins forbidden in the sixth commandment?

A. The sins forbidden in the sixth commandment are, all taking away the life of ourselves, [1] or of others, [2] except in case of public justice, [3] lawful war, [4] or necessary defence; [5] the neglecting or withdrawing the lawful and necessary means of preservation of life; [6] sinful anger, [7] hatred, [8] envy, [9] desire of revenge; [10] all excessive passions, [11] distracting cares; [12] immoderate use of meat, drink, [13] labour, [14] and recreations; [15] provoking words, [16] oppression, [17] quarreling, [18] striking, wounding, [19] and whatsoever else tends to the destruction of the life of any. [20]

Proofs

[1] **Acts 16:28:** But Paul cried with a loud voice, saying, Do thyself no harm: for we are all here.

[2] **Genesis 9:6:** Whoso sheddeth man's blood, by man shall his blood be shed: for in the image of God made he man.

[3] **Numbers 35:31, 33:** Moreover ye shall take no satisfaction for the life of a murderer, which *is* guilty of death: but he shall be surely put to death … So ye shall not pollute the land wherein ye *are*: for blood it defileth the land: and the land cannot be cleansed of the blood that is shed therein, but by the blood of him that shed it.

[4] **Jeremiah 48:10:** Cursed *be* he that doeth the work of the LORD deceitfully, and cursed *be* he that keepeth back his sword from blood. **Deuteronomy 20:1:** When thou goest out to battle against thine enemies, and seest horses, and chariots, *and* a people more than thou, be not afraid of them: for the LORD thy God *is* with thee, which brought thee up out of the land of Egypt. [See the rest of the chapter.]

[5] **Exodus 22:2-3:** If a thief be found breaking up, and be smitten that he die, *there shall* no blood *be shed* for him. If the sun be risen upon him, *there shall be* blood *shed* for him; *for* he should make full restitution; if he have nothing, then he shall be sold for his theft.

[6] **Matthew 25:42-43:** For I was an hungered, and ye gave me no meat: I was thirsty, and ye gave me no drink: I was a stranger, and ye took me not in: naked, and ye clothed me not: sick, and in prison, and ye visited me not. **James 2:15-16:** If a brother or sister be naked, and destitute of daily food, And one of you say unto them, Depart in peace, be *ye* warmed and filled; notwithstanding ye give them not those things which are needful to the body; what *doth it* profit? **Ecclesiastes 6:1-2:** There is an evil which I have seen under the sun, and it *is* common among men: A man to whom God hath given riches, wealth, and honour, so that he wanteth nothing for his soul of all that

he desireth, yet God giveth him not power to eat thereof, but a stranger eateth it: this is vanity, and it *is* an evil disease.

[7] **Matthew 5:22:** But I say unto you, That whosoever is angry with his brother without a cause shall be in danger of the judgment: and whosoever shall say to his brother, Raca, shall be in danger of the council: but whosoever shall say, Thou fool, shall be in danger of hell fire.

[8] **1 John 3:15:** Whosoever hateth his brother is a murderer: and ye know that no murderer hath eternal life abiding in him. **Leviticus 19:17:** Thou shalt not hate thy brother in thine heart: thou shalt in any wise rebuke thy neighbour, and not suffer sin upon him.

[9] **Proverbs 14:30:** A sound heart *is* the life of the flesh: but envy the rottenness of the bones.

[10] **Romans 12:19:** Dearly beloved, avenge not yourselves, but *rather* give place unto wrath: for it is written, Vengeance *is* mine; I will repay, saith the Lord.

[11] **Ephesians 4:31:** Let all bitterness, and wrath, and anger, and clamour, and evil speaking, be put away from you, with all malice …

[12] **Matthew 6:31, 34:** Therefore take no thought, saying, What shall we eat? or, What shall we drink? or, Wherewithal shall we be clothed? … Take therefore no thought for the morrow: for the morrow shall take thought for the things of itself. Sufficient unto the day *is* the evil thereof.

[13] **Luke 21:34:** And take heed to yourselves, lest at any time your hearts be overcharged with surfeiting, and drunkenness, and cares of this life, and *so* that day come upon you unawares. **Romans 13:13:** Let us walk honestly, as in the day; not in rioting and drunkenness, not in chambering and wantonness, not in strife and envying.

[14] **Ecclesiastes 12:12:** And further, by these, my son, be admonished: of making many books *there is* no end; and much study *is* a weariness of the flesh. **Ecclesiastes 2:22-23:** For what hath man of all his labour, and of the vexation of his heart, wherein he hath laboured under the sun? For all his days *are* sorrows, and his travail grief; yea, his heart taketh not rest in the night. This is also vanity.

[15] **Isaiah 5:12:** And the harp, and the viol, the tabret, and pipe, and wine, are in their feasts: but they regard not the work of the LORD, neither consider the operation of his hands.

[16] **Proverbs 15:1:** A soft answer turneth away wrath: but grievous words stir up anger. **Proverbs 12:18:** There is that speaketh like the piercings of a sword: but the tongue of the wise *is* health.

[17] **Ezekiel 18:18:** *As for* his father, because he cruelly oppressed, spoiled his brother by violence, and did *that* which *is* not good among his people, lo, even he shall die in his iniquity. **Exodus 1:14:** And they made their lives bitter with hard bondage, in mortar, and in brick, and in all manner of service in the field: all their service, wherein they made them serve, *was* with rigour.

[18] **Galatians 5:15:** But if ye bite and devour one another, take heed that ye be not consumed one of another. **Proverbs 23:29:** Who hath woe? who hath sorrow? who hath contentions? who hath babbling? who hath wounds without cause? who hath redness of eyes?

[19] **Numbers 35:16-18, 21:** And if he smite him with an instrument of iron, so that he die, he *is* a murderer: the murderer shall surely be put to death. And if he smite him with throwing a stone, wherewith he may die, and he die, he *is* a murderer: the murderer shall surely be put to death. Or *if* he smite him with an hand weapon of wood, wherewith he may die, and he die, he *is* a murderer: the murderer shall surely be put to death ... Or in enmity smite him with his hand, that he die: he that smote *him* shall surely be put to death; *for* he *is* a murderer: the revenger of blood shall slay the murderer, when he meeteth him.

[20] **Exodus 21:18-36** [containing laws for smiters, for an hurt by chance, for an ox that goreth, and for him that is an occasion of harm].

137. Which is the seventh commandment?

A. The seventh commandment is, *Thou shalt not commit adultery*. [1]

Proof

[1] **Exodus 20:14:** Thou shalt not commit adultery.

138. What are the duties required in the seventh commandment?

A. The duties required in the seventh commandment are, chastity in body, mind, affections, [1] words, [2] and behaviour; [3] and the preservation of it in ourselves and others; [4] watchfulness over the eyes and all the senses; [5] temperance, [6] keeping of chaste company, [7] modesty in apparel; [8] marriage by those that have not the gift of continency, [9] conjugal love, [10] and cohabitation; [11]diligent labour in our callings; [12] shunning all occasions of uncleanness, and resisting temptations thereunto. [13]

Proofs

[1] **1 Thessalonians 4:4:** That every one of you should know how to possess his vessel in sanctification and honour ...**Job 31:1:** I made a covenant with mine eyes: why then should I think upon a maid? **1 Corinthians 7:34:** There is difference *also* between a wife and a virgin. The unmarried woman careth for the things of the Lord, that she may be holy both in body and in spirit: but she that is married careth for the things of the world, how she may please *her* husband.

[2] **Colossians 4:6:** Let your speech *be* alway with grace, seasoned with salt, that ye may know how ye ought to answer every man.

[3] **1 Peter 3:2:** While they behold your chaste conversation *coupled* with fear.

[4] **1 Corinthians 7:2, 35-36:** Nevertheless, *to avoid* fornication, let every man have his own wife, and let every woman have her own husband ... And this I speak for your own profit; not that I may cast a snare upon you, but for that which is comely, and that ye may attend upon the Lord without distraction. But if any man think that he behaveth himself uncomely toward his virgin, if she pass the flower of *her* age, and need so require, let him do what he will, he sinneth not: let them marry.

[5] **Job 31:1:** I made a covenant with mine eyes; why then should I think upon a maid?

[6] **Acts 24:24-25:** And after certain days, when Felix came with his wife Drusilla, which was a Jewess, he sent for Paul, and heard him concerning the faith in Christ. And as he reasoned of righteousness, temperance, and judgment to come, Felix trembled, and answered, Go thy way for this time; when I have a convenient season, I will call for thee.

[7] **Proverbs 2:16-20:** To deliver thee from the strange woman, *even* from the stranger *which* flattereth with her words; Which forsaketh the guide of her youth, and forgetteth the covenant of her God. For her

house inclineth unto death, and her paths unto the dead. None that go unto her return again, neither take they hold of the paths of life. That thou mayest walk in the way of good *men*, and keep the paths of the righteous.

[8] **1 Timothy 2:9:** In like manner also, that women adorn themselves in modest apparel, with shamefacedness and sobriety; not with broided hair, or gold, or pearls, or costly array.

[9] **1 Corinthians 7:2, 9:** Nevertheless, *to avoid* fornication, let every man have his own wife, and let every woman have her own husband … But if they cannot contain, let them marry: for it is better to marry than to burn.

[10] **Proverbs 5:19-20:** *Let her be as* the loving hind and pleasant roe; let her breasts satisfy thee at all times; and be thou ravished always with her love. And why wilt thou, my son, be ravished with a strange woman, and embrace the bosom of a stranger?

[11] **1 Peter 3:7:** Likewise, ye husbands, dwell with *them* according to knowledge, giving honour unto the wife, as unto the weaker vessel, and as being heirs together of the grace of life; that your prayers be not hindered.

[12] **Proverbs 31:11, 27-28:** The heart of her husband doth safely trust in her, so that he shall have no need of spoil … She looketh well to the ways of her household, and eateth not the bread of idleness. Her children arise up, and call her blessed; her husband *also*, and he praiseth her.

[13] **Proverbs 5:8:** Remove thy way far from her, and come not nigh the door of her house … **Genesis 39:8-10:** But he refused, and said unto his master's wife, Behold, my master wotteth not what *is* with me in the house, and he hath committed all that he hath to my hand; *There is* none greater in this house than I; neither hath he kept back any thing from me but thee, because thou *art* his wife: how then can I do this great wickedness, and sin against God? And it came to pass, as she spake to Joseph day by day, that he hearkened not unto her, to lie by her, *or* to be with her.

139. What are the sins forbidden in the seventh commandment?

A. The sins forbidden in the seventh commandment, besides the neglect of the duties required, [1] are, adultery, fornication, [2] rape, incest, [3] sodomy, and all unnatural lusts; [4] all unclean imaginations, thoughts, purposes, and affections; [5] all corrupt or filthy communications, or listening thereunto; [6] wanton looks, [7] impudent or light behaviour, immodest apparel; [8] prohibiting of lawful, [9] and dispensing with unlawful marriages; [10] allowing, tolerating, keeping of stews, and resorting to them; [11] entangling vows of single life, [12] undue delay of marriage, [13] having more wives or husbands than one at the same time; [14] unjust divorce, [15] or desertion; [16] idleness, gluttony, drunkenness, [17]unchaste company; [18] lascivious songs, books, pictures, dancings, stage plays; [19] and all other provocations to, or acts of uncleanness, either in ourselves or others. [20]

Proofs

[1] **Proverbs 5:7:** Hear me now therefore, O ye children, and depart not from the words of my mouth.

[2] **Hebrews 13:4:** Marriage *is* honourable in all, and the bed undefiled: but whoremongers and adulterers God will judge. **Galatians 5:19:** Now the works of the flesh are manifest, which are *these*; Adultery, fornication, uncleanness, lasciviousness ...

[3] **2 Samuel 13:14:** Howbeit he would not hearken unto her voice: but, being stronger than she, forced her, and lay with her. **1 Corinthians 5:1:** It is reported commonly *that there is* fornication among you, and such fornication as is not so much as named among the Gentiles, that one should have his father's wife.

[4] **Romans 1:24, 26-27:** Wherefore God also gave them up to uncleanness through the lusts of their own hearts, to dishonour their own bodies between themselves ... For this cause God gave them up unto vile affections: for even their women did change the natural use into that which is against nature: And likewise also the men, leaving the natural use of the woman, burned in their lust one toward another; men with men working that which is unseemly, and receiving in themselves that recompense of their error which was meet. **Leviticus 20:15-16:** And if a man lie with a beast, he shall surely be put to death: and ye shall slay the beast. And if a woman approach unto any beast, and lie down thereto, thou shalt kill the

woman, and the beast: they shall surely be put to death; their blood *shall be* upon them.

[5] **Matthew 5:28:** But I say unto you, That whosoever looketh on a woman to lust after her hath committed adultery with her already in his heart. **Matthew 15:19:** For out of the heart proceed evil thoughts, murders, adulteries, fornications, thefts, false witness, blasphemies ... **Colossians 3:5:** Mortify therefore your members which are upon the earth; fornication, uncleanness, inordinate affection, evil concupiscence, and covetousness, which is idolatry ...

[6] **Ephesians 5:3-4:** But fornication, and all uncleanness, or covetousness, let it not be once named among you, as becometh saints; Neither filthiness, nor foolish talking, nor jesting, which are not convenient: but rather giving of thanks. **Proverbs 7:5, 21-22:** That they may keep thee from the strange woman, from the stranger *which* flattereth with her words ... With her much fair speech she caused him to yield, with the flattering of her lips she forced him. He goeth after her straightway, as an ox goeth to the slaughter, or as a fool to the correction of the stocks ...

[7] **Isaiah 3:16:** Moreover the LORD saith, Because the daughters of Zion are haughty, and walk with stretched forth necks and wanton eyes, walking and mincing as they go, and making a tinkling with their feet ... **2 Peter 2:14:** Having eyes full of adultery, and that cannot cease from sin; beguiling unstable souls: an heart they have exercised with covetous practices; cursed children ...

[8] **Proverbs 7:10, 13:** And, behold, there met him a woman with the attire of an harlot, and subtil of heart ... So she caught him, and kissed him, *and* with an impudent face said unto him ...

[9] **1 Timothy 4:3:** Forbidding to marry, *and commanding* to abstain from meats, which God hath created to be received with thanksgiving of them which believe and know the truth.

[10] **Leviticus 18:1-21. Mark 6:18:** For John had said unto Herod, It is not lawful for thee to have thy brother's wife. **Malachi 2:11-12:** Judah hath dealt treacherously, and an abomination is committed in Israel and in Jerusalem; for Judah hath profaned the holiness of the LORD which he loved, and hath married the daughter of a strange god. The LORD will cut off the man that doeth this, the master and the scholar,

out of the tabernacles of Jacob, and him that offereth an offering unto the LORD of hosts.

[11] **1 Kings 15:12:** And he took away the sodomites out of the land, and removed all the idols that his fathers had made. **2 Kings 23:7:** And he brake down the houses of the sodomites, that *were* by the house of the LORD, where the women wove hangings for the grove. **Deuteronomy 23:17-18:** There shall be no whore of the daughters of Israel, nor a sodomite of the sons of Israel. Thou shalt not bring the hire of a whore, or the price of a dog, into the house of the LORD thy God for any vow: for even both these *are* abomination unto the LORD thy God. **Leviticus 19:29:** Do not prostitute thy daughter, to cause her to be a whore; lest the land fall to whoredom, and the land become full of wickedness. **Jeremiah 5:7:** How shall I pardon thee for this? thy children have forsaken me, and sworn by *them that are* no gods: when I had fed them to the full, they then committed adultery, and assembled themselves by troops in the harlots' houses. **Proverbs 7:24-27:** Hearken unto me now therefore, O ye children, and attend to the words of my mouth. Let not thine heart decline to her ways, go not astray in her paths. For she hath cast down many wounded: yea, many strong *men* have been slain by her. Her house *is* the way to hell, going down to the chambers of death.

[12] **Matthew 19:10-11:** His disciples say unto him, If the case of the man be so with *his* wife, it is not good to marry. But he said unto them, All *men* cannot receive this saying, save *they* to whom it is given.

[13] **1 Corinthians 7:7-9:** For I would that all men were even as I myself. But every man hath his proper gift of God, one after this manner, and another after that. I say therefore to the unmarried and widows, It is good for them if they abide even as I. But if they cannot contain, let them marry: for it is better to marry than to burn. **Genesis 38:26:** And Judah acknowledged *them*, and said, She hath been more righteous than I; because that I gave her not to Shelah my son. And he knew her again no more.

[14] **Malachi 2:14-15:** Yet ye say, Wherefore? Because the LORD hath been witness between thee and the wife of thy youth, against whom thou hast dealt treacherously: yet *is* she thy companion, and the wife of thy covenant. And did not he make one? Yet had he the residue of the spirit. And wherefore one? That he might seek a godly seed. Therefore take heed to your spirit, and let none deal treacherously

against the wife of his youth. **Matthew 19:5:** And said, For this cause shall a man leave father and mother, and shall cleave to his wife: and they twain shall be one flesh …

[15] **Malachi 2:16:** For the LORD, the God of Israel, saith that he hateth putting away: for *one* covereth violence with his garment, saith the LORD of hosts: therefore take heed to your spirit, that ye deal not treacherously. **Matthew 5:32:** But I say unto you, That whosoever shall put away his wife, saving for the cause of fornication, causeth her to commit adultery: and whosoever shall marry her that is divorced committeth adultery.

[16] **1 Corinthians 7:12-13:** But to the rest speak I, not the Lord: If any brother hath a wife that believeth not, and she be pleased to dwell with him, let him not put her away. And the woman which hath an husband that believeth not, and if he be pleased to dwell with her, let her not leave him.

[17] **Ezekiel 16:49:** Behold, this was the iniquity of thy sister Sodom, pride, fulness of bread, and abundance of idleness was in her and in her daughters, neither did she strengthen the hand of the poor and needy. **Proverbs 23:30-33:** They that tarry long at the wine; they that go to seek mixed wine. Look not thou upon the wine when it is red, when it giveth his colour in the cup, *when* it moveth itself aright. At the last it biteth like a serpent, and stingeth like an adder. Thine eyes shall behold strange women, and thine heart shall utter perverse things.

[18] **Genesis 39:10:** And it came to pass, as she spake to Joseph day by day, that he hearkened not unto her, to lie by her, *or* to be with her. **Proverbs 5:8:** Remove thy way far from her, and come not nigh the door of her house …

[19] **Ephesians 5:4:** Neither filthiness, nor foolish talking, nor jesting, which are not convenient: but rather giving of thanks. **Ezekiel 23:14-16:** And *that* she increased her whoredoms: for when she saw men portrayed upon the wall, the images of the Chaldeans pourtrayed with vermilion, Girded with girdles upon their loins, exceeding in dyed attire upon their heads, all of them princes to look to, after the manner of the Babylonians of Chaldea, the land of their nativity: And as soon as she saw them with her eyes, she doted upon them, and sent messengers unto them into Chaldea. **Isaiah 23:15-17:** And it shall come to pass in that day, that Tyre shall be forgotten seventy years,

according to the days of one king: after the end of seventy years shall Tyre sing as an harlot. Take an harp, go about the city, thou harlot that hast been forgotten; make sweet melody, sing many songs, that thou mayest be remembered. And it shall come to pass after the end of seventy years, that the LORD will visit Tyre, and she shall turn to her hire, and shall commit fornication with all the kingdoms of the world upon the face of the earth. **Isaiah 3:16:** Moreover the LORD saith, Because the daughters of Zion are haughty, and walk with stretched forth necks and wanton eyes, walking and mincing as they go, and making a tinkling with their feet … **Mark 6:22:** And when the daughter of the said Herodias came in, and danced, and pleased Herod and them that sat with him, the king said unto the damsel, Ask of me whatsoever thou wilt, and I will give it thee. **Romans 13:13:** Let us walk honestly, as in the day; not in rioting and drunkenness, not in chambering and wantonness, not in strife and envying. **1 Peter 4:3:** For the time past of our life may suffice us to have wrought the will of the Gentiles, when we walked in lasciviousness, lusts, excess of wine, revellings, banquetings, and abominable idolatries.

[20] **2 Kings 9:30:** And when Jehu was come to Jezreel, Jezebel heard *of it*; and she painted her face, and tired her head, and looked out at a window. [Compare with] **Jeremiah 4:30:** And *when* thou *art* spoiled, what wilt thou do? Though thou clothest thyself with crimson, though thou deckest thee with ornaments of gold, though thou rentest thy face with painting, in vain shalt thou make thyself fair; thy lovers will despise thee, they will seek thy life. [And with] **Ezekiel 23:40:** And furthermore, that ye have sent for men to come from far, unto whom a messenger *was* sent; and, lo, they came: for whom thou didst wash thyself, paintedst thy eyes, and deckedst thyself with ornaments …

140. Which is the eighth commandment?

A. The eighth commandment is, *Thou shalt not steal.* [1]

Proof

[1] **Exodus 20:15:** Thou shalt not steal.

141. What are the duties required in the eighth commandment?

A. The duties required in the eighth commandment are, truth, faithfulness, and justice in contracts and commerce between man and man; [1] rendering to everyone his due; restitution of goods unlawfully detained from the right owners thereof; [2] giving and lending freely, according to our abilities, and the necessities of others; [3] moderation of our judgments, wills, and affections concerning worldly goods; [4] a provident care and study to get, [5] keep, use, and dispose these things which are necessary and convenient for the sustentation of our nature, and suitable to our condition; [6] a lawful calling, [7] and diligence in it; [8] frugality; [9] avoiding unnecessary lawsuits, [10] and suretiship, or other like engagements; [11] and an endeavour, by all just and lawful means, to procure, preserve, and further the wealth and outward estate of others, as well as our own. [12]

Proofs

[1] **Psalm 15:2, 4:** He that walketh uprightly, and worketh righteousness, and speaketh the truth in his heart ... In whose eyes a vile person is contemned; but he honoureth them that fear the Lord. *He that* sweareth to *his own* hurt, and changeth not. **Zechariah 7:4, 10:** Then came the word of the Lord of hosts unto me, saying ... And oppress not the widow, nor the fatherless, the stranger, nor the poor; and let none of you imagine evil against his brother in your heart. **Zechariah 8:16-17:** These *are* the things that ye shall do; Speak ye every man the truth to his neighbour; execute the judgment of truth and peace in your gates: And let none of you imagine evil in your hearts against his neighbour; and love no false oath: for all these *are things* that I hate, saith the Lord. **Romans 13:7:** Render therefore to all their dues: tribute to whom tribute *is due*; custom to whom custom; fear to whom fear; honour to whom honour.

[2] **Leviticus 6:2-5:** If a soul sin, and commit a trespass against the Lord, and lie unto his neighbour in that which was delivered him to keep, or in fellowship, or in a thing taken away by violence, or hath deceived his neighbour; Or have found that which was lost, and lieth concerning it, and sweareth falsely; in any of all these that a man doeth, sinning therein: Then it shall be, because he hath sinned, and is guilty, that he shall restore that which he took violently away, or the thing which he hath deceitfully gotten, or that which was delivered him to keep, or the lost thing which he found, Or all that about which he hath sworn falsely; he shall even restore it in the principal, and shall add the

fifth part more thereto, *and* give it unto him to whom it appertaineth, in the day of his trespass offering. [Compare with] **Luke 19:8:** And Zacchaeus stood, and said unto the Lord; Behold, Lord, the half of my goods I give to the poor; and if I have taken any thing from any man by false accusation, I restore *him* fourfold.

[3] **Luke 6:30, 38:** Give to every man that asketh of thee; and of him that taketh away thy goods ask *them* not again ... Give, and it shall be given unto you; good measure, pressed down, and shaken together, and running over, shall men give into your bosom. For with the same measure that ye mete withal it shall be measured to you again. **1 John 3:17:** But whoso hath this world's good, and seeth his brother have need, and shutteth up his bowels *of compassion* from him, how dwelleth the love of God in him? **Ephesians 4:28:** Let him that stole steal no more: but rather let him labour, working with *his* hands the thing which is good, that he may have to give to him that needeth. **Galatians 6:10:** As we have therefore opportunity, let us do good unto all *men*, especially unto them who are of the household of faith.

[4] **1 Timothy 6:6-9:** But godliness with contentment is great gain. For we brought nothing into *this* world, *and it is* certain we can carry nothing out. And having food and raiment let us be therewith content. But they that will be rich fall into temptation and a snare, and *into* many foolish and hurtful lusts, which drown men in destruction and perdition. **Galatians 6:14:** But God forbid that I should glory, save in the cross of our Lord Jesus Christ, by whom the world is crucified unto me, and I unto the world.

[5] **1 Timothy 5:8:** But if any provide not for his own, and specially for those of his own house, he hath denied the faith, and is worse than an infidel.

[6] **Proverbs 27:23-27:** Be thou diligent to know the state of thy flocks, *and* look well to thy herds. For riches are not for ever: and doth the crown *endure* to every generation? The hay appeareth, and the tender grass sheweth itself, and herbs of the mountains are gathered. The lambs *are* for thy clothing, and the goats *are* the price of the field. And *thou shalt have* goats' milk enough for thy food, for the food of thy household, and *for* the maintenance for thy maidens. **Ecclesiastes 2:24:** *There is* nothing better for a man, *than* that he should eat and drink, and *that* he should make his soul enjoy good in his labour. This also I saw, that it

was from the hand of God. **Ecclesiastes 3:12-13:** I know that *there is* no good in them, but for *a man* to rejoice, and to do good in his life. And also that every man should eat and drink, and enjoy the good of all his labour, it *is* the gift of God. **1 Timothy 6:17-18:** Charge them that are rich in this world, that they be not highminded, nor trust in uncertain riches, but in the living God, who giveth us richly all things to enjoy; That they do good, that they be rich in good works, ready to distribute, willing to communicate ... **Isaiah 38:1:** In those days was Hezekiah sick unto death. And Isaiah the prophet the son of Amoz came unto him, and said unto him, Thus saith the LORD, Set thine house in order: for thou shalt die, and not live. **Matthew 11:8:** But what went ye out for to see? A man clothed in soft raiment? behold, they that wear soft *clothing* are in kings' houses.

[7] **1 Corinthians 7:20:** Let every man abide in the same calling wherein he was called. **Genesis 2:15:** And the LORD God took the man, and put him into the garden of Eden to dress it and to keep it. **Genesis 3:19:** In the sweat of thy face shalt thou eat bread, till thou return unto the ground; for out of it wast thou taken: for dust thou *art*, and unto dust shalt thou return.

[8] **Ephesians 4:28:** Let him that stole steal no more: but rather let him labour, working with *his* hands the thing which is good, that he may have to give to him that needeth. **Proverbs 10:4:** He becometh poor that dealeth *with* a slack hand: but the hand of the diligent maketh rich.

[9] **John 6:12:** When they were filled, he said unto his disciples, Gather up the fragments that remain, that nothing be lost. **Proverbs 21:20:** *There is* treasure to be desired and oil in the dwelling of the wise; but a foolish man spendeth it up.

[10] **1 Corinthians 6:1-9:** Dare any of you, having a matter against another, go to law before the unjust, and not before the saints? Do ye not know that the saints shall judge the world? and if the world shall be judged by you, are ye unworthy to judge the smallest matters? Know ye not that we shall judge angels? how much more things that pertain to this life? If then ye have judgments of things pertaining to this life, set them to judge who are least esteemed in the church. I speak to your shame. Is it so, that there is not a wise man among you? no, not one that shall be able to judge between his brethren? But brother goeth to law with brother, and that before the unbelievers. Now therefore there is utterly a fault among you, because ye go to law one with another. Why

do ye not rather take wrong? why do ye not rather *suffer yourselves* to be defrauded? Nay, ye do wrong, and defraud, and that *your* brethren. Know ye not that the unrighteous shall not inherit the kingdom of God? Be not deceived: neither fornicators, nor idolaters, nor adulterers, nor effeminate, nor abusers of themselves with mankind …

[11] **Proverbs 6:1-6:** My son, if thou be surety for thy friend, if thou hast stricken thy hand with a stranger, Thou art snared with the words of thy mouth, thou art taken with the words of thy mouth. Do this now, my son, and deliver thyself, when thou art come into the hand of thy friend; go, humble thyself, and make sure thy friend. Give not sleep to thine eyes, nor slumber to thine eyelids. Deliver thyself as a roe from the hand *of the hunter*, and as a bird from the hand of the fowler. Go to the ant, thou sluggard; consider her ways, and be wise … **Proverbs 11:15:** He that is surety for a stranger shall smart *for it*: and he that hateth suretiship is sure.

[12] **Leviticus 25:35:** And if thy brother be waxen poor, and fallen in decay with thee; then thou shalt relieve him: *yea, though he be* a stranger, or a sojourner; that he may live with thee. **Deuteronomy 22:1-4:** Thou shalt not see thy brother's ox or his sheep go astray, and hide thyself from them: thou shalt in any case bring them again unto thy brother. And if thy brother *be* not nigh unto thee, or if thou know him not, then thou shalt bring it unto thine own house, and it shall be with thee until thy brother seek after it, and thou shalt restore it to him again. In like manner shalt thou do with his ass; and so shalt thou do with his raiment; and with all lost thing of thy brother's, which he hath lost, and thou hast found, shalt thou do likewise: thou mayest not hide thyself. Thou shalt not see thy brother's ass or his ox fall down by the way, and hide thyself from them: thou shalt surely help him to lift *them* up again. **Exodus 23:4-5:** If thou meet thine enemy's ox or his ass going astray, thou shalt surely bring it back to him again. If thou see the ass of him that hateth thee lying under his burden, and wouldest forbear to help him, thou shalt surely help with him. **Genesis 47:14, 20:** And Joseph gathered up all the money that was found in the land of Egypt, and in the land of Canaan, for the corn which they bought: and Joseph brought the money into Pharaoh's house … And Joseph bought all the land of Egypt for Pharaoh; for the Egyptians sold every man his field, because the famine prevailed over them: so the land became Pharaoh's. **Philippians 2:4:** Look not every man on his own things, but every

man also on the things of others. **Matthew 22:39:** And the second *is* like unto it, Thou shalt love thy neighbour as thyself.

142. What are the sins forbidden in the eighth commandment

A. The sins forbidden in the eighth commandment, besides the neglect of the duties required, [1] are, theft, [2]robbery, [3] man-stealing, [4] and receiving any thing that is stolen; [5] fraudulent dealing, [6] false weights and measures, [7] removing landmarks, [8] injustice and unfaithfulness in contracts between man and man, [9] or in matters of trust; [10] oppression, [11] extortion, [12] usury, [13] bribery, [14] vexatious lawsuits, [15] unjust inclosures and depopulations; [16] ingrossing commodities to enhance the price: [17] unlawful callings, [18] and all other unjust or sinful ways of taking or withholding from our neighbour what belongs to him, or of enriching ourselves; [19] covetousness; [20] inordinate prizing and affecting worldly goods; [21] distrustful and distracting cares and studies in getting, keeping, and using them; [22] envying at the prosperity of others; [23] as likewise idleness, [24] prodigality, wasteful gaming; and all other ways whereby we do unduly prejudice our own outward estate, [25] and defrauding ourselves of the due use and comfort of that estate which God hath given us. [26]

Proofs

[1] **James 2:15-16:** If a brother or sister be naked, and destitute of daily food, And one of you say unto them, Depart in peace, be *ye* warmed and filled; notwithstanding ye give them not those things which are needful to the body; what *doth it* profit? **1 John 3:17:** But whoso hath this world's good, and seeth his brother have need, and shutteth up his bowels *of compassion* from him, how dwelleth the love of God in him?

[2] **Ephesians 4:28:** Let him that stole steal no more: but rather let him labour, working with *his* hands the thing which is good, that he may have to give to him that needeth.

[3] **Psalm 62:10:** Trust not in oppression, and become not vain in robbery: if riches increase, set not your heart *upon them*.

[4] **1 Timothy 1:10:** For whoremongers, for them that defile themselves with mankind, for menstealers, for liars, for perjured persons, and if there be any other thing that is contrary to sound doctrine …

[5] **Proverbs 29:24:** Whoso is partner with a thief hateth his own soul: he heareth cursing, and bewrayeth *it* not. **Psalm 50:18:** When thou sawest a thief, then thou consentedst with him, and hast been partaker with adulterers.

[6] **1 Thessalonians 4:6:** That no *man* go beyond and defraud his brother in *any* matter: because that the Lord *is* the avenger of all such, as we also have forewarned you and testified.

[7] **Proverbs 11:1:** A false balance *is* abomination to the LORD: but a just weight *is* his delight. **Proverbs 20:10:** Divers weights, *and* divers measures, both of them *are* alike abomination to the LORD.

[8] **Deuteronomy 19:14:** Thou shalt not remove thy neighbour's landmark, which they of old time have set in thine inheritance, which thou shalt inherit in the land that the LORD thy God giveth thee to possess it. **Proverbs 23:10:** Remove not the old landmark; and enter not into the fields of the fatherless …

[9] **Amos 8:5:** Saying, When will the new moon be gone, that we may sell corn? and the sabbath, that we may set forth wheat, making the ephah small, and the shekel great, and falsifying the balances by deceit? **Psalm 37:21:** The wicked borroweth, and payeth not again: but the righteous sheweth mercy, and giveth.

[10] **Luke 16:10-12:** He that is faithful in that which is least is faithful also in much: and he that is unjust in the least is unjust also in much. If therefore ye have not been faithful in the unrighteous mammon, who will commit to your trust the true *riches*? And if ye have not been faithful in that which is another man's, who shall give you that which is your own?

[11] **Ezekiel 22:29:** The people of the land have used oppression, and exercised robbery, and have vexed the poor and needy: yea, they have oppressed the stranger wrongfully. **Leviticus 25:17:** Ye shall not therefore oppress one another; but thou shalt fear thy God: for I *am* the LORD your God.

[12] **Matthew 23:25:** Woe unto you, scribes and Pharisees, hypocrites! for ye make clean the outside of the cup and of the platter, but within they are full of extortion and excess. **Ezekiel 22:12:** In thee have they

taken gifts to shed blood; thou hast taken usury and increase, and thou hast greedily gained of thy neighbours by extortion, and hast forgotten me, saith the Lord GOD.

[13] **Psalm 15:5:** *He that* putteth not out his money to usury, nor taketh reward against the innocent. He that doeth these *things* shall never be moved.

[14] **Job 15:34:** For the congregation of hypocrites *shall be* desolate, and fire shall consume the tabernacles of bribery.

[15] **1 Corinthians 6:6-8:** But brother goeth to law with brother, and that before the unbelievers. Now therefore there is utterly a fault among you, because ye go to law one with another. Why do ye not rather take wrong? why do ye not rather *suffer yourselves to* be defrauded? Nay, ye do wrong, and defraud, and that *your* brethren. **Proverbs 3:29-30:** Devise not evil against thy neighbour, seeing he dwelleth securely by thee. Strive not with a man without cause, if he have done thee no harm.

[16] **Isaiah 5:8:** Woe unto them that join house to house, that lay field to field, till *there be* no place, that they may be placed alone in the midst of the earth! **Micah 2:2:** And they covet fields, and take *them* by violence; and houses, and take *them* away: so they oppress a man and his house, even a man and his heritage.

[17] **Proverbs 11:26:** He that withholdeth corn, the people shall curse him: but blessing *shall be* upon the head of him that selleth *it*.

[18] **Acts 19:19, 24-25:** Many of them also which used curious arts brought their books together, and burned them before all *men*: and they counted the price of them, and found *it* fifty thousand *pieces* of silver ... For a certain *man* named Demetrius, a silversmith, which made silver shrines for Diana, brought no small gain unto the craftsmen; Whom he called together with the workmen of like occupation, and said, Sirs, ye know that by this craft we have our wealth.

[19] **Job 20:19:** Because he hath oppressed *and* hath forsaken the poor; *because* he hath violently taken away an house which he builded not ... **James 5:4:** Behold, the hire of the labourers who have reaped down your fields, which is of you kept back by fraud, crieth: and the cries of them which have reaped are entered into the ears of the Lord of sabaoth. **Proverbs 21:6:** The getting of treasures by a lying tongue *is* a vanity tossed to and fro of them that seek death.

[20] **Luke 12:15:** And he said unto them, Take heed, and beware of covetousness: for a man's life consisteth not in the abundance of the things which he possesseth.

[21] **1 Timothy 6:5:** Perverse disputings of men of corrupt minds, and destitute of the truth, supposing that gain is godliness: from such withdraw thyself. **Colossians 3:2:** Set your affection on things above, not on things on the earth. **Proverbs 23:5:** Wilt thou set thine eyes upon that which is not? for *riches* certainly make themselves wings; they fly away as an eagle toward heaven. **Psalm 62:10:** Trust not in oppression, and become not vain in robbery: if riches increase, set not your heart *upon them*.

[22] **Matthew 6:25, 31, 34:** Therefore I say unto you, Take no thought for your life, what ye shall eat, or what ye shall drink; nor yet for your body, what ye shall put on. Is not the life more than meat, and the body than raiment? … Therefore take no thought, saying, What shall we eat? or, What shall we drink? or, Wherewithal shall we be clothed? … Take therefore no thought for the morrow: for the morrow shall take thought for the things of itself. Sufficient unto the day *is* the evil thereof. **Ecclesiastes 5:12:** The sleep of a labouring man *is* sweet, whether he eat little or much: but the abundance of the rich will not suffer him to sleep.

[23] **Psalm 73:3:** For I was envious at the foolish, *when* I saw the prosperity of the wicked. **Psalm 37:1, 7:** Fret not thyself because of evildoers, neither be thou envious against the workers of iniquity … Rest in the Lord, and wait patiently for him: fret not thyself because of him who prospereth in his way, because of the man who bringeth wicked devices to pass.

[24] **2 Thessalonians 3:11:** For we hear that there are some which walk among you disorderly, working not at all, but are busybodies. **Proverbs 18:9:** He also that is slothful in his work is brother to him that is a great waster.

[25] **Proverbs 21:17:** He that loveth pleasure *shall be* a poor man: he that loveth wine and oil shall not be rich. **Proverbs 23:20-21:** Be not among winebibbers; among riotous eaters of flesh: For the drunkard and the glutton shall come to poverty: and drowsiness shall clothe *a man* with rags. **Proverbs 28:19:** He that tilleth his land shall have plenty of bread: but he that followeth after vain *persons* shall have poverty enough.

[26] **Ecclesiastes 4:8:** There is one *alone*, and *there is* not a second; yea, he hath neither child nor brother: yet *is there* no end of all his labour; neither is his eye satisfied with riches; neither *saith he*, For whom do I labour, and bereave my soul of good? This *is* also vanity, yea, it *is* a sore travail. **Ecclesiastes 6:2:** A man to whom God hath given riches, wealth, and honour, so that he wanteth nothing for his soul of all that he desireth, yet God giveth him not power to eat thereof, but a stranger eateth it: this *is* vanity, and it *is* an evil disease. **1 Timothy 5:8:** But if any provide not for his own, and specially for those of his own house, he hath denied the faith, and is worse than an infidel.

143. Which is the ninth commandment?

A. The ninth commandment is, *Thou shalt not bear false witness against thy neighbour.* [1]

Proof

[1] **Exodus 20:16:** Thou shalt not bear false witness against thy neighbour.

144. What are the duties required in the ninth commandment?

A. The duties required in the ninth commandment are, the preserving and promoting of truth between man and man, [1] and the good name of our neighbour, as well as our own; [2] appearing and standing for the truth; [3]and from the heart, [4] sincerely, [5] freely, [6] clearly, [7] and fully, [8] speaking the truth, and only the truth, in matters of judgment and justice, [9] and in all other things whatsoever; [10] a charitable esteem of our neighbours; [11] loving, desiring, and rejoicing in their good name; [12] sorrowing for, [13] and covering of their infirmities; [14] freely acknowledging of their gifts and graces, [15] defending their innocency; [16] a ready receiving of a good report, [17] and unwillingness to admit of an evil report, [18] concerning them; discouraging tale-bearers, [19] flatterers, [20] and slanderers; [21] love and care of our own good name, and defending it when need requireth; [22] keeping of lawful promises; [23] studying and practising of whatsoever things are true, honest, lovely, and of good report. [24]

Proofs

[1] **Zechariah 8:16:** These *are* the things that ye shall do; Speak ye every man the truth to his neighbour; execute the judgment of truth and peace in your gates …

[2] **3 John 12:** Demetrius hath good report of all *men*, and of the truth itself: yea, and we *also* bear record; and ye know that our record is true.

[3] **Proverbs 31:8-9:** Open thy mouth for the dumb in the cause of all such as are appointed to destruction. Open thy mouth, judge righteously, and plead the cause of the poor and needy.

[4] **Psalm 15:2:** He that walketh uprightly, and worketh righteousness, and speaketh the truth in his heart.

[5] **2 Chronicles 19:9:** And he charged them, saying, Thus shall ye do in the fear of the LORD, faithfully, and with a perfect heart.

[6] **1 Samuel 19:4-5:** And Jonathan spake good of David unto Saul his father, and said unto him, Let not the king sin against his servant, against David; because he hath not sinned against thee, and because his works *have been* to thee-ward very good: For he did put his life in his hand, and slew the Philistine, and the LORD wrought a great salvation for all Israel: thou sawest *it*, and didst rejoice: wherefore then wilt thou sin against innocent blood, to slay David without a cause?

[7] **Joshua 7:19:** And Joshua said unto Achan, My son, give, I pray thee, glory to the LORD God of Israel, and make confession unto him; and tell me now what thou hast done; hide *it* not from me.

[8] **2 Samuel 14:18-20:** Then the king answered and said unto the woman, Hide not from me, I pray thee, the thing that I shall ask thee. And the woman said, Let my lord the king now speak. And the king said, *Is not* the hand of Joab with thee in all this? And the woman answered and said, *As* thy soul liveth, my lord the king, none can turn to the right hand or to the left from ought that my lord the king hath spoken: for thy servant Joab, he bade me, and he put all these words in the mouth of thine handmaid: To fetch about this form of speech hath thy servant Joab done this thing: and my lord *is* wise, according to the wisdom of an angel of God, to know all *things* that *are* in the earth.

[9] **Leviticus 19:15:** Ye shall do no unrighteousness in judgment: thou shalt not respect the person of the poor, nor honour the person of the mighty: *but* in righteousness shalt thou judge thy neighbour.

Proverbs 14:5, 25: A faithful witness will not lie: but a false witness will utter lies … A true witness delivereth souls: but a deceitful *witness* speaketh lies.

[10] **2 Corinthians 1:17-18:** When I therefore was thus minded, did I use lightness? or the things that I purpose, do I purpose according to the flesh, that with me there should be yea yea, and nay nay? But *as* God *is* true, our word toward you was not yea and nay. **Ephesians 4:25:** Wherefore putting away lying, speak every man truth with his neighbour: for we are members one of another.

[11] **Hebrews 6:9:** But, beloved, we are persuaded better things of you, and things that accompany salvation, though we thus speak. **1 Corinthians 13:7:** Beareth all things, believeth all things, hopeth all things, endureth all things.

[12] **Romans 1:8:** First, I thank my God through Jesus Christ for you all, that your faith is spoken of throughout the whole world. **2 John 4:** I rejoiced greatly that I found of thy children walking in truth, as we have received a commandment from the Father. **3 John 3-4:** For I rejoiced greatly, when the brethren came and testified of the truth that is in thee, even as thou walkest in the truth. I have no greater joy than to hear that my children walk in truth.

[13] **2 Corinthians 2:4:** For out of much affliction and anguish of heart I wrote unto you with many tears; not that ye should be grieved, but that ye might know the love which I have more abundantly unto you. **2 Corinthians 12:21:** *And* lest, when I come again, my God will humble me among you, and *that* I shall bewail many which have sinned already, and have not repented of the uncleanness and fornication and lasciviousness which they have committed.

[14] **Proverbs 17:9:** He that covereth a transgression seeketh love; but he that repeateth a matter separateth *very* friends. **1 Peter 4:8:** And above all things have fervent charity among yourselves: for charity shall cover the multitude of sins.

[15] **1 Corinthians 1:4-5, 7:** I thank my God always on your behalf, for the grace of God which is given you by Jesus Christ; That in every thing ye are enriched by him, in all utterance, and *in* all knowledge … So that ye come behind in no gift; waiting for the coming of our Lord Jesus Christ … **2 Timothy 1:4-5:** Greatly desiring to see thee, being mindful of thy tears, that I may be filled with joy; When I call to remembrance

the unfeigned faith that is in thee, which dwelt first in thy grandmother Lois, and thy mother Eunice; and I am persuaded that in thee also.

[16] **1 Samuel 22:14:** Then Ahimelech answered the king, and said, And who *is so* faithful among all thy servants as David, which is the king's son in law, and goeth at thy bidding, and is honourable in thine house?

[17] **1 Corinthians 13:6-7:** Rejoiceth not in iniquity, but rejoiceth in the truth; Beareth all things, believeth all things, hopeth all things, endureth all things.

[18] **Psalm 15:3:** *He that* backbiteth not with his tongue, nor doeth evil to his neighbour, nor taketh up a reproach against his neighbour.

[19] **Proverbs 25:23:** The north wind driveth away rain: so *doth* an angry countenance a backbiting tongue.

[20] **Proverbs 26:24-25:** He that hateth dissembleth with his lips, and layeth up deceit within him; When he speaketh fair, believe him not: for *there are* seven abominations in his heart.

[21] **Psalm 101:5:**Whoso privily slandereth his neighbour, him will I cut off: him that hath an high look and a proud heart will not I suffer.

[22] **Proverbs 22:1:** A *good* name *is* rather to be chosen than great riches, *and* loving favour rather than silver and gold. **John 8:49:** Jesus answered, I have not a devil; but I honour my Father, and ye do dishonour me.

[23] **Psalm 15:4:** In whose eyes a vile person is contemned; but he honoureth them that fear the LORD. *He that* sweareth to *his own* hurt, and changeth not.

[24] **Philippians 4:8:** Finally, brethren, whatsoever things are true, whatsoever things *are* honest, whatsoever things *are* just, whatsoever things *are* pure, whatsoever things *are* lovely, whatsoever things *are* of good report; if *there be* any virtue, and if *there be* any praise, think on these things.

145. What are the sins forbidden in the ninth commandment?

A. The sins forbidden in the ninth commandment are, all prejudicing the truth, and the good name of our neighbours, as well as our own, [1] especially in public judicature; [2] giving false evidence, [3] suborning false witnesses, [4] wittingly appearing and pleading for an evil cause, outfacing and overbearing the truth; [5] passing unjust sentence, [6] calling evil good, and good evil; rewarding the wicked according to the work of the righteous, and the righteous according to the work of the wicked; [7] forgery, [8] concealing the truth, undue silence in a just cause, [9] and holding our peace when iniquity calleth for either a reproof from ourselves, [10] or complaint to others; [11] speaking the truth unseasonably, [12] or maliciously to a wrong end, [13] or perverting it to a wrong meaning, [14] or in doubtful and equivocal expressions, to the prejudice of truth or justice; [15] speaking untruth, [16] lying, [17] slandering, [18] backbiting, [19] detracting, tale bearing, [20] whispering, [21] scoffing, [22] reviling, [23] rash, [24] harsh, [25] and partial censuring; [26] misconstructing intentions, words, and actions; [27] flattering, [28] vain-glorious boasting; [29] thinking or speaking too highly or too meanly of ourselves or others; [30] denying the gifts and graces of God; [31] aggravating smaller faults; [32] hiding, excusing, or extenuating of sins, when called to a free confession; [33] unnecessary discovering of infirmities; [34] raising false rumours, [35] receiving and countenancing evil reports, [36] and stopping our ears against just defence; [37] evil suspicion; [38] envying or grieving at the deserved credit of any, [39] endeavouring or desiring to impair it, [40] rejoicing in their disgrace and infamy; [41] scornful contempt, [42] fond admiration; [43] breach of lawful promises; [44] neglecting such things as are of good report, [45] and practising, or not avoiding ourselves, or not hindering what we can in others, such things as procure an ill name. [46]

Proofs

[1] **1 Samuel 17:28:** And Eliab his eldest brother heard when he spake unto the men; and Eliab's anger was kindled against David, and he said, Why camest thou down hither? and with whom hast thou left those few sheep in the wilderness? I know thy pride, and the naughtiness of thine heart; for thou art come down that thou mightest see the battle.

2 Samuel 16:3: And the king said, And where *is* thy master's son? And Ziba said unto the king, Behold, he abideth at Jerusalem: for he said, To day shall the house of Israel restore me the kingdom of my father. **2 Samuel 1:9-10, 15-16:** He said unto me again, Stand, I pray thee, upon me, and slay me: for anguish is come upon me, because my life is yet whole in me. So I stood upon him, and slew him, because I was sure that he could not live after that he was fallen: and I took the crown that *was* upon his head, and the bracelet that *was* on his arm, and have brought them hither unto my lord ... And David called one of the young men, and said, Go near, *and* fall upon him. And he smote him that he died. And David said unto him, Thy blood *be* upon thy head; for thy mouth hath testified against thee, saying, I have slain the LORD's anointed.

[2] **Leviticus 19:15:** Ye shall do no unrighteousness in judgment: thou shalt not respect the person of the poor, nor honour the person of the mighty: *but* in righteousness shalt thou judge thy neighbour. **Habakkuk 1:4:** Therefore the law is slacked, and judgment doth never go forth: for the wicked doth compass about the righteous; therefore wrong judgment proceedeth.

[3] **Proverbs 19:5:** A false witness shall not be unpunished, and *he that* speaketh lies shall not escape. **Proverbs 6:16, 19:** These six *things* doth the LORD hate: yea, seven *are* an abomination unto him ... A false witness *that* speaketh lies, and he that soweth discord among brethren.

[4] **Acts 6:13:** And set up false witnesses, which said, This man ceaseth not to speak blasphemous words against this holy place, and the law ...

[5] **Jeremiah 9:3, 5:** And they bend their tongues like their bow for lies: but they are not valiant for the truth upon the earth; for they proceed from evil to evil, and they know not me, saith the LORD ... And they will deceive every one his neighbour, and will not speak the truth: they have taught their tongue to speak lies, *and* weary themselves to commit iniquity. **Acts 24:2, 5:** And when he was called forth, Tertullus began to accuse *him*, saying, Seeing that by thee we enjoy great quietness, and that very worthy deeds are done unto this nation by thy providence ... For we have found this man a pestilent *fellow*, and a mover of sedition among all the Jews throughout the world, and a ringleader of the sect of the Nazarenes ... **Psalm 12:3-4:** The LORD shall cut off all flattering lips, *and* the tongue that speaketh proud things: Who

have said, With our tongue will we prevail; our lips *are* our own: who *is* lord over us? **Psalm 52:1-4:** Why boastest thou thyself in mischief, O mighty man? the goodness of God *endureth* continually. Thy tongue deviseth mischiefs; like a sharp razor, working deceitfully. Thou lovest evil more than good; *and* lying rather than to speak righteousness. Selah. Thou lovest all devouring words, O *thou* deceitful tongue.

[6] **Proverbs 17:15:** He that justifieth the wicked, and he that condemneth the just, even they both *are* abomination to the LORD. **1 Kings 21:9-14:** And she wrote in the letters, saying, Proclaim a fast, and set Naboth on high among the people: And set two men, sons of Belial, before him, to bear witness against him, saying, Thou didst blaspheme God and the king. And *then* carry him out, and stone him, that he may die. And the men of his city, *even* the elders and the nobles who were the inhabitants in his city, did as Jezebel had sent unto them, *and* as it *was* written in the letters which she had sent unto them. They proclaimed a fast, and set Naboth on high among the people. And there came in two men, children of Belial, and sat before him: and the men of Belial witnessed against him, *even* against Naboth, in the presence of the people, saying, Naboth did blaspheme God and the king. Then they carried him forth out of the city, and stoned him with stones, that he died. Then they sent to Jezebel, saying, Naboth is stoned, and is dead.

[7] **Isaiah 5:23:** Which justify the wicked for reward, and take away the righteousness of the righteous from him!

[8] **Psalm 119:69:** The proud have forged a lie against me: *but* I will keep thy precepts with *my* whole heart. **Luke 19:8:** And Zacchaeus stood, and said unto the Lord; Behold, Lord, the half of my goods I give to the poor; and if I have taken any thing from any man by false accusation, I restore *him* fourfold. **Luke 16:5-7:** So he called every one of his lord's debtors *unto him*, and said unto the first, How much owest thou unto my lord? And he said, An hundred measures of oil. And he said unto him, Take thy bill, and sit down quickly, and write fifty. Then said he to another, And how much owest thou? And he said, An hundred measures of wheat. And he said unto him, Take thy bill, and write fourscore.

[9] **Leviticus 5:1:** And if a soul sin, and hear the voice of swearing, and *is* a witness, whether he hath seen or known *of it*; if he do not utter *it*, then he shall bear his iniquity. **Deuteronomy 13:8:** Thou

shalt not consent unto him, nor hearken unto him; neither shall thine eye pity him, neither shalt thou spare, neither shalt thou conceal him ... **Acts 5:3, 8-9:** But Peter said, Ananias, why hath Satan filled thine heart to lie to the Holy Ghost, and to keep back *part* of the price of the land? ... And Peter answered unto her, Tell me whether ye sold the land for so much? And she said, Yea, for so much. Then Peter said unto her, How is it that ye have agreed together to tempt the Spirit of the Lord? behold, the feet of them which have buried thy husband *are* at the door, and shall carry thee out. **2 Timothy 4:16:** At my first answer no man stood with me, but all *men* forsook me: *I pray God* that it may not be laid to their charge.

[10] **1 Kings 1:6:** And his father had not displeased him at any time in saying, Why hast thou done so? and he also *was a* very goodly *man*; and *his mother* bare him after Absalom.**Leviticus 19:17:** Thou shalt not hate thy brother in thine heart: thou shalt in any wise rebuke thy neighbour, and not suffer sin upon him.

[11] **Isaiah 59:4:** None calleth for justice, nor *any* pleadeth for truth: they trust in vanity, and speak lies; they conceive mischief, and bring forth iniquity.

[12] **Proverbs 29:11:** A fool uttereth all his mind: but a wise *man* keepeth it in till afterwards.

[13] **1 Samuel 22:9-10:** Then answered Doeg the Edomite, which was set over the servants of Saul, and said, I saw the son of Jesse coming to Nob, to Ahimelech the son of Ahitub. And he inquired of the Lord for him and gave him victuals, and gave him the sword of Goliath the Philistine. [Compare with] **Psalm 52:1-5:** Why boastest thou thyself in mischief, O mighty man? the goodness of God *endureth* continually. Thy tongue deviseth mischiefs; like a sharp razor, working deceitfully. Thou lovest evil more than good; *and* lying rather than to speak righteousness. Selah. Thou lovest all devouring words, O *thou* deceitful tongue. God shall likewise destroy thee for ever, he shall take thee away, and pluck thee out of *thy* dwelling place, and root thee out of the land of the living. Selah.

[14] **Psalm 56:5:** Every day they wrest my words: all their thoughts *are* against me for evil. **John 2:19:** Jesus answered and said unto them, Destroy this temple, and in three days I will raise it up. [Compare with] **Matthew 26:60-61:** But found none: yea, though many false witnesses

came, *yet* found they none. At the last came two false witnesses, And said, This *fellow* said, I am able to destroy the temple of God, and to build it in three days.

[15] **Genesis 3:5:** For God doth know that in the day ye eat thereof, then your eyes shall be opened, and ye shall be as gods, knowing good and evil. **Genesis 26:7, 9:** And the men of the place asked *him* of his wife; and he said, She *is* my sister: for he feared to say, *She is* my wife; lest, *said he*, the men of the place should kill me for Rebekah; because she *was* fair to look upon … And Abimelech called Isaac, and said, Behold, of a surety she *is* thy wife: and how saidst thou, She *is* my sister? And Isaac said unto him, Because I said, Lest I die for her.

[16] **Isaiah 59:13:** In transgressing and lying against the LORD, and departing away from our God, speaking oppression and revolt, conceiving and uttering from the heart words of falsehood.

[17] **Leviticus 19:11:** Ye shall not steal, neither deal falsely, neither lie one to another. **Colossians 3:9:** Lie not one to another, seeing that ye have put off the old man with his deeds …

[18] **Psalm 50:20:** Thou sittest *and* speakest against thy brother; thou slanderest thine own mother's son.

[19] **Psalm 15:3:** *He that* backbiteth not with his tongue, nor doeth evil to his neighbour, nor taketh up a reproach against his neighbour. **James 4:11:** Speak not evil one of another, brethren. He that speaketh evil of *his* brother, and judgeth his brother, speaketh evil of the law, and judgeth the law: but if thou judge the law, thou art not a doer of the law, but a judge. **Jeremiah 38:4:** Therefore the princes said unto the king, We beseech thee, let this man be put to death: for thus he weakeneth the hands of the men of war that remain in this city, and the hands of all the people, in speaking such words unto them: for this man seeketh not the welfare of this people, but the hurt.

[20] **Leviticus 19:16:** Thou shalt not go up and down *as* a talebearer among thy people: neither shalt thou stand against the blood of thy neighbour: I *am* the LORD.

[21] **Romans 1:29-30:** Being filled with all unrighteousness, fornication, wickedness, covetousness, maliciousness; full of envy, murder, debate, deceit, malignity; whisperers, Backbiters, haters of God, despiteful, proud, boasters, inventors of evil things, disobedient to parents …

[22] **Genesis 21:9:** And Sarah saw the son of Hagar the Egyptian, which she had born unto Abraham, mocking. **Galatians 4:29:** But as then he that was born after the flesh persecuted him *that was* born after the Spirit, even so *it is* now.

[23] **1 Corinthians 6:10:** Nor thieves, nor covetous, nor drunkards, nor revilers, nor extortioners, shall inherit the kingdom of God.

[24] **Matthew 7:1:** Judge not, that ye be not judged.

[25] **Acts 28:4:** And when the barbarians saw the *venomous* beast hang on his hand, they said among themselves, No doubt this man is a murderer, whom, though he hath escaped the sea, yet vengeance suffereth not to live.

[26] **Genesis 38:24:** And it came to pass about three months after, that it was told Judah, saying, Tamar thy daughter in law hath played the harlot; and also, behold, she *is* with child by whoredom. And Judah said, Bring her forth, and let her be burnt. **Romans 2:1:** Therefore thou art inexcusable, O man, whosoever thou art that judgest: for wherein thou judgest another, thou condemnest thyself; for thou that judgest doest the same things.

[27] **Nehemiah 6:6-8:** Wherein *was* written, It is reported among the heathen, and Gashmu saith *it, that* thou and the Jews think to rebel: for which cause thou buildest the wall, that thou mayest be their king, according to these words. And thou hast also appointed prophets to preach of thee at Jerusalem, saying, *There is* a king in Judah: and now shall it be reported to the king according to these words. Come now therefore, and let us take counsel together. Then I sent unto him, saying, There are no such things done as thou sayest, but thou feignest them out of thine own heart. **Romans 3:8:** And not *rather*, (as we be slanderously reported, and as some affirm that we say,) Let us do evil, that good may come? whose damnation is just. **Psalm 69:10:** When I wept, *and chastened* my soul with fasting, that was to my reproach. **1 Samuel 1:13-15:** Now Hannah, she spake in her heart; only her lips moved, but her voice was not heard: therefore Eli thought she had been drunken. And Eli said unto her, How long wilt thou be drunken? put away thy wine from thee. And Hannah answered and said, No, my lord, I *am* a woman of a sorrowful spirit: I have drunk neither wine nor strong drink, but have poured out my soul before the LORD. **2 Samuel 10:3:** And the princes of the children

of Ammon said unto Hanun their lord, Thinkest thou that David doth honour thy father, that he hath sent comforters unto thee? hath not David *rather* sent his servants unto thee to search the city, and to spy it out, and to overthrow it?

[28] **Psalm 12:2-3:** They speak vanity every one with his neighbour: *with* flattering lips *and* with a double heart do they speak. The LORD shall cut off all flattering lips, *and* the tongue that speaketh proud things ...

[29] **2 Timothy 3:2:** For men shall be lovers of their own selves, covetous, boasters, proud, blasphemers, disobedient to parents, unthankful, unholy ...

[30] **Luke 18:9, 11:** And he spake this parable unto certain which trusted in themselves that they were righteous, and despised others ... The Pharisee stood and prayed thus with himself, God, I thank thee, that I am not as other men *are*, extortioners, unjust, adulterers, or even as this publican. **Romans 12:16:** *Be* of the same mind one toward another. Mind not high things, but condescend to men of low estate. Be not wise in your own conceits. **1 Corinthians 4:6:** And these things, brethren, I have in a figure transferred to myself and *to* Apollos for your sakes; that ye might learn in us not to think *of men* above that which is written, that no one of you be puffed up for one against another. **Acts 12:22:** And the people gave a shout, *saying, It is* the voice of a god, and not of a man. **Exodus 4:10-14:** And Moses said unto the LORD, O my Lord, I *am* not eloquent, neither heretofore, nor since thou hast spoken unto thy servant: but I *am* slow of speech, and of a slow tongue. And the LORD said unto him, Who hath made man's mouth? or who maketh the dumb, or deaf, or the seeing, or the blind? have not I the LORD? Now therefore go, and I will be with thy mouth, and teach thee what thou shalt say. And he said, O my Lord, send, I pray thee, by the hand *of him whom* thou wilt send. And the anger of the LORD was kindled against Moses, and he said, *Is* not Aaron the Levite thy brother? I know that he can speak well. And also, behold, he cometh forth to meet thee: and when he seeth thee, he will be glad in his heart.

[31] **Job 27:5-6:** God forbid that I should justify you: till I die I will not remove mine integrity from me. My righteousness I hold fast, and will not let it go: my heart shall not reproach *me* so long as I live. **Job 4:6:** *Is* not *this* thy fear, thy confidence, thy hope, and the uprightness of thy ways?

[32] **Matthew 7:3-5:** And why beholdest thou the mote that is in thy brother's eye, but considerest not the beam that is in thine own eye? Or how wilt thou say to thy brother, Let me pull out the mote out of thine eye; and, behold, a beam *is* in thine own eye? Thou hypocrite, first cast out the beam out of thine own eye; and then shalt thou see clearly to cast out the mote out of thy brother's eye.

[33] **Proverbs 28:13:** He that covereth his sins shall not prosper: but whoso confesseth and forsaketh *them* shall have mercy. **Proverbs 30:20:** Such *is* the way of an adulterous woman; she eateth, and wipeth her mouth, and saith, I have done no wickedness. **Genesis 3:12-13:** And the man said, The woman whom thou gavest *to be* with me, she gave me of the tree, and I did eat. And the LORD God said unto the woman, What *is* this *that* thou hast done? And the woman said, The serpent beguiled me, and I did eat. **Jeremiah 2:35:** Yet thou sayest, Because I am innocent, surely his anger shall turn from me. Behold, I will plead with thee, because thou sayest, I have not sinned. **2 Kings 5:25:** But he went in, and stood before his master. And Elisha said unto him, Whence *comest thou*, Gehazi? And he said, Thy servant went no whither. **Genesis 4:9:** And the LORD said unto Cain, Where *is* Abel thy brother? And he said, I know not: *Am* I my brother's keeper?

[34] **Genesis 9:22:** And Ham, the father of Canaan, saw the nakedness of his father, and told his two brethren without. **Proverbs 25:9-10.** Debate thy cause with thy neighbour *himself*; and discover not a secret to another: Lest he that heareth *it* put thee to shame, and thine infamy turn not away.

[35] **Exodus 23:1:** Thou shalt not raise a false report: put not thine hand with the wicked to be an unrighteous witness.

[36] **Proverbs 29:12:** If a ruler hearken to lies, all his servants *are* wicked.

[37] **Acts 7:56-57:** And said, Behold, I see the heavens opened, and the Son of man standing on the right hand of God. Then they cried out with a loud voice, and stopped their ears, and ran upon him with one accord ... **Job 31:13-14:** If I did despise the cause of my man-servant or of my maidservant, when they contended with me; What then shall I do when God riseth up? and when he visiteth, what shall I answer him?

[38] **1 Corinthians 13:5:** Doth not behave itself unseemly, seeketh not her own, is not easily provoked, thinketh no evil ... **1 Timothy 6:4.** He is proud, knowing nothing, but doting about questions and strifes of words, whereof cometh envy, strife, railings, evil surmisings.

[39] **Numbers 11:29:** And Moses said unto him, Enviest thou for my sake? would God that all the LORD's people were prophets, *and* that the LORD would put his spirit upon them! **Matthew 21:15:** And when the chief priests and scribes saw the wonderful things that he did, and the children crying in the temple, and saying, Hosanna to the son of David; they were sore displeased.

[40] **Ezra 4:12-13:** Be it known unto the king, that the Jews which came up from thee to us are come unto Jerusalem, building the rebellious and the bad city, and have set up the walls *thereof*, and joined the foundations. Be it known now unto the king, that, if this city be builded, and the walls set up *again, then* will they not pay toll, tribute, and custom, and *so* thou shalt endamage the revenue of the kings.

[41] **Jeremiah 48:27:** For was not Israel a derision unto thee? was he found among thieves? for since thou spakest of him, thou skippedst for joy.

[42] **Psalm 35:15-16, 21:** But in mine adversity they rejoiced, and gathered themselves together: *yea*, the abjects gathered themselves together against me, and I knew *it* not; they did tear *me*, and ceased not: With hypocritical mockers in feasts, they gnashed upon me with their teeth ... Yea, they opened their mouth wide against me, *and* said, Aha, aha, our eye hath seen *it*. **Matthew 27:28-29:** And they stripped him, and put on him a scarlet robe. And when they had platted a crown of thorns, they put *it* upon his head, and a reed in his right hand: and they bowed the knee before him, and mocked him, saying, Hail, King of the Jews!

[43] **Jude 16:** These are murmurers, complainers, walking after their own lusts; and their mouth speaketh great swelling *words*, having men's persons in admiration because of advantage. **Acts 12:22:** And the people gave a shout, *saying, It is* the voice of a god, and not of a man.

[44] **Romans 1:31:** Without understanding, covenantbreakers, without natural affection, implacable, unmerciful ... **2 Timothy 3:3:** Without natural affection, trucebreakers, false accusers, incontinent, fierce, despisers of those that are good ...

[45] **1 Samuel 2:24:** Nay, my sons; for *it is* no good report that I hear: ye make the LORD's people to transgress.

[46] **2 Samuel 13:12-13:** And she answered him, Nay, my brother, do not force me; for no such thing ought to be done in Israel: do not thou this folly. And I, whither shall I cause my shame to go? and as for thee, thou shalt be as one of the fools in Israel. Now therefore, I pray thee, speak unto the king; for he will not withhold me from thee. **Proverbs 5:8-9:** Remove thy way far from her, and come not nigh the door of her house: Lest thou give thine honour unto others, and thy years unto the cruel ... **Proverbs 6:33:** A wound and dishonour shall he get; and his reproach shall not be wiped away.

146. Which is the tenth commandment?

A. The tenth commandment is, *Thou shalt not covet thy neighbour's house, thou shall not covet thy neighbour's wife, nor his man-servant, nor his maid-servant, nor his ox, nor his ass, nor any thing that is thy neighbour's.* [1]

Proof

Exodus 20:17: Thou shalt not covet thy neighbour's house, thou shalt not covet thy neighbour's wife, nor his manservant, nor his maidservant, nor his ox, nor his ass, nor any thing that *is* thy neighbour's. [1]

147. What are the duties required in the tenth commandment?

A. The duties required in the tenth commandment are, such a full contentment with our own condition, [1] and such a charitable frame of the whole soul toward our neighbour, as that all our inward motions and affections touching him, tend unto, and further all that good which is his. [2]

Proofs

[1] **Hebrews 13:5:** *Let your* conversation *be* without covetousness; *and be* content with such things as ye have: for he hath said, I will never leave thee, nor forsake thee. **1 Timothy 6:6:** But godliness with contentment is great gain.

[2] **Job 31:29:** If I rejoiced at the destruction of him that hated me, or lifted up myself when evil found him ... **Romans 12:15:** Rejoice with them that do rejoice, and weep with them that weep. **Psalm 122:7-9:** Peace *be* within thy walls, *and* prosperity within

thy palaces. For my brethren and companions' sakes, I will now say, Peace be within thee. Because of the house of the LORD our God I will seek thy good. **1 Timothy 1:5:** Now the end of the commandment is charity out of a pure heart, and *of* a good conscience, and *of* faith unfeigned ... **Esther 10:3:** For Mordecai the Jew *was* next unto king Ahasuerus, and great among the Jews, and accepted of the multitude of his brethren, seeking the wealth of his people, and speaking peace to all his seed. **1 Corinthians 13:4-7:** Charity suffereth long, *and* is kind; charity envieth not; charity vaunteth not itself, is not puffed up, Doth not behave itself unseemly, seeketh not her own, is not easily provoked, thinketh no evil; Rejoiceth not in iniquity, but rejoiceth in the truth; Beareth all things, believeth all things, hopeth all things, endureth all things.

148. What are the sins forbidden in the tenth commandment?

A. The sins forbidden in the tenth commandment are, discontentment with our own estate; [1] envying [2] and grieving at the good of our neighbour, [3] together with all inordinate motions and affections to anything that is his. [4]

Proofs

[1] **1 Kings 21:4:** And Ahab came into his house heavy and displeased because of the word which Naboth the Jezreelite had spoken to him: for he had said, I will not give thee the inheritance of my fathers. And he laid him down upon his bed, and turned away his face, and would eat no bread. **Esther 5:13:** Yet all this availeth me nothing, so long as I see Mordecai the Jew sitting at the king's gate. **1 Corinthians 10:10:** Neither murmur ye, as some of them also murmured, and were destroyed of the destroyer.

[2] **Galatians 5:26:** Let us not be desirous of vain glory, provoking one another, envying one another. **James 3:14, 16:** But if ye have bitter envying and strife in your hearts, glory not, and lie not against the truth ... For where envying and strife *is*, there *is* confusion and every evil work.

[3] **Psalm 112:9-10:** He hath dispersed, he hath given to the poor; his righteousness endureth for ever; his horn shall be exalted with honour. The wicked shall see *it*, and be grieved; he shall gnash with his teeth, and melt away: the desire of the wicked shall perish. **Nehemiah 2:10:** When Sanballat the Horonite, and Tobiah the servant, the Ammonite, heard

of it, it grieved them exceedingly that there was come a man to seek the welfare of the children of Israel.

[4] **Romans 7:7-8:** What shall we say then? *Is the* law sin? God forbid. Nay, I had not known sin, but by the law: for I had not known lust, except the law had said, Thou shalt not covet. But sin, taking occasion by the commandment, wrought in me all manner of concupiscence. For without the law sin *was* dead. **Romans 13:9:** For this, Thou shalt not commit adultery, Thou shalt not kill, Thou shalt not steal, Thou shalt not bear false witness, Thou shalt not covet; and if *there be* any other commandment, it is briefly comprehended in this saying, namely, Thou shalt love thy neighbour as thyself. **Colossians 3:5:** Mortify therefore your members which are upon the earth; fornication, uncleanness, inordinate affection, evil concupiscence, and covetousness, which is idolatry … **Deuteronomy 5:21:** Neither shalt thou desire thy neighbour's wife, neither shalt thou covet thy neighbour's house, his field, or his manservant, or his maidservant, his ox, or his ass, or any *thing* that *is* thy neighbour's.

149. Is any man able perfectly to keep the commandments of God?

A. No man is able, either of himself, [1] or by any grace received in this life, perfectly to keep the commandments of God; [2] but doth daily break them in thought, [3] word, and deed. [4]

Proofs

[1] **James 3:2:** For in many things we offend all. If any man offend not in word, the same *is* a perfect man, *and* able also to bridle the whole body. **John 15:5**: I am the vine, ye *are* the branches: He that abideth in me, and I in him, the same bringeth forth much fruit: for without me ye can do nothing. **Romans 8:3:** For what the law could not do, in that it was weak through the flesh, God sending his own Son in the likeness of sinful flesh, and for sin, condemned sin in the flesh …

[2] **Ecclesiastes 7:20:** For *there is* not a just man upon earth, that doeth good, and sinneth not. **1 John 1:8, 10:** If we say that we have no sin, we deceive ourselves, and the truth is not in us … If we say that we have not sinned, we make him a liar, and his word is not in us. **Galatians 5:17:** For the flesh lusteth against the Spirit, and the Spirit against the flesh: and these are contrary the one to the other: so that ye cannot do the things that ye would. **Romans 7:18-19:** For

I know that in me (that is, in my flesh,) dwelleth no good thing: for to will is present with me; but *how* to perform that which is good I find not. For the good that I would I do not: but the evil which I would not, that I do.

[3] **Genesis 6:5:** And God saw that the wickedness of man *was* great in the earth, and *that* every imagination of the thoughts of his heart *was* only evil continually. **Genesis 8:21:** And the LORD smelled a sweet savour; and the LORD said in his heart, I will not again curse the ground any more for man's sake; for the imagination of man's heart *is* evil from his youth; neither will I again smite any more every thing living, as I have done.

[4] **Romans 3:9-19:** What then? are we better *than they*? No, in no wise: for we have before proved both Jews and Gentiles, that they are all under sin; As it is written, There is none righteous, no, not one: There is none that understandeth, there is none that seeketh after God. They are all gone out of the way, they are together become unprofitable; there is none that doeth good, no, not one. Their throat *is* an open sepulchre; with their tongues they have used deceit; the poison of asps *is* under their lips: Whose mouth *is* full of cursing and bitterness: Their feet are swift to shed blood: Destruction and misery *are* in their ways: And the way of peace have they not known: There is no fear of God before their eyes. Now we know that what things soever the law saith, it saith to them who are under the law: that every mouth may be stopped, and all the world may become guilty before God. **James 3:2-13:** For in many things we offend all …

150. Are all transgressions of the law of God equally heinous in themselves, and in the sight of God?

A. All transgressions of the law of God are not equally heinous; but some sins in themselves, and by reason of several aggravations, are more heinous in the sight of God than others. [1]

Proofs

[1] **John 19:11:** Jesus answered, Thou couldest have no power *at all* against me, except it were given thee from above: therefore he that delivered me unto thee hath the greater sin. **Ezekiel 8:6, 13, 15:** He said furthermore unto me, Son of man, seest thou what they do? *even* the great abominations that the house of Israel committeth here, that I should go far off from my sanctuary? but turn thee yet again, *and* thou

shalt see greater abominations ... He said also unto me, Turn thee yet again, *and* thou shalt see greater abominations that they do ... Then said he unto me, Hast thou seen this, O son of man? turn thee yet again, *and* thou shalt see greater abominations than these. **1 John 5:16:** If any man see his brother sin a sin *which is* not unto death, he shall ask, and he shall give him life for them that sin not unto death. There is a sin unto death: I do not say that he shall pray for it. **Psalm 78:17, 32, 56:** And they sinned yet more against him by provoking the most High in the wilderness ... For all this they sinned still, and believed not for his wondrous works ...Yet they tempted and provoked the most high God, and kept not his testimonies ...

151. What are those aggravations that make some sins more heinous than others?

A. Sins receive their aggravations,

1. From the persons offending [1] if they be of riper age, [2] greater experience or grace, [3] eminent for profession, [4] gifts, [5] place, [6] office, [7] guides to others, [8] and whose example is likely to be followed by others. [9]
2. From the parties offended: [10] if immediately against God, [11] his attributes, [12] and worship; [13] against Christ, and his grace; [14] the Holy Spirit, [15] his witness, [16] and workings; [17] against superiors, men of eminency, [18] and such as we stand especially related and engaged unto; [19] against any of the saints, [20] particularly weak brethren, [21] the souls of them, or any other, [22]and the common good of all or many. [23]
3. From the nature and quality of the offence: [24] if it be against the express letter of the law, [25] break many commandments, contain in it many sins: [26] if not only conceived in the heart, but breaks forth in words and actions, [27] scandalize others, [28] and admit of no reparation: [29] if against means, [30] mercies, [31] judgments, [32] light of nature, [33] conviction of conscience, [34] public or private admonition, [35] censures of the church, [36] civil punishments; [37] and our prayers,

purposes, promises, [38] vows, [39] covenants, [40] and engagements to God or men: [41] if done deliberately, [42] wilfully, [43] presumptuously, [44] impudently, [45] boastingly, [46] maliciously, [47] frequently, [48] obstinately, [49] with delight, [50] continuance, [51] or relapsing after repentance. [52]

4. From circumstances of time [53] and place: [54] if on the Lord's day, [55] or other times of divine worship; [56] or immediately before [57] or after these, [58] or other helps to prevent or remedy such miscarriages; [59] if in public, or in the presence of others, who are thereby likely to be provoked or defiled. [60]

Proofs

[1] **Jeremiah 2:8:** The priests said not, Where *is* the LORD? and they that handle the law knew me not: the pastors also transgressed against me, and the prophets prophesied by Baal, and walked after *things that* do not profit.

[2] **Job 32:7, 9:** I said, Days should speak, and multitude of years should teach wisdom … Great men are not *always* wise: neither do the aged understand judgment. **Ecclesiastes 4:13:** Better *is* a poor and a wise child than an old and foolish king, who will no more be admonished.

[3] **1 Kings 11:4, 9:** For it came to pass, when Solomon was old, *that* his wives turned away his heart after other gods: and his heart was not perfect with the LORD his God, as *was* the heart of David his father … And the LORD was angry with Solomon, because his heart was turned from the LORD God of Israel, which had appeared unto him twice …

[4] **2 Samuel 12:14:** Howbeit, because by this deed thou hast given great occasion to the enemies of the LORD to blaspheme, the child also *that is* born unto thee shall surely die. **1 Corinthians 5:1:** It is reported commonly *that there is* fornication among you, and such fornication as is not so much as named among the Gentiles, that one should have his father's wife.

[5] **James 4:17:** Therefore to him that knoweth to do good, and doeth *it* not, to him it is sin. **Luke 12:47-48:** And that servant, which knew his lord's will, and prepared not *himself,* neither did according to his will, shall be beaten with many *stripes*. But he that knew not, and did

commit things worthy of stripes, shall be beaten with few *stripes*. For unto whomsoever much is given, of him shall be much required: and to whom men have committed much, of him they will ask the more.

[6] **Jeremiah 5:4-5:** Therefore I said, Surely these *are* poor; they are foolish: for they know not the way of the LORD, *nor* the judgment of their God. I will get me unto the great men, and will speak unto them; for they have known the way of the LORD, *and* the judgment of their God: but these have altogether broken the yoke, *and* burst the bonds.

[7] **2 Samuel 12:7-9:** And Nathan said to David, Thou *art* the man. Thus saith the LORD God of Israel, I anointed thee king over Israel, and I delivered thee out of the hand of Saul; And I gave thee thy master's house, and thy master's wives into thy bosom, and gave thee the house of Israel and of Judah; and if *that had been* too little, I would moreover have given unto thee such and such things. Wherefore hast thou despised the commandment of the LORD, to do evil in his sight? thou hast killed Uriah the Hittite with the sword, and hast taken his wife *to be* thy wife, and hast slain him with the sword of the children of Ammon. **Ezekiel 8:11-12:** And there stood before them seventy men of the ancients of the house of Israel, and in the midst of them stood Jaazaniah the son of Shaphan, with every man his censer in his hand; and a thick cloud of incense went up. Then said he unto me, Son of man, hast thou seen what the ancients of the house of Israel do in the dark, every man in the chambers of his imagery? for they say, The LORD seeth us not; the LORD hath forsaken the earth.

[8] **Romans 2:17-24:** Behold, thou art called a Jew, and restest in the law, and makest thy boast of God, And knowest *his* will, and approvest the things that are more excellent, being instructed out of the law; And art confident that thou thyself art a guide of the blind, a light of them which are in darkness, An instructor of the foolish, a teacher of babes, which hast the form of knowledge and of the truth in the law. Thou therefore which teachest another, teachest thou not thyself? thou that preachest a man should not steal, dost thou steal? Thou that sayest a man should not commit adultery, dost thou commit adultery? thou that abhorrest idols, dost thou commit sacrilege? Thou that makest thy boast of the law, through breaking the law dishonourest thou God? For the name of God is blasphemed among the Gentiles through you, as it is written.

[9] **Galatians 2:11-14:** But when Peter was come to Antioch, I withstood him to the face, because he was to be blamed. For before that certain came from James, he did eat with the Gentiles: but when they were come, he withdrew and separated himself, fearing them which were of the circumcision. And the other Jews dissembled likewise with him; insomuch that Barnabas also was carried away with their dissimulation. But when I saw that they walked not uprightly according to the truth of the gospel, I said unto Peter before *them* all, If thou, being a Jew, livest after the manner of Gentiles, and not as do the Jews, why compellest thou the Gentiles to live as do the Jews?

[10] **Matthew 21:38-39:** But when the husbandmen saw the son, they said among themselves, This is the heir; come, let us kill him, and let us seize on his inheritance. And they caught him, and cast *him* out of the vineyard, and slew *him*.

[11] **1 Samuel 2:25:** If one man sin against another, the judge shall judge him: but if a man sin against the LORD, who shall intreat for him? Notwithstanding they hearkened not unto the voice of their father, because the LORD would slay them. **Acts 5:4:** Whiles it remained, was it not thine own? and after it was sold, was it not in thine own power? why hast thou conceived this thing in thine heart? thou hast not lied unto men, but unto God. **Psalm 51:4:** Against thee, thee only, have I sinned, and done *this* evil in thy sight: that thou mightest be justified when thou speakest, *and* be clear when thou judgest.

[12] **Romans 2:4:** Or despisest thou the riches of his goodness and forbearance and longsuffering; not knowing that the goodness of God leadeth thee to repentance?

[13] **Malachi 1:8:** And if ye offer the blind for sacrifice, *is it* not evil? and if ye offer the lame and sick, *is it* not evil? offer it now unto thy governor; will he *be* pleased with thee, or accept thy person? saith the LORD of hosts. **Malachi 1:14:** But cursed *be* the deceiver, which hath in his flock a male, and voweth, and sacrificeth unto the LORD a corrupt thing: for I *am* a great King, saith the LORD of hosts, and my name *is* dreadful among the heathen.

[14] **Hebrews 2:2-3:** For if the word spoken by angels was stedfast, and every transgression and disobedience received a just recompense of reward; How shall we escape, if we neglect so great salvation; which at the first began to be spoken by the Lord, and was confirmed unto us

by them that heard *him*. **Hebrews 12:25:** See that ye refuse not him that speaketh. For if they escaped not who refused him that spake on earth, much more *shall not* we escape, if we turn away from him that *speaketh* from heaven …

[15] **Hebrews 10:29:** Of how much sorer punishment, suppose ye, shall he be thought worthy, who hath trodden under foot the Son of God, and hath counted the blood of the covenant, wherewith he was sanctified, an unholy thing, and hath done despite unto the Spirit of grace? **Matthew 12:31-32:** Wherefore I say unto you, All manner of sin and blasphemy shall be forgiven unto men: but the blasphemy *against* the *Holy* Ghost shall not be forgiven unto men. And whosoever speaketh a word against the Son of man, it shall be forgiven him: but whosoever speaketh against the Holy Ghost, it shall not be forgiven him, neither in this world, neither in the *world* to come.

[16] **Ephesians 4:30:** And grieve not the holy Spirit of God, whereby ye are sealed unto the day of redemption.

[17] **Hebrews 6:4-6:** For *it is* impossible for those who were once enlightened, and have tasted of the heavenly gift, and were made partakers of the Holy Ghost, And have tasted the good word of God, and the powers of the world to come, If they shall fall away, to renew them again unto repentance; seeing they crucify to themselves the Son of God afresh, and put *him* to an open shame.

[18] **Jude 8:** Likewise also these *filthy* dreamers defile the flesh, despise dominion, and speak evil of dignities. **Numbers 12:8-9:** With him will I speak mouth to mouth, even apparently, and not in dark speeches; and the similitude of the LORD shall he behold: wherefore then were ye not afraid to speak against my servant Moses? And the anger of the LORD was kindled against them; and he departed. **Isaiah 3:5:** And the people shall be oppressed, every one by another, and every one by his neighbour: the child shall behave himself proudly against the ancient, and the base against the honourable.

[19] **Proverbs 30:17:** The eye *that* mocketh at *his* father, and despiseth to obey *his* mother, the ravens of the valley shall pick it out, and the young eagles shall eat it. **2 Corinthians 12:15:** And I will very gladly spend and be spent for you; though the more abundantly I love you, the less I be loved. **Psalm 55:12-15:** For *it was* not an enemy *that* reproached me; then I could have borne *it*: neither *was it* he that hated me *that* did

magnify *himself* against me; then I would have hid myself from him: But *it was* thou, a man mine equal, my guide, and mine acquaintance. We took sweet counsel together, *and* walked unto the house of God in company. Let death seize upon them, *and* let them go down quick into hell: for wickedness *is* in their dwellings, *and* among them.

[20] **Zephaniah 2:8, 10-11:** I have heard the reproach of Moab, and the revilings of the children of Ammon, whereby they have reproached my people, and magnified *themselves* against their border … This shall they have for their pride, because they have reproached and magnified *themselves* against the people of the LORD of hosts. The LORD *will be* terrible unto them: for he will famish all the gods of the earth; and *men* shall worship him, every one from his place, *even* all the isles of the heathen. **Matthew 18:6:** But whoso shall offend one of these little ones which believe in me, it were better for him that a millstone were hanged about his neck, and *that* he were drowned in the depth of the sea. **1 Corinthians 6:8:** Nay, ye do wrong, and defraud, and that *your* brethren. **Revelation 17:6:** And I saw the woman drunken with the blood of the saints, and with the blood of the martyrs of Jesus: and when I saw her, I wondered with great admiration.

[21] **1 Corinthians 8:11-12:** And through thy knowledge shall the weak brother perish, for whom Christ died? But when ye sin so against the brethren, and wound their weak conscience, ye sin against Christ. **Romans 14:13, 15, 21:** Let us not therefore judge one another any more: but judge this rather, that no man put a stumblingblock or an occasion to fall in *his* brother's way … But if thy brother be grieved with *thy* meat, now walkest thou not charitably. Destroy not him with thy meat, for whom Christ died … *It is* good neither to eat flesh, nor to drink wine, nor *any thing* whereby thy brother stumbleth, or is offended, or is made weak.

[22] **Ezekiel 13:19:** And will ye pollute me among my people for handfuls of barley and for pieces of bread, to slay the souls that should not die, and to save the souls alive that should not live, by your lying to my people that hear *your* lies? **1 Corinthians 8:12:** But when ye sin so against the brethren, and wound their weak conscience, ye sin against Christ. **Revelation 18:12-13:** The merchandise of gold, and silver, and precious stones, and of pearls, and fine linen, and purple, and silk, and scarlet, and all thyine wood, and all manner vessels of ivory, and all manner vessels of most precious wood, and of brass, and iron, and

marble, And cinnamon, and odours, and ointments, and frankincense, and wine, and oil, and fine flour, and wheat, and beasts, and sheep, and horses, and chariots, and slaves, and souls of men. **Matthew 23:15:** Woe unto you, scribes and Pharisees, hypocrites! for ye compass sea and land to make one proselyte, and when he is made, ye make him twofold more the child of hell than yourselves.

[23] **1 Thessalonians 2:15-16:** Who both killed the Lord Jesus, and their own prophets, and have persecuted us; and they please not God, and are contrary to all men: Forbidding us to speak to the Gentiles that they might be saved, to fill up their sins alway: for the wrath is come upon them to the uttermost. **Joshua 22:20:** Did not Achan the son of Zerah commit a trespass in the accursed thing, and wrath fell on all the congregation of Israel? and that man perished not alone in his iniquity.

[24] **Proverbs 6:30-33:** *Men* do not despise a thief, if he steal to satisfy his soul when he is hungry; But *if* he be found, he shall restore sevenfold; he shall give all the substance of his house. *But* whoso committeth adultery with a woman lacketh understanding: he *that* doeth it destroyeth his own soul. A wound and dishonour shall he get; and his reproach shall not be wiped away.

[25] **Ezra 9:10-12:** And now, O our God, what shall we say after this? for we have forsaken thy commandments, Which thou hast commanded by thy servants the prophets, saying, The land, unto which ye go to possess it, is an unclean land with the filthiness of the people of the lands, with their abominations, which have filled it from one end to another with their uncleanness. Now therefore give not your daughters unto their sons, neither take their daughters unto your sons, nor seek their peace or their wealth for ever: that ye may be strong, and eat the good of the land, and leave *it* for an inheritance to your children for ever. **1 Kings 11:9-10:** And the LORD was angry with Solomon, because his heart was turned from the LORD God of Israel, which had appeared unto him twice, And had commanded him concerning this thing, that he should not go after other gods: but he kept not that which the LORD commanded.

[26] **Colossians 3:5:** Mortify therefore your members which are upon the earth; fornication, uncleanness, inordinate affection, evil concupiscence, and covetousness, which is idolatry ... **1 Timothy 6:10:** For the love of money is the root of all evil: which while some coveted after, they have erred from the faith, and pierced themselves through

with many sorrows. **Proverbs 5:8-12:** Remove thy way far from her, and come not nigh the door of her house: Lest thou give thine honour unto others, and thy years unto the cruel: Lest strangers be filled with thy wealth; and thy labours *be* in the house of a stranger; And thou mourn at the last, when thy flesh and thy body are consumed, And say, How have I hated instruction, and my heart despised reproof … **Proverbs 6:32-33:** *But* whoso committeth adultery with a woman lacketh understanding: he *that* doeth it destroyeth his own soul. A wound and dishonour shall he get; and his reproach shall not be wiped away. **Joshua 7:21:** When I saw among the spoils a goodly Babylonish garment, and two hundred shekels of silver, and a wedge of gold of fifty shekels weight, then I coveted them, and took them; and, behold, they *are* hid in the earth in the midst of my tent, and the silver under it.

[27] **James 1:14-15:** But every man is tempted, when he is drawn away of his own lust, and enticed. Then when lust hath conceived, it bringeth forth sin: and sin, when it is finished, bringeth forth death. **Matthew 5:22:** But I say unto you, That whosoever is angry with his brother without a cause shall be in danger of the judgment: and whosoever shall say to his brother, Raca, shall be in danger of the council: but whosoever shall say, Thou fool, shall be in danger of hell fire. **Micah 2:1:** Woe to them that devise iniquity, and work evil upon their beds! when the morning is light, they practise it, because it is in the power of their hand.

[28] **Matthew 18:7:** Woe unto the world because of offences! for it must needs be that offences come; but woe to that man by whom the offence cometh! **Romans 2:23-24:**Thou that makest thy boast of the law, through breaking the law dishonourest thou God? For the name of God is blasphemed among the Gentiles through you, as it is written.

[29] **Deuteronomy 22:22, 28-29:** If a man be found lying with a woman married to an husband, then they shall both of them die, *both* the man that lay with the woman, and the woman: so shalt thou put away evil from Israel … If a man find a damsel *that is* a virgin, which is not betrothed, and lay hold on her, and lie with her, and they be found; Then the man that lay with her shall give unto the damsel's father fifty *shekels* of silver, and she shall be his wife; because he hath humbled her, he may not put her away all his days. **Proverbs 6:32-35:** *But* whoso committeth adultery with a woman lacketh understanding: he *that*

doeth it destroyeth his own soul. A wound and dishonour shall he get; and his reproach shall not be wiped away. For jealousy *is* the rage of a man: therefore he will not spare in the day of vengeance. He will not regard any ransom; neither will he rest content, though thou givest many gifts.

[30] **Matthew 11:21-24:** Woe unto thee, Chorazin! woe unto thee, Bethsaida! for if the mighty works, which were done in you, had been done in Tyre and Sidon, they would have repented long ago in sackcloth and ashes. But I say unto you, It shall be more tolerable for Tyre and Sidon at the day of judgment, than for you. And thou, Capernaum, which art exalted unto heaven, shalt be brought down to hell: for if the mighty works, which have been done in thee, had been done in Sodom, it would have remained until this day. But I say unto you, That it shall be more tolerable for the land of Sodom in the day of judgment, than for thee. **John 15:22:** If I had not come and spoken unto them, they had not had sin: but now they have no cloak for their sin.

[31] **Isaiah 1:3:** The ox knoweth his owner, and the ass his master's crib: *but* Israel doth not know, my people doth not consider. **Deuteronomy 32:6:** Do ye thus requite the LORD, O foolish people and unwise? *is* not he thy father *that* hath bought thee? hath he not made thee, and established thee?

[32] **Amos 4:8-11:** So two *or* three cities wandered unto one city, to drink water; but they were not satisfied: yet have ye not returned unto me, saith the LORD. I have smitten you with blasting and mildew: when your gardens and your vineyards and your fig trees and your olive trees increased, the palmerworm devoured *them*: yet have ye not returned unto me, saith the LORD. I have sent among you the pestilence after the manner of Egypt: your young men have I slain with the sword, and have taken away your horses; and I have made the stink of your camps to come up unto your nostrils: yet have ye not returned unto me, saith the LORD. I have overthrown *some* of you, as God overthrew Sodom and Gomorrah, and ye were as a firebrand plucked out of the burning: yet have ye not returned unto me, saith the LORD. **Jeremiah 5:3:** O LORD, *are* not thine eyes upon the truth? thou hast stricken them, but they have not grieved; thou hast consumed them, *but* they have refused to receive correction: they have made their faces harder than a rock; they have refused to return.

[33] **Romans 1:26-27:** For this cause God gave them up unto vile affections: for even their women did change the natural use into that which is against nature: And likewise also the men, leaving the natural use of the woman, burned in their lust one toward another; men with men working that which is unseemly, and receiving in themselves that recompense of their error which was meet.

[34] **Romans 1:32:** Who knowing the judgment of God, that they which commit such things are worthy of death, not only do the same, but have pleasure in them that do them. **Daniel 5:22:** And thou his son, O Belshazzar, hast not humbled thine heart, though thou knewest all this … **Titus 3:10-11:** A man that is an heretick after the first and second admonition reject; Knowing that he that is such is subverted, and sinneth, being condemned of himself.

[35] **Proverbs 29:1:** He, that being often reproved hardeneth *his* neck, shall suddenly be destroyed, and that without remedy.

[36] **Titus 3:10:** A man that is an heretick after the first and second admonition reject … **Matthew 18:17:** And if he shall neglect to hear them, tell *it* unto the church: but if he neglect to hear the church, let him be unto thee as an heathen man and a publican.

[37] **Proverbs 27:22:** Though thou shouldest bray a fool in a mortar among wheat with a pestle, *yet* will not his foolishness depart from him. **Proverbs 23:35:** They have stricken me, *shalt thou say*, and I was not sick; they have beaten me, *and* I felt *it* not: when shall I awake? I will seek it yet again.

[38] **Psalm 78:34-37:** When he slew them, then they sought him: and they returned and inquired early after God. And they remembered that God *was* their rock, and the high God their redeemer … Nevertheless they did flatter him with their mouth, and they lied unto him with their tongues. For their heart was not right with him, neither were they stedfast in his covenant. **Jeremiah 2:20:** For of old time I have broken thy yoke, *and* burst thy bands; and thou saidst, I will not transgress; when upon every high hill and under every green tree thou wanderest, playing the harlot. **Jeremiah 42:5-6, 20-21:** Then they said to Jeremiah, The Lord be a true and faithful witness between us, if we do not even according to all things for the which the Lord thy God shall send thee to us. Whether *it be* good, or whether *it be* evil, we will obey the voice of the Lord our God, to whom we send thee; that it

may be well with us, when we obey the voice of the LORD our God … For ye dissembled in your hearts, when ye sent me unto the Lord your God, saying, Pray for us unto the LORD our God; and according unto all that the LORD our God shall say, so declare unto us, and we will do *it*. And *now* I have this day declared *it* to you; but ye have not obeyed the voice of the LORD your God, nor any *thing* for the which he hath sent me unto you.

[39] **Ecclesiastes 5:4-6:** When thou vowest a vow unto God, defer not to pay it; for *he hath* no pleasure in fools: pay that which thou hast vowed. Better *is it* that thou shouldest not vow, than that thou shouldest vow and not pay. Suffer not thy mouth to cause thy flesh to sin; neither say thou before the angel, that it *was* an error: wherefore should God be angry at thy voice, and destroy the work of thine hands? **Proverbs 20:25**: *It is* a snare to the man *who* devoureth *that which is* holy, and after vows to make enquiry.

[40] **Leviticus 26:25:** And I will bring a sword upon you, that shall avenge the quarrel of *my* covenant: and when ye are gathered together within your cities, I will send the pestilence among you; and ye shall be delivered into the hand of the enemy.

[41] **Proverbs 2:17:** Which forsaketh the guide of her youth, and forgetteth the covenant of her God. **Ezekiel 7:18-19:** They shall also gird *themselves* with sackcloth, and horror shall cover them; and shame *shall be* upon all faces, and baldness upon all their heads. They shall cast their silver in the streets, and their gold shall be removed: their silver and their gold shall not be able to deliver them in the day of the wrath of the LORD: they shall not satisfy their souls, neither fill their bowels: because it is the stumblingblock of their iniquity.

[42] **Psalm 36:4:** He deviseth mischief upon his bed; he setteth himself in a way *that is not* good; he abhorreth not evil.

[43] **Jeremiah 6:16:** Thus saith the LORD, Stand ye in the ways, and see, and ask for the old paths, where *is* the good way, and walk therein, and ye shall find rest for your souls. But they said, We will not walk *therein*.

[44] **Numbers 15:30:** But the soul that doeth *ought* presumptuously, *whether he be* born in the land, or a stranger, the same reproacheth the LORD; and that soul shall be cut off from among his people. **Exodus 21:14:** But if a man come presumptuously upon his neighbour, to slay him with guile; thou shalt take him from mine altar, that he may die.

[45] **Jeremiah 3:3:** Therefore the showers have been withholden, and there hath been no latter rain; and thou hadst a whore's forehead, thou refusedst to be ashamed. **Proverbs 7:13:** So she caught him, and kissed him, *and* with an impudent face said unto him …

[46] **Psalm 52:1:** Why boastest thou thyself in mischief, O mighty man? the goodness of God *endureth* continually.

[47] **3 John 10:** Wherefore, if I come, I will remember his deeds which he doeth, prating against us with malicious words …

[48] **Numbers 14:22:** Because all those men which have seen my glory, and my miracles, which I did in Egypt and in the wilderness, and have tempted me now these ten times, and have not hearkened to my voice …

[49] **Zechariah 7:11-12:** But they refused to hearken, and pulled away the shoulder, and stopped their ears, that they should not hear. Yea, they made their hearts *as* an adamant stone, lest they should hear the law, and the words which the LORD of hosts hath sent in his spirit by the former prophets: therefore came a great wrath from the LORD of hosts.

[50] **Proverbs 2:14:** Who rejoice to do evil, *and* delight in the frowardness of the wicked …

[51] **Isaiah 57:17:** For the iniquity of his covetousness was I wroth, and smote him: I hid me, and was wroth, and he went on frowardly in the way of his heart.

[52] **Jeremiah 34:8-11:** *This is* the word that came unto Jeremiah from the LORD, after that the king Zedekiah had made a covenant with all the people which *were* at Jerusalem, to proclaim liberty unto them; That every man should let his manservant, and every man his maidservant, *being* an Hebrew or an Hebrewess, go free; that none should serve himself of them, *to wit*, of a Jew his brother. Now when all the princes, and all the people, which had entered into the covenant, heard that every one should let his manservant, and every one his maidservant, go free, that none should serve themselves of them any more, then they obeyed, and let *them* go. But afterward they turned, and caused the servants and the handmaids, whom they had let go free, to return, and brought them into subjection for servants and for handmaids. **2 Peter 2:20-22:** For if after they have escaped the pollutions of the world through the knowledge of the Lord and Saviour Jesus Christ, they are again entangled therein, and overcome, the latter end is worse with them than the beginning. For it had been better for

them not to have known the way of righteousness, than, after they have known *it*, to turn from the holy commandment delivered unto them. But it is happened unto them according to the true proverb, The dog *is* turned to his own vomit again; and the sow that was washed to her wallowing in the mire.

[53] **2 Kings 5:26:** And he said unto him, Went not mine heart *with thee*, when the man turned again from his chariot to meet thee? *Is it* a time to receive money, and to receive garments, and oliveyards, and vineyards, and sheep, and oxen, and menservants, and maidservants?

[54] **Jeremiah 7:10:** And come and stand before me in this house, which is called by my name, and say, We are delivered to do all these abominations ... **Isaiah 26:10:** Let favour be shewed to the wicked, *yet* will he not learn righteousness; in the land of uprightness will he deal unjustly, and will not behold the majesty of the LORD.

[55] **Ezekiel 23:37-39:** That they have committed adultery, and blood *is* in their hands, and with their idols have they committed adultery, and have also caused their sons, whom they bare unto me, to pass for them through *the fire*, to devour *them*. Moreover this they have done unto me: they have defiled my sanctuary in the same day, and have profaned my sabbaths. For when they had slain their children to their idols, then they came the same day into my sanctuary to profane it; and, lo, thus have they done in the midst of mine house.

[56] **Isaiah 58:3-5:** Wherefore have we fasted, *say they*, and thou seest not? *wherefore* have we afflicted our soul, and thou takest no knowledge? Behold, in the day of your fast ye find pleasure, and exact all your labours. Behold, ye fast for strife and debate, and to smite with the fist of wickedness: ye shall not fast as *ye do this* day, to make your voice to be heard on high. Is it such a fast that I have chosen? a day for a man to afflict his soul? *is it* to bow down his head as a bulrush, and to spread sackcloth and ashes *under him*? wilt thou call this a fast, and an acceptable day to the LORD? **Numbers 25:6-7:** And, behold, one of the children of Israel came and brought unto his brethren a Midianitish woman in the sight of Moses, and in the sight of all the congregation of the children of Israel, who *were* weeping *before* the door of the tabernacle of the congregation. And when Phinehas, the son of Eleazar, the son of Aaron the priest, saw *it*, he rose up from among the congregation, and took a javelin in his hand ...

[57] **1 Corinthians 11:20-21:** When ye come together therefore into one place, *this* is not to eat the Lord's supper. For in eating every one taketh before *other* his own supper: and one is hungry, and another is drunken.

[58] **Jeremiah 7:8-10:** Behold, ye trust in lying words, that cannot profit. Will ye steal, murder, and commit adultery, and swear falsely, and burn incense unto Baal, and walk after other gods whom ye know not; And come and stand before me in this house, which is called by my name, and say, We are delivered to do all these abominations? **Proverbs 7:14-15:** *I have* peace offerings with me; this day have I payed my vows. Therefore came I forth to meet thee, diligently to seek thy face, and I have found thee. **John 13:27, 30:** And after the sop Satan entered into him. Then said Jesus unto him, That thou doest, do quickly … He then having received the sop went immediately out: and it was night.

[59] **Ezra 9:13-14:** And after all that is come upon us for our evil deeds, and for our great trespass, seeing that thou our God hast punished us less than our iniquities *deserve*, and hast given us *such* deliverance as this; Should we again break thy commandments, and join in affinity with the people of these abominations? wouldest not thou be angry with us till thou hadst consumed *us*, so that *there should be* no remnant nor escaping?

[60] **2 Samuel 16:22:** So they spread Absalom a tent upon the top of the house; and Absalom went in unto his father's concubines in the sight of all Israel. **1 Samuel 2:22-24:** Now Eli was very old, and heard all that his sons did unto all Israel; and how they lay with the women that assembled *at* the door of the tabernacle of the congregation. And he said unto them, Why do ye such things? for I hear of your evil dealings by all this people. Nay, my sons; for *it is* no good report that I hear: ye make the LORD's people to transgress.

152. What doth every sin deserve at the hands of God?

A. Every sin, even the least, being against the sovereignty, [1] goodness, [2] and holiness of God, [3] and against his righteous law, [4] deserveth his wrath and curse, [5] both in this life, [6] and that which is to come; [7] and cannot be expiated but by the blood of Christ. [8]

Proofs

[1] **James 2:10–11:** For whosoever shall keep the whole law, and yet offend in one *point*, he is guilty of all. For he that said, Do not commit adultery, said also, Do not kill. Now if thou commit no adultery, yet if thou kill, thou art become a transgressor of the law.

[2] **Exodus 20:1–2:** And God spake all these words, saying, I *am* the LORD thy God, which have brought thee out of the land of Egypt, out of the house of bondage.

[3] **Habakkuk 1:13:** *Thou art* of purer eyes than to behold evil, and canst not look on iniquity: wherefore lookest thou upon them that deal treacherously, *and* holdest thy tongue when the wicked devoureth *the man that is* more righteous than he? **Leviticus 10:3:** Then Moses said unto Aaron, This *is it* that the LORD spake, saying, I will be sanctified in them that come nigh me, and before all the people I will be glorified. And Aaron held his peace. **Leviticus 11:44–45:** For I *am* the LORD your God: ye shall therefore sanctify yourselves, and ye shall be holy; for I *am* holy: neither shall ye defile yourselves with any manner of creeping thing that creepeth upon the earth. For I *am* the LORD that bringeth you up out of the land of Egypt, to be your God: ye shall therefore be holy, for I *am* holy.

[4] **1 John 3:4:** Whosoever committeth sin transgresseth also the law: for sin is the transgression of the law. **Romans 7:12:** Wherefore the law *is* holy, and the commandment holy, and just, and good.

[5] **Ephesians 5:6:** Let no man deceive you with vain words: for because of these things cometh the wrath of God upon the children of disobedience. **Galatians 3:10:** For as many as are of the works of the law are under the curse: for it is written, Cursed *is* every one that continueth not in all things which are written in the book of the law to do them.

[6] **Lamentations 3:39:** Wherefore doth a living man complain, a man for the punishment of his sins? **Deuteronomy 28:15–18:** But it shall come to pass, if thou wilt not hearken unto the voice of the LORD thy God, to observe to do all his commandments and his statutes which I command thee this day; that all these curses shall come upon thee, and overtake thee: Cursed *shalt* thou *be* in the city, and cursed *shalt* thou *be* in the field. Cursed *shall be* thy basket and thy store …

[7] **Matthew 25:41:** Then shall he say also unto them on the left hand, Depart from me, ye cursed, into everlasting fire, prepared for the devil and his angels …

[8] **Hebrews 9:22:** And almost all things are by the law purged with blood; and without shedding of blood is no remission. **1 Peter 1:18-19:** Forasmuch as ye know that ye were not redeemed with corruptible things, as silver and gold, from your vain conversation *received* by tradition from your fathers; But with the precious blood of Christ, as of a lamb without blemish and without spot …

153. What doth God require of us, that we may escape his wrath and curse due to us by reason of the transgression of the law?

A. That we may escape the wrath and curse of God due to us by reason of the transgression of the law, he requireth of us repentance toward God, and faith toward our Lord Jesus Christ, [1] and the diligent use of the outward means whereby Christ communicates to us the benefits of his mediation. [2]

Proofs

[1] **Acts 20:21:** Testifying both to the Jews, and also to the Greeks, repentance toward God, and faith toward our Lord Jesus Christ. **Matthew 3:7-8:** But when he saw many of the Pharisees and Sadducees come to his baptism, he said unto them, O generation of vipers, who hath warned you to flee from the wrath to come? Bring forth therefore fruits meet for repentance … **Luke 13:3, 5:** I tell you, Nay: but, except ye repent, ye shall all likewise perish. **Acts 16:30-31:** And brought them out, and said, Sirs, what must I do to be saved? And they said, Believe on the Lord Jesus Christ, and thou shalt be saved, and thy house. **John 3:16, 18:** For God so loved the world, that he gave his only begotten Son, that whosoever believeth in him should not perish, but have everlasting life … He that believeth on him is not condemned: but he that believeth not is condemned already, because he hath not believed in the name of the only begotten Son of God.

[2] **Proverbs 2:1-5:** My son, if thou wilt receive my words, and hide my commandments with thee; So that thou incline thine ear unto wisdom, *and* apply thine heart to understanding; Yea, if thou criest after knowledge, *and* liftest up thy voice for understand-

ing; If thou seekest her as silver, and searchest for her as *for* hid treasures; Then shalt thou understand the fear of the LORD, and find the knowledge of God. **Proverbs 8:33-36:** Hear instruction, and be wise, and refuse it not. Blessed *is* the man that heareth me, watching daily at my gates, waiting at the posts of my doors. For whoso findeth me findeth life, and shall obtain favour of the LORD. But he that sinneth against me wrongeth his own soul: all they that hate me love death.

154. What are the outward means whereby Christ communicates to us the benefits of his mediation?

A. The outward and ordinary means whereby Christ communicates to his church the benefits of his mediation, are all his ordinances; especially the Word, sacraments, and prayer; all which are made effectual to the elect for their salvation. [1]

Proofs

[1] **Matthew 28:19-20:** Go ye therefore, and teach all nations, baptizing them in the name of the Father, and of the Son, and of the Holy Ghost: Teaching them to observe all things whatsoever I have commanded you: and, lo, I am with you alway, *even* unto the end of the world. Amen. **Acts 2:42, 46-47:** And they continued stedfastly in the apostles' doctrine and fellowship, and in breaking of bread, and in prayers ... And they, continuing daily with one accord in the temple, and breaking bread from house to house, did eat their meat with gladness and singleness of heart, Praising God, and having favour with all the people. And the Lord added to the church daily such as should be saved.

155. How is the Word made effectual to salvation?

A. The Spirit of God maketh the reading, but especially the preaching of the Word, an effectual means of enlightening, [1] convincing, and humbling sinners; [2] of driving them out of themselves, and drawing them unto Christ; [3] of conforming them to his image, [4]and subduing them to his will; [5] of strengthening them against temptations and corruptions; [6] of building them up in grace, [7] and establishing their hearts in holiness and comfort through faith unto salvation. [8]

Proofs

[1] **Nehemiah 8:8:** So they read in the book in the law of God distinctly, and gave the sense, and caused *them* to understand the reading. **Acts 26:18:** To open their eyes, *and* to turn *them* from darkness to light, and *from* the power of Satan unto God, that they may receive forgiveness of sins, and inheritance among them which are sanctified by faith that is in me. **Psalm 19:8:** The statutes of the LORD *are* right, rejoicing the heart: the commandment of the LORD *is* pure, enlightening the eyes.

[2] **1 Corinthians 14:24-25:** But if all prophesy, and there come in one that believeth not, or *one* unlearned, he is convinced of all, he is judged of all: And thus are the secrets of his heart made manifest; and so falling down on *his* face he will worship God, and report that God is in you of a truth. **2 Chronicles 34:18-19, 26-28:** Then Shaphan the scribe told the king, saying, Hilkiah the priest hath given me a book. And Shaphan read it before the king. And it came to pass, when the king had heard the words of the law, that he rent his clothes … And as for the king of Judah, who sent you to inquire of the LORD, so shall ye say unto him, Thus saith the LORD God of Israel *concerning* the words which thou hast heard; Because thine heart was tender, and thou didst humble thyself before God, when thou heardest his words against this place, and against the inhabitants thereof, and humbledst thyself before me, and didst rend thy clothes, and weep before me; I have even heard *thee* also, saith the LORD. Behold, I will gather thee to thy fathers, and thou shalt be gathered to thy grave in peace …

[3] **Acts 2:37, 41:** Now when they heard *this*, they were pricked in their heart, and said unto Peter and to the rest of the apostles, Men *and* brethren, what shall we do?... Then they that gladly received his word were baptized: and the same day there were added *unto them* about three thousand souls. **Acts 8:27-30, 35-38:** And he arose and went: and, behold, a man of Ethiopia, an eunuch of great authority under Candace queen of the Ethiopians, who had the charge of all her treasure, and had come to Jerusalem for to worship, Was returning, and sitting in his chariot read Esaias the prophet. Then the Spirit said unto Philip, Go near, and join thyself to this chariot. And Philip ran thither to *him*, and heard him read the prophet Esaias, and said, Understandest thou what thou readest? … Then Philip opened his mouth, and began at the same scripture, and preached unto him Jesus. And as they went on *their* way, they came unto a certain water: and the eunuch said, See, *here* is

water; what doth hinder me to be baptized? And Philip said, If thou believest with all thine heart, thou mayest. And he answered and said, I believe that Jesus Christ is the Son of God. And he commanded the chariot to stand still: and they went down both into the water, both Philip and the eunuch; and he baptized him.

[4] **2 Corinthians 3:18:** But we all, with open face beholding as in a glass the glory of the Lord, are changed into the same image from glory to glory, *even* as by the Spirit of the Lord.

[5] **2 Corinthians 10:4-6:** (For the weapons of our warfare *are* not carnal, but mighty through God to the pulling down of strong holds;) Casting down imaginations, and every high thing that exalteth itself against the knowledge of God, and bringing into captivity every thought to the obedience of Christ; And having in a readiness to revenge all disobedience, when your obedience is fulfilled. **Romans 6:17:** But God be thanked, that ye were the servants of sin, but ye have obeyed from the heart that form of doctrine which was delivered you.

[6] **Matthew 4:4, 7, 10:** But he answered and said, It is written, Man shall not live by bread alone, but by every word that proceedeth out of the mouth of God ... Jesus said unto him, It is written again, Thou shalt not tempt the Lord thy God ... Then saith Jesus unto him, Get thee hence, Satan: for it is written, Thou shalt worship the Lord thy God, and him only shalt thou serve. **Ephesians 6:16-17:** Above all, taking the shield of faith, wherewith ye shall be able to quench all the fiery darts of the wicked. And take the helmet of salvation, and the sword of the Spirit, which is the word of God ... **Psalm 19:11:** Moreover by them is thy servant warned: *and* in keeping of them *there is* great reward. **1 Corinthians 10:11:** Now all these things happened unto them for ensamples: and they are written for our admonition, upon whom the ends of the world are come.

[7] **Acts 20:32:** And now, brethren, I commend you to God, and to the word of his grace, which is able to build you up, and to give you an inheritance among all them which are sanctified. **2 Timothy 3:15-17:** And that from a child thou hast known the holy scriptures, which are able to make thee wise unto salvation through faith which is in Christ Jesus. All scripture *is* given by inspiration of God, and *is* profitable for doctrine, for reproof, for correction, for

instruction in righteousness: That the man of God may be perfect, thoroughly furnished unto all good works.

[8] **Romans 16:25:** Now to him that is of power to stablish you according to my gospel, and the preaching of Jesus Christ, according to the revelation of the mystery, which was kept secret since the world began … **1 Thessalonians 3:2, 10-11, 13:** And sent Timotheus, our brother, and minister of God, and our fellow-labourer in the gospel of Christ, to establish you, and to comfort you concerning your faith … Night and day praying exceedingly that we might see your face, and might perfect that which is lacking in your faith? Now God himself and our Father, and our Lord Jesus Christ, direct our way unto you … To the end he may stablish your hearts unblameable in holiness before God, even our Father, at the coming of our Lord Jesus Christ with all his saints. **Romans 15:4:** For whatsoever things were written aforetime were written for our learning, that we through patience and comfort of the scriptures might have hope. **Romans 10:13-17:** For whosoever shall call upon the name of the Lord shall be saved. How then shall they call on him in whom they have not believed? and how shall they believe in him of whom they have not heard? and how shall they hear without a preacher? And how shall they preach, except they be sent? as it is written, How beautiful are the feet of them that preach the gospel of peace, and bring glad tidings of good things! But they have not all obeyed the gospel. For Esaias saith, Lord, who hath believed our report? So then faith *cometh* by hearing, and hearing by the word of God. **Romans 1:16:** For I am not ashamed of the gospel of Christ: for it is the power of God unto salvation to every one that believeth; to the Jew first, and also to the Greek.

156. Is the Word of God to be read by all?

A. Although all are not to be permitted to read the Word publicly to the congregation, [1] yet all sorts of people are bound to read it apart by themselves, [2] and with their families: [3] to which end, the holy scriptures are to be translated out of the original into vulgar languages. [4]

Proofs

[1] **Deuteronomy 31:9, 11-13:** And Moses wrote this law, and delivered it unto the priests the sons of Levi, which bare the ark of the covenant of the LORD, and unto all the elders of Israel … When all Israel

is come to appear before the LORD thy God in the place which he shall choose, thou shalt read this law before all Israel in their hearing. Gather the people together, men, and women, and children, and thy stranger that *is* within thy gates, that they may hear, and that they may learn, and fear the LORD your God, and observe to do all the words of this law: And *that* their children, which have not known *any thing*, may hear, and learn to fear the LORD your God, as long as ye live in the land whither ye go over Jordan to possess it. **Nehemiah 8:2-3:** And Ezra the priest brought the law before the congregation both of men and women, and all that could hear with understanding, upon the first day of the seventh month. And he read therein before the street that *was* before the water gate from the morning until midday, before the men and the women, and those that could understand; and the ears of all the people *were attentive* unto the book of the law. **Nehemiah 9:3-5:** And they stood up in their place, and read in the book of the law of the LORD their God *one* fourth part of the day; and *another* fourth part they confessed, and worshipped the LORD their God. Then stood up upon the stairs, of the Levites, Jeshua, and Bani ... and cried with a loud voice unto the LORD their God. Then the Levites, Jeshua, and Kadmiel ... said, Stand up *and* bless the LORD your God for ever and ever: and blessed be thy glorious name, which is exalted above all blessing and praise.

[2] **Deuteronomy 17:19:** And it shall be with him, and he shall read therein all the days of his life: that he may learn to fear the LORD his God, to keep all the words of this law and these statutes, to do them ... **Revelation 1:3:** Blessed *is* he that readeth, and they that hear the words of this prophecy, and keep those things which are written therein: for the time *is* at hand. **John 5:39:** Search the scriptures; for in them ye think ye have eternal life: and they are they which testify of me. **Isaiah 34:16:** Seek ye out of the book of the LORD, and read: no one of these shall fail ...

[3] **Deuteronomy 6:6-9:** And these words, which I command thee this day, shall be in thine heart: And thou shalt teach them diligently unto thy children, and shalt talk of them when thou sittest in thine house, and when thou walkest by the way, and when thou liest down, and when thou risest up. And thou shalt bind them for a sign upon thine hand, and they shall be as frontlets between thine eyes. And thou shalt write them upon the posts of thy house, and on thy gates. **Genesis 18:17, 19:** And the LORD said, Shall I hide from Abraham that thing which I do ...

For I know him, that he will command his children and his household after him, and they shall keep the way of the LORD, to do justice and judgment; that the LORD may bring upon Abraham that which he hath spoken of him. **Psalm 78:5-7:** For he established a testimony in Jacob, and appointed a law in Israel, which he commanded our fathers, that they should make them known to their children: That the generation to come might know *them, even* the children *which* should be born; *who* should arise and declare *them* to their children: That they might set their hope in God, and not forget the works of God, but keep his commandments …

[4] **1 Corinthians 14:6, 9, 11-12, 15-16, 24, 27-28:** Now, brethren, if I come unto you speaking with tongues, what shall I profit you, except I shall speak to you either by revelation, or by knowledge, or by prophesying, or by doctrine … So likewise ye, except ye utter by the tongue words easy to be understood, how shall it be known what is spoken? for ye shall speak into the air … Therefore if I know not the meaning of the voice, I shall be unto him that speaketh a barbarian, and he that speaketh *shall be* a barbarian unto me. Even so ye, forasmuch as ye are zealous of spiritual *gifts*, seek that ye may excel to the edifying of the church … What is it then? I will pray with the spirit, and I will pray with the understanding also: I will sing with the spirit, and I will sing with the understanding also. Else when thou shalt bless with the spirit, how shall he that occupieth the room of the unlearned say Amen at thy giving of thanks, seeing he understandeth not what thou sayest … But if all prophesy, and there come in one that believeth not, or *one* unlearned, he is convinced of all, he is judged of all … If any man speak in an *unknown* tongue, *let it be* by two, or at the most *by* three, and *that* by course; and let one interpret. But if there be no interpreter, let him keep silence in the church; and let him speak to himself, and to God.

157. How is the Word of God to be read?

A. The holy Scriptures are to be read with an high and reverent esteem of them; [1] with a firm persuasion that they are the very Word of God, [2] and that he only can enable us to understand them; [3] with desire to know, believe, and obey the will of God revealed in them; [4] with diligence, [5] and attention to the matter and scope of them; [6] with meditation, [7] application, [8] self-denial, [9] and prayer. [10]

Proofs

[1] **Psalm 19:10:** More to be desired *are they* than gold, yea, than much fine gold: sweeter also than honey and the honeycomb. **Nehemiah 8:3-6, 10:** And he read therein before the street that *was* before the water gate from the morning until midday, before the men and the women, and those that could understand; and the ears of all the people *were attentive* unto the book of the law. And Ezra the scribe stood upon a pulpit of wood, which they had made for the purpose; and beside him stood Mattithiah, and Shema, and Anaiah, and Urijah, and Hilkiah, and Maaseiah, on his right hand; and on his left hand, Pedaiah, and Mishael, and Malchiah, and Hashum, and Hashbadana, Zechariah, *and* Meshullam. And Ezra opened the book in the sight of all the people; (for he was above all the people;) and when he opened it, all the people stood up: And Ezra blessed the LORD, the great God. And all the people answered, Amen, Amen, with lifting up their hands: and they bowed their heads, and worshipped the LORD with *their* faces to the ground ... **Exodus 24:7:** And he took the book of the covenant, and read in the audience of the people: and they said, All that the LORD hath said will we do, and be obedient. **2 Chronicles 34:27:** Because thine heart was tender, and thou didst humble thyself before God, when thou heardest his words against this place, and against the inhabitants thereof, and humbledst thyself before me, and didst rend thy clothes, and weep before me; I have even heard *thee* also, saith the LORD. **Isaiah 66:2:** For all those *things* hath mine hand made, and all those *things* have been, saith the LORD: but to this *man* will I look, *even* to *him that is* poor and of a contrite spirit, and trembleth at my word.

[2] **2 Peter 1:19-21:** We have also a more sure word of prophecy; whereunto ye do well that ye take heed, as unto a light that shineth in a dark place, until the day dawn, and the day star arise in your hearts: Knowing this first, that no prophecy of the scripture is of any private interpretation. For the prophecy came not in old time by the will of man: but holy men of God spake *as they were* moved by the Holy Ghost.

[3] **Luke 24:45:** Then opened he their understanding, that they might understand the scriptures ... **2 Corinthians 3:13-16:** And not as Moses, *which* put a vail over his face, that the children of Israel could not stedfastly look to the end of that which is abolished: But their minds were blinded: for until this day remaineth the same veil untaken away in the reading of the old testament; which veil is done

away in Christ. But even unto this day, when Moses is read, the veil is upon their heart. Nevertheless when it shall turn to the Lord, the veil shall be taken away.

[4] **Deuteronomy 17:19, 20:** And it shall be with him, and he shall read therein all the days of his life: that he may learn to fear the LORD his God, to keep all the words of this law and these statutes, to do them: That his heart be not lifted up above his brethren, and that he turn not aside from the commandment, *to* the right hand, or *to* the left: to the end that he may prolong *his* days in his kingdom, he, and his children, in the midst of Israel.

[5] **Acts 17:11:** These were more noble than those in Thessalonica, in that they received the word with all readiness of mind, and searched the scriptures daily, whether those things were so.

[6] **Acts 8:30, 34:** And Philip ran thither to *him*, and heard him read the prophet Esaias, and said, Understandest thou what thou readest ... And the eunuch answered Philip, and said, I pray thee, of whom speaketh the prophet this? of himself, or of some other man? **Luke 10:26-28:** He said unto him, What is written in the law? how readest thou? And he answering said, Thou shalt love the Lord thy God with all thy heart, and with all thy soul, and with all thy strength, and with all thy mind; and thy neighbour as thyself. And he said unto him, Thou hast answered right: this do, and thou shalt live.

[7] **Psalm 1:2:** But his delight *is* in the law of the LORD; and in his law doth he meditate day and night. **Psalm 119:97:** O how love I thy law! it *is* my meditation all the day.

[8] **2 Chronicles 34:21:** Go, inquire of the LORD for me, and for them that are left in Israel and in Judah, concerning the words of the book that is found: for great *is* the wrath of the LORD that is poured out upon us, because our fathers have not kept the word of the LORD, to do after all that is written in this book.

[9] **Proverbs 3:5:** Trust in the LORD with all thine heart; and lean not unto thine own understanding. **Deuteronomy 33:3:** Yea, he loved the people; all his saints *are* in thy hand: and they sat down at thy feet; *every one* shall receive of thy words.

[10] **Proverbs 2:1-6:** My son, if thou wilt receive my words, and hide my commandments with thee; So that thou incline thine ear unto wisdom, *and* apply thine heart to understanding; Yea, if thou criest

after knowledge, *and* liftest up thy voice for understanding; If thou seekest her as silver, and searchest for her as *for* hid treasures; Then shalt thou understand the fear of the LORD, and find the knowledge of God. For the LORD giveth wisdom: out of his mouth *cometh* knowledge and understanding. **Psalm 119:18:** Open thou mine eyes, that I may behold wondrous things out of thy law. **Nehemiah 8:6, 8:** And Ezra blessed the LORD, the great God. And all the people answered, Amen, Amen, with lifting up their hands: and they bowed their heads, and worshipped the LORD with *their* faces to the ground ... So they read in the book in the law of God distinctly, and gave the sense, and caused *them* to understand the reading.

158. By whom is the Word of God to be preached?

A. The Word of God is to be preached only by such as are sufficiently gifted, [1] and also duly approved and called to that office. [2]

Proofs

[1] **1 Timothy 3:2, 6:** A bishop then must be blameless, the husband of one wife, vigilant, sober, of good behaviour, given to hospitality, apt to teach ... Not a novice, lest being lifted up with pride he fall into the condemnation of the devil. **Ephesians 4:8-11:** Wherefore he saith, When he ascended up on high, he led captivity captive, and gave gifts unto men. (Now that he ascended, what is it but that he also descended first into the lower parts of the earth? He that descended is the same also that ascended up far above all heavens, that he might fill all things.) And he gave some, apostles; and some, prophets; and some, evangelists; and some, pastors and teachers ... **Hosea 4:6:** My people are destroyed for lack of knowledge: because thou hast rejected knowledge, I will also reject thee, that thou shalt be no priest to me: seeing thou hast forgotten the law of thy God, I will also forget thy children. **Malachi 2:7:** For the priest's lips should keep knowledge, and they should seek the law at his mouth: for he *is* the messenger of the LORD of hosts. **2 Corinthians 3:6:** Who also hath made us able ministers of the new testament; not of the letter, but of the spirit: for the letter killeth, but the spirit giveth life.

[2] **Jeremiah 14:15:** Therefore thus saith the LORD concerning the prophets that prophesy in my name, and I sent them not, yet they say, Sword and famine shall not be in this land; By sword and famine shall

those prophets be consumed. **Romans 10:15:** And how shall they preach, except they be sent? as it is written, How beautiful are the feet of them that preach the gospel of peace, and bring glad tidings of good things! **Hebrews 5:4:** And no man taketh this honour unto himself, but he that is called of God, as *was* Aaron. **1 Corinthians 12:28-29:** And God hath set some in the church, first apostles, secondarily prophets, thirdly teachers, after that miracles, then gifts of healings, helps, governments, diversities of tongues. *Are* all apostles? *are* all prophets? are all teachers? *are* all workers of miracles? **1 Timothy 3:10:** And let these also first be proved; then let them use the office of a deacon, being *found* blameless. **1 Timothy 4:14:** Neglect not the gift that is in thee, which was given thee by prophecy, with the laying on of the hands of the presbytery. **1 Timothy 5:22:** Lay hands suddenly on no man, neither be partaker of other men's sins: keep thyself pure.

159. How is the Word of God to be preached by those that are called thereunto?

A. They that are called to labour in the ministry of the Word, are to preach sound doctrine, [1] diligently, [2] in season and out of season; [3] plainly, [4] not in the enticing words of man's wisdom, but in demonstration of the Spirit, and of power; [5] faithfully, [6] making known the whole counsel of God; [7] wisely, [8] applying themselves to the necessities and capacities of the hearers; [9] zealously, [10] with fervent love to God [11] and the souls of his people; [12] sincerely, [13] aiming at his glory, [14] and their conversion, [15] edification, [16] and salvation. [17]

Proofs

[1] **Titus 2:1, 8:** But speak thou the things which become sound doctrine ... Sound speech, that cannot be condemned; that he that is of the contrary part may be ashamed, having no evil thing to say of you.

[2] **Acts 18:25:** This man was instructed in the way of the Lord; and being fervent in the spirit, he spake and taught diligently the things of the Lord, knowing only the baptism of John.

[3] **2 Timothy 4:2:** Preach the word; be instant in season, out of season; reprove, rebuke, exhort with all longsuffering and doctrine.

[4] **1 Corinthians 14:19:** Yet in the church I had rather speak five words with my understanding, that *by my voice* I might teach others also, than ten thousand words in an *unknown* tongue.

[5] **1 Corinthians 2:4:** And my speech and my preaching *was* not with enticing words of man's wisdom, but in demonstration of the Spirit and of power …

[6] **Jeremiah 23:28:** The prophet that hath a dream, let him tell a dream; and he that hath my word, let him speak my word faithfully. What *is* the chaff to the wheat? saith the Lord. **1 Corinthians 4:1–2.** Let a man so account of us, as of the ministers of Christ, and stewards of the mysteries of God. Moreover it is required in stewards, that a man be found faithful.

[7] **Acts 20:27:** For I have not shunned to declare unto you all the counsel of God.

[8] **Colossians 1:28:** Whom we preach, warning every man, and teaching every man in all wisdom; that we may present every man perfect in Christ Jesus … **2 Timothy 2:15:** Study to shew thyself approved unto God, a workman that needeth not to be ashamed, rightly dividing the word of truth.

[9] **1 Corinthians 3:2:** I have fed you with milk, and not with meat: for hitherto ye were not able *to bear it*, neither yet now are ye able. **Hebrews 5:12–14:** For when for the time ye ought to be teachers, ye have need that one teach you again which *be* the first principles of the oracles of God; and are become such as have need of milk, and not of strong meat. For every one that useth milk *is* unskilful in the word of righteousness: for he is a babe. But strong meat belongeth to them that are of full age, *even* those who by reason of use have their senses exercised to discern both good and evil. **Luke 12:42:** And the Lord said, Who then is that faithful and wise steward, whom *his* lord shall make ruler over his household, to give *them their* portion of meat in due season?

[10] **Acts 18:25:** This man was instructed in the way of the Lord; and being fervent in the spirit, he spake and taught diligently the things of the Lord, knowing only the baptism of John.

[11] **2 Corinthians 5:13–14:** For whether we be beside ourselves, *it is* to God: or whether we be sober, *it is* for your cause. For the love of Christ constraineth us; because we thus judge, that if one died for all,

then were all dead ... **Philippians 1:15-17:** Some indeed preach Christ even of envy and strife; and some also of good will: The one preach Christ of contention, not sincerely, supposing to add affliction to my bonds: But the other of love, knowing that I am set for the defence of the gospel.

[12] **Colossians 4:12:** Epaphras, who is *one* of you, a servant of Christ, saluteth you, always labouring fervently for you in prayers, that ye may stand perfect and complete in all the will of God. **2 Corinthians 12:15:** And I will very gladly spend and be spent for you; though the more abundantly I love you, the less I be loved.

[13] **2 Corinthians 2:17:** For we are not as many, which corrupt the word of God: but as of sincerity, but as of God, in the sight of God speak we in Christ. **2 Corinthians 4:2:** But have renounced the hidden things of dishonesty, not walking in craftiness, nor handling the word of God deceitfully; but by manifestation of the truth commending ourselves to every man's conscience in the sight of God.

[14] **1 Thessalonians 2:4-6:** But as we were allowed of God to be put in trust with the gospel, even so we speak; not as pleasing men, but God, which trieth our hearts. For neither at any time used we flattering words, as ye know, nor a cloak of covetousness; God *is* witness: Nor of men sought we glory, neither of you, nor *yet* of others, when we might have been burdensome, as the apostles of Christ. **John 7:18:** He that speaketh of himself seeketh his own glory: but he that seeketh his glory that sent him, the same is true, and no unrighteousness is in him.

[15] **1 Corinthians 9:19-22:** For though I be free from all *men*, yet have I made myself servant unto all, that I might gain the more. And unto the Jews I became as a Jew, that I might gain the Jews; to them that are under the law, as under the law, that I might gain them that are under the law; To them that are without law, as without law, (being not without law to God, but under the law to Christ,) that I might gain them that are without law. To the weak became I as weak, that I might gain the weak: I am made all things to all *men*, that I might by all means save some.

[16] **2 Corinthians 12:19:** Again, think ye that we excuse ourselves unto you? we speak before God in Christ: but *we do* all things, dearly beloved, for your edifying. **Ephesians 4:12:** For the perfecting of

the saints, for the work of the ministry, for the edifying of the body of Christ …

[17] **1 Timothy 4:16:** Take heed unto thyself, and unto the doctrine; continue in them: for in doing this thou shalt both save thyself, and them that hear thee. **Acts 26:16-18:** But rise, and stand upon thy feet: for I have appeared unto thee for this purpose, to make thee a minister and a witness both of these things which thou hast seen, and of those things in the which I will appear unto thee; Delivering thee from the people, and *from* the Gentiles, unto whom now I send thee, To open their eyes, *and* to turn *them* from darkness to light, and *from* the power of Satan unto God, that they may receive forgiveness of sins, and inheritance among them which are sanctified by faith that is in me.

160. What is required of those that hear the Word preached?

A. It is required of those that hear the Word preached, that they attend upon it with diligence, [1] preparation, [2] and prayer; [3] examine what they hear by the Scriptures; [4] receive the truth with faith, [5] love, [6] meekness, [7] and readiness of mind, [8] as the Word of God; [9] meditate, [10] and confer of it; [11] hide it in their hearts, [12] and bring forth the fruit of it in their lives. [13]

Proofs

[1] **Proverbs 8:34:** Blessed *is* the man that heareth me, watching daily at my gates, waiting at the posts of my doors.

[2] **1 Peter 2:1-2:** Wherefore laying aside all malice, and all guile, and hypocrisies, and envies, and all evil speakings, As newborn babes, desire the sincere milk of the word, that ye may grow thereby … **Luke 8:18:** Take heed therefore how ye hear: for whosoever hath, to him shall be given; and whosoever hath not, from him shall be taken even that which he seemeth to have.

[3] **Psalm 119:18:** Open thou mine eyes, that I may behold wondrous things out of thy law. **Ephesians 6:18-19:** Praying always with all prayer and supplication in the Spirit, and watching thereunto with all perseverance and supplication for all saints; And for me, that utterance may be given unto me, that I may open my mouth boldly, to make known the mystery of the gospel …

[4] **Acts 17:11:** These were more noble than those in Thessalonica, in that they received the word with all readiness of mind, and searched the scriptures daily, whether those things were so.

[5] **Hebrews 4:2:** For unto us was the gospel preached, as well as unto them: but the word preached did not profit them, not being mixed with faith in them that heard *it*.

[6] **2 Thessalonians 2:10:** And with all deceivableness of unrighteousness in them that perish; because they received not the love of the truth, that they might be saved.

[7] **James 1:21:** Wherefore lay apart all filthiness and superfluity of naughtiness, and receive with meekness the engrafted word, which is able to save your souls.

[8] **Acts 17:11:** These were more noble than those in Thessalonica, in that they received the word with all readiness of mind, and searched the scriptures daily, whether those things were so.

[9] **1 Thessalonians 2:13:** For this cause also thank we God without ceasing, because, when ye received the word of God which ye heard of us, ye received *it* not *as* the word of men, but as it is in truth, the word of God, which effectually worketh also in you that believe.

[10] **Luke 9:44:** Let these sayings sink down into your ears: for the Son of man shall be delivered into the hands of men. **Hebrews 2:1:** Therefore we ought to give the more earnest heed to the things which we have heard, lest at any time we should let *them* slip.

[11] **Luke 24:14:** And they talked together of all these things which had happened. **Deuteronomy 6:6-7:** And these words, which I command thee this day, shall be in thine heart: And thou shalt teach them diligently unto thy children, and shalt talk of them when thou sittest in thine house, and when thou walkest by the way, and when thou liest down, and when thou risest up.

[12] **Proverbs 2:1:** My son, if thou wilt receive my words, and hide my commandments with thee ... **Psalm 119:11:** Thy word have I hid in mine heart, that I might not sin against thee.

[13] **Luke 8:15:** But that on the good ground are they, which in an honest and good heart, having heard the word, keep *it*, and bring forth fruit with patience. **James 1:25:** But whoso looketh into the perfect law of liberty, and continueth *therein*, he being

not a forgetful hearer, but a doer of the work, this man shall be blessed in his deed.

161. How do the sacraments become effectual means of salvation?

A. The sacraments become effectual means of salvation, not by any power in themselves, or any virtue derived from the piety or intention of him by whom they are administered, but only by the working of the Holy Ghost, and the blessing of Christ, by whom they are instituted. [1]

Proofs

[1] **1 Peter 3:21:** The like figure whereunto *even* baptism doth also now save us (not the putting away of the filth of the flesh, but the answer of a good conscience toward God,) by the resurrection of Jesus Christ ... **Acts 8:13, 23:** Then Simon himself believed also: and when he was baptized, he continued with Philip, and wondered, beholding the miracles and signs which were done ...For I perceive that thou art in the gall of bitterness, and *in* the bond of iniquity. **1 Corinthians 3:6-7:** I have planted, Apollos watered; but God gave the increase. So then neither is he that planteth any thing, neither he that watereth; but God that giveth the increase. **1 Corinthians 12:13:** For by one Spirit are we all baptized into one body, whether *we be* Jews or Gentiles, whether *we be* bond or free; and have been all made to drink into one Spirit.

162. What is a sacrament?

A. A sacrament is an holy ordinance instituted by Christ in his church, [1] to signify, seal, and exhibit [2] unto those that are within the covenant of grace, [3] the benefits of his mediation; [4] to strengthen and increase their faith, and all other graces; [5] to oblige them to obedience; [6] to testify and cherish their love and communion one with another; [7] and to distinguish them from those that are without. [8]

Proofs

[1] **Genesis 17:7, 10:** And I will establish my covenant between me and thee and thy seed after thee in their generations for an everlasting covenant, to be a God unto thee, and to thy seed after

thee ... This *is* my covenant, which ye shall keep, between me and you and thy seed after thee; Every man child among you shall be circumcised. **Exodus 12** [containing the institution of the passover]. **Matthew 28:19:** Go ye therefore, and teach all nations, baptizing them in the name of the Father, and of the Son, and of the Holy Ghost ... **Matthew 26:26-28:** And as they were eating, Jesus took bread, and blessed *it*, and brake *it*, and gave *it* to the disciples, and said, Take, eat; this is my body. And he took the cup, and gave thanks, and gave *it* to them, saying, Drink ye all of it; For this is my blood of the new testament, which is shed for many for the remission of sins.

[2] **Romans 4:11:** And he received the sign of circumcision, a seal of the righteousness of the faith which *he had yet* being uncircumcised: that he might be the father of all them that believe, though they be not circumcised; that righteousness might be imputed unto them also ... **1 Corinthians 11:24-25:** And when he had given thanks, he brake *it*, and said, Take, eat: this is my body, which is broken for you: this do in remembrance of me. After the same manner also *he took* the cup, when he had supped, saying, This cup is the new testament in my blood: this do ye, as oft as ye drink *it*, in remembrance of me.

[3] **Romans 15:8:** Now I say that Jesus Christ was a minister of the circumcision for the truth of God, to confirm the promises *made* unto the fathers ... **Exodus 12:48:** And when a stranger shall sojourn with thee, and will keep the passover to the LORD, let all his males be circumcised, and then let him come near and keep it; and he shall be as one that is born in the land: for no uncircumcised person shall eat thereof.

[4] **Acts 2:38:** Then Peter said unto them, Repent, and be baptized every one of you in the name of Jesus Christ for the remission of sins, and ye shall receive the gift of the Holy Ghost. **1 Corinthians 10:16:** The cup of blessing which we bless, is it not the communion of the blood of Christ? The bread which we break, is it not the communion of the body of Christ?

[5] **Romans 4:11:** And he received the sign of circumcision, a seal of the righteousness of the faith which *he had yet* being uncircumcised: that he might be the father of all them that believe, though they be not circumcised; that righteousness might be imputed unto them also ... **Galatians 3:27:** For as many of you as have been baptized into Christ have put on Christ.

[6] **Romans 6:3-4:** Know ye not, that so many of us as were baptized into Jesus Christ were baptized into his death? Therefore we are buried with him by baptism into death: that like as Christ was raised up from the dead by the glory of the Father, even so we also should walk in newness of life. **1 Corinthians 10:21:** Ye cannot drink the cup of the Lord, and the cup of devils: ye cannot be partakers of the Lord's table, and of the table of devils.

[7] **Ephesians 4:2-5:** With all lowliness and meekness, with long-suffering, forbearing one another in love; Endeavouring to keep the unity of the Spirit in the bond of peace. *There is* one body, and one Spirit, even as ye are called in one hope of your calling; One Lord, one faith, one baptism ... **1 Corinthians 12:13:** For by one Spirit are we all baptized into one body, whether *we be* Jews or Gentiles, whether *we be* bond or free; and have been all made to drink into one Spirit.

[8] **Ephesians 2:11-12:** Wherefore remember, that ye *being* in time past Gentiles in the flesh, who are called Uncircumcision by that which is called the Circumcision in the flesh made by hands; That at that time ye were without Christ, being aliens from the commonwealth of Israel, and strangers from the covenants of promise, having no hope, and without God in the world ... **Genesis 34:14:** And they said unto them, We cannot do this thing, to give our sister to one that is uncircumcised; for that *were* a reproach unto us ...

163. What are the parts of a sacrament?

A. The parts of the sacrament are two; the one an outward and sensible sign, used according to Christ's own appointment; the other an inward and spiritual grace thereby signified. [1]

Proofs

[1] **Matthew 3:11:** I indeed baptize you with water unto repentance: but he that cometh after me is mightier than I, whose shoes I am not worthy to bear: he shall baptize you with the Holy Ghost, and *with* fire ... **1 Peter 3:21:** The like figure whereunto *even* baptism doth also now save us (not the putting away of the filth of the flesh, but the answer of a good conscience toward God,) by the resurrection of Jesus Christ ... **Romans 2:28-29:** For he is not a Jew, which is one outwardly; neither *is that* circumcision, which is outward in the flesh: But he is a Jew, which is one inwardly; and circumcision is that of the

heart, in the spirit, *and* not in the letter; whose praise *is* not of men, but of God.

164. How many sacraments hath Christ instituted in his church under the New Testament?

A. Under the New Testament Christ hath instituted in his church only two sacraments, baptism and the Lord's Supper. [1]

Proofs

[1] **Matthew 28:19:** Go ye therefore, and teach all nations, baptizing them in the name of the Father, and of the Son, and of the Holy Ghost … **1 Corinthians 11:20, 23:** When ye come together therefore into one place, *this* is not to eat the Lord's supper … For I have received of the Lord that which also I delivered unto you, That the Lord Jesus the *same* night in which he was betrayed took bread … **Matthew 26:26-28:** And as they were eating, Jesus took bread, and blessed *it*, and brake *it*, and gave *it* to the disciples, and said, Take, eat; this is my body. And he took the cup, and gave thanks, and gave *it* to them, saying, Drink ye all of it; For this is my blood of the new testament, which is shed for many for the remission of sins.

165. What is baptism?

A. Baptism is a sacrament of the New Testament, wherein Christ hath ordained the washing with water in the name of the Father, and of the Son, and of the Holy Ghost, [1] to be a sign and seal of ingrafting into himself, [2] of remission of sins by his blood, [3] and regeneration by his Spirit; [4] of adoption, [5] and resurrection unto everlasting life; [6] and whereby the parties baptized are solemnly admitted into the visible church, [7] and enter into an open and professed engagement to be wholly and only the Lord's. [8]

Proofs

[1] **Matthew 28:19:** Go ye therefore, and teach all nations, baptizing them in the name of the Father, and of the Son, and of the Holy Ghost …

[2] **Galatians 3:27:** For as many of you as have been baptized into Christ have put on Christ.

[3] **Mark 1:4:** John did baptize in the wilderness, and preach the baptism of repentance for the remission of sins. **Revelation 1:5:** And from Jesus Christ, *who is* the faithful witness, *and* the first begotten of the dead, and the prince of the kings of the earth. Unto him that loved us, and washed us from our sins in his own blood …

[4] **Titus 3:5:** Not by works of righteousness which we have done, but according to his mercy he saved us, by the washing of regeneration, and renewing of the Holy Ghost … **Ephesians 5:26:** That he might sanctify and cleanse it with the washing of water by the word …

[5] **Galatians 3:26-27:** For ye are all the children of God by faith in Christ Jesus. For as many of you as have been baptized into Christ have put on Christ.

[6] **1 Corinthians 15:29:** Else what shall they do which are baptized for the dead, if the dead rise not at all? why are they then baptized for the dead? **Romans 6:5:** For if we have been planted together in the likeness of his death, we shall be also *in the likeness of his* resurrection …

[7] **1 Corinthians 12:13:** For by one Spirit are we all baptized into one body, whether *we be* Jews or Gentiles, whether *we be* bond or free; and have been all made to drink into one Spirit.

[8] **Romans 6:4:** Therefore we are buried with him by baptism into death: that like as Christ was raised up from the dead by the glory of the Father, even so we also should walk in newness of life.

166. Unto whom is baptism to be administered?

A. Baptism is not to be administered to any that are out of the visible church, and so strangers from the covenant of promise, till they profess their faith in Christ, and obedience to him, [1] but infants descending from parents, either both, or but one of them, professing faith in Christ, and obedience to him, are in that respect within the covenant, and to be baptized. [2]

Proofs

[1] **Acts 8:36-37:** And as they went on *their* way, they came unto a certain water: and the eunuch said, See, *here is* water; what doth hinder me to be baptized? And Philip said, If thou believest with all thine heart, thou mayest. And he answered and said, I believe that Jesus Christ is the Son of God. **Acts 2:38:** Then Peter said unto them, Repent, and be

baptized every one of you in the name of Jesus Christ for the remission of sins, and ye shall receive the gift of the Holy Ghost.

[2] **Genesis 17:7, 9:** And I will establish my covenant between me and thee and thy seed after thee in their generations for an everlasting covenant, to be a God unto thee, and to thy seed after thee … And God said unto Abraham, Thou shalt keep my covenant therefore, thou, and thy seed after thee in their generations. [Compare with] **Galatians 3:9, 14:** So then they which be of faith are blessed with faithful Abraham … That the blessing of Abraham might come on the Gentiles through Jesus Christ; that we might receive the promise of the Spirit through faith. [And with] **Colossians 2:11-12:** In whom also ye are circumcised with the circumcision made without hands, in putting off the body of the sins of the flesh by the circumcision of Christ: Buried with him in baptism, wherein also ye are risen with *him* through the faith of the operation of God, who hath raised him from the dead. [And with] **Acts 2:38-39:** Then Peter said unto them, Repent, and be baptized every one of you in the name of Jesus Christ for the remission of sins, and ye shall receive the gift of the Holy Ghost. For the promise is unto you, and to your children, and to all that are afar off, *even* as many as the Lord our God shall call. [And with] **Romans 4:11-12:** And he received the sign of circumcision, a seal of the righteousness of the faith which *he had yet* being uncircumcised: that he might be the father of all them that believe, though they be not circumcised; that righteousness might be imputed unto them also: And the father of circumcision to them who are not of the circumcision only, but who also walk in the steps of that faith of our father Abraham, which *he had* being *yet* uncircumcised. **1 Corinthians 7:14:** For the unbelieving husband is sanctified by the wife, and the unbelieving wife is sanctified by the husband: else were your children unclean; but now are they holy. **Matthew 28:19:** Go ye therefore, and teach all nations, baptizing them in the name of the Father, and of the Son, and of the Holy Ghost … **Luke 18:15-16:** And they brought unto him also infants, that he would touch them: but when *his* disciples saw *it*, they rebuked them. But Jesus called them *unto him*, and said, Suffer little children to come unto me, and forbid them not: for of such is the kingdom of God. **Romans 11:16:** For if the firstfruit *be* holy, the lump *is* also *holy*: and if the root *be* holy, so *are* the branches.

167. How is our baptism to be improved by us?

A. The needful but much neglected duty of improving our baptism, is to be performed by us all our life long, especially in the time of temptation, and when we are present at the administration of it to others; [1] by serious and thankful consideration of the nature of it, and of the ends for which Christ instituted it, the privileges and benefits conferred and sealed thereby, and our solemn vow made therein; [2] by being humbled for our sinful defilement, our falling short of, and walking contrary to, the grace of baptism, and our engagements; [3] by growing up to assurance of pardon of sin, and of all other blessings sealed to us in that sacrament; [4] by drawing strength from the death and resurrection of Christ, into whom we are baptized, for the mortifying of sin, and quickening of grace; [5] and by endeavouring to live by faith, [6] to have our conversation in holiness and righteousness, [7] as those that have therein given up their names to Christ; [8] and to walk in brotherly love, as being baptized by the same Spirit into one body. [9]

Proofs

[1] **Colossians 2:11-12:** In whom also ye are circumcised with the circumcision made without hands, in putting off the body of the sins of the flesh by the circumcision of Christ: Buried with him in baptism, wherein also ye are risen with *him* through the faith of the operation of God, who hath raised him from the dead. **Romans 6:4, 6, 11:** Therefore we are buried with him by baptism into death: that like as Christ was raised up from the dead by the glory of the Father, even so we also should walk in newness of life ... Knowing this, that our old man is crucified with *him*, that the body of sin might be destroyed, that henceforth we should not serve sin ... Likewise reckon ye also yourselves to be dead indeed unto sin, but alive unto God through Jesus Christ our Lord.

[2] **Romans 6:3-5:** Know ye not, that so many of us as were baptized into Jesus Christ were baptized into his death? Therefore we are buried with him by baptism into death: that like as Christ was raised up from the dead by the glory of the Father, even so we also should walk in

newness of life. For if we have been planted together in the likeness of his death, we shall be also *in the likeness* of *his* resurrection.

[3] **1 Corinthians 1:11-13:** For it hath been declared unto me of you, my brethren, by them *which are of the house* of Chloe, that there are contentions among you. Now this I say, that every one of you saith, I am of Paul; and I of Apollos; and I of Cephas; and I of Christ. Is Christ divided? was Paul crucified for you? or were ye baptized in the name of Paul? **Romans 6:2-3:** God forbid. How shall we, that are dead to sin, live any longer therein? Know ye not, that so many of us as were baptized into Jesus Christ were baptized into his death?

[4] **Romans 4:11-12:** And he received the sign of circumcision, a seal of the righteousness of the faith which *he had yet* being uncircumcised: that he might be the father of all them that believe, though they be not circumcised; that righteousness might be imputed unto them also: And the father of circumcision to them who are not of the circumcision only, but who also walk in the steps of that faith of our father Abraham, which *he had* being *yet* uncircumcised. **1 Peter 3:21:** The like figure whereunto *even* baptism doth also now save us (not the putting away of the filth of the flesh, but the answer of a good conscience toward God,) by the resurrection of Jesus Christ ...

[5] **Romans 6:3-5:** Know ye not, that so many of us as were baptized into Jesus Christ were baptized into his death? Therefore we are buried with him by baptism into death: that like as Christ was raised up from the dead by the glory of the Father, even so we also should walk in newness of life. For if we have been planted together in the likeness of his death, we shall be also *in the likeness* of *his* resurrection ...

[6] **Galatians 3:26-27:** For ye are all the children of God by faith in Christ Jesus. For as many of you as have been baptized into Christ have put on Christ.

[7] **Romans 6:22:** But now being made free from sin, and become servants to God, ye have your fruit unto holiness, and the end everlasting life.

[8] **Acts 2:38:** Then Peter said unto them, Repent, and be baptized every one of you in the name of Jesus Christ for the remission of sins, and ye shall receive the gift of the Holy Ghost.

[9] **1 Corinthians 12:13, 25-27:** For by one Spirit are we all baptized into one body, whether *we be* Jews or Gentiles, whether *we be* bond or

free; and have been all made to drink into one Spirit ... That there should be no schism in the body; but *that* the members should have the same care one for another. And whether one member suffer, all the members suffer with it; or one member be honoured, all the members rejoice with it. Now ye are the body of Christ, and members in particular.

168. What is the Lord's Supper?

A. The Lord's Supper is a sacrament of the New Testament, [1] wherein, by giving and receiving bread and wine according to the appointment of Jesus Christ, his death is showed forth; and they that worthily communicate feed upon his body and blood, to their spiritual nourishment and growth in grace; [2] have their union and communion with him confirmed; [3] testify and renew their thankfulness, [4] and engagement to God, [5] and their mutual love and fellowship each with the other, as members of the same mystical body. [6]

Poofs

[1] **Luke 22:20:** Likewise also the cup after supper, saying, This cup *is* the new testament in my blood, which is shed for you.

[2] **Matthew 26:26-28:** And as they were eating, Jesus took bread, and blessed *it*, and brake *it*, and gave *it* to the disciples, and said, Take, eat; this is my body. And he took the cup, and gave thanks, and gave *it* to them, saying, Drink ye all of it; For this is my blood of the new testament, which is shed for many for the remission of sins. **1 Corinthians 11:23-26:** For I have received of the Lord that which also I delivered unto you, That the Lord Jesus the *same* night in which he was betrayed took bread: And when he had given thanks, he brake *it*, and said, Take, eat: this is my body, which is broken for you: this do in remembrance of me. After the same manner also *he took* the cup, when he had supped, saying, This cup is the new testament in my blood: this do ye, as oft as ye drink *it*, in remembrance of me. For as often as ye eat this bread, and drink this cup, ye do shew the Lord's death till he come.

[3] **1 Corinthians 10:16:** The cup of blessing which we bless, is it not the communion of the blood of Christ? The bread which we break, is it not the communion of the body of Christ?

[4] **1 Corinthians 11:24:** And when he had given thanks, he brake *it*, and said, Take, eat: this is my body, which is broken for you: this do in remembrance of me.

[5] **1 Corinthians 10:14-16, 21:** Wherefore, my dearly beloved, flee from idolatry. I speak as to wise men; judge ye what I say. The cup of blessing which we bless, is it not the communion of the blood of Christ? The bread which we break, is it not the communion of the body of Christ? ... Ye cannot drink the cup of the Lord, and the cup of devils: ye cannot be partakers of the Lord's table, and of the table of devils.

[6] **1 Corinthians 10:17:** For we *being* many are one bread, *and* one body: for we are all partakers of that one bread.

169. How hath Christ appointed bread and wine to be given and received in the sacrament of the Lord's Supper?

A. Christ hath appointed the ministers of his Word, in the administration of this sacrament of the Lord's Supper, to set apart the bread and wine from common use, by the word of institution, thanksgiving, and prayer; to take and break the bread, and to give both the bread and the wine to the communicants: who are, by the same appointment, to take and eat the bread, and to drink the wine, in thankful remembrance that the body of Christ was broken and given, and his blood shed, for them. [1]

Proofs

[1] **1 Corinthians 11:23-24:** For I have received of the Lord that which also I delivered unto you, That the Lord Jesus the *same* night in which he was betrayed took bread: And when he had given thanks, he brake *it*, and said, Take, eat: this is my body, which is broken for you: this do in remembrance of me. **Matthew 26:26-28:** And as they were eating, Jesus took bread, and blessed *it*, and brake *it,* and gave *it* to the disciples, and said, Take, eat; this is my body. And he took the cup, and gave thanks, and gave *it* to them, saying, Drink ye all of it; For this is my blood of the new testament, which is shed for many for the remission of sins. **Mark 14:22-24:** And as they did eat, Jesus took bread, and blessed, and brake *it*, and gave to them, and said, Take, eat: this is my body. And he took the cup, and when he had given thanks, he gave *it* to

them: and they all drank of it. And he said unto them, This is my blood of the new testament, which is shed for many. **Luke 22:19-20:** And he took bread, and gave thanks, and brake *it*, and gave unto them, saying, This is my body which is given for you: this do in remembrance of me. Likewise also the cup after supper, saying, This cup *is* the new testament in my blood, which is shed for you.

170. How do they that worthily communicate in the Lord's Supper feed upon the body and blood of Christ therein?

A. As the body and blood of Christ are not corporally or carnally present in, with, or under the bread and wine in the Lord's Supper, [1] and yet are spiritually present to the faith of the receiver, no less truly and really than the elements themselves are to their outward senses; [2] so they that worthily communicate in the sacrament of the Lord's Supper, do therein feed upon the body and blood of Christ, not after a corporal and carnal, but in a spiritual manner; yet truly and really, [3] while by faith they receive and apply unto themselves Christ crucified, and all the benefits of his death. [4]

Proofs

[1] **Acts 3:21:** Whom the heaven must receive until the times of restitution of all things, which God hath spoken by the mouth of all his holy prophets since the world began.

[2] **Matthew 26:26, 28:** And as they were eating, Jesus took bread, and blessed *it*, and brake *it*, and gave *it* to the disciples, and said, Take, eat; this is my body ... For this is my blood of the new testament, which is shed for many for the remission of sins.

[3] **1 Corinthians 11:24-29:** And when he had given thanks, he brake *it*, and said, Take, eat: this is my body, which is broken for you: this do in remembrance of me. After the same manner also *he took* the cup, when he had supped, saying, This cup is the new testament in my blood: this do ye, as oft as ye drink *it*, in remembrance of me. For as often as ye eat this bread, and drink this cup, ye do shew the Lord's death till he come. Wherefore whosoever shall eat this bread, and drink this cup of the Lord, unworthily, shall be guilty of the body and blood of the Lord. But let a man examine himself, and so let him eat of *that* bread, and drink of *that* cup. For he that eateth and

drinketh unworthily, eateth and drinketh damnation to himself, not discerning the Lord's body.

[4] **1 Corinthians 10:16:** The cup of blessing which we bless, is it not the communion of the blood of Christ? The bread which we break, is it not the communion of the body of Christ?

171. How are they that receive the sacrament of the Lord's Supper to prepare themselves before they come unto it?

A. They that receive the sacrament of the Lord's Supper are, before they come, to prepare themselves thereunto, by examining themselves [1] of their being in Christ, [2] of their sins and wants; [3] of the truth and measure of their knowledge, [4] faith, [5] repentance; [6] love to God and the brethren, [7] charity to all men, [8] forgiving those that have done them wrong; [9] of their desires after Christ, [10] and of their new obedience; [11] and by renewing the exercise of these graces, [12] by serious meditation, [13] and fervent prayer. [14]

Proofs

[1] **1 Corinthians 11:28:** But let a man examine himself, and so let him eat of *that* bread, and drink of *that* cup.

[2] **2 Corinthians 13:5:** Examine yourselves, whether ye be in the faith; prove your own selves. Know ye not your own selves, how that Jesus Christ is in you, except ye be reprobates?

[3] **1 Corinthians 5:7:** Purge out therefore the old leaven, that ye may be a new lump, as ye are unleavened. For even Christ our passover is sacrificed for us ... [Compare with] **Exodus 12:15:** Seven days shall ye eat unleavened bread; even the first day ye shall put away leaven out of your houses: for whosoever eateth leavened bread from the first day until the seventh day, that soul shall be cut off from Israel.

[4] **1 Corinthians 11:29:** For he that eateth and drinketh unworthily, eateth and drinketh damnation to himself, not discerning the Lord's body.

[5] **2 Corinthians 13:5:** Examine yourselves, whether ye be in the faith; prove your own selves. Know ye not your own selves, how that

Jesus Christ is in you, except ye be reprobates? **Matthew 26:28:** For this is my blood of the new testament, which is shed for many for the remission of sins.

[6] **Zechariah 12:10:** And I will pour upon the house of David, and upon the inhabitants of Jerusalem, the spirit of grace and of supplications: and they shall look upon me whom they have pierced, and they shall mourn for him, as one mourneth for his only *son*, and shall be in bitterness for him, as one that is in bitterness for *his* firstborn. **1 Corinthians 11:31:** For if we would judge ourselves, we should not be judged.

[7] **1 Corinthians 10:16-17:** The cup of blessing which we bless, is it not the communion of the blood of Christ? The bread which we break, is it not the communion of the body of Christ? For we *being* many are one bread, *and* one body: for we are all partakers of that one bread. **Acts 2:46-47:** And they, continuing daily with one accord in the temple, and breaking bread from house to house, did eat their meat with gladness and singleness of heart, Praising God, and having favour with all the people. And the Lord added to the church daily such as should be saved.

[8] **1 Corinthians 5:8:** Therefore let us keep the feast, not with old leaven, neither with the leaven of malice and wickedness; but with the unleavened *bread* of sincerity and truth. **1 Corinthians 11:18, 20:** For first of all, when ye come together in the church, I hear that there be divisions among you; and I partly believe it ... When ye come together therefore into one place, *this* is not to eat the Lord's supper.

[9] **Matthew 5:23-24:** Therefore if thou bring thy gift to the altar, and there rememberest that thy brother hath ought against thee; Leave there thy gift before the altar, and go thy way; first be reconciled to thy brother, and then come and offer thy gift.

[10] **Isaiah 55:1:** Ho, every one that thirsteth, come ye to the waters, and he that hath no money; come ye, buy, and eat; yea, come, buy wine and milk without money and without price. **John 7:37:** In the last day, that great *day* of the feast, Jesus stood and cried, saying, If any man thirst, let him come unto me, and drink.

[11] **1 Corinthians 5:7-8:** Purge out therefore the old leaven, that ye may be a new lump, as ye are unleavened. For even Christ our passover is sacrificed for us: Therefore let us keep the feast, not with

old leaven, neither with the leaven of malice and wickedness; but with the unleavened *bread* of sincerity and truth.

[12] **1 Corinthians 11:25-26, 28:** After the same manner also *he took* the cup, when he had supped, saying, This cup is the new testament in my blood: this do ye, as oft as ye drink *it*, in remembrance of me. For as often as ye eat this bread, and drink this cup, ye do shew the Lord's death till he come ... But let a man examine himself, and so let him eat of *that* bread, and drink of that cup. **Hebrews 10:21-22:** And *having* an high priest over the house of God; Let us draw near with a true heart in full assurance of faith, having our hearts sprinkled from an evil conscience, and our bodies washed with pure water. **Hebrews 10:24:** And let us consider one another to provoke unto love and to good works ... **Psalm 26:6:** I will wash mine hands in innocency: so will I compass thine altar, O LORD...

[13] **1 Corinthians 11:24-25:** And when he had given thanks, he brake *it*, and said, Take, eat: this is my body, which is broken for you: this do in remembrance of me. After the same manner also *he took* the cup, when he had supped, saying, This cup is the new testament in my blood: this do ye, as oft as ye drink *it*, in remembrance of me.

[14] **2 Chronicles 30:18-19:** For a multitude of the people, *even* many of Ephraim, and Manasseh, Issachar, and Zebulun, had not cleansed themselves, yet did they eat the passover otherwise than it was written. But Hezekiah prayed for them, saying, The good LORD pardon every one *That* prepareth his heart to seek God, the LORD God of his fathers, though *he be* not *cleansed* according to the purification of the sanctuary. **Matthew 26:26:** And as they were eating, Jesus took bread, and blessed *it*, and brake *it*, and gave *it* to the disciples, and said, Take, eat; this is my body.

172. May one who doubteth of his being in Christ, or of his due preparation, come to the Lord's Supper?

A. One who doubteth of his being in Christ, or of his due preparation to the sacrament of the Lord's Supper, may have true interest in Christ, though he be not yet assured thereof; [1] and in God's account hath it, if he be duly affected with the apprehension of the want of it, [2] and unfeignedly desires to be found in Christ, [3] and to depart from iniquity: [4] in which case (because promises are made, and this sacrament is appointed, for the relief even of weak and doubting Christians) [5] he is to bewail his unbelief, [6] and labour to have his doubts resolved; [7] and, so doing, he may and ought to come to the Lord's Supper, that he may be further strengthened. [8]

Proofs

[1] Isaiah 50:10: Who *is* among you that feareth the LORD, that obeyeth the voice of his servant, that walketh *in* darkness, and hath no light? let him trust in the name of the LORD, and stay upon his God. **1 John 5:13:** These things have I written unto you that believe on the name of the Son of God; that ye may know that ye have eternal life, and that ye may believe on the name of the Son of God. **Psalm 88:** O LORD God of my salvation, I have cried day *and* night before thee: Let my prayer come before thee: incline thine ear unto my cry; For my soul is full of troubles: and my life draweth nigh unto the grave. I am counted with them that go down into the pit: I am as a man *that hath* no strength: Free among the dead, like the slain that lie in the grave, whom thou rememberest no more: and they are cut off from thy hand. Thou hast laid me in the lowest pit, in darkness, in the deeps. Thy wrath lieth hard upon me, and thou hast afflicted *me* with all thy waves. Selah. Thou hast put away mine acquaintance far from me; thou hast made me an abomination unto them: *I am* shut up, and I cannot come forth. Mine eye mourneth by reason of affliction: LORD, I have called daily upon thee, I have stretched out my hands unto thee. Wilt thou shew wonders to the dead? shall the dead arise *and* praise thee? Selah. Shall thy lovingkindness be declared in the grave? or thy faithfulness in destruction? Shall thy wonders be known in the dark? and thy righteousness in the land of forgetfulness? But unto thee have I cried, O LORD; and in the morning shall my prayer prevent thee. LORD, why castest thou off my soul? why hidest thou thy face from me? I *am* afflicted and ready to die from *my* youth up: *while* I suffer thy terrors I am distracted. Thy fierce wrath goeth over me; thy terrors have cut me off. They came round about me daily like water; they compassed me about together. Lover and friend hast thou put far from me, *and* mine acquaintance into darkness. **Psalm 77:1–4, 7–10:** I cried unto God with my voice, *even* unto God with my voice; and he gave ear unto me. In the day of my trouble I sought the Lord: my sore ran in the night, and ceased not: my soul refused to be comforted. I remembered God, and was troubled: I complained, and my spirit was overwhelmed. Selah. Thou holdest mine eyes waking: I am so troubled that I cannot speak … Will the Lord cast off for ever? and will he be favourable no more? Is his mercy clean gone for ever? doth *his* promise fail for evermore? Hath God forgotten to be gracious? hath he in anger shut up his tender mercies? Selah. And I said, This *is* my infirmity: *but I will remember* the years of the right hand of the most High. **Jonah 2:4, 7:** Then I said, I am cast out of thy sight; yet I will look again toward thy holy temple … When my soul fainted within me I remembered the Lord: and my prayer came in unto thee, into thine holy temple.

[2] **Isaiah 54:7-10:** For a small moment have I forsaken thee; but with great mercies will I gather thee. In a little wrath I hid my face from thee for a moment; but with everlasting kindness will I have mercy on thee, saith the Lord thy Redeemer. For this *is as* the waters of Noah unto me: for *as* I have sworn that the waters of Noah should no more go over the earth; so have I sworn that I would not be wroth with thee, nor rebuke thee. For the mountains shall depart, and the hills be removed; but my kindness shall not depart from thee, neither shall the covenant of my peace be removed, saith the Lord that hath mercy on thee. **Matthew 5:3-4:** Blessed *are* the poor in spirit: for theirs is the kingdom of heaven. Blessed *are* they that mourn: for they shall be comforted. **Psalm 31:22:** For I said in my haste, I am cut off from before thine eyes: nevertheless thou heardest the voice of my supplications when I cried unto thee. **Psalm 73:13, 22-23:** Verily I have cleansed my heart *in* vain, and washed my hands in innocency … So foolish *was* I, and ignorant: I was *as* a beast before thee. Nevertheless I *am* continually with thee: thou hast holden *me* by my right hand.

[3] **Philippians 3:8-9:** Yea doubtless, and I count all things *but* loss for the excellency of the knowledge of Christ Jesus my Lord: for whom I have suffered the loss of all things, and do count them *but* dung, that I may win Christ, And be found in him, not having mine own righteousness, which is of the law, but that which is through the faith of Christ, the righteousness which is of God by faith … **Psalm 10:17:** Lord, thou hast heard the desire of the humble: thou wilt prepare their heart, thou wilt cause thine ear to hear … **Psalm 42:1-2, 5, 11:** As the hart panteth after the water brooks, so panteth my soul after thee, O God.

My soul thirsteth for God, for the living God: when shall I come and appear before God? … Why art thou cast down, O my soul? and *why* art thou disquieted in me? hope thou in God: for I shall yet praise him *for* the help of his countenance … Why art thou cast down, O my soul? and why art thou disquieted within me? hope thou in God: for I shall yet praise him, *who is* the health of my countenance, and my God.

[4] **2 Timothy 2:19:** Nevertheless the foundation of God standeth sure, having this seal, The Lord knoweth them that are his. And, Let every one that nameth the name of Christ depart from iniquity. **Isaiah 50:10:** Who *is* among you that feareth the LORD, that obeyeth the voice of his servant, that walketh *in* darkness, and hath no light? let him trust in the name of the LORD, and stay upon his God. **Psalm 66:18-20:** If I regard iniquity in my heart, the Lord will not hear *me:* *But* verily God hath heard *me*; he hath attended to the voice of my prayer. Blessed *be* God, which hath not turned away my prayer, nor his mercy from me.

[5] **Isaiah 40:11, 29, 31:** He shall feed his flock like a shepherd: he shall gather the lambs with his arm, and carry *them* in his bosom, *and* shall gently lead those that are with young … He giveth power to the faint; and to *them that have* no might he increaseth strength … But they that wait upon the LORD shall renew their strength; they shall mount up with wings as eagles; they shall run, and not be weary; *and* they shall walk, and not faint. **Matthew 11:28:** Come unto me, all *ye* that labour and are heavy laden, and I will give you rest. **Matthew 12:20:** A bruised reed shall he not break, and smoking flax shall he not quench, till he send forth judgment unto victory. **Matthew 26:28:** For this is my blood of the new testament, which is shed for many for the remission of sins.

[6] **Mark 9:24:** And straightway the father of the child cried out, and said with tears, Lord, I believe; help thou mine unbelief.

[7] **Acts 2:37:** Now when they heard *this*, they were pricked in their heart, and said unto Peter and to the rest of the apostles, Men *and* brethren, what shall we do? **Acts 16:30:** And brought them out, and said, Sirs, what must I do to be saved?

[8] **Romans 4:11:** And he received the sign of circumcision, a seal of the righteousness of the faith which *he had* yet being uncircumcised: that he might be the father of all them that believe, though they be

not circumcised; that righteousness might be imputed unto them also … **1 Corinthians 11:28:** But let a man examine himself, and so let him eat of *that* bread, and drink of *that* cup.

173. May any who profess the faith, and desire to come to the Lord's Supper, be kept from it?

A. Such as are found to be ignorant or scandalous, notwithstanding their profession of the faith, and desire to come to the Lord's Supper, may and ought to be kept from that sacrament, by the power which Christ hath left in his church, [1] until they receive instruction, and manifest their reformation. [2]

Proofs

[1] **1 Corinthians 11:27-34:** Wherefore whosoever shall eat this bread, and drink *this* cup of the Lord, unworthily, shall be guilty of the body and blood of the Lord. But let a man examine himself, and so let him eat of *that* bread, and drink of *that* cup. For he that eateth and drinketh unworthily, eateth and drinketh damnation to himself, not discerning the Lord's body. For this cause many *are* weak and sickly among you, and many sleep. For if we would judge ourselves, we should not be judged. But when we are judged, we are chastened of the Lord, that we should not be condemned with the world. Wherefore, my brethren, when ye come together to eat, tarry one for another. And if any man hunger, let him eat at home; that ye come not together unto condemnation. And the rest will I set in order when I come. [Compare with] **Matthew 7:6:** Give not that which is holy unto the dogs, neither cast ye your pearls before swine, lest they trample them under their feet, and turn again and rend you. [And with] **1 Corinthians 5:** It is reported commonly *that there is* fornication among you, and such fornication as is not so much as named among the Gentiles, that one should have his father's wife. And ye are puffed up, and have not rather mourned, that he that hath done this deed might be taken away from among you. For I verily, as absent in body, but present in spirit, have judged already, as though I were present, *concerning* him that hath so done this deed, In the name of our Lord Jesus Christ, when ye are gathered together, and my spirit, with the power of our Lord Jesus Christ, To deliver such an one unto Satan for the destruction of the flesh, that the spirit may be saved in the day of the Lord Jesus. Your glorying *is* not good. Know ye not

that a little leaven leaveneth the whole lump? Purge out therefore the old leaven, that ye may be a new lump, as ye are unleavened. For even Christ our passover is sacrificed for us: Therefore let us keep the feast, not with old leaven, neither with the leaven of malice and wickedness; but with the unleavened *bread* of sincerity and truth. I wrote unto you in an epistle not to company with fornicators: Yet not altogether with the fornicators of this world, or with the covetous, or extortioners, or with idolaters; for then must ye needs go out of the world. But now I have written unto you not to keep company, if any man that is called a brother be a fornicator, or covetous, or an idolater, or a railer, or a drunkard, or an extortioner; with such an one no not to eat. For what have I to do to judge them also that are without? do not ye judge them that are within? But them that are without God judgeth. Therefore put away from among yourselves that wicked person. [And with] **Jude 23:** And others save with fear, pulling *them* out of the fire; hating even the garment spotted by the flesh. [And with] **1 Timothy 5:22:** Lay hands suddenly on no man, neither be partaker of other men's sins: keep thyself pure.

[2] **2 Corinthians 2:7:** So that contrariwise ye *ought* rather to forgive *him*, and comfort *him*, lest perhaps such a one should be swallowed up with overmuch sorrow.

174. What is required of them that receive the sacrament of the Lord's Supper in the time of the administration of it?

A. It is required of them that receive the sacrament of the Lord's Supper, that, during the time of the administration of it, with all holy reverence and attention they wait upon God in that ordinance, [1] diligently observe the sacramental elements and actions, [2] heedfully discern the Lord's body, [3] and affectionately meditate on his death and sufferings, [4] and thereby stir up themselves to a vigorous exercise of their graces; [5] in judging themselves, [6] and sorrowing for sin; [7] in earnest hungering and thirsting after Christ, [8] feeding on him by faith, [9] receiving of his fullness, [10] trusting in his merits, [11] rejoicing in his love, [12] giving thanks for his grace; [13] in renewing of their covenant with God, [14] and love to all the saints. [15]

Proofs

[1] **Leviticus 10:3:** Then Moses said unto Aaron, This *is it* that the LORD spake, saying, I will be sanctified in them that come nigh me, and before all the people I will be glorified. And Aaron held his peace. **Hebrews 12:28:** Wherefore we receiving a kingdom which cannot be moved, let us have grace, whereby we may serve God acceptably with reverence and godly fear … **Psalm 5:7:** But as for me, I will come *into* thy house in the multitude of thy mercy: *and* in thy fear will I worship toward thy holy temple. **1 Corinthians 11:17, 26-27:** Now in this that I declare *unto you* I praise *you* not, that ye come together not for the better, but for the worse … For as often as ye eat this bread, and drink this cup, ye do shew the Lord's death till he come. Wherefore whosoever shall eat this bread, and drink *this* cup of the Lord, unworthily, shall be guilty of the body and blood of the Lord.

[2] **Exodus 24:8:** And Moses took the blood, and sprinkled *it* on the people, and said, Behold the blood of the covenant, which the LORD hath made with you concerning all these words. [Compare with] **Matthew 26:28:** For this is my blood of the new testament, which is shed for many for the remission of sins.

[3] **1 Corinthians 11:29:** For he that eateth and drinketh unworthily, eateth and drinketh damnation to himself, not discerning the Lord's body.

[4] **Luke 22:19:** And he took bread, and gave thanks, and brake *it*, and gave unto them, saying, This is my body which is given for you: this do in remembrance of me.

[5] **1 Corinthians 11:26:** For as often as ye eat this bread, and drink this cup, ye do shew the Lord's death till he come. **1 Corinthians 10:3-5, 11, 14:** And did all eat the same spiritual meat; And did all drink the same spiritual drink: for they drank of that spiritual Rock that followed them: and that Rock was Christ. But with many of them God was not well pleased: for they were overthrown in the wilderness … Now all these things happened unto them for ensamples: and they are written for our admonition, upon whom the ends of the world are come … Wherefore, my dearly beloved, flee from idolatry.

[6] **1 Corinthians 11:31:** For if we would judge ourselves, we should not be judged.

[7] **Zechariah 12:10:** And I will pour upon the house of David, and upon the inhabitants of Jerusalem, the spirit of grace and of supplications: and they shall look upon me whom they have pierced, and they shall mourn for him, as one mourneth for *his* only *son*, and shall be in bitterness for him, as one that is in bitterness for *his* firstborn.

[8] **Revelation 22:17:** And the Spirit and the bride say, Come. And let him that heareth say, Come. And let him that is athirst come. And whosoever will, let him take the water of life freely.

[9] **John 6:35:** And Jesus said unto them, I am the bread of life: he that cometh to me shall never hunger; and he that believeth on me shall never thirst.

[10] **John 1:16:** And of his fulness have all we received, and grace for grace.

[11] **Philippians 3:9:** And be found in him, not having mine own righteousness, which is of the law, but that which is through the faith of Christ, the righteousness which is of God by faith …

[12] **Psalm 63:4-5:** Thus will I bless thee while I live: I will lift up my hands in thy name. My soul shall be satisfied as *with* marrow and fatness; and my mouth shall praise *thee* with joyful lips … **2 Chronicles 30:21:** And the children of Israel that were present at Jerusalem, kept the feast of unleavened bread seven days with great gladness: and the Levites and the priests praised the LORD day by day, *singing* with loud instruments unto the LORD.

[13] **Psalm 22:26:** The meek shall eat and be satisfied: they shall praise the LORD that seek him: your heart shall live for ever.

[14] **Jeremiah 50:5:** They shall ask the way to Zion with their faces thitherward, *saying*, Come, and let us join ourselves to the LORD in a perpetual covenant *that* shall not be forgotten. **Psalm 50:5:** Gather my saints together unto me; those that have made a covenant with me by sacrifice.

[15] **Acts 2:42:** And they continued stedfastly in the apostles' doctrine and fellowship, and in breaking of bread, and in prayers.

175. What is the duty of Christians, after they have received the sacrament of the Lord's Supper?

A. The duty of Christians, after they have received the sacrament of the Lord's Supper, is seriously to consider how they have behaved themselves therein, and with what success; [1] if they find quickening and comfort, to bless God for it, [2] beg the continuance of it, [3] watch against relapses, [4] fulfill their vows, [5] and encourage themselves to a frequent attendance on that ordinance: [6] but if they find no present benefit, more exactly to review their preparation to, and carriage at, the sacrament; [7] in both which, if they can approve themselves to God and their own consciences, they are to wait for the fruit of it in due time: [8] but, if they see they have failed in either, they are to be humbled, [9] and to attend upon it afterwards with more care and diligence. [10]

Proofs

[1] **Psalm 28:7:** The LORD *is* my strength and my shield; my heart trusted in him, and I am helped: therefore my heart greatly rejoiceth; and with my song will I praise him. **Psalm 85:8:** I will hear what God the LORD will speak: for he will speak peace unto his people, and to his saints: but let them not turn again to folly. **1 Corinthians 11:7, 30-31:** For a man indeed ought not to cover *his* head, forasmuch as he is the image and glory of God: but the woman is the glory of the man ... For this cause many *are* weak and sickly among you, and many sleep. For if we would judge ourselves, we should not be judged.

[2] **2 Chronicles 30:21-23, 25-26:** And the children of Israel that were present at Jerusalem, kept the feast of unleavened bread seven days with great gladness: and the Levites and the priests praised the LORD day by day, *singing* with loud instruments unto the LORD. And Hezekiah spake comfortably unto all the Levites that taught the good knowledge of the LORD: and they did eat throughout the feast seven days, offering peace offerings, and making confession to the LORD God of their fathers. And the whole assembly took counsel to keep other seven days: and they kept *other* seven days with gladness ... And all the congregation of Judah, with the priests and the Levites, and all the congregation that came out of Israel, and the strangers that came out of the land of Israel, and that dwelt in Judah, rejoiced. So there was great joy in Jerusalem: for since the time of Solomon the son of David king of Israel *there was* not the like in Jerusalem. **Acts 2:42, 46-47:** And they continued stedfastly in the apostles' doctrine and fellowship, and in breaking of bread, and in prayers ... And they, continuing daily with

one accord in the temple, and breaking bread from house to house, did eat their meat with gladness and singleness of heart, Praising God, and having favour with all the people. And the Lord added to the church daily such as should be saved.

[3] **Psalm 36:10:** O continue thy lovingkindness unto them that know thee; and thy righteousness to the upright in heart. **Song of Solomon 3:4:** *It was* but a little that I passed from them, but I found him whom my soul loveth: I held him, and would not let him go, until I had brought him into my mother's house, and into the chamber of her that conceived me. **1 Chronicles 29:18:** O LORD God of Abraham, Isaac, and of Israel, our fathers, keep this for ever in the imagination of the thoughts of the heart of thy people, and prepare their heart unto thee …

[4] **1 Corinthians 10:3-5, 12:** And did all eat the same spiritual meat; And did all drink the same spiritual drink: for they drank of that spiritual Rock that followed them: and that Rock was Christ. But with many of them God was not well pleased: for they were overthrown in the wilderness … Wherefore let him that thinketh he standeth take heed lest he fall.

[5] **Psalm 50:14:** Offer unto God thanksgiving; and pay thy vows unto the most High …

[6] **1 Corinthians 11:25-26:** After the same manner also *he took* the cup, when he had supped, saying, This cup is the new testament in my blood: this do ye, as oft as ye drink *it*, in remembrance of me. For as often as ye eat this bread, and drink this cup, ye do shew the Lord's death till he come. **Acts 2:42, 46:** And they continued stedfastly in the apostles' doctrine and fellowship, and in breaking of bread, and in prayers … And they, continuing daily with one accord in the temple, and breaking bread from house to house, did eat their meat with gladness and singleness of heart …

[7] **Song of Solomon 5:1-6:** I am come into my garden, my sister, *my* spouse: I have gathered my myrrh with my spice; I have eaten my honeycomb with my honey; I have drunk my wine with my milk: eat, O friends; drink, yea, drink abundantly, O beloved. I sleep, but my heart waketh: *it is* the voice of my beloved that knocketh, *saying*, Open to me, my sister, my love, my dove, my undefiled: for my head is filled with dew, *and* my locks with the drops of the night. I have put

off my coat; how shall I put it on? I have washed my feet; how shall I defile them? My beloved put in his hand by the hole *of the door*, and my bowels were moved for him. I rose up to open to my beloved; and my hands dropped with myrrh, and my fingers *with* sweet smelling myrrh, upon the handles of the lock. I opened to my beloved; but my beloved had withdrawn himself, *and* was gone: my soul failed when he spake: I sought him, but I could not find him; I called him, but he gave me no answer. **Ecclesiastes 5:1-6:** Keep thy foot when thou goest to the house of God, and be more ready to hear, than to give the sacrifice of fools: for they consider not that they do evil. Be not rash with thy mouth, and let not thine heart be hasty to utter *any* thing before God: for God *is* in heaven, and thou upon earth: therefore let thy words be few. For a dream cometh through the multitude of business; and a fool's voice *is known* by multitude of words. When thou vowest a vow unto God, defer not to pay it; for *he hath* no pleasure in fools: pay that which thou hast vowed. Better *is it* that thou shouldest not vow, than that thou shouldest vow and not pay. Suffer not thy mouth to cause thy flesh to sin; neither say thou before the angel, that it was an error: wherefore should God be angry at thy voice, and destroy the work of thine hands?

[8] **Psalm 123:1-2:** Unto thee lift I up mine eyes, O thou that dwellest in the heavens. Behold, as the eyes of servants *look* unto the hand of their masters, *and* as the eyes of a maiden unto the hand of her mistress; so our eyes *wait* upon the LORD our God, until that he have mercy upon us. **Psalm 42:5, 8:** Why art thou cast down, O my soul? and *why* art thou disquieted in me? hope thou in God: for I shall yet praise him *for* the help of his countenance ... Yet the LORD will command his lovingkindness in the daytime, and in the night his song *shall be* with me, *and* my prayer unto the God of my life. **Psalm 43:3-5:** O send out thy light and thy truth: let them lead me; let them bring me unto thy holy hill, and to thy tabernacles. Then will I go unto the altar of God, unto God my exceeding joy: yea, upon the harp will I praise thee, O God my God. Why art thou cast down, O my soul? and why art thou disquieted within me? hope in God: for I shall yet praise him, *who is* the health of my countenance, and my God.

[9] **2 Chronicles 30:18-19:** For a multitude of the people, *even* many of Ephraim, and Manasseh, Issachar, and Zebulun, had not cleansed themselves, yet did they eat the passover otherwise than it was written.

But Hezekiah prayed for them, saying, The good LORD pardon every one *That* prepareth his heart to seek God, the LORD God of his fathers, though *he be* not *cleansed* according to the purification of the sanctuary. **Isaiah 1:16, 18:** Wash you, make you clean; put away the evil of your doings from before mine eyes; cease to do evil ... Come now, and let us reason together, saith the LORD: though your sins be as scarlet, they shall be as white as snow; though they be red like crimson, they shall be as wool.

[10] **2 Corinthians 7:11:** For behold this selfsame thing, that ye sorrowed after a godly sort, what carefulness it wrought in you, yea, *what* clearing of yourselves, yea, *what* indignation, yea, *what* fear, yea, *what* vehement desire, yea, *what* zeal, yea, *what* revenge! In all *things* ye have approved yourselves to be clear in this matter. **1 Chronicles 15:12-14:** And said unto them, Ye *are* the chief of the fathers of the Levites: sanctify yourselves, *both* ye and your brethren, that ye may bring up the ark of the LORD God of Israel unto *the place that* I have prepared for it. For because ye *did it* not at the first, the LORD our God made a breach upon us, for that we sought him not after the due order. So the priests and the Levites sanctified themselves to bring up the ark of the LORD God of Israel.

176. Wherein do the sacraments of baptism and the Lord's Supper agree?

A. The sacraments of baptism and the Lord's Supper agree, in that the author of both is God; [1] the spiritual part of both is Christ and his benefits; [2] both are seals of the same covenant, [3] are to be dispensed by ministers of the gospel, and by none other; [4] and to be continued in the church of Christ until his second coming. [5]

Proofs

[1] **Matthew 28:19:** Go ye therefore, and teach all nations, baptizing them in the name of the Father, and of the Son, and of the Holy Ghost ... **1 Corinthians 11:23:** For I have received of the Lord that which also I delivered unto you, That the Lord Jesus the *same* night in which he was betrayed took bread ...

[2] **Romans 6:3-4:** Know ye not, that so many of us as were baptized into Jesus Christ were baptized into his death? Therefore we are buried

with him by baptism into death: that like as Christ was raised up from the dead by the glory of the Father, even so we also should walk in newness of life. **1 Corinthians 10:16:** The cup of blessing which we bless, is it not the communion of the blood of Christ? The bread which we break, is it not the communion of the body of Christ?

[3] **Romans 4:11:** And he received the sign of circumcision, a seal of the righteousness of the faith which *he had yet* being uncircumcised: that he might be the father of all them that believe, though they be not circumcised; that righteousness might be imputed unto them also ... [Compare with] **Colossians 2:12:** Buried with him in baptism, wherein also ye are risen with *him* through the faith of the operation of God, who hath raised him from the dead. **Matthew 26:27-28:** And he took the cup, and gave thanks, and gave *it* to them, saying, Drink ye all of it; For this is my blood of the new testament, which is shed for many for the remission of sins.

[4] **John 1:33:** And I knew him not: but he that sent me to baptize with water, the same said unto me, Upon whom thou shalt see the Spirit descending, and remaining on him, the same is he which baptizeth with the Holy Ghost. **Matthew 28:19:** Go ye therefore, and teach all nations, baptizing them in the name of the Father, and of the Son, and of the Holy Ghost ... **1 Corinthians 11:23:** For I have received of the Lord that which also I delivered unto you, That the Lord Jesus the *same* night in which he was betrayed took bread ... **1 Corinthians 4:1:** Let a man so account of us, as of the ministers of Christ, and stewards of the mysteries of God. **Hebrews 5:4:** And no man taketh this honour unto himself, but he that is called of God, as *was* Aaron.

[5] **Matthew 28:19-20:** Go ye therefore, and teach all nations, baptizing them in the name of the Father, and of the Son, and of the Holy Ghost: Teaching them to observe all things whatsoever I have commanded you: and, lo, I am with you alway, *even* unto the end of the world. Amen. **1 Corinthians 11:26:** For as often as ye eat this bread, and drink this cup, ye do shew the Lord's death till he come.

177. Wherein do the sacraments of baptism and the Lord's Supper differ?

A. The sacraments of baptism and the Lord's Supper differ, in that baptism is to be administered but once, with water, to be a sign and seal of our regeneration and ingrafting into Christ, [1] and that even to infants; [2] whereas the Lord's Supper is to be administered often, in the elements of bread and wine, to represent and exhibit Christ as spiritual nourishment to the soul, [3] and to confirm our continuance and growth in him, [4] and that only to such as are of years and ability to examine themselves. [5]

Proofs

[1] **Matthew 3:11:** I indeed baptize you with water unto repentance: but he that cometh after me is mightier than I, whose shoes I am not worthy to bear: he shall baptize you with the Holy Ghost, and *with* fire ... **Titus 3:5:** Not by works of righteousness which we have done, but according to his mercy he saved us, by the washing of regeneration, and renewing of the Holy Ghost ... **Galatians 3:27:** For as many of you as have been baptized into Christ have put on Christ.

[2] **Genesis 17:7, 9:** And I will establish my covenant between me and thee and thy seed after thee in their generations for an everlasting covenant, to be a God unto thee, and to thy seed after thee ... And God said unto Abraham, Thou shalt keep my covenant therefore, thou, and thy seed after thee in their generations. **Acts 2:38–39**:Then Peter said unto them, Repent, and be baptized every one of you in the name of Jesus Christ for the remission of sins, and ye shall receive the gift of the Holy Ghost. For the promise is unto you, and to your children, and to all that are afar off, *even* as many as the Lord our God shall call. **1 Corinthians 7:14:** For the unbelieving husband is sanctified by the wife, and the unbelieving wife is sanctified by the husband: else were your children unclean; but now are they holy.

[3] **1 Corinthians 11:23–26:** For I have received of the Lord that which also I delivered unto you, That the Lord Jesus the *same* night in which he was betrayed took bread: And when he had given thanks, he brake *it*, and said, Take, eat: this is my body, which is broken for you: this do in remembrance of me. After the same manner also *he took* the cup, when he had supped, saying, This cup is the new testament in my blood: this do ye, as oft as ye drink *it*, in remembrance of me. For as often as ye eat this bread, and drink this cup, ye do shew the Lord's death till he come.

[4] **1 Corinthians 10:16:** The cup of blessing which we bless, is it not the communion of the blood of Christ? The bread which we break, is it not the communion of the body of Christ?

[5] **1 Corinthians 11:28-29:** But let a man examine himself, and so let him eat of *that* bread, and drink of *that* cup. For he that eateth and drinketh unworthily, eateth and drinketh damnation to himself, not discerning the Lord's body.

178. What is prayer?

A. Prayer is an offering up of our desires unto God, [1] in the name of Christ, [2] by the help of his Spirit; [3] with confession of our sins, [4] and thankful acknowledgment of his mercies. [5]

Proofs

[1] **Psalm 62:8:** Trust in him at all times; ye people, pour out your heart before him: God *is* a refuge for us. Selah.

[2] **John 16:23:** And in that day ye shall ask me nothing. Verily, verily, I say unto you, Whatsoever ye shall ask the Father in my name, he will give *it* you.

[3] **Romans 8:26:** Likewise the Spirit also helpeth our infirmities: for we know not what we should pray for as we ought: but the Spirit itself maketh intercession for us with groanings which cannot be uttered.

[4] **Psalm 32:5-6:** I acknowledged my sin unto thee, and mine iniquity have I not hid. I said, I will confess my transgressions unto the LORD; and thou forgavest the iniquity of my sin. Selah. For this shall every one that is godly pray unto thee in a time when thou mayest be found: surely in the floods of great waters they shall not come nigh unto him. **Daniel 9:4.** And I prayed unto the LORD my God, and made my confession, and said, O Lord, the great and dreadful God, keeping the covenant and mercy to them that love him, and to them that keep his commandments …

[5] **Philippians 4:6:** Be careful for nothing; but in every thing by prayer and supplication with thanksgiving let your requests be made known unto God.

179. Are we to pray unto God only?

A. God only being able to search the hearts, [1] hear the requests, [2] pardon the sins, [3] and fulfill the desires of all; [4]

and only to be believed in, [5] and worshipped with religious worship; [6] prayer, which is a special part thereof, [7] is to be made by all to him alone, [8] and to none other. [9]

Proofs

[1] **1 Kings 8:39:** Then hear thou in heaven thy dwelling place, and forgive, and do, and give to every man according to his ways, whose heart thou knowest; (for thou, *even* thou only, knowest the hearts of all the children of men;) ... **Acts 1:24:** And they prayed, and said, Thou, Lord, which knowest the hearts of all *men*, shew whether of these two thou hast chosen ... **Romans 8:27:** And he that searcheth the hearts knoweth what *is* the mind of the Spirit, because he maketh intercession for the saints according to the will of God.

[2] **Psalm 65:2:** O thou that hearest prayer, unto thee shall all flesh come.

[3] **Micah 7:18:** Who *is* a God like unto thee, that pardoneth iniquity, and passeth by the transgression of the remnant of his heritage? he retaineth not his anger for ever, because he delighteth *in* mercy.

[4] **Psalm 145:18-19:** The LORD *is* nigh unto all them that call upon him, to all that call upon him in truth. He will fulfil the desire of them that fear him: he also will hear their cry, and will save them.

[5] **Romans 10:14:** How then shall they call on him in whom they have not believed? and how shall they believe in him of whom they have not heard? and how shall they hear without a preacher?

[6] **Matthew 4:10:** Then saith Jesus unto him, Get thee hence, Satan: for it is written, Thou shalt worship the Lord thy God, and him only shalt thou serve.

[7] **1 Corinthians 1:2:** Unto the church of God which is at Corinth, to them that are sanctified in Christ Jesus, called *to be* saints, with all that in every place call upon the name of Jesus Christ our Lord, both theirs and ours ...

[8] **Psalm 50:15:** And call upon me in the day of trouble: I will deliver thee, and thou shalt glorify me.

[9] **Romans 10:14:** How then shall they call on him in whom they have not believed? and how shall they believe in him of whom they have not heard? and how shall they hear without a preacher?

180. What is it to pray in the name of Christ?

A. To pray in the name of Christ is, in obedience to his command, and in confidence on his promises, to ask mercy for his sake; [1] not by bare mentioning of his name, [2] but by drawing our encouragement to pray, and our boldness, strength, and hope of acceptance in prayer, from Christ and his mediation. [3]

Proofs

[1] **John 14:13-14:** And whatsoever ye shall ask in my name, that will I do, that the Father may be glorified in the Son. If ye shall ask any thing in my name, I will do *it*. **John 16:24:** Hitherto have ye asked nothing in my name: ask, and ye shall receive, that your joy may be full. **Daniel 9:17:** Now therefore, O our God, hear the prayer of thy servant, and his supplications, and cause thy face to shine upon thy sanctuary that is desolate, for the Lord's sake.

[2] **Matthew 7:21:** Not every one that saith unto me, Lord, Lord, shall enter into the kingdom of heaven; but he that doeth the will of my Father which is in heaven.

[3] **Hebrews 4:14-16:** Seeing then that we have a great high priest, that is passed into the heavens, Jesus the Son of God, let us hold fast *our* profession. For we have not an high priest which cannot be touched with the feeling of our infirmities; but was in all points tempted like as *we are, yet* without sin. Let us therefore come boldly unto the throne of grace, that we may obtain mercy, and find grace to help in time of need. **1 John 5:13-15:** These things have I written unto you that believe on the name of the Son of God; that ye may know that ye have eternal life, and that ye may believe on the name of the Son of God. And this is the confidence that we have in him, that, if we ask any thing according to his will, he heareth us: And if we know that he hear us, whatsoever we ask, we know that we have the petitions that we desired of him.

181. Why are we to pray in the name of Christ?

A. The sinfulness of man, and his distance from God by reason thereof, being so great, as that we can have no access into his presence without a mediator; [1] and there being none in heaven or earth appointed to, or fit for, that glorious work but Christ alone, [2] we are to pray in no other name but his only. [3]

Proofs

[1] **John 14:6:** Jesus saith unto him, I am the way, the truth, and the life: no man cometh unto the Father, but by me. **Isaiah 59:2:** But your iniquities have separated between you and your God, and your sins have hid *his* face from you, that he will not hear. **Ephesians 3:12**: In whom we have boldness and access with confidence by the faith of him.

[2] **John 6:27:** Labour not for the meat which perisheth, but for that meat which endureth unto everlasting life, which the Son of man shall give unto you: for him hath God the Father sealed. **Hebrews 7:25-27:** Wherefore he is able also to save them to the uttermost that come unto God by him, seeing he ever liveth to make intercession for them. For such an high priest became us, *who is* holy, harmless, undefiled, separate from sinners, and made higher than the heavens; Who needeth not daily, as those high priests, to offer up sacrifice, first for his own sins, and then for the people's: for this he did once, when he offered up himself. **1 Timothy 2:5:** For *there is* one God, and one mediator between God and men, the man Christ Jesus ...

[3] **Colossians 3:17:** And whatsoever ye do in word or deed, *do* all in the name of the Lord Jesus, giving thanks to God and the Father by him. **Hebrews 13:15:** By him therefore let us offer the sacrifice of praise to God continually, that is, the fruit of *our* lips giving thanks to his name.

182. How doth the Spirit help us to pray?

A. We not knowing what to pray for as we ought, the Spirit helpeth our infirmities, by enabling us to understand both for whom, and what, and how prayer is to be made; and by working and quickening in our hearts (although not in all persons, nor at all times, in the same measure) those apprehensions, affections, and graces which are requisite for the right performance of that duty. [1]

Proofs

[1] **Romans 8:26-27:** Likewise the Spirit also helpeth our infirmities: for we know not what we should pray for as we ought: but the Spirit itself maketh intercession for us with groanings which cannot be uttered. And he that searcheth the hearts knoweth what *is* the mind of the Spirit, because he maketh intercession for the saints according

to *the will of* God. **Psalm 10:17:** LORD, thou hast heard the desire of the humble: thou wilt prepare their heart, thou wilt cause thine ear to hear ... **Zechariah 12:10:** And I will pour upon the house of David, and upon the inhabitants of Jerusalem, the spirit of grace and of supplications: and they shall look upon me whom they have pierced, and they shall mourn for him, as one mourneth for *his* only *son*, and shall be in bitterness for him, as one that is in bitterness for *his* firstborn.

183. For whom are we to pray?

A. We are to pray for the whole church of Christ upon earth; [1] for magistrates, [2] and ministers; [3] for ourselves, [4] our brethren, [5] yea, our enemies; [6] and for all sorts of men living, [7] or that shall live hereafter; [8] but not for the dead, [9] nor for those that are known to have sinned the sin unto death. [10]

Proofs

[1] **Ephesians 6:18:** Praying always with all prayer and supplication in the Spirit, and watching thereunto with all perseverance and supplication for all saints ... **Psalm 28:9:** Save thy people, and bless thine inheritance: feed them also, and lift them up for ever.

[2] **1 Timothy 2:1-2:** I exhort therefore, that, first of all, supplications, prayers, intercessions, *and* giving of thanks, be made for all men; For kings, and *for* all that are in authority; that we may lead a quiet and peaceable life in all godliness and honesty.

[3] **Colossians 4:3:** Withal praying also for us, that God would open unto us a door of utterance, to speak the mystery of Christ, for which I am also in bonds ...

[4] **Genesis 32:11:** Deliver me, I pray thee, from the hand of my brother, from the hand of Esau: for I fear him, lest he will come and smite me, *and* the mother with the children.

[5] **James 5:16:** Confess *your* faults one to another, and pray one for another, that ye may be healed. The effectual fervent prayer of a righteous man availeth much.

[6] **Matthew 5:44:** But I say unto you, Love your enemies, bless them that curse you, do good to them that hate you, and pray for them which despitefully use you, and persecute you ...

[7] **1 Timothy 2:1-2:** I exhort therefore, that, first of all, supplications, prayers, intercessions, *and* giving of thanks, be made for all men; For kings, and *for* all that are in authority; that we may lead a quiet and peaceable life in all godliness and honesty.

[8] **John 17:20:** Neither pray I for these alone, but for them also which shall believe on me through their word ... **2 Samuel 7:29:** Therefore now let it please thee to bless the house of thy servant, that it may continue for ever before thee: for thou, O Lord GOD, hast spoken *it*: and with thy blessing let the house of thy servant be blessed for ever.

[9] **2 Samuel 12:21-23:** Then said his servants unto him, What thing *is* this that thou hast done? thou didst fast and weep for the child, *while it was* alive; but when the child was dead, thou didst rise and eat bread. And he said, While the child was yet alive, I fasted and wept: for I said, Who can tell *whether* GOD will be gracious to me, that the child may live? But now he is dead, wherefore should I fast? can I bring him back again? I shall go to him, but he shall not return to me.

[10] **1 John 5:16:** If any man see his brother sin a sin *which is* not unto death, he shall ask, and he shall give him life for them that sin not unto death. There is a sin unto death: I do not say that he shall pray for it.

184. For what things are we to pray?

A. We are to pray for all things tending to the glory of God, [1] the welfare of the church, [2] our own [3] or others' good; [4] but not for anything that is unlawful. [5]

Proofs

[1] **Matthew 6:9:** After this manner therefore pray ye: Our Father which art in heaven, Hallowed be thy name.

[2] **Psalm 51:18:** Do good in thy good pleasure unto Zion: build thou the walls of Jerusalem. **Psalm 122:6:** Pray for the peace of Jerusalem: they shall prosper that love thee.

[3] **Matthew 7:11:** If ye then, being evil, know how to give good gifts unto your children, how much more shall your Father which is in heaven give good things to them that ask him?

[4] **Psalm 125:4:** Do good, O LORD, unto *those that be* good, and to *them that are* upright in their hearts.

[5] **1 John 5:14:** And this is the confidence that we have in him, that, if we ask any thing according to his will, he heareth us ...

185. How are we to pray?

A. We are to pray with an awful apprehension of the majesty of God, [1] and deep sense of our own unworthiness, [2] necessities, [3] and sins; [4] with penitent, [5] thankful, [6] and enlarged hearts; [7] with understanding, [8] faith, [9] sincerity, [10] fervency, [11] love, [12] and perseverance, [13] waiting upon him, [14] with humble submission to his will. [15]

Proofs

[1] **Ecclesiastes 5:1:** Keep thy foot when thou goest to the house of God, and be more ready to hear, than to give the sacrifice of fools: for they consider not that they do evil.

[2] **Genesis 18:27:** And Abraham answered and said, Behold now, I have taken upon me to speak unto the Lord, which *am but* dust and ashes ... **Genesis 32:10:** I am not worthy of the least of all the mercies, and of all the truth, which thou hast shewed unto thy servant; for with my staff I passed over this Jordan; and now I am become two bands.

[3] **Luke 15:17-19:** And when he came to himself, he said, How many hired servants of my father's have bread enough and to spare, and I perish with hunger! I will arise and go to my father, and will say unto him, Father, I have sinned against heaven, and before thee, And am no more worthy to be called thy son: make me as one of thy hired servants.

[4] **Luke 18:13-14:** And the publican, standing afar off, would not lift up so much as *his* eyes unto heaven, but smote upon his breast, saying, God be merciful to me a sinner. I tell you, this man went down to his house justified *rather* than the other: for every one that exalteth himself shall be abased; and he that humbleth himself shall be exalted.

[5] **Psalm 51:17:** The sacrifices of God *are* a broken spirit: a broken and a contrite heart, O God, thou wilt not despise.

[6] **Philippians 4:6:** Be careful for nothing; but in every thing by prayer and supplication with thanksgiving let your requests be made known unto God.

[7] **1 Samuel 1:15:** And Hannah answered and said, No, my lord, I *am* a woman of a sorrowful spirit: I have drunk neither wine nor strong drink, but have poured out my soul before the LORD. **1 Samuel 2:1:** And Hannah prayed, and said, My heart rejoiceth in the LORD, mine horn is

exalted in the LORD: my mouth is enlarged over mine enemies; because I rejoice in thy salvation.

[8] **1 Corinthians 14:15:** What is it then? I will pray with the spirit, and I will pray with the understanding also: I will sing with the spirit, and I will sing with the understanding also.

[9] **Mark 11:24:** Therefore I say unto you, What things soever ye desire, when ye pray, believe that ye receive *them*, and ye shall have *them*. **James 1:6:** But let him ask in faith, nothing wavering. For he that wavereth is like a wave of the sea driven with the wind and tossed.

[10] **Psalm 145:18:** The LORD *is* nigh unto all them that call upon him, to all that call upon him in truth. **Psalm 17:1:** Hear the right, O LORD, attend unto my cry, give ear unto my prayer, *that goeth* not out of feigned lips.

[11] **James 5:16:** Confess *your* faults one to another, and pray one for another, that ye may be healed. The effectual fervent prayer of a righteous man availeth much.

[12] **1 Timothy 2:8:** I will therefore that men pray every where, lifting up holy hands, without wrath and doubting.

[13] **Ephesians 6:18:** Praying always with all prayer and supplication in the Spirit, and watching thereunto with all perseverance and supplication for all saints …

[14] **Micah 7:7:** Therefore I will look unto the LORD; I will wait for the God of my salvation: my God will hear me.

[15] **Matthew 26:39:** And he went a little farther, and fell on his face, and prayed, saying, O my Father, if it be possible, let this cup pass from me: nevertheless not as I will, but as thou *wilt*.

186. What rule hath God given for our direction in the duty of prayer?

A. The whole Word of God is of use to direct us in the duty of prayer; [1] but the special rule of direction is that form of prayer which our Saviour Christ taught his disciples, commonly called *The Lord's Prayer*. [2]

Proofs

[1] **1 John 5:14:** And this is the confidence that we have in him, that, if we ask any thing according to his will, he heareth us …

[2] **Matthew 6:9-13:** After this manner therefore pray ye: Our Father which art in heaven, Hallowed be thy name. Thy kingdom come. Thy will be done in earth, as *it is* in heaven. Give us this day our daily bread. And forgive us our debts, as we forgive our debtors. And lead us not into temptation, but deliver us from evil: For thine is the kingdom, and the power, and the glory, for ever. Amen. **Luke 11:2-4:** And he said unto them, When ye pray, say, Our Father which art in heaven, Hallowed be thy name. Thy kingdom come. Thy will be done, as in heaven, so in earth. Give us day by day our daily bread. And forgive us our sins; for we also forgive every one that is indebted to us. And lead us not into temptation; but deliver us from evil.

187. How is the Lord's Prayer to be used?

A. The Lord's Prayer is not only for direction, as a pattern, according to which we are to make other prayers; but may also be used as a prayer, so that it be done with understanding, faith, reverence, and other graces necessary to the right performance of the duty of prayer. [1]

Proofs

[1] **Matthew 6:9:** After this manner therefore pray ye: Our Father which art in heaven, Hallowed be thy name … [Compare with] **Luke 11:2:** And he said unto them, When ye pray, say, Our Father which art in heaven, Hallowed be thy name. Thy kingdom come. Thy will be done, as in heaven, so in earth.

188. Of how many parts doth the Lord's prayer consist?

A. The Lord's Prayer consists of three parts; a preface, petitions, and a conclusion.

189. What doth the preface of the Lord's Prayer teach us?

A. The preface of the Lord's Prayer (contained in these words, *Our Father which art in heaven*,[1]) teacheth us, when we pray, to draw near to God with confidence of his fatherly goodness, and our interest therein; [2] with reverence, and all other childlike dispositions, [3] heavenly affections, [4] and due apprehensions of his sovereign power, majesty, and gracious condescension: [5] as also, to pray with and for others. [6]

Proofs

[1] **Matthew 6:9:** After this manner therefore pray ye: Our Father which art in heaven, Hallowed be thy name.

[2] **Luke 11:13:** If ye then, being evil, know how to give good gifts unto your children: how much more shall *your* heavenly Father give the Holy Spirit to them that ask him? **Romans 8:15:** For ye have not received the spirit of bondage again to fear; but ye have received the Spirit of adoption, whereby we cry, Abba, Father.

[3] **Isaiah 64:9:** Be not wroth very sore, O LORD, neither remember iniquity for ever: behold, see, we beseech thee, we *are* all thy people.

[4] **Psalm 123:1:** Unto thee lift I up mine eyes, O thou that dwellest in the heavens. **Lamentations 3:41:** Let us lift up our heart with *our* hands unto God in the heavens.

[5] **Isaiah 63:15-16:** Look down from heaven, and behold from the habitation of thy holiness and of thy glory: where *is* thy zeal and thy strength, the sounding of thy bowels and of thy mercies toward me? are they restrained? Doubtless thou *art* our father, though Abraham be ignorant of us, and Israel acknowledge us not: thou, O LORD, *art* our father, our redeemer; thy name *is* from everlasting. **Nehemiah 1:4-6:** And it came to pass, when I heard these words, that I sat down and wept, and mourned *certain* days, and fasted, and prayed before the God of heaven, And said, I beseech thee, O LORD God of heaven, the great and terrible God, that keepeth covenant and mercy for them that love him and observe his commandments: Let thine ear now be attentive, and thine eyes open, that thou mayest hear the prayer of thy servant, which I pray before thee now, day and night, for the children of Israel thy servants, and confess the sins of the children of Israel, which we have sinned against thee: both I and my father's house have sinned.

[6] **Acts 12:5:** Peter therefore was kept in prison: but prayer was made without ceasing of the church unto God for him.

190. What do we pray for in the first petition?

A. In the first petition, (which is, *Hallowed by thy name*, [1]) acknowledging the utter inability and indisposition that is in ourselves and all men to honour God aright, [2] we pray, that God would by his grace enable and incline us and others to know, to acknowledge, and highly to esteem him, [3] his titles, [4] attributes, [5] ordinances, Word, [6] works, and whatsoever he is pleased to make himself known by; [7] and to glorify him in thought, word, [8] and deed: [9] that he would prevent and remove atheism, [10] ignorance, [11] idolatry, [12] profaneness, [13] and whatsoever is dishonorable to him; [14] and, by his over-ruling providence, direct and dispose of all things to his own glory. [15]

Proofs

[1] **Matthew 6:9:** After this manner therefore pray ye: Our Father which art in heaven, Hallowed be thy name.

[2] **2 Corinthians 3:5:** Not that we are sufficient of ourselves to think any thing as of ourselves; but our sufficiency *is* of God … **Psalm 51:15:** O Lord, open thou my lips; and my mouth shall shew forth thy praise.

[3] **Psalm 67:2-3:** That thy way may be known upon earth, thy saving health among all nations. Let the people praise thee, O God; let all the people praise thee.

[4] **Psalm 83:18:** That *men* may know that thou, whose name alone *is* JEHOVAH, *art* the most high over all the earth.

[5] **Psalm 86:10-13, 15:** For thou *art* great, and doest wondrous things: thou *art* God alone. Teach me thy way, O LORD; I will walk in thy truth: unite my heart to fear thy name. I will praise thee, O Lord my God, with all my heart: and I will glorify thy name for evermore. For great *is* thy mercy toward me: and thou hast delivered my soul from the lowest hell … But thou, O Lord, *art* a God full of compassion, and gracious, longsuffering, and plenteous in mercy and truth.

[6] **2 Thessalonians 3:1:** Finally, brethren, pray for us, that the word of the Lord may have *free* course, and be glorified, even as *it is* with you … **Psalm 147:19-20:** He sheweth his word unto Jacob, his statutes and his judgments unto Israel. He hath not dealt so with any nation: and *as for his* judgments, they have not known them. Praise ye the LORD. **Psalm 138:1-3:** I will praise thee with my whole heart: before the gods will I sing praise unto thee. I will worship toward thy holy temple, and praise thy name for thy lovingkindness and for thy truth: for thou hast magnified thy word above all thy name. In the day when

I cried thou answeredst me, *and* strengthenedst me *with* strength in my soul. **2 Corinthians 2:14-15:** Now thanks *be* unto God, which always causeth us to triumph in Christ, and maketh manifest the savour of his knowledge by us in every place. For we are unto God a sweet savour of Christ, in them that are saved, and in them that perish ...

[7] **Psalm 145:** I will extol thee, my God, O king ... **Psalm 8:** O Lord our Lord, how excellent *is* thy name in all the earth ...

[8] **Psalm 103:1:** Bless the Lord, O my soul: and all that is within me, *bless* his holy name. **Psalm 19:14:** Let the words of my mouth, and the meditation of my heart, be acceptable in thy sight, O Lord, my strength, and my redeemer.

[9] **Philippians 1:9, 11:** And this I pray, that your love may abound yet more and more in knowledge and *in* all judgment ... Being filled with the fruits of righteousness, which are by Jesus Christ, unto the glory and praise of God.

[10] **Psalm 67:1-4:** God be merciful unto us, and bless us; *and* cause his face to shine upon us; Selah. That thy way may be known upon earth, thy saving health among all nations. Let the people praise thee, O God; let all the people praise thee. O let the nations be glad and sing for joy: for thou shalt judge the people righteously, and govern the nations upon earth. Selah.

[11] **Ephesians 1:17-18:** That the God of our Lord Jesus Christ, the Father of glory, may give unto you the spirit of wisdom and revelation in the knowledge of him: The eyes of your understanding being enlightened; that ye may know what is the hope of his calling, and what the riches of the glory of his inheritance in the saints ...

[12] **Psalm 97:7:** Confounded be all they that serve graven images, that boast themselves of idols: worship him, all *ye* gods.

[13] **Psalm 74:18, 22-23:** Remember this, *that* the enemy hath reproached, O Lord, and *that* the foolish people have blasphemed thy name ... Arise, O God, plead thine own cause: remember how the foolish man reproacheth thee daily. Forget not the voice of thine enemies: the tumult of those that rise up against thee increaseth continually.

[14] **2 Kings 19:15-16:** And Hezekiah prayed before the Lord, and said, O Lord God of Israel, which dwellest *between* the cherubims, thou art the God, *even* thou alone, of all the kingdoms of the earth;

thou hast made heaven and earth. LORD, bow down thine ear, and hear: open, LORD, thine eyes, and see: and hear the words of Sennacherib, which hath sent him to reproach the living God.

[15] **2 Chronicles 20:6, 10-12:** And said, O LORD God of our fathers, art not thou God in heaven? and rulest *not* thou over all the kingdoms of the heathen? and in thine hand *is there not* power and might, so that none is able to withstand thee ... And now, behold, the children of Ammon and Moab and mount Seir, whom thou wouldest not let Israel invade, when they came out of the land of Egypt, but they turned from them, and destroyed them not; Behold, *I say, how* they reward us, to come to cast us out of thy possession, which thou hast given us to inherit. O our God, wilt thou not judge them? for we have no might against this great company that cometh against us; neither know we what to do: but our eyes *are* upon thee. **Psalm 83:** Keep not thou silence, O God: hold not thy peace ... **Psalm 140:4, 8:** Keep me, O LORD, from the hands of the wicked; preserve me from the violent man; who have purposed to overthrow my goings ... Grant not, O LORD, the desires of the wicked: further not his wicked device; *lest* they exalt themselves. Selah.

191. What do we pray for in the second petition?

A. In the second petition, (which is, *Thy kingdom come*, [1]) acknowledging ourselves and all mankind to be by nature under the dominion of sin and Satan, [2] we pray, that the kingdom of sin and Satan may be destroyed, [3] the gospel propagated throughout the world, [4] the Jews called, [5] the fullness of the Gentiles brought in; [6] the church furnished with all gospel-officers and ordinances, [7] purged from corruption, [8] countenanced and maintained by the civil magistrate: [9] that the ordinances of Christ may be purely dispensed, and made effectual to the converting of those that are yet in their sins, and the confirming, comforting, and building up of those that are already converted: [10] that Christ would rule in our hearts here, [11] and hasten the time of his second coming, and our reigning with him forever: [12] and that he would be pleased so to exercise the kingdom of his power in all the world, as may best conduce to these ends. [13]

Proofs

[1] **Matthew 6:10:** Thy kingdom come. Thy will be done in earth, as *it is* in heaven.

[2] **Ephesians 2:2-3:** Wherein in time past ye walked according to the course of this world, according to the prince of the power of the air, the spirit that now worketh in the children of disobedience: Among whom also we all had our conversation in times past in the lusts of our flesh, fulfilling the desires of the flesh and of the mind; and were by nature the children of wrath, even as others.

[3] **Psalm 68:1, 18:** Let God arise, let his enemies be scattered: let them also that hate him flee before him … Thou hast ascended on high, thou hast led captivity captive: thou hast received gifts for men; yea, *for* the rebellious also, that the LORD God might dwell *among them*. **Revelation 12:10-11:** And I heard a loud voice saying in heaven, Now is come salvation, and strength, and the kingdom of our God, and the power of his Christ: for the accuser of our brethren is cast down, which accused them before our God day and night. And they overcame him by the blood of the Lamb, and by the word of their testimony; and they loved not their lives unto the death.

[4] **2 Thessalonians 3:1:** Finally, brethren, pray for us, that the word of the Lord may have *free* course, and be glorified, even as it is with you …

[5] **Romans 10:1:** Brethren, my heart's desire and prayer to God for Israel is, that they might be saved.

[6] **John 17:9, 20:** I pray for them: I pray not for the world, but for them which thou hast given me; for they are thine … Neither pray I for these alone, but for them also which shall believe on me through their word … **Romans 11:25-26:** For I would not, brethren, that ye should be ignorant of this mystery, lest ye should be wise in your own conceits; that blindness in part is happened to Israel, until the fulness of the Gentiles be come in. And so all Israel shall be saved: as it is written, There shall come out of Sion the Deliverer, and shall turn away ungodliness from Jacob … **Psalm 67:** God be merciful unto us, and bless us; *and* cause his face to shine upon us; Selah. That thy way may be known upon earth, thy saving health among all nations. Let the people praise thee, O God; let all the people praise thee. O let the nations be glad and sing for joy: for thou shalt judge the people righteously, and govern the nations upon earth. Selah. Let the people

praise thee, O God; let all the people praise thee. *Then* shall the earth yield her increase; *and* God, *even* our own God, shall bless us. God shall bless us; and all the ends of the earth shall fear him.

[7] **Matthew 9:38:** Pray ye therefore the Lord of the harvest, that he will send forth labourers into his harvest. **2 Thessalonians 3:1:** Finally, brethren, pray for us, that the word of the Lord may have *free* course, and be glorified, even as *it is* with you ...

[8] **Malachi 1:11:** For from the rising of the sun even unto the going down of the same my name *shall be* great among the Gentiles; and in every place incense *shall be* offered unto my name, and a pure offering: for my name *shall be* great among the heathen, saith the LORD of hosts. **Zephaniah 3:9:** For then will I turn to the people a pure language, that they may all call upon the name of the LORD, to serve him with one consent.

[9] **1 Timothy 2:1-2:** I exhort therefore, that, first of all, supplications, prayers, intercessions, *and* giving of thanks, be made for all men; For kings, and *for* all that are in authority; that we may lead a quiet and peaceable life in all godliness and honesty.

[10] **Acts 4:29-30:** And now, Lord, behold their threatenings: and grant unto thy servants, that with all boldness they may speak thy word, By stretching forth thine hand to heal; and that signs and wonders may be done by the name of thy holy child Jesus. **Ephesians 6:18-20:** Praying always with all prayer and supplication in the Spirit, and watching thereunto with all perseverance and supplication for all saints; And for me, that utterance may be given unto me, that I may open my mouth boldly, to make known the mystery of the gospel, For which I am an ambassador in bonds: that therein I may speak boldly, as I ought to speak. **Romans 15:29-30, 32:** And I am sure that, when I come unto you, I shall come in the fulness of the blessing of the gospel of Christ. Now I beseech you, brethren, for the Lord Jesus Christ's sake, and for the love of the Spirit, that ye strive together with me in *your* prayers to God for me ... That I may come unto you with joy by the will of God, and may with you be refreshed. **2 Thessalonians 1:11:** Wherefore also we pray always for you, that our God would count you worthy of *this* calling, and fulfil all the good pleasure of *his* goodness, and the work of faith with power ... **2 Thessalonians 2:16-17:** Now our Lord Jesus Christ himself, and God, even our Father, which hath loved us, and

hath given *us* everlasting consolation and good hope through grace, Comfort your hearts, and stablish you in every good word and work.

[11] **Ephesians 3:14-20:** For this cause I bow my knees unto the Father of our Lord Jesus Christ, Of whom the whole family in heaven and earth is named, That he would grant you, according to the riches of his glory, to be strengthened with might by his Spirit in the inner man; That Christ may dwell in your hearts by faith; that ye, being rooted and grounded in love, May be able to comprehend with all saints what *is* the breadth, and length, and depth, and height; And to know the love of Christ, which passeth knowledge, that ye might be filled with all the fulness of God. Now unto him that is able to do exceeding abundantly above all that we ask or think, according to the power that worketh in us ...

[12] **Revelation 22:20:** He which testifieth these things saith, Surely I come quickly. Amen. Even so, come, Lord Jesus.

[13] **Isaiah 64:1-2:** Oh that thou wouldest rend the heavens, that thou wouldest come down, that the mountains might flow down at thy presence ... As *when* the melting fire burneth, the fire causeth the waters to boil, to make thy name known to thine adversaries, *that* the nations may tremble at thy presence! **Revelation 4:8-11:** And the four beasts had each of them six wings about *him*; and *they were* full of eyes within: and they rest not day and night, saying, Holy, holy, holy, Lord God Almighty, which was, and is, and is to come. And when those beasts give glory and honour and thanks to him that sat on the throne, who liveth for ever and ever, The four and twenty elders fall down before him that sat on the throne, and worship him that liveth for ever and ever, and cast their crowns before the throne, saying, Thou art worthy, O Lord, to receive glory and honour and power: for thou hast created all things, and for thy pleasure they are and were created.

192. What do we pray for in the third petition?

A. In the third petition, (which is, *Thy will be done in earth as it is in heaven*, [1]) acknowledging, that by nature we and all men are not only utterly unable and unwilling to know and do the will of God, [2] but prone to rebel against his Word, [3] to repine and murmur against his providence, [4] and wholly inclined to do the will of the flesh, and of the devil: [5] we pray, that God would by his Spirit take away from ourselves and others all blindness, [6] weakness, [7] indisposedness, [8] and perverseness of heart; [9] and by his grace make us able and willing to know, do , and submit to his will in all things, [10] with the like humility, [11] cheerfulness, [12]faithfulness, [13] diligence, [14] zeal, [15] sincerity, [16] and constancy, [17] as the angels do in heaven. [18]

Proofs

[1] **Matthew 6:10:** Thy kingdom come. Thy will be done in earth, as *it is* in heaven.

[2] **Romans 7:18:** For I know that in me (that is, in my flesh,) dwelleth no good thing: for to will is present with me; but *how* to perform that which is good I find not. **Job 21:14:** Therefore they say unto God, Depart from us; for we desire not the knowledge of thy ways. **1 Corinthians 2:14:** But the natural man receiveth not the things of the Spirit of God: for they are foolishness unto him: neither can he know *them*, because they are spiritually discerned.

[3] **Romans 8:7:** Because the carnal mind *is* enmity against God: for it is not subject to the law of God, neither indeed can be.

[4] **Exodus 17:7:** And he called the name of the place Massah, and Meribah, because of the chiding of the children of Israel, and because they tempted the LORD, saying, Is the LORD among us, or not? **Numbers 14:2:** And all the children of Israel murmured against Moses and against Aaron: and the whole congregation said unto them, Would God that we had died in the land of Egypt! or would God we had died in this wilderness!

[5] **Ephesians 2:2:** Wherein in time past ye walked according to the course of this world, according to the prince of the power of the air, the spirit that now worketh in the children of disobedience …

[6] **Ephesians 1:17-18:** That the God of our Lord Jesus Christ, the Father of glory, may give unto you the spirit of wisdom and revelation in the knowledge of him: The eyes of your understanding being enlightened; that ye may know what is the hope of his calling, and what the riches of the glory of his inheritance in the saints …

[7] **Ephesians 3:16:** That he would grant you, according to the riches of his glory, to be strengthened with might by his Spirit in the inner man …

[8] **Matthew 26:40-41:** And he cometh unto the disciples, and findeth them asleep, and saith unto Peter, What, could ye not watch with me one hour? Watch and pray, that ye enter not into temptation: the spirit indeed *is* willing, but the flesh *is* weak.

[9] **Jeremiah 31:18-19:** I have surely heard Ephraim bemoaning himself *thus*; Thou hast chastised me, and I was chastised, as a bullock unaccustomed *to the yoke*: turn thou me, and I shall be turned; for thou *art* the LORD my God. Surely after that I was turned, I repented; and after that I was instructed, I smote upon *my* thigh: I was ashamed, yea, even confounded, because I did bear the reproach of my youth.

[10] **Psalm 119:1, 8, 35-36:** Blessed *are* the undefiled in the way, who walk in the law of the LORD … I will keep thy statutes: O forsake me not utterly … Make me to go in the path of thy commandments; for therein do I delight. Incline my heart unto thy testimonies, and not to covetousness. **Acts 21:14:** And when he would not be persuaded, we ceased, saying, The will of the Lord be done.

[11] **Micah 6:8:** He hath shewed thee, O man, what *is* good; and what doth the LORD require of thee, but to do justly, and to love mercy, and to walk humbly with thy God?

[12] **Psalm 100:2:** Serve the LORD with gladness: come before his presence with singing. **Job 1:21:** And said, Naked came I out of my mother's womb, and naked shall I return thither: the LORD gave, and the LORD hath taken away; blessed be the name of the LORD. **2 Samuel 15:25-26:** And the king said unto Zadok, Carry back the ark of God into the city: if I shall find favour in the eyes of the LORD, he will bring me again, and shew me *both* it, and his habitation: But if he thus say, I have no delight in thee; behold, *here am I*, let him do to me as seemeth good unto him.

[13] **Isaiah 38:3:** And said, Remember now, O LORD, I beseech thee, how I have walked before thee in truth and with a perfect heart, and have done *that which is* good in thy sight. And Hezekiah wept sore.

[14] **Psalm 119:4-5:** Thou hast commanded *us* to keep thy precepts diligently. O that my ways were directed to keep thy statutes!

[15] **Romans 12:11:** Not slothful in business; fervent in spirit; serving the Lord …

[16] **Psalm 119:80:** Let my heart be sound in thy statutes; that I be not ashamed.

[17] **Psalm 119:112:** I have inclined mine heart to perform thy statutes alway, *even unto* the end.

[18] **Isaiah 6:2-3:** Above it stood the seraphims: each one had six wings; with twain he covered his face, and with twain he covered his feet, and with twain he did fly. And one cried unto another, and said, Holy, holy, holy, *is* the LORD of hosts: the whole earth *is* full of his glory. **Psalm 103:20-21:** Bless the LORD, ye his angels, that excel in strength, that do his commandments, hearkening unto the voice of his word. Bless ye the LORD, all *ye* his hosts; ye ministers of his, that do his pleasure. **Matthew 18:10:** Take heed that ye despise not one of these little ones; for I say unto you, That in heaven their angels do always behold the face of my Father which is in heaven.

193. What do we pray for in the fourth petition?

A. In the fourth petition,(which is, *Give us this day our daily bread*, [1]) acknowledging, that in Adam, and by our own sin, we have forfeited our right to all the outward blessings of this life, and deserve to be wholly deprived of them by God, and to have them cursed to us in the use of them; [2] and that neither they of themselves are able to sustain us, [3] nor we to merit, [4] or by our own industry to procure them; [5] but prone to desire, [6] get, [7] and use them unlawfully: [8] we pray for ourselves and others, that both they and we, waiting upon the providence of God from day to day in the use of lawful means, may, of his free gift, and as to his fatherly wisdom shall seem best, enjoy a competent portion of them; [9] and have the same continued and blessed unto us in our holy and comfortable use of them, [10] and contentment in them; [11] and be kept from all things that are contrary to our temporal support and comfort. [12]

Proofs

[1] **Matthew 6:11:** Give us this day our daily bread.

[2] **Genesis 2:17.** But of the tree of the knowledge of good and evil, thou shalt not eat of it: for in the day that thou eatest thereof thou shalt surely die. **Genesis 3:17:** And unto Adam he said, Because thou hast hearkened unto the voice of thy wife, and hast eaten of the tree, of which I commanded thee, saying, Thou shalt not eat of it: cursed

is the ground for thy sake; in sorrow shalt thou eat *of* it all the days of thy life … **Romans 8:20-22:** For the creature was made subject to vanity, not willingly, but by reason of him who hath subjected *the same* in hope, Because the creature itself also shall be delivered from the bondage of corruption into the glorious liberty of the children of God. For we know that the whole creation groaneth and travaileth in pain together until now. **Jeremiah 5:25:** Your iniquities have turned away these *things*, and your sins have withholden good *things* from you. **Deuteronomy 28:15-17:** But it shall come to pass, if thou wilt not hearken unto the voice of the LORD thy God, to observe to do all his commandments and his statutes which I command thee this day; that all these curses shall come upon thee, and overtake thee: Cursed *shalt* thou *be* in the city, and cursed *shalt* thou *be* in the field. Cursed *shall be* thy basket and thy store …

[3] **Deuteronomy 8:3:** And he humbled thee, and suffered thee to hunger, and fed thee with manna, which thou knewest not, neither did thy fathers know; that he might make thee know that man doth not live by bread only, but by every *word* that proceedeth out of the mouth of the LORD doth man live.

[4] **Genesis 32:10:** I am not worthy of the least of all the mercies, and of all the truth, which thou hast shewed unto thy servant; for with my staff I passed over this Jordan; and now I am become two bands.

[5] **Deuteronomy 8:17-18:** And thou say in thine heart, My power and the might of *mine* hand hath gotten me this wealth. But thou shalt remember the LORD thy God: for *it is* he that giveth thee power to get wealth, that he may establish his covenant which he sware unto thy fathers, as *it is* this day.

[6] **Jeremiah 6:13:** For from the least of them even unto the greatest of them every one *is* given to covetousness; and from the prophet even unto the priest every one dealeth falsely.**Mark 7:21-22:** For from within, out of the heart of men, proceed evil thoughts, adulteries, fornications, murders, Thefts, covetousness, wickedness, deceit, lasciviousness, an evil eye, blasphemy, pride, foolishness …

[7] **Hosea 12:7:** *He is* a merchant, the balances of deceit *are* in his hand: he loveth to oppress.

[8] **James 4:3:** Ye ask, and receive not, because ye ask amiss, that ye may consume *it* upon your lusts.

[9] **Genesis 43:12-14:** And take double money in your hand; and the money that was brought again in the mouth of your sacks, carry *it* again in your hand; peradventure it *was* an oversight: Take also your brother, and arise, go again unto the man: And God Almighty give you mercy before the man, that he may send away your other brother, and Benjamin. If I be bereaved *of my children*, I am bereaved. **Genesis 28:20:** And Jacob vowed a vow, saying, If God will be with me, and will keep me in this way that I go, and will give me bread to eat, and raiment to put on ... **Ephesians 4:28:** Let him that stole steal no more: but rather let him labour, working with *his* hands the thing which is good, that he may have to give to him that needeth. **2 Thessalonians 3:11-12:** For we hear that there are some which walk among you disorderly, working not at all, but are busybodies. Now them that are such we command and exhort by our Lord Jesus Christ, that with quietness they work, and eat their own bread. **Philippians 4:6:** Be careful for nothing; but in every thing by prayer and supplication with thanksgiving let your requests be made known unto God.

[10] **1 Timothy 4:3-5:** Forbidding to marry, *and commanding* to abstain from meats, which God hath created to be received with thanksgiving of them which believe and know the truth. For every creature of God *is* good, and nothing to be refused, if it be received with thanksgiving: For it is sanctified by the word of God and prayer.

[11] **1 Timothy 6:6-8:** But godliness with contentment is great gain. For we brought nothing into *this* world, *and it is* certain we can carry nothing out. And having food and raiment let us be therewith content.

[12] **Proverbs 30:8-9:** Remove far from me vanity and lies: give me neither poverty nor riches; feed me with food convenient for me: Lest I be full, and deny *thee*, and say, Who *is* the LORD? or lest I be poor, and steal, and take the name of my God *in vain*.

194. What do we pray for in the fifth petition?

A. In the fifth petition, (which is, *Forgive us our debts, as we forgive our debtors*, [1]) acknowledging, that we and all others are guilty both of original and actual sin, and thereby become debtors to the justice of God; and that neither we, nor any other creature, can make the least satisfaction for that debt: [2] we pray for ourselves and others, that God of his free grace would, through the obedience and satisfaction of Christ, apprehended and applied by faith, acquit us both from the guilt and punishment of sin, [3] accept us in his Beloved; [4] continue his favour and grace to us, [5] pardon our daily failings, [6] and fill us with peace and joy, in giving us daily more and more assurance of forgiveness; [7] which we are the rather emboldened to ask, and encouraged to expect, when we have this testimony in ourselves, that we from the heart forgive others their offences. [8]

Proofs

[1] **Matthew 6:12:** And forgive us our debts, as we forgive our debtors.

[2] **Romans 3:9-22:** What then? are we better *than they*? No, in no wise: for we have before proved both Jews and Gentiles, that they are all under sin; As it is written, There is none righteous, no, not one: There is none that understandeth, there is none that seeketh after God. They are all gone out of the way, they are together become unprofitable; there is none that doeth good, no, not one ... Now we know that what things soever the law saith, it saith to them who are under the law: that every mouth may be stopped, and all the world may become guilty before God ... **Matthew 18:24-25:** And when he had begun to reckon, one was brought unto him, which owed him ten thousand talents. But forasmuch as he had not to pay, his lord commanded him to be sold, and his wife, and children, and all that he had, and payment to be made. **Psalm 130:3-4:** If thou, LORD, shouldest mark iniquities, O Lord, who shall stand? But *there is* forgiveness with thee, that thou mayest be feared.

[3] **Romans 3:24-26:** Being justified freely by his grace through the redemption that is in Christ Jesus: Whom God hath set forth *to be* a propitiation through faith in his blood, to declare his righteousness for the remission of sins that are past, through the forbearance of God; To declare, *I say*, at this time his righteousness: that he might be just, and the justifier of him which believeth in Jesus. **Hebrews 9:22:** And almost all things are by the law purged with blood; and without shedding of blood is no remission.

[4] **Ephesians 1:6-7:** To the praise of the glory of his grace, wherein he hath made us accepted in the beloved. In whom we have redemption through his blood, the forgiveness of sins, according to the riches of his grace ...

[5] **2 Peter 1:2:** Grace and peace be multiplied unto you through the knowledge of God, and of Jesus our Lord …

[6] **Hosea 14:2:** Take with you words, and turn to the LORD: say unto him, Take away all iniquity, and receive *us* graciously: so will we render the calves of our lips. **Jeremiah 14:7:** O LORD, though our iniquities testify against us, do thou *it* for thy name's sake: for our backslidings are many; we have sinned against thee.

[7] **Romans 15:13:** Now the God of hope fill you with all joy and peace in believing, that ye may abound in hope, through the power of the Holy Ghost. **Psalm 51:7-10, 12:** Purge me with hyssop, and I shall be clean: wash me, and I shall be whiter than snow. Make me to hear joy and gladness; *that* the bones *which* thou hast broken may rejoice. Hide thy face from my sins, and blot out all mine iniquities. Create in me a clean heart, O God; and renew a right spirit within me … Restore unto me the joy of thy salvation; and uphold me *with thy* free spirit.

[8] **Luke 11:4:** And forgive us our sins; for we also forgive every one that is indebted to us. And lead us not into temptation; but deliver us from evil. **Matthew 6:14-15:** For if ye forgive men their trespasses, your heavenly Father will also forgive you: But if ye forgive not men their trespasses, neither will your Father forgive your trespasses. **Matthew 18:35:** So likewise shall my heavenly Father do also unto you, if ye from your hearts forgive not every one his brother their trespasses.

195. What do we pray for in the sixth petition?

A. In the sixth petition, (which is, *And lead us not into temptation, but deliver us from evil*, [1]) acknowledging, that the most wise, righteous, and gracious God, for divers holy and just ends, may so order things, that we may be assaulted, foiled, and for a time led captive by temptations; [2] that Satan, [3] the world, [4] and the flesh, are ready powerfully to draw us aside, and ensnare us; [5] and that we, even after the pardon of our sins, by reason of our corruption, [6] weakness, and want of watchfulness, [7] are not only subject to be tempted, and forward to expose ourselves unto temptations, [8] but also of ourselves unable and unwilling to resist them, to recover out of them, and to improve them; [9] and worthy to be left under the power of them: [10] we pray, that God would so overrule the world and all in it, [11] subdue the flesh, [12] and restrain Satan, [13] order all things, [14] bestow and bless all means of grace, [15] and quicken us to watchfulness in the use of them, that we and all his people may by his providence be kept from being tempted to sin; [16] or, if tempted, that by his Spirit we may be powerfully supported and enabled to stand in the hour of temptation; [17] or when fallen, raised again and recovered out of it, [18] and have a sanctified use and improvement thereof: [19] that our sanctification and salvation may be perfected, [20] Satan trodden under our feet, [21] and we fully freed from sin, temptation, and all evil, forever. [22]

Proofs

[1] **Matthew 6:13:** And lead us not into temptation, but deliver us from evil: For thine is the kingdom, and the power, and the glory, for ever. Amen.

[2] **2 Chronicles 32:31:** Howbeit in *the business of* the ambassadors of the princes of Babylon, who sent unto him to inquire of the wonder that was *done* in the land, God left him, to try him, that he might know all *that was* in his heart.

[3] **1 Chronicles 21:1:** And Satan stood up against Israel, and provoked David to number Israel.

[4] **Luke 21:34:** And take heed to yourselves, lest at any time your hearts be overcharged with surfeiting, and drunkenness, and cares of this life, and *so* that day come upon you unawares. **Mark 4:19:** And the cares of this world, and the deceitfulness of riches, and the lusts of other things entering in, choke the word, and it becometh unfruitful.

[5] **James 1:14:** But every man is tempted, when he is drawn away of his own lust, and enticed.

[6] **Galatians 5:17:** For the flesh lusteth against the Spirit, and the Spirit against the flesh: and these are contrary the one to the other: so that ye cannot do the things that ye would.

[7] **Matthew 26:41:** Watch and pray, that ye enter not into temptation: the spirit indeed *is* willing, but the flesh *is* weak.

[8] **Matthew 26:69-72:** Now Peter sat without in the palace: and a damsel came unto him, saying, Thou also wast with Jesus of Galilee. But he denied before *them* all, saying, I know not what thou sayest. And when he was gone out into the porch, another *maid* saw him, and said unto them that were there, This *fellow* was also with Jesus of Nazareth. And again he denied with an oath, I do not know the man. **Galatians 2:11-14:** But when Peter was come to Antioch, I withstood him to the face, because he was to be blamed. For before that certain came from James, he did eat with the Gentiles: but when they were come, he withdrew and separated himself, fearing them which were of the circumcision. And the other Jews dissembled likewise with him; insomuch that Barnabas also was carried away with their dissimulation. But when I saw that they walked not uprightly according to the truth of the gospel, I said unto Peter before *them* all, If thou, being a Jew, livest after the manner of Gentiles, and not as do the Jews, why compellest thou the Gentiles to live as do the Jews? **2 Chronicles 18:3:** And Ahab king of Israel said unto Jehoshaphat king of Judah, Wilt thou go with me to Ramothgilead? And he answered him, I *am* as thou *art*, and my people as thy people; and *we will be* with thee in the war. [Compare with] **2 Chronicles 19:2:** And Jehu the son of Hanani the seer went out to meet him, and said to king Jehoshaphat, Shouldest thou help the ungodly, and love them that hate the LORD? therefore *is* wrath upon thee from before the LORD.

[9] **Romans 7:23-24:** But I see another law in my members, warring against the law of my mind, and bringing me into captivity to the law of sin which is in my members. O wretched man that I am! who shall deliver me from the body of this death? **1 Chronicles 21:1-4:** And Satan stood up against Israel, and provoked David to number Israel. And David said to Joab and to the rulers of the people, Go, number Israel from Beersheba even to Dan; and bring the number of them to me, that I may know *it*. And Joab answered, The LORD make his people an hundred times so many more as they *be*: but, my lord the king, *are* they not all my lord's servants? why then doth my lord require this thing? why will he be a cause of trespass to Israel? Nevertheless the king's word prevailed against Joab. Wherefore Joab departed, and went throughout all Israel, and came to Jerusalem. **2 Chronicles 16:7-10:** And at that time Hanani the seer came to Asa king of Judah, and said unto him, Because thou hast relied on the king of Syria, and not relied on the

LORD thy God, therefore is the host of the king of Syria escaped out of thine hand. Were not the Ethiopians and the Lubims a huge host, with very many chariots and horsemen? yet, because thou didst rely on the LORD, he delivered them into thine hand. For the eyes of the LORD run to and fro throughout the whole earth, to shew himself strong in the behalf of *them* whose heart *is* perfect toward him. Herein thou hast done foolishly: therefore from henceforth thou shalt have wars. Then Asa was wroth with the seer, and put him in a prison house; for *he was* in a rage with him because of this *thing*. And Asa oppressed some of the people the same time.

[10] **Psalm 81:11-12:** But my people would not hearken to my voice; and Israel would none of me. So I gave them up unto their own hearts' lust: *and* they walked in their own counsels.

[11] **John 17:15:** I pray not that thou shouldest take them out of the world, but that thou shouldest keep them from the evil.

[12] **Psalm 51:10:** Create in me a clean heart, O God; and renew a right spirit within me. **Psalm 119:133:** Order my steps in thy word: and let not any iniquity have dominion over me.

[13] **2 Corinthians 12:7-8:** And lest I should be exalted above measure through the abundance of the revelations, there was given to me a thorn in the flesh, the messenger of Satan to buffet me, lest I should be exalted above measure. For this thing I besought the Lord thrice, that it might depart from me.

[14] **1 Corinthians 10:12-13:** Wherefore let him that thinketh he standeth take heed lest he fall. There hath no temptation taken you but such as is common to man: but God *is* faithful, who will not suffer you to be tempted above that ye are able; but will with the temptation also make a way to escape, that ye may be able to bear *it*.

[15] **Hebrews 13:20-21:** Now the God of peace, that brought again from the dead our Lord Jesus, that great shepherd of the sheep, through the blood of the everlasting covenant, Make you perfect in every good work to do his will, working in you that which is wellpleasing in his sight, through Jesus Christ; to whom *be* glory for ever and ever. Amen.

[16] **Matthew 26:41:** Watch and pray, that ye enter not into temptation: the spirit indeed *is* willing, but the flesh *is* weak. **Psalm 19:13:** Keep back thy servant also from presumptuous *sins*; let them not have

dominion over me: then shall I be upright, and I shall be innocent from the great transgression.

[17] **Ephesians 3:14-17:** For this cause I bow my knees unto the Father of our Lord Jesus Christ, Of whom the whole family in heaven and earth is named, That he would grant you, according to the riches of his glory, to be strengthened with might by his Spirit in the inner man; That Christ may dwell in your hearts by faith; that ye, being rooted and grounded in love ... **1 Thessalonians 3:13:** To the end he may stablish your hearts unblameable in holiness before God, even our Father, at the coming of our Lord Jesus Christ with all his saints. **Jude 24:** Now unto him that is able to keep you from falling, and to present *you* faultless before the presence of his glory with exceeding joy ...

[18] **Psalm 51:12:** Restore unto me the joy of thy salvation; and uphold me *with thy* free spirit.

[19] **1 Peter 5:8-10:** Be sober, be vigilant; because your adversary the devil, as a roaring lion, walketh about, seeking whom he may devour: Whom resist stedfast in the faith, knowing that the same afflictions are accomplished in your brethren that are in the world. But the God of all grace, who hath called us unto his eternal glory by Christ Jesus, after that ye have suffered a while, make you perfect, stablish, strengthen, settle *you*.

[20] **2 Corinthians 13:7, 9:** Now I pray to God that ye do no evil; not that we should appear approved, but that ye should do that which is honest, though we be as reprobates ... For we are glad, when we are weak, and ye are strong: and this also we wish, *even* your perfection.

[21] **Romans 16:20:** And the God of peace shall bruise Satan under your feet shortly. The grace of our Lord Jesus Christ *be* with you. Amen. **Zechariah 3:2:** And the LORD said unto Satan, The LORD rebuke thee, O Satan; even the LORD that hath chosen Jerusalem rebuke thee: *is* not this a brand plucked out of the fire? **Luke 22:31-32:** And the Lord said, Simon, Simon, behold, Satan hath desired *to have* you, that he may sift *you* as wheat: But I have prayed for thee, that thy faith fail not: and when thou art converted, strengthen thy brethren.

[22] **John 17:15:** I pray not that thou shouldest take them out of the world, but that thou shouldest keep them from the evil. **1 Thessalonians 5:23:** And the very God of peace sanctify you

wholly; and *I pray God* your whole spirit and soul and body be preserved blameless unto the coming of our Lord Jesus Christ.

196. What doth the conclusion of the Lord's Prayer teach us?

A. The conclusion of the Lord's Prayer, (which is, *For thine is the kingdom, and the power, and the glory, for ever. Amen.* [1]) teacheth us to enforce our petitions with arguments, [2] which are to be taken, not from any worthiness in ourselves, or in any other creature, but from God; [3] and with our prayers to join praises, [4] ascribing to God alone eternal sovereignty, omnipotency, and glorious excellency; [5] in regard whereof, as he is able and willing to help us, [6] so we by faith are emboldened to plead with him that he would, [7] and quietly to rely upon him, that he will fulfil our requests. [8] And, to testify this our desire and assurance, we say, Amen. [9]

Proofs

[1] **Matthew 6:13:** And lead us not into temptation, but deliver us from evil: For thine is the kingdom, and the power, and the glory, for ever. Amen.

[2] **Romans 15:30:** Now I beseech you, brethren, for the Lord Jesus Christ's sake, and for the love of the Spirit, that ye strive together with me in *your* prayers to God for me ...

[3] **Daniel 9:4, 7-9, 16-19:** And I prayed unto the LORD my God, and made my confession, and said, O Lord, the great and dreadful God, keeping the covenant and mercy to them that love him, and to them that keep his commandments ... O Lord, righteousness *belongeth* unto thee, but unto us confusion of faces, as at this day ... O Lord, to us *belongeth* confusion of face, to our kings, to our princes, and to our fathers, because we have sinned against thee. To the Lord our God *belong* mercies and forgivenesses, though we have rebelled against him ... O Lord, according to all thy righteousness, I beseech thee, let thine anger and thy fury be turned away from thy city Jerusalem ... Now therefore, O our God, hear the prayer of thy servant, and his supplications, and cause thy face to shine upon thy sanctuary that is desolate, for the Lord's sake. O my God, incline thine ear, and hear; open thine eyes, and behold our desolations, and the city which is called by thy name: for we do not present our supplications before thee for

our righteousnesses, but for thy great mercies. O Lord, hear; O Lord, forgive; O Lord, hearken and do; defer not, for thine own sake, O my God: for thy city and thy people are called by thy name.

[4] **Philippians 4:6:** Be careful for nothing; but in every thing by prayer and supplication with thanksgiving let your requests be made known unto God.

[5] **1 Chronicles 29:10-13:** Wherefore David blessed the LORD before all the congregation: and David said, Blessed *be* thou, LORD God of Israel our father, for ever and ever. Thine, O LORD, *is* the greatness, and the power, and the glory, and the victory, and the majesty: for all *that is* in the heaven and in the earth *is thine*; thine *is* the kingdom, O LORD, and thou art exalted as head above all. Both riches and honour *come* of thee, and thou reignest over all; and in thine hand *is* power and might; and in thine hand *it is* to make great, and to give strength unto all. Now therefore, our God, we thank thee, and praise thy glorious name.

[6] **Ephesians 3:20-21:** Now unto him that is able to do exceeding abundantly above all that we ask or think, according to the power that worketh in us, Unto him *be* glory in the church by Christ Jesus throughout all ages, world without end. Amen. **Luke 11:13:** If ye then, being evil, know how to give good gifts unto your children: how much more shall *your* heavenly Father give the Holy Spirit to them that ask him?

[7] **2 Chronicles 20:6, 11:** And said, O LORD God of our fathers, *art* not thou God in heaven? and rulest *not* thou over all the kingdoms of the heathen? and in thine hand *is there not* power and might, so that none is able to withstand thee? ... Behold, *I say, how* they reward us, to come to cast us out of thy possession, which thou hast given us to inherit.

[8] **2 Chronicles 14:11:** And Asa cried unto the LORD his God, and said, LORD, *it is* nothing with thee to help, whether with many, or with them that have no power: help us, O LORD our God; for we rest on thee, and in thy name we go against this multitude. O LORD, thou *art* our God; let not man prevail against thee.

[9] **1 Corinthians 14:16:** Else when thou shalt bless with the spirit, how shall he that occupieth the room of the unlearned say Amen at thy giving of thanks, seeing he understandeth not what thou sayest? **Revelation 22:20-21:** He which testifieth these things saith, Surely I come quickly. Amen. Even so, come, Lord Jesus. The grace of our Lord Jesus Christ *be* with you all. Amen.

The
Shorter
Catechism

The Shorter Catechism

Roderick Lawson

- A classic – valued by the church for over three centuries
- An in-depth explanation of the Christian faith
- Beautifully textured hardback cover. With Ribbon

The Westminster Assembly of 1643 to 1649 produced three documents of lasting value to the Church: *The Westminster Confession of Faith, The Larger Catechism*, and *The Shorter Catechism*.

Since then, *The Shorter Catechism* has become well known as a manual of doctrine for both children and adults who require an introduction to the Christian faith. It is an ideal way to give structure to the discipling of new believers. This edition contains the addition of scripture proof texts and notes by Roderick Lawson.

ISBN 978-1-78191-810-4

KEY QUESTIONS AND ANSWERS
ON THE CHRISTIAN FAITH
THE
SHORTER
CATECHISM
WITH SCRIPTURE PROOFS AND
NOTES BY RODERICK LAWSON

The Shorter Catechism

Roderick Lawson

- An introduction to the Christian faith
- Created by the Westminster Assembly in the 17th century
- Paperback edition. Contains proof texts
- Well known manual of doctrine for all those requiring an introduction to the Christian Faith.

This edition contains the addition of scripture proofs in full & notes by Roderick Lawson. The Westminster shorter catechism has been an effective tool for teaching the Christian faith to young and old for over 300 years and is still used in Presbyterian and other reformed churches to this day.

This is one of the most popular editions as it contains proof texts to aid a parent or teacher in their instruction.

ISBN 978-1-85792-288-2

HERITAGE

AN EXPOSITION ON THE SHORTER CATECHISM

WHAT IS THE CHIEF END OF MAN?

INCLUDES THE WESTMINSTER CONFESSION AND THE LONGER CATECHISM

ALEXANDER WHYTE

An Exposition on the Shorter Catechism

What is the Chief End of Man?

Alexander Whyte

Alexander Whyte (1836-1921) is best known for his books on Bible Characters. A leading Scottish Churchman of the nineteenth and early twentieth centuries it is only to be expected that he turned his mind to the Shorter Catechism – that summary of Christian doctrine that was taught in schools and homes across Scotland and throughout the world. In a question and answer format the Shorter Catechism was written with uneducated layman in mind. Simple, direct and brief it was memorised by millions of people from all backgrounds. Its spiritual value has been proved again and again as it provides a base of solid Christian teaching that has stood the test of time.

This exposition is a treasure, as it adds some background and some explanation to the brevity that is obviously necessary in a catechism. Quoting from a wide range of Reformed and Puritan authors, Whyte provides useful application and illustrations that help illuminate the answers and will help us apply them to our lives.

ISBN 978-1-85792-250-9

Marianne Ross

LOVE

THE SHORTER CATECHISM ACTIVITY BOOK

Learning the Truth with Puzzles

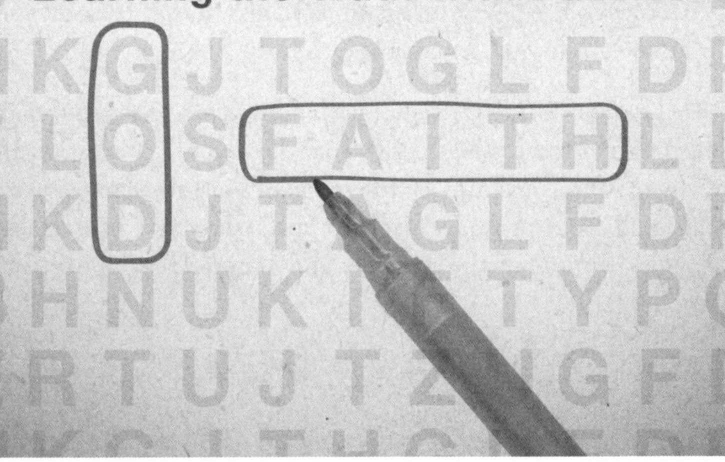

The Shorter Catechism Activity Book

Learning the Truth with Puzzles

Marianne Ross

Using the familiar puzzle formats children use in school such as word searches, crossword puzzles and codes this book will help children to work through the Westminster Shorter Catechism – one of the church's statements of faith. Not only will they enjoy completing these work sheets; the truths that are presented here will be a strong foundation for their future life. The shorter catechism covers the following important doctrines:

God; Sin; Christ; The ten commandments; Baptism; The Lord's Supper and The Lord's prayer.

ISBN 978-1-84550-722-0

Christian Focus Publications

Our mission statement –

STAYING FAITHFUL
In dependence upon God we seek to impact the world through literature faithful to His infallible Word, the Bible. Our aim is to ensure that the Lord Jesus Christ is presented as the only hope to obtain forgiveness of sin, live a useful life and look forward to heaven with Him.

Our books are published in four imprints:

CHRISTIAN FOCUS

Popular works including biographies, commentaries, basic doctrine and Christian living.

CHRISTIAN HERITAGE

Books representing some of the best material from the rich heritage of the church.

MENTOR

Books written at a level suitable for Bible College and seminary students, pastors, and other serious readers. The imprint includes commentaries, doctrinal studies, examination of current issues and church history.

CF4•K

Children's books for quality Bible teaching and for all age groups: Sunday school curriculum, puzzle and activity books; personal and family devotional titles, biographies and inspirational stories – Because you are never too young to know Jesus!

Christian Focus Publications Ltd,
Geanies House, Fearn, Ross-shire,
IV20 1TW, Scotland, United Kingdom.
www.christianfocus.com